Mastering Core TOEFL iBT / TOEIC Words

Newly updated 1,650 words that have frequently appeared on the TOEFL iBT test since 2011

 William H. Shin

 OLD STONE PRESS

Mastering Core TOEFL iBT/ TOEIC WORDS with William H. Shin
Copyright © 2014 William H. Shin

All rights reserved. No part of this book may be reproduced or utilized in any form
or by any means, electronic or mechanical, including photocopying, audio recording,
or by any information storage and retrieval system, without permission in writing
from the publisher, Old Stone Press, an imprint of J. H. Clark and Associates, Inc.,
520 Old Stone Lane, Louisville, Kentucky 40207, www.oldstonepress.com, or by the author,
William H. Shin, Knowledge Tree LLC, New Jersey, except in the case of brief quotations
embodied in critical articles and reviews.

Library of Congress Cataloging-in-Publication Data has been applied for.
Mastering Core TOEFL iBT/ TOEIC WORDS with William H. Shin

ISBN 978-1-938462-08-5

Published by Old Stone Press
Louisville, Kentucky 40207
First Edition, 2014
Printed in the United States of America

TOEFL is a trademark of ETS (Educational Testing Service), a private non-profit organization, which designs and administers the tests. TOEFL is a standardized test of English language proficiency for non-native English language speakers wishing to enroll in universities using English as the main/dominant medium of communication. The test is accepted by many English-speaking academic and professional institutions. TOEFL is one of the two major English-language tests in the world, the other being the IELTS.

PRAISE FOR THE BOOK

❝ Whenever my students ask me about the way to improve their TOEFL iBT/ TOEIC scores, I tell them to expand their vocabulary most of all. Vocabulary is the key to listening as well as reading. Only if you know the word can you hear it and then understand what it means. The publication of Mastering Core TOEFL iBT/ TOEIC Words with William H. Shin *allows me now to recommend an excellent guide to my students when I emphasize the importance of vocabulary. Packed with words frequently presented on the TOEFL iBT/ TOEIC, the book will help students to learn the essential words day by day and master them in only about a month. The drill at the end of each day's vocabulary is a must.* ❞

Wonkyung Yang, PhD
General English Program
Seoul Women's University, Seoul, Korea

PRAISE FOR THE BOOK

❝Mastering Core TOEFL iBT/ TOEIC Words with William H. Shin *is an amazing book which helps students achieve two goals, preparing for the TOEFL iBT/ TOEIC and SAT, simultaneously. Above all, this book has the great advantage of showing a perfectly feasible way to start using a 33-day schedule and drills for the student wandering in the maze of words. The carefully selected example sentences also guide students into the exact path.*❞

Hee Jeong Son, MD, PhD
Associate Professor
Chief of Department of Anesthesiology
Kangwon National University, College of Medicine, Korea

""*William H. Shin's* Mastering Core TOEFL iBT/ TOEIC Words *includes 1,650 essential words with synonyms, antonyms, and succinct examples that students can easily memorize. I would highly recommend the book for my nursing students who wish to study in the US. From Day 1 to Day 33, students will surely feel moderately challenged with the book's drills. 50 words and 20 questions per day should be a doable, step-by-step routine for vocabulary learners. Besides the clear definition of words, including three to four synonyms and antonyms for each word gives this book an edge over other vocabulary books with relatively fewer synonyms and antonyms. Further, it shows the level of difficulty with asterisks (*), which will add to the students' self-confidence once they master the words. With this book, I am confident that students will find themselves upgraded in reading comprehension skills as well as general English proficiency.*""

Daewon Ko
Professor, Business and Law, Kunsan College of Nursing, Korea
Stanford University (MBA, 1993); Valparaiso University (JD, 2006)

Introduction

This book contains as many as 1,650 core TOEFL iBT/ TOEIC words along with synonyms, definitions, example sentences, and 29 different reviews provided by my colleagues and students. In order to help students preparing for the TOEFL iBT/ TOEIC to memorize the words more effectively, certain words have stars (*), which indicate the degrees of diffculty of memorizing them. Based on my long-term TOEFL/ TOEIC teaching experience, students preparing for the TOEFL iBT/ TOEIC must precisely learn the definitions of the core TOEFL iBT/ TOEIC words in this book to enhance their TOEFL iBT/ TOEIC scores. Once students have memorized all the words, they will be able to start dealing with questions from the reading, writing, listening, and speaking sections more easily and efficiently. I have no doubt that this book will enable students to become better TOEFL iBT/ TOEIC test takers.

    I have been working as a TOEFL iBT and TOEFL CBT instructor for more than 15 years in both New York and New Jersey in the US. In addition, I have made a ceaseless and indefatigable effort to analyze the TOEFL iBT/ TOEIC questions on a daily basis in order to become a better TOEFL iBT/ TOEIC lecturer and to meet my students' demands as well. Ultimately, it led me to start and complete this book. I am certain that this book will play a tremendously positive role in helping students boost their TOEFL iBT/ TOEIC scores.

    I will always be grateful to my former and current TOEFL iBT/ TOEIC students, colleagues, and pianist, Lynn. Particularly, I would like to express my gratitude to Hoon, who designed the cover. Without their help, I would not be able to publish it. I would like to dedicate *Mastering Core TOEFL iBT/ TOEIC Words with William H. Shin* to them.

William H. Shin

TOEFL iBT/ TOEIC WORDS (Day 1)

1. **Arresting** [uh-**rest**-ting]
   adj def: capable of attracting attention or interest.
       synonyms: interesting, consuming, engaging
       antonyms: boring, dry, heavy, monotonous
       Greg always makes an *arresting* smile whenever he meets with his girlfriend.

2. **Classify** [**klas**-uh-fahy]
   verb def: to arrange or organize by classes; order according to class.
       synonyms: allocate, arrange, assort
       antonyms: derange, disarray, disorder
       Jason has made tremendous and continuous effort to *classify* a variety of his personal matters into one.

3. **Extend** [ik-**stend**]
   verb def: to stretch out to the full length.
       synonyms: add to, aggrandize, amplify, augment
       antonyms: abridge, condense, contract
       Lauren *extended* the measuring tape as far as it would go.

4. **Equatorial** [ee-kwuh-**tawr**-ee-uh l]
   adj def: near an equator.
       synonyms: tropical, central
       A great number of the tourists from the United States of America appear to enjoy *equatorial* temperatures.

5. **Transition** [tran-zish-*uh*n]
   noun def: movement, passage, or change from one position, state. (**)
       synonyms: alteration, conversion, evolution
       antonyms: beginning, conclusion, finish, stagnation
       Gregory made a difficult *transition* from enlisted man to officer.

6. **Erode** [ih-**rohd**]
   verb def: to eat into or away; destroy by slow consumption.
       synonyms: deteriorate, wear away, abrade, corrode
       antonyms: build, construct
       It is common sense that battery acid *erodes* the engine.

7. **Thrive** [thrahyv]
   verb def: to grow or develop vigorously; flourish. (***)
       synonyms: advance, arrive, blossom
       antonyms: decline, fail, languish
       The adolescents *thrived* in Asia.

TOEFL iBT/ TOEIC WORDS (Day 1)

8. Annual [an-yoo-uhl]
   adj def: pertaining to a year; yearly.
        synonyms: each year, once a year
        Clara was surprised to find out that she was capable of making more than $50,000 *annual* income.

9. Precipitation [pri-sip-i-tey-shuhn]
   noun def: a headlong rush or fall; abrupt, impulsive haste; total amount of rainfall a year. (***)
        synonyms: condensation, rainfall
        antonyms: dryness
        It has been generally believed that rainforests in Africa receive more annual *precipitation* than any other place in the world.

10. Foster [faw-ster]
   verb def: to promote the growth or development of. (*)
        synonyms: advance, cultivate, encourage, forward
        antonyms: condemn, discourage
        The record agent *fostered* the development of his clients by sending them to singing lessons.

11. Endure [en-door]
   verb def: to hold out against; to sustain without impairment or yielding.
        synonyms: abide, accustom, allow, brook
        antonyms: discontinue
        Peter appeared to *endure* great financial pressure with equanimity.

12. Boost [boost]
   noun def: a lifting or raising by pushing from behind or below.
        synonyms: increase, addition, breakthrough, improvement
        antonyms: blow, decrease, hindrance, setback
        There has been a tremendous *boost* in food prices for the past several years.

13. Retreat [ree-treet]
   verb def: to withdraw.
        synonyms: to evacuate, fight, retire, withdraw
        antonyms: to advance, arrive, come
        The general ordered his soldiers to *retreat* from the fierce battlefield.

14. Hibernate [hi-ber-neyt]
   verb def: to spend the winter in close quarters. (***)
        synonyms: hide, lie torpid
        Bears spend the winter *hibernating* in caves.

TOEFL iBT/ TOEIC WORDS (Day 1)

15. Forge [fawrj]
    verb def: to form by concentrated effort. (**)
        Forging ahead and finishing the job require a burst of energy and patience.

16. Vertical [**vur**-ti-kuhl]
    adj def: upright; plumb.
        synonyms: erect, perpendicular, sheer, upward
        antonyms: horizontal, prone
        A variety of *vertical* trees in the mountain reminded Penny of her interest when she was an elementary student.

17. Descend [dih-**send**]
    verb def: to go or pass from a higher to a lower place. (*)
        synonyms: collapse, crash, decline, dismount
        antonyms: ascend, go up, increase
        The climbers slowly *descended* from the mountaintop.

18. Migrate [**mahy**-greyt]
    verb def: to move from one region to another.
        synonyms: drift, emigrate, leave, roam
        antonyms: stay
        A great number of migratory birds *migrate* southward in the winter.

19. Camouflage [**kam**-uh-flahzh]
    noun def: result of obscuring things to deceive an enemy. (***)
        synonyms: disguise, conceal, cover, deceit
        antonyms: reveal, show, uncover
        Drab plumage provides the bird with *camouflage* against predators.

20. Retain [ri-**teyn**]
    verb def: to hold; to keep possession of.
        synonyms: bear in mind, detain, contain
        antonyms: free, let go, loose
        Many people in China still tend to *retain* their old customs.

21. Cluster [**kluhs**-ter]
    noun def: a group of things or persons close together.
        synonyms: array, assemblage, bundle, pack
        antonyms: individual, one
        There was a *cluster* of tourists in front of Buckingham Palace.

22. Tolerate [**tol**-uh-reyt]
    verb def: to allow the existence, presence, practice.
        synonyms: accept, admit, consent, brook

TOEFL iBT/ TOEIC WORDS (Day 1)

   antonyms: check, disallow, disapprove
   It is true that Ellen can *tolerate* laziness, but not incompetence.

23. Inclement [in-klem-uh-nt]
   adj def: severe; rough; harsh.
      synonyms: bitter, nasty, brutal, foul
      antonyms: clear, mild, sunny
   Inclement weather prevented Charlie from riding a horse, which had been his long-time favorite outdoor activity.

24. Fluctuate [fluhk-choo-eyt]
   verb def: to change continuously; to shift back and forth. (**)
      synonyms: vacillate, change, alter
      antonyms: hold, persist, remain
   The price of gold has *fluctuated* dramatically for the last several months due to economic decline.

25. Vary [vair-ee]
   verb def: to show diversity; be different.
      synonyms: alter, assort, convert, fluctuate
      antonym: remain, stay
   The age at which children are ready to read *varies*.

26. Exacerbate [ig-zas-er-beyt]
   verb def: to increase the severity, bitterness. (****)
      synonyms: infuriate, aggravate, annoy, embitter
      antonyms: aid, calm, comfort
   It is unwise to take aspirin to relieve heartburn; instead of providing relief, the drug will only *exacerbate* the problem.

27. Suppress [suh-pres]
   verb def: to put an end to the activities. (**)
      synonyms: restrain, abolish, annihilate, censor
      antonyms: encourage, release
   The leader of the Democratic Party *suppressed* the Communist party.

28. Befuddle [bih-fuhd-l]
   verb def: to confuse, as with glib statement. (***)
      synonyms: confuse, addle, baffle, fluster
      antonyms: clear up, explain
   It is firmly believed that politicians *befuddled* the public with campaign promises.

TOEFL iBT/ TOEIC WORDS (Day 1)

29. Proclaim [proh-kleym]
   verb def: to announce; to declare officially.
       synonyms: advertise, blazon, affirm, announce
       antonyms: conceal, hide
       The United States of America immediately *proclaimed* war right after Japan attacked Pearl Harbor.

30. Regain [ree-geyn]
   verb def: to get back; recover.
       synonyms: achieve, reacquire
       antonyms: forfeit, lose
       Peter slowly *regained* his health by eating healthy food as well as exercising on a daily basis.

31. Refrain [ri-freyn]
   verb def: to abstain from an impulse to say so or do. (***)
       synonyms: cease, check, forgo, avoid
       antonyms: do, go ahead, jump in
       Catherine *refrained* from telling John what she thought in order to avoid an unwanted conflict.

32. Withstand [with-stand]
   verb def: to stand or hold out against.
       synonyms: endure, brace, combat, confront
       antonyms: surrender, yield
       It is extremely difficult for Brian to *withstand* the temptation of smoking seven cigarettes a day.

33. Flee [flee]
   verb def: to run away; to move swiftly.
       synonyms: abscond, avoid, evade
       antonyms: face, meet, stand, stay
       Susan decided to *flee* from her husband, for her husband never appeared to treat her fairly.

34. Seethe [seeth]
   verb def: to surge; to foam as if boiling. (****)
       synonyms: be furious, be inclined, be livid, be mad
       antonyms: be happy
       John *seethed* with indignation.

35. Disguise [dis-gahyz]
   verb def: to change the appearance of in order to conceal identity.
       synonyms: affect, change, cloak, camouflage

TOEFL iBT/ TOEIC WORDS (Day 1)

antonyms: expose, open, represent, reveal
The King was frequently *disguised* as a peasant.

36. Reckon [rek-uhn]
verb def: to esteem; to consider, as in number or amount.
synonyms: add up, evaluate, account, appraise
antonyms: neglect, subtract
An umpire was *reckoned* an authority on the field.

37. Enrich [en-rich]
verb def: to supply with riches, wealth, abundance.
synonyms: improve, embellish, adorn, aggrandize
antonyms: decrease, deplete, impoverish
Perry studied every night in order to expand and *enrich* his knowledge of Russian language and literature.

38. Overcome [oh-ver-kuhm]
verb def: to get the better of in a struggle or conflict.
synonyms: conquered, defeated, overwhelmed
antonyms: to be indifferent, unconcerned, unmoved
By doing exercise three times a week, Gerardo *overcame* his physical weakness.

39. Exclude [ik-sklood]
verb def: to keep or shut out; prevent the entrance of.
synonyms: expel, forbid, ban, block
antonyms: accept, add, allow, include
Employees and their relatives were *excluded* from participation in the contest.

40. Ignite [ig-nahyt]
verb def: to kindle; to set on fire. (***)
synonyms: burn, kindle, inflame
antonyms: extinguish, put out
The spilled gasoline was *ignited* by the carelessly thrown cigarette butt.

41. Scatter [skat-er]
verb def: to throw loosely about. (**)
synonyms: disperse, cast, diffuse
antonyms: collect, gather
The police *scattered* a crowd, who were gathering to protest against the existing government.

TOEFL iBT/ TOEIC WORDS (Day 1)

42. Clasp [klasp]
   verb def: to seize; to grasp; to grip.
        synonyms: buckle, clamp, clinch, embrace
        antonyms: let go, loose
       David *clasped* his wife's hand gently.

43. Extol [ik-**stol**]
   verb def: to praise highly; to laud; to eulogize. (***)
        synonyms: acclaim, applause, brag, celebrate
        antonyms: blame, criticize
       The salesman *extolled* the virtues of the used car he was trying to convince the customer to buy.

44. Enliven [en-**lahy**-vuhn]
   verb def: to make vigorous or active; to make cheerful.
        synonyms: inspire, vitalize, animate, brighten
        antonyms: bore, dull, enervate, exhaust
       Flowers and decorations *enliven* any room.

45. Coax [kohks]
   verb def: to manipulate to a desired end by adroit handling or persistent effort. (****)
        synonyms: persuade, allure, beguile, blandish
       Kevin attempted to *coax* a raise from his boss.

46. Imprudent [im-**prood**-nt]
   adj def: lacking discretion, wisdom, or good judgment. (*****)
       It's politically *imprudent* to stir up such controversy during an election year.

47. Abstruse [ab-**stroos**]
   adj def: hard to understand; recondite. (***)
        synonyms: abstract, complex, complicated, deep
        antonyms: clear, concrete, lucid, obvious
       The philosopher's elucidation was so clear that he turned an *abstruse* subject into one his audience could grasp.

48. Synthetic [sin-**thet**-ik]
   adj def: amalgamated; coalesced; compounded.
        synonyms: artificial, constructed, counterfeit, fabricated
        antonyms: genuine, natural, real
       Most winter boots are made of *synthetic* leather.

TOEFL iBT/ TOEIC WORDS (Day 1)

49. Endeavor [en-dev-er]
   verb def: to exert oneself to try to affect something.
        synonyms: aim, effort, aspire, assay
        Mr. Clark always *endeavors* to keep everything well organized in his apartment.

        As urbanization advanced, it swept away the distinctive physical and social characteristics of the culture of the past, substituting undifferentiated built environments and standardized patterns of dress and behavior. Hand camera users *endeavored* to reaffirm individuality and arrest time in the face of the encroaching depersonalization of existence.
                — Naomi Rosenblum, *A World History of Photography*, 1989

50. Viable [vahy-uh-buhl]
   adj def: capable of living. (****)
        synonyms: reasonable, practicable, doable
        antonyms: impossible, unachievable, impractical
        Catherine suggested a *viable* solution to the problem we were facing.

Drill 1

1. The word **arresting** is closest in meaning to

    A) apprehend
    B) befuddled
    C) attractive
    D) repair

2. The word **foster** is closest in meaning to

    A) proclaim
    B) regains
    C) promote
    D) refrain

3. The word **endure** is closest in meaning to

    A) withstand
    B) lapse
    C) flee
    D) seethe

4. The phrase **cope with** is closest in meaning to

    A) reckon
    B) enrich
    C) overcome
    D) exclude

5. The word **disperse** is closest in meaning to

    A) ignition
    B) cycle
    C) shudder
    D) scatter

Drill 1

6. The word **exacerbate** is closest in meaning to

    A) etch
    B) extol
    C) clasp
    D) worsen

7. The word **suppress** is closest in meaning to

    A) encourage
    B) release
    C) viable
    D) restrain

8. The word **flee** is closest in meaning to

    A) extol
    B) escape
    C) linger
    D) withstand

9. The word **seethe** is closest in meaning to

    A) furious
    B) happy
    C) flourish
    D) abate

10. The word **enrich** is closest in meaning to

    A) deplete
    B) impoverish
    C) embellish
    D) astounding

Drill 1

11. The word **extol** is closest in meaning to

    A) annual
    B) praise
    C) banal
    D) erode

12. The word **offspring** is closest in meaning to

    A) deluge
    B) extol
    C) flourish
    D) descendent

13. The word **inclement** is closest in meaning to

    A) harsh
    B) incite
    C) meticulous
    D) spawn

14. The word **thrive** is closest in meaning to

    A) linger
    B) myriad
    C) prosper
    D) niche

15. The word **camouflage** is closest in meaning to

    A) outset
    B) hide
    C) prompt
    D) requisite

Drill 1

16. The word **retain** is closest in meaning to

    A) hold
    B) aloft
    C) forecast
    D) dispose

17. The word **migrate** is closest in meaning to

    A) collapse
    B) abate
    C) shift
    D) inert

18. The word **transition** is closest in meaning to

    A) depict
    B) glaze
    C) periphery
    D) movement

19. The word **forge** is closest in meaning to

    A) glean
    B) seek
    C) luster
    D) form

20. The word **reckon** is closest in meaning to?

    A) consider
    B) emit
    C) imprudent
    D) jaunt

1. C 2. C 3. A 4. C 5. D 6. D 7. D 8. B 9. A 10. C
11. B 12. D 13 .A 14. C 15. B 16. A 17. C 18. D 19. D 20. A

TOEFL iBT/ TOEIC WORDS (Day 2)

1. Perceive [per-**seev**]
    verb def: to become aware of.
        synonyms: notice, apprehend, behold, descry
        antonyms: miss, neglect
    That was an excellent idea, but I *perceived* difficulties in putting it into practice.

2. Banal [buh-**nal**]
    adj def: devoid of freshness or originality; hackneyed; trite. (***)
        synonyms: bromide, clichéd, dull, conventional
        antonyms: fresh, new, original
    It is interesting that there were *banal* and sophomoric treatments of courage on the frontier.

3. Elaborate [ih-**lab**-er-it]
    adj def: worked out with great care and nicety of detail.
        synonyms: intricate, involved, careful, complex
        antonyms: general, normal, regular, simple
    Tommy made an *elaborate* preparation for the meeting scheduled for tomorrow because he was in charge of it.

4. Extravagance [ik-**strav**-uh-guhns]
    noun def: excessive or unnecessary expenditure. (***)
        synonyms: indulgence, amenity
        antonyms: economy, moderation
    That sports car Donald purchased last week was an absolutely inexcusable *extravagance* to his friends.

5. Ostentatious [os-ten-**tey**-shuhs]
    adj def: characterized by or given to pretentious or conspicuous show. (***)
        synonyms: flashy, showy, boastful, flamboyant
        antonyms: modest, plain, quiet
    Her family has always considered Joyce an *ostentatious* dresser.

6. Prominent [**prom**-uh-nuhnt]
    adj def: standing out as to be seen easily.
        synonyms: arresting, bulging
        antonyms: depressed, invisible, obscured
    Her eyes are her most *prominent* feature.

TOEFL iBT/ TOEIC WORDS (Day 2)

7. Categorize [**kat**-i-guh-rahyz]
   verb def: to arrange in categories.
        synonyms: assort, classify, identify
        Peter seems to be obsessed with *categorizing* things around him.

8. Rigid [**rij**-id]
   adj def: stiff; unyielding; not pliant.
        synonyms: adamant, austere, changeless
        antonyms: bending, flexible, lenient
        Students in a boarding school need to meet *rigid* specifications and regulations.

9. Confine [kuhn-**fahyn**]
   verb def: to enclose within boundaries or bounds. (***)
        synonyms: circumscribe, constrain, delimit
        antonyms: free, liberate, release
        Patricia *confined* her efforts to finishing the book she had started two years ago.

10. Distinguish [dih-**sting**-gwish]
   verb def: to recognize as distinct or different.
        synonyms: analyze, ascertain, classify, collate
        It is hard to *distinguish* Jennifer from her twin sister.

11. Agitate [**aj**-i-teyt]
   verb def: to move; to shake; to disturb. (**)
        synonyms: beat, churn, convulse, disturb
        antonyms: calm, lull, quiet, soothe
        The machine *agitated* the mixture.

12. Esoteric [es-uh-**ter**-ik]
   adj def: belonging to a select few. (****)
        synonyms: obscure, abstruse, arcane, cryptic
        antonyms: common, known, obvious
        The poetry John read is full of *esoteric* allusions.

13. Secular [**sek**-yuh-ler]
   adj def: pertaining to worldly things.
        synonyms: civil, earthly, lay, material
        antonyms: godly, holy, religious

TOEFL iBT/ TOEIC WORDS (Day 2)

Phillip showed numerous *secular* interests.

14. Illiterate [ih-**lit**-er-it]
   adj def: unable to read and write.
        synonyms: ignorant, unenlightened
        antonyms: able, educated, learned, literate
       Albert is musically *illiterate* because he didn't have a chance to learn it.

15. Prevail [pri-**veyl**]
   verb def: to be widespread, current, or prediminant
        synonyms: dominate, control, abound
        antonyms: lose, surrender
       The soldiers *prevailed* over their enemies in the battle.

16. Entrench [en-**trench**]
   verb def: to place in a position of strength.
        synonyms: establish, anchor, confirm, define
       It is fortunate that Paul was able to *entrench* his proposition to the company behind undeniable fact.

17. Identity [ahy-**den**-ti-tee]
   noun def: the condition of being oneself or itself.
        synonyms: recognition, label, description, determination
        antonyms: confusion, mistake
       Sam doubted his own *identity*.

18. Embellish [em-**bel**-ish]
   verb def: to beautify by or as if by ornamentation. (**)
        synonyms: adorn, amplify, array, bedeck, elaborate
        antonyms: deface, disfigure, mar, simplify
       Justine decided to hire someone to *embellish* her apartment on 5th Avenue.

19. Magnificent [mag-**nif**-uh-suhnt]
   adj def: making a splendid appearance or show.
        synonyms: glorious, arresting, august, brilliant, elegant
        antonyms: offensive, poor, ugly
       Magnificent scenery made Tim extremely happy and speechless.

TOEFL iBT/ TOEIC WORDS (Day 2)

20. Prompt [prompt]
adj def: at once; without delay.
    synonyms: early, alert, apt, brisk, eager
    antonyms: late, negligent, tardy, slow
A *prompt* reply by John gave me a chance to do my task more effectively.

21. Indulge [in-dulhji]
verb def: to yield to an inclination or desire.
    synonyms: delight, favor, foster, gratify
    antonyms: resist
Sophie usually *indulged* her appetite for sweets.

22. Utilize [yoot-l-ahyz]
verb def: put to use.
    synonyms: advance, apply, bestow, employ
The villagers *utilized* a stream to power the mill.

23. Outset [out-set]
noun def: the beginning; start.
Stephen wanted to explain the situation at the *outset*.

24. Engrave [en-greyv]
verb def: to carve, cut, or etch into a material.
    synonyms: bite, chisel
That image Otis happened to observe was *engraved* on his mind.

25. Derive [dih-rahyv]
verb def: to receive from a source or origin.
    synonyms: acquire, arrive, assume, determine
    antonyms: create, invent
It is believed that the linguistic roots of many English words *derive* from those of Latin words.

26. Ethereal [ih-theer-ee-uhl]
adj def: light; airy; tenuous. (**)
    synonyms: delicate, celestial, divine, fairy
    antonyms: earthy, indelicate, worldly
Byron created an *ethereal* world through his poetic imagination.

TOEFL iBT/ TOEIC WORDS (Day 2)

27. Effervescent [ef-er-**ves**-uhnt]
   adj def: vivacious; gay; lively; sparkling. (****)
      synonyms: airy, bouncy, elastic, expansive
      antonyms: flat, stale
   Tina's *effervescent* personality made her perfect for the job of game show host.

28. Stark [stahrk]
   adj def: sheer, utter, downright.
      synonyms: absolute, complete, consummate
      anonyms: indefinite
   Nancy bought posters to liven up her *stark* new apartment, although she couldn't afford furniture.

29. Undercurrent [**uhn**-der-kur-uhnt]
   noun def: a tendency underlying or at variance with the obvious.
      synonyms: atmosphere, aura, direction, eddy, flavor
   Even in his friendly remarks, anyone in the room could sense an *undercurrent* of hostility.

30. Exaggerate [ig-**zaj**-uh-reyt]
   verb def: to magnify beyond the limits of truth. (*)
      synonyms: overstate, embellish, amplify, brag, caricature
      antonyms: depreciate, minimize, reduce, understate
   Sarah seemed to *exaggerate* the difficulties of a situation.

31. Alleviate [uh-**lee**-vee-eyt]
   verb def: to lessen: to mitigate; to make easier. (***)
      synonyms: relieve, lessen, allay, assuage, ease, lighten
      antonyms: aggravate, heighten, increase
   Taking pain medication *alleviates* severe pain.

32. Outing [**ou**-ting]
   noun def: a pleasure trip; excursion; picnic.
      synonyms: drive, excursion, expedition, jaunt, junket
   Most of the students wanted to participate in the annual *outing* for the senior class.

TOEFL iBT/ TOEIC WORDS (Day 2)

33. Cherub [cher-uhb]
   adj def: a child with a sweet, chubby innocent face. (**)
   synonyms: angel, seraph, beautiful infant
   Her *cherubic* appearance made people think that her personality was also sweet, when the opposite was true.

34. Integrate [in-ti-greyt]
   verb def: to bring together.
   synonyms: mix, amalgamate, articulate, assimilate, attune
   antonyms: divide, separate
   The principal *integrated* a previously racially segregated school.

35. Diverse [dih-vurs]
   adj def: made up of different kind or forms. (*)
   synonyms: different, various, assorted, contrary
   antonyms: alike, conforming, identical
   German higher education is as *diverse* as its countryside, cities, and towns.

   We can adapt to new problems in ways that other species cannot. It is this ability that enabled our ancestors to spread over the globe, displacing other hominids and many other species along the way. Our cultures and individual behaviors are so successfully *diverse* that humans are more like an entire ecosystem than a single species.
   —Barbara Oakley, *Evil Genes*, (2007) 2008

36. Asymmetrical [ey-suh-me-trik-kel]
   adj def: not identical on both sides of a central line. (***)
   synonyms: uneven, awry, crooked, unbalanced
   The hairstylist was shocked to find that the two sides of his customer's hair were *asymmetrical*.

37. Perfunctory [per-fuhngk-tuh-ree]
   adj def: performed merely as a routine duty, hasty and superficial
   synonyms: routine
   In his lecture, Sr. Smith revealed himself to be a merely *perfunctory* speaker.

38. Discard [dih-skarrd]
   verb def: to cast aside or dispose of; to get rid of. (**)
   synonyms: abandon, abdicate, banish, cancel
   antonyms: embrace, keep, retain

TOEFL iBT/ TOEIC WORDS (Day 2)

The CEO of the company *discarded* the documents on his own instead of having his secretary destroy them.

39. Undoubtable [uhn-**dout**-uh-buhl]
adj def: not called in question; undisputed.
His statement was considered *undoubtable*.

40. Meticulous [muh-**tik**-yuh-luhs]
adj def: taking or showing extreme care about minute detail. (***)
    synonyms: accurate, cautious, exact, fastidious
    antonyms: careless, messy, sloppy
Most of the students in class paid *meticulous* attention to the lecture delivered by Professor DeFazio.

41. Conspicuous [kuhn-**spik**-yoo-uhs]
adj def: attracting special attention. (*)
    synonyms: obvious, apparent, clear, distinct
    antonyms: concealed, hidden, imperceptible
Jason seemed to be extremely uncomfortable about his *conspicuous* weight gain.

Conspicuous species of large organisms with small populations are vulnerable—and several fishes and marine mammals, including Steller's sea cow, have succumbed.
    — Stephen Jay Gould, *Natural History*, June 1991

42. Disfigure [dis-**fig**-yer]
verb def: to mar the appearance or beauty of.
    synonyms: blemish, damage, deface, defile
    antonyms: adorn, decorate, ornament
My town was completely *disfigured* by tasteless new office buildings.

43. Depict [dih-**pikt**]
verb def: to describe in detail; to delineate.
    synonyms: render, delineate, illustrate, image
Susan tried to *depict* scenery as lively as she could.

44. Exemplify [ig-**zem**-pluh-fahy]
verb def: to furnish or serve as an example of.
    synonyms: cite, demonstrate

TOEFL iBT/ TOEIC WORDS (Day 2)

The plays of Wilde *exemplify* the comedy of manners.

45. Deem [deem]
    verb def: to form or have an opinion. (**)
        synonyms: regard, consider, account, allow
        The king did not *deem* the issue unimportant.

46. Profound [pruh-**found**]
    adj def: penetrating into subjects of thought or knowledge.
        synonyms: abstruse, deep, discerning, enlightened
        antonyms: ignorant, stupid
        Dr. Westwood has been known as a *profound* thinker since he started to teach at the university.

47. Incite [in-**sahyt**]
    verb def: to stir; to encourage; to urge; to stimulate.
        synonyms: encourage, abet, activate, actuate, agitate
        antonyms: delay, deter, discourage, prohibit
        A demagogue *incited* a crowd to riot.

48. Incontrovertible [in-kon-truh-**vur**-tuh-buhl]
    adj def: not disputable; not open to question or dispute. (**)
        synonyms: accurate, authentic, certain, established
        antonyms: changeable, uncertain, variable
        Kenny spent a whole weekend in order to prepare an *incontrovertible* business proposal to his boss.

49. Inconsequential [in-kon-si-**kwen**-shuhl]
    adj def: insignificant; illogical.
        synonyms: not of major significance
        antonyms: substantial, major
        Unfortunately, the case study conducted by Mr. Holliday turned out to be of *inconsequential* significance.

50. Encode [en-**kohd**]
    verb def: to convert into code.
        synonyms: encrypt, cipher, conceal
        antonyms: decode
        Credit card companies *encode* cardholder information in the credit cards before the cards are mailed out to the cardholders.

Drill 2

1. The word **prominence** is closest in meaning to

    A) agreement
    B) clemence
    C) prestige
    D) overturn

2. The word **outset** is closest in meaning to

    A) vagary
    B) outline
    C) regard
    D) beginning

3. The word **undoubtable** is closest in meaning to

    A) unsightly
    B) surely
    C) unrelentingly
    D) hollowly

4. The word **profound** is closest in meaning to

    A) feverish
    B) grand
    C) abstruse
    D) jubilant

5. The word **incited** is closest in meaning to

    A) roused
    B) grieved
    C) unveiled
    D) whittled

Drill 2

6. The word **incontrovertible** is closest in meaning to

    A) pleasining
    B) indistinct
    C) complimentary
    D) manifest

7. The word **discard** is closest in meaning to

    A) desert
    B) suppress
    C) tolerance
    D) vary

8. The word **deem** is closest in meaning to

    A) withstand
    B) consider
    C) proclaim
    D) rapid

9. The word **inconsequential** is closest in meaning to

    A) transition
    B) unify
    C) not important
    D) voracious

10. The word **confine** is closest in meaning to

    A) alleviate
    B) limit
    C) renounce
    D) clasp

Drill 2

11. The word **stark** is closest in meaning to

    A) coax
    B) empty
    C) distinguish
    D) enrich

12. The word **agitate** is closest in meaning to

    A) forge
    B) hibernate
    C) illiterate
    D) stir up

13. The word **extravagance** is closest in meaning to

    A) luxurious
    B) magnificent
    C) ordain
    D) pursuit

14. The word **alleviate** is closest in meaning to

    A) prevail
    B) reckon
    C) lessen
    D) stagnant

15. The word **effervescence** is closest in meaning to

    A) undercurrent
    B) liveliness
    C) vex
    D) adjacent

Drill 2

16. The word **banal** is closest in meaning to

    A) ethnic
    B) hinder
    C) hazard
    D) cliché

17. The word **ostentatious** is closest in meaning to

    A) showy
    B) induce
    C) liaison
    D) myriad

18. The word **prevail** is closest in meaning to

    A) mutate
    B) endow
    C) control
    D) afflict

19. The word **secular** is closest in meaning to

    A) abuse
    B) worldly
    C) dwindle
    D) embitter

20. The word **embellish** is closest in meaning to

    A) alter
    B) extend
    C) exacerbate
    D) decorate

1. C 2. D 3. B 4. C 5. A 6. D 7. A 8. B 9. C 10. B
11. B 12. D 13. A 14. C 15. B 16. D 17. A 18. C 19. B 20. D

TOEFL iBT/ TOEIC WORDS (Day 3)

1. Astonishing [uh-**ston**-i-shing]
    adj def: causing astonishment. (**)
        synonyms: amazing, astounding, impressive, marvelous
        antonyms: boring, dull, expected
        Stephen displayed an *astonishing* lack of concern for others.

2. Array [uh-**rey**]
    verb def: to place in proper or desired order.
        synonyms: align, exhibit, display
        Tiffany *arrayed* herself in furs and diamond.

3. Inhabit [in-**hab**-it]
    verb def: to dwell; to cohabit.
        synonyms: abide, dwell, locate, lodge
        antonyms: depart, leave, move, vacate
        Several different species of birds and animals *inhabit* the island.

4. Requisite [**rek**-wuh-zit]
    adj def: required or necessary for a particular purpose. (***)
        The recently released reference book is the *requisite* material for students to prepare for the upcoming TOEFL iBT/ TOEIC tests.

5. Linger [**ling**-ger]
    verb def: to remain or stay on in a place longer than is usual.
        synonyms: loiter, delay, amble, crawl
        antonyms: go, hurry, rush
        Roxanne *lingered* awhile after the party.

6. Constraint [kuhn-**streynt**]
    noun def: limitation; restriction.
        synonyms: coercion, compulsion, duress
        antonyms: freedom
        A group of students standing in front of the administration building demanded freedom from *constraint*.

7. Deter [dih-**ter**]
    verb def: to discourage from acting. (*****)
        synonyms: avert, block, dampen, forestall
        antonyms: instigate, encourage, persuade, promote
        Lynn *deterred* her daughter from going out at night.

TOEFL iBT/ TOEIC WORDS (Day 3)

Rick Wagoner, CEO of General Motors, the automaker in most imminent danger of failure, gave lawmakers three reasons Chapter 11 isn't an option. First, the special financing that usually tides companies over through reorganization is so scarce right now that GM might not be able to get enough to keep functioning. Second, the stigma of bankruptcy would *deter* consumers from buying GM cars. Third, GM is already in the midst of a dramatic reorganization that will pave the way to a profitable future.
—Justin Fox, *Time*, 1 Dec. 2008

8. Stagnate [stag-nayt]
   verb def: to become motionless; to fail to grow. (***)
      synonyms: constipate, decay, decline, idle
      antonyms: grow, strengthen
   High costs have caused the building industries to *stagnate*.

9. Desiccate [des-i-keyt]
   verb def: to dry up; to dehydrate. (****)
      synonyms: dehydrate, dry, evaporate, parch
      antonyms: moisten, wet
   In fact, the package of fruit had been *desiccated* for the past three weeks before it was sold to the customer.

10. Adjacent [uh-jey-suhnt]
   adj def: abutting; bordering.
      synonyms: beside, alongside, contiguous
      antonyms: apart, away, detached, distant
   The motel Catherine was staying in is *adjacent* to the highway.

11. Internecine [in-ter-nee-seen]
   adj def: pertaining to conflict or struggle within a group. (**)
      synonyms: exterminatory, deadly, mutually destructive
   The disadvantage of *internecine* chemical weapons is that they are devastating to both sides in a conflict.

12. Variegate [vair-ee-i-geyt]
   verb def: to make varied in appearance as by adding different colors. (***)
   Tiffany decided to paint her room in *variegated* colors.

TOEFL iBT/ TOEIC WORDS (Day 3)

13. Adapt [uh-**dapt**]
    verb def: to make suitable to requirements.
        synonyms: acclimate, accommodate, alter, change
        antonyms: disarrange, disorder, disturb
    Although it may be difficult at first, Charles has no choice but to *adapt* to the new computer system.

14. Flourish [**flur**-ish]
    verb def: to thrive; to achieve; to be successful; prosper.
        synonyms: amplify, augment, bloom, burgeon, develop
        antonyms: cease, languish, to be stunted, fail to thrive
    It is no exaggeration to say that local markets have *flourished* in recent years.

15. Exploit [**ex**-sploit]
    verb def: advance or further through exploitation.
        synonyms: achievement, adventure, attachment, deed
    Tom *exploited* his new movie through a series of guest appearances.

16. Niche [nich]
    noun def: a place or position suitable or appropriate for a person. (***)
    Hannah fortunately discovered a *niche* for herself right after college.

> To succeed in this new world, you have to sell yourself. You go to a brand-name college, not to imbibe the wisdom of its professors, but to make impressions and connections. You pick a *niche* that can bring attention to yourself and then develop your personal public relations efforts to let the world know who you are.
>   — Alan Wolfe, *New York Times Book Review*, 7 Jan. 2001

17. Diversity [dih-**vur**-si-tee]
    noun def: the state or fact of being diverse; difference.
        synonyms: assortment, divergence, medley, multifarious
        antonyms: identicalness, sameness, similarity
    New York City is well known for its cultural *diversity*.

18. Pursuit [per-**soot**]
    noun def: the act of pursuing.
        synonyms: chase, search, following, hunt
        antonyms: retreat, surrender

TOEFL iBT/ TOEIC WORDS (Day 3)

A huge group of dogs was running into the woods in *pursuit* of a wounded bear.

19. Agile [aj-uhl]
   adj def: quick or fast in movement. (**)
       synonyms: active, acute, alert, brisk
       antonyms: brittle, clumsy, stiff
   The *agile* monkey leapt onto the table and snatched the boy's banana away in the blink of an eye.

20. Sustenance [suhs-tuh-nuhns]
   noun def: means of support; maintenance.
       synonyms: aid, food
   Brian draws spiritual *sustenance* from daily church attendance.

21. Myriad [mir-ee-uh-d]
   noun def: indefinitely great number. (****)
       synonyms: innumerable, countless, endless
       antonyms: calculable, limited, measurable
   My boss said that they were necessary in order to comply with the *myriad* of regulations imposed on the industry.

   Mr. McCullough hails Adams for being uncannily prescient ... foreseeing a *myriad* of developments, from the difficulty of defeating the British ... to the divisive consequences of slavery.
   — Michiko Kakutani, *New York Times*, 22 May 2001

22. Rapid [rap-id]
   adj def: occurring within a short time.
       synonyms: active, agile, brisk, expeditious
       antonyms: languishing, leisurely, slow
   Scientists are getting deeply concerned about the *rapid* disappearance of the island's coral reefs.

23. Enormous [ih-nawr-muhs]
   adj def: greatly exceeding the common size.
       synonyms: astronomic, colossal, excessive, gigantic
       antonyms: insignificant, little, minute. tiny
   Liana made an *enormous* effort to improve her test skills and strategies in order to earn excellent standardized test scores.

TOEFL iBT/ TOEIC WORDS (Day 3)

24. Spectacular [spek-**tak**-yuh-ler]
    adj def: given to impressive.
        synonyms: wonderful, amazing, astonishing, breathtaking
        antonyms: normal, ordinary, regular, usual
        The autumn foliage is *spectacular*.

25. Courtship [**kawrt**-ship]
    noun def: the act or process of courting.
        synonyms: dating, engagement, lovemaking
        Some animals often show aggression during *courtship*.

26. Entice [en-**tahys**]
    verb def: to lead on by exciting hope or desire. (***)
        synonyms: allure, persuade, attract
        antonyms: disgust, dissuade, repel, repulse
    A surprisingly large number of people were *enticed* westward by dreams of gold.

27. Spawn [spawn]
    verb def: give birth to; give rise to. (**)
        synonyms: produce, bring forth, create, generate
        antonyms: destroy
    Tim's sudden disappearance *spawned* many different and unbelievable rumors.

28. Endemic [en-**dem**-ik]
    adj def: natural to or characteristic of a specific people. (***)
        synonyms: native, local, regional
    Divorce has become so *endemic* in our society that a whole lore has risen up around it: that divorce is a temporary crisis; that so many children have experienced their parents' divorce that children nowadays do not worry much about it; that in fact it makes things easier, and it is itself a mere rite of passage; that if the parents feel better, so will the children.
        — Elisabeth Lasch-Quinn, *New Republic*, 6 May 2002

29. Alternate [**awl**-ter-neyt]
    verb def: to interchange repeatedly.
        synonyms: to be intermittent, periodic, recurring
    Day *alternates* with night.

TOEFL iBT/ TOEIC WORDS (Day 3)

30. Incredible [in-**kred**-uh-buhl]
   adj def: not credible; hard to believe.
        synonyms: absurd, flimsy, implausible, impossible
        antonyms: credible, plausible, tenable
        The plot of the story Joan is writing seems to be *incredible*.

31. Indigenous [in-**dij**-uh-nuhs]
   adj def: originating in and characteristic of a particular region. (***)
        synonyms: aboriginal, native
        antonyms: alien, foreign
        Viking invaders quickly subdued the *indigenous* population, known as the Picts.
        — Jared M. Diamond, *Collapse*, 2005

32. Voracious [vaw-**rey**-shuhs]
   adj def: craving or consuming large quantities. (****)
        synonyms: greedy, avid, covetous, hungry
        antonyms: quenched, satisfied
        Jack had a *voracious* eating behavior when he was an elementary school student.

33. Hefty [**hef**-tee]
   adj def: heavy; large; big.
        synonyms: big, bulky, ample, awkward
        antonyms: slight, small, thin, tiny
        Stephen carried many *hefty* books in his backpack.

34. Constitute [**kahn**-sti-toot]
   verb def: to compose; to be made up of.
        synonyms: comprise, aggregate, complement, complete
        Mortar *constituted* of lime and sand.

35. Unify [**yoo**-nuh-fahy]
   verb def: to make or become a single unit.
        synonyms: affiliate, ally, associate, combine
        Dr. Schmidt *unified* conflicting theories by introducing new research findings.

TOEFL iBT/ TOEIC WORDS (Day 3)

36. Encroach [en-**krohch**]
    verb def: to advance beyond proper limits.
        synonyms: infringe, interfere, intervene
        antonyms: keep off
    It has been acknowledged that the urban areas *encroach* on the suburb every year.

37. Dwell [dwell]
    verb def: to live or stay as a permanent resident.
        synonyms: abide, exist, inhabit, locate
    Jessica *dwelled* with a farm family as an exchange student in Germany.

38. Deluge [**del**-yooj]
    noun def: great flood of water inundation. (**)
        synonyms: avalanche, barrage, cataclysm, overflowing.
    The *deluge* caused severe mudslides that completely destroyed the village.

39. Implacable [im-**plak**-uh-buhl]
    adj def: unable to be mollified or pacified. (***)
        synonyms: merciless, inexorable, cruel
        antonyms: kind, merciful, nice
    The Senator had an *implacable* hatred for his political opponents.

40. Exigent [**ex**-si-juh-nt]
    adj def: needing immediate action; urgently pressing.
        synonyms: urgent, pressing, acute, burning, clamorous
        antonyms: ordinary, usual
    The patient was losing blood so rapidly that it was *exigent* to stop the source of the bleeding.

41. Illusory [ih-**loo**-suh-ree]
    adj def: causing illusion; misleading; unreal.
        synonyms: deceptive, chimerical, delusory, fallacious
        antonyms: genuine, real
    Ms. Kennedy sometimes believed in an *illusory* sense of security.

42. Avert [uh-**vurt**]
    verb def: to avoid; to obviate. (***)
        synonyms: avoid, deflect, deter, divert
        antonyms: aid, help

TOEFL iBT/ TOEIC WORDS (Day 3)

In order to *avert* a car accident, Alex took a rest as often as he could while driving from New York to Florida last summer.

43. Bemoan [bih-**mohn**]
verb def: to express distress or grief.
> synonyms: complain, deplore, grieve, lament
> antonyms: be happy, gloat

Sarah *bemoaned* the fact that she failed to pass the exam she had taken.

44. Ordain [awr-**deyn**]
verb def: to invest with ministerial or sacerdotal authority. (**)
> synonyms: anoint, appoint, commission, consecrate
> antonyms: cancel, disavow, void

Stephanie sat proudly in the front row to watch her mother be *ordained* as the first female minister in the church's history.

45. Protract [proh-**trakt**]
verb def: to draw out or lengthen.
> synonyms: extend, continue, delay, drag out
> antonyms: abbreviate, curtail, shorten

The project has been *protracted* by a group of protesters.

46. Marvel [**mahr**-vuhl]
noun def: something that causes wonder.
> synonyms: curiosity, miracle, phenomenon

The newly constructed building was an engineering *marvel*.

47. Spoof [spoof]
noun def: mocking imitation of someone or something.
> synonyms: trick, mockery, bluff, burlesque

The show Tom watched on TV last night was a *spoof* of college life.

48. Restrict [ri-**strikt**]
verb def: to confine or keep within limits, as of space.
> synonyms: confine, limit, bound, check, circumscribe
> antonyms: enlarge, expand, free, release

The doctor told Susan to *restrict* the amount of sugar she consumes on a daily basis.

49. Pity [pit-ee]
    noun def: sympathetic or kindly sorrow evoked by suffering. (**)
        synonyms: charity, clemency, comfort, compassion
        antonyms: disdain, malevolence, mercilessness
    Brian felt deep *pity* for the fact that his best friend, Carl, was unable to earn enough money to support his parents financially.

50. Vex [veks]
    verb def: to irritate; to annoy; to provoke. (***)
        synonyms: abrade, afflict, aggravate, agitate
        antonyms: aid, assist, help, soothe
    The loud noise from the street *vexed* Paul, for he couldn't concentrate on his study for tomorrow's exam.

TOEFL iBT/ TOEIC WORDS (Day 3)

❝ *Studying vocabulary may seem to be endless work that demands vigorous effort. For this reason, many don't even know what to do or where to start —they are simply overwhelmed. They get frustrated and consequently lose focus. This masterpiece in studying vocabulary clearly shows the right and shortest track for accomplishing this formidable task in a very realistic and achievable way by offering the 33-day plan. This text is exceptionally well organized and handy! If you have experienced difficulty in finding a proper text for vocabulary study, I would strongly recommend Mr Shin's* Mastering Core TOEFL iBT/ TOEIC words, *without hesitation ...* ❞

Yunho Cho, PhD
Professor and Head of Department of Mechanical System Design
Pusan National University, Korea

Drill 3

1. The word **inhabit** is closest in meaning to

    A) unify
    B) encroach on
    C) dwell in
    D) deluge

2. The word **stable** is closest in meaning to

    A) implacable
    B) steady
    C) exigent
    D) illusory

3. The word **deter** is closest in meaning to

    A) avert
    B) bemoan
    C) ordain
    D) protract

4. The word **constraint** is closest in meaning to

    A) marvel
    B) spoofs
    C) restrictions
    D) splinters

5. The word **requisite** is closest in meaning to

    A) necessary
    B) spoilable
    C) piteous
    D) encouraging

Drill 3

6. The word **entice** is closest in meaning to

    A) vex
    B) enliven
    C) coax
    D) revive

7. The word **immense** is closest in meaning to

    A) exact
    B) enormous
    C) imprudent
    D) abstruse

8. The word **veracious** is closest in meaning to

    A) abstain
    B) truthful
    C) carping
    D) exacerbate

9. The word **indigenous** is closest in meaning to

    A) disdain
    B) efficacious
    C) native
    D) impeccable

10. The word **alternate** is closest in meaning to

    A) change
    B) nonchalant
    C) pallid
    D) ostracize

Drill 3

11. The word **internecine** is closest in meaning to

    A) deadly
    B) obsolete
    C) scrupulous
    D) refutable

12. The word **agile** is closest in meaning to

    A) relevance
    B) turbulent
    C) usurp
    D) moving fast

13. The word **myriad** is closest in meaning to

    A) sagacious
    B) numerous
    C) sedentary
    D) oblivious

14. The word **hefty** is closest in meaning to

    A) obsessive
    B) incremental
    C) strong
    D) gregarious

15. The word **sustenance** is closest in meaning to

    A) nourishment
    B) grandiose
    C) whimsical
    D) tactile

Drill 3

16. The word **linger** is closest in meaning to

    A) emanate
    B) garner
    C) delay
    D) hibernate

17. The word **stagnate** is closest in meaning to

    A) harness
    B) idle
    C) novice
    D) torment

18. The word **desiccate** is closest in meaning to

    A) dry
    B) triumph
    C) wither
    D) hinge

19. The word **adjacent** is closest in meaning to

    A) infest
    B) embrace
    C) next to
    D) emend

20. The word **niche** is closest in meaning to

    A) elate
    B) compartment
    C) ignite
    D) outset

1. C 2. B 3. A 4. C 5. A 6. C 7. B 8. B 9. C 10. A
11. A 12. D 13. B 14. C 15. A 16. C 17. B 18. A 19. C 20. B

TOEFL iBT/ TOEIC WORDS (Day 4)

1. Endeavor [en-**dev**-er]
    verb def: to exert oneself to do.
        synonyms: aim, effort, exertion
        Kim constantly *endeavored* in order to improve her TOEFL iBT test scores.

2. Dominate [**dom**-uh-neyt]
    verb def: to rule over; govern.
        synonyms: boss, command, control, dictate
        antonyms: follow, submit, surrender
        The company Alex and Paul established has *dominated* the IT market for more than a decade.

3. Viable [**vahy**-uh-buhl]
    adj def: capable of living. (****)
        synonyms: applicable, feasible, practical
        antonyms: impossible, unbelievable, unreasonable
    The desert is not a *viable* place for planting trees.

        The departure point for a *viable* peace deal—either with Syria or the Palestinians—must not be based purely on what the political traffic in Israel will bear, but on the requirements of all sides.
        Aaron David Miller, *Newsweek*, 12 Jan. 2009

4. Jeopardy [**jep**-er-dee]
    noun def: risk of or exposure to loss.
        synonyms: danger, trouble, accident, hazard
        antonyms: protection, safety
    Moor and Scott as local fire fighters routinely put their lives in *jeopardy* by executing daring rescues.

5. Allocate [**al**-uh-keyt]
    verb def: to set apart for a particular purpose.
        synonyms: assign, allot, apportion, appropriate, designate
        antonyms: keep, keep together
    The CEO intentionally *allocated* a considerable amount of funds for new projects in order to save his company in the future.

6. Obtain [uhb-**teyn**]
    verb def: to come into possession of.
        synonyms: get, acquire, access, accomplish, achieve

TOEFL iBT/ TOEIC WORDS (Day 4)

antonyms: forfeit, forsake, lose, sacrifice
It appeared to be impossible for Charles to *obtain* the information he desperately needed.

7. Adequate [adi-kwit]
adj def: as good as necessary for some requirement or purpose. (**)
synonyms: enough, capable, requisite, sufficient, suitable
antonyms: inadequate, insufficient, unfit, unqualified
Paul provided the plants in the garden with an *adequate* amount of water.

8. Procreate [proh-kree-yet]
verb def: to beget; generate.
synonyms: breed, conceive, create
antonyms: kill
A drive to *procreate* is inherent in the makeup of all human beings.

9. Designate [dez-ig-neyt]
verb def: to make or point out; to indicate.
synonyms: allocate, appoint, assign, authorize
Steve was *designated* as an executive officer of the company two years ago.

10. Precedent [pres-i-duhnt]
noun def: decision or case that serves as a guide or justification. (**)
synonyms: antecedent, authority, criterion, exemplar
There was no legal *precedent* for the judge to follow in this case.

11. Divert [dih-vurt]
verb def: to turn aside; draw off.
synonyms: alter, avert, change, deflect, pivot
antonyms: maintain, stay
They were charged with illegally *diverting* public funds for private use.

12. Ample [am-phul]
noun def: fully sufficient or more than adequate for the purposes.
synonyms: abounding, abundant, bountiful, capacious, commodious, enough
antonyms: insufficient, meager, not enough
The apartment Jenny just moved in has *ample* storage space.

TOEFL iBT/ TOEIC WORDS (Day 4)

13. Encompass [en-**kuhm**-puhs]
   verb def: to form a circle about. (**)
       synonyms: surround, circumscribe, beset, compass, enclose
       antonyms: exclude
       The baron *encompassed* his castle with a moat.

14. Biennial [bahy-**en**-ee-uhl]
   adj def: happening every two years.
       There are many different kinds of *biennial* plants in the world.

15. Vertebrate [**vur**-tuh-brit]
   adj def: having a backbone or spinal column.
       Watching *vertebrate* animals in the zoo has been John's favorite activity since he was a child.

16. Squander [**skwan**-der]
   verb def: to spend or use wastefully. (****)
       synonyms: consume, dissipate, be wasteful
       antonyms: hoard, save, set aside
       Alex had no regret about *squandering* his father's hard-earned fortune.

17. Fertile [**fur**-tl]
   adj def: productive; prolific. (**)
       synonyms: bountiful, breeding, fecund
       antonyms: barren, impotent, infertile, sterile
       Thanks to the *fertile* soil, Andrew was able to grow eggplant in his garden.

18. Inseminate [in-**sem**-uh-neyt]
   verb def: to introduce semen into. (***)
       Some women have to be artificially *inseminated* in order to become pregnant.

19. Plague [pleyg]
   verb def: to trouble; annoy; torment in any manner. (**)
       synonyms: afflict, bother, fret, gall
       antonyms: aid, assist, help, please
       Thomas has been *plagued* by allergies all his life.

TOEFL iBT/ TOEIC WORDS (Day 4)

20. Aggressive [uih-**gres**-iv]
  adj def: tending toward unprovoked offensive.
    synonyms: belligerent, hostile, assailing
    antonyms: calm, easy-going, laid-back
  A football player needs a more *aggressive* style of play than a soccer player.

21. Penetrate [**pen**-i-treyt]
  verb def: to pierce or pass through or into. (***)
    synonyms: access, bore, break in, crack
    antonyms: exit, take out, withdraw
  The roots of these plants have been known to *penetrate* to a depth of more than 15 feet.

22. Expose [ik-**spohz**]
  verb def: to lay open to danger, attack, harm.
    synonyms: reveal, air, bare
    antonyms: conceal, cover, hide
  The shingles had fallen off, *exposing* the wood underneath.

23. Foible [**foi**-buhl]
  noun def. minor weakness
    synonyms: frailty, quirk, peculiarity
  One of Linda's *foibles* is her habit of licking the center of an Oreo cookie.

24. Adversary [**ad**-ver-ser-ee]
  noun def: a person or force that opposes or attacks. (**)
    synonyms: opponent, bandit, competitor, contestant
    antonyms: ally, assistant, friend, helper
  His political *adversaries* put forth a lot of effort to stop him from winning the nomination.

  He's a very smart criminal who pushes emotional buttons to get what he wants. He's quite a worthy *adversary* for Mac and the team.
  —*TV Guide*, 2-8 June 2008

25. Fleet [fleet]
  noun def: a large group of ships, airplanes, trucks.
    synonyms: armada, naval force, warships
  John has owned a *fleet* of trucks and cabs for the last twenty years.

TOEFL iBT/ TOEIC WORDS (Day 4)

26. Adverse [ad-**vurs**]
    adj def: unfavorable; antagonistic in purpose or effect. (*)
        synonyms: conflicting, contrary, detrimental, inimical, injurious
        antonyms: advantageous, aiding, auspicious, fortunate
    An *adverse* wind caused us to sleep over in an unknown cave.

27. Dwindle [dwin-dl]
    verb def: to become smaller and smaller. (***)
        synonyms: abate, decay, contract
        antonyms: develop, enlarge, expand
    Jackie's habit of wasting money has *dwindled* her fortune inherited from her parents.

28. Delay [dih-**ley**]
    verb def: to put off to a later time; defer.
        synonyms: deferment, interruption, hindrance
        antonyms: advance, dispatch, expedite
    Josh had a tendency to *delay* his work until it was too late to be completed in time.

29. Intimidate [in-**tim**-i-deyt]
    verb def: to make timid; fill with fear.
        synonyms: frighten, threaten, appall, bluster
        antonyms: assist, encourage, help
    Tebow had tried to *intimidate* his opponents before the game started.

30. Ruthless [**rooth**-lis]
    adj def: no mercy; cruel; without pity or compassion.
        synonyms: mean, callous, heartless, cruel
        antonyms: compassionate, considerate, gentle
    A *ruthless* tyrant harmed numerous innocent people.

31. Offspring [**awf**-spring]
    noun def: children or young of a particular parent.
        synonyms: descendent, lineage, offshoot, progeny
        antonyms: parent
    It is said that a newly released product is the *offspring* of an inventive mind.

TOEFL iBT/ TOEIC WORDS (Day 4)

32. Hinder [**hin**-der]
   verb def: to cause delay, interruption, or difficulty. (**)
        synonyms: balk, block, burden, check
        antonyms: advance, aid, assist, encourage
       The storm *hindered* us from reaching the top of the mountain.

33. Mitigate [**mit**-i-geyt]
   verb def: to lessen in force or intensity. (*****)
        synonyms: abate, allay, alleviate, appease
        antonyms: aggravate, incite, increase, intensify
       A judge may *mitigate* a sentence if she decides that a person committed a crime out of need.

       At the far end of the room is a sliding glass door, taped with an X to *mitigate* shattering. The framing is flimsy, and rattles from mortar rounds even a half-mile away.
                              — William Langewiesche, *Atlantic*, May 2005

34. Exert [ig-**zurt**]
   verb def: to apply strenuous, vigorous effort or action. (**)
        synonyms: apply, employ, exercise, expand
       Kenny *exerted* every effort on the business project he was in charge of.

35. Torment [**tawr**-ment]
   verb def: to afflict with great bodily or mental suffering; pain.
        synonyms: affliction, agony, anguish, bane, excruciation
        antonyms: contentment, glee, happiness, joy
       Lauren has been *tormented* with unbearable physical pain for the past two decades.

36. Lust [luhst]
   noun def: a passionate or overmastering desire or craving. (**)
        synonyms: passion, avidity, covetousness, craving
        antonyms: disgust, disenchantment
       Tina was frequently driven by a *lust* of power.

37. Ferocious [fuh-**roh**-shuhs]
   adj def: savagely fierce. (**)
        synonyms: violent, barbaric, feral, implacable
        antonyms: gentle, innocent, kind, mild

A *ferocious* wind virtually completely destroyed many buildings and municipal facilities.

38. Audacious [aw-**dey**-shuhs]
adj def: extremely bold or daring. (****)
   synonyms: reckless, brave, cheeky, courageous
   antonyms: cautious, humble, meek
   "And you, your majesty, may kiss my bum!" replied the *audacious* peasant.

   Whatever made him think his *audacious* fiction would sell—especially after a lifetime of literary marginalization—is a mystery, but he has certainly been vindicated. With a rush of work that he did not begin publishing until he was in his forties, he won literary fame in Europe and Latin America.
   — Valerie Sayers, *Commonweal*, 13 July 2007

39. Stun [stuhn]
verb def: to deprive of consciousness or strength.
   synonyms: shock, amaze, astonish, astound
   A teacher was *stunned* by a Jefferson's GPA.

40. Bloat [bloht]
verb def: to inflate; make vain or conceited.
   synonyms: billow, dilate, distend, enlarge
   antonyms: deflate, shrink, shrivel
   The promotion has *bloated* his ego to an alarming degree.

41. Inveigle [in-**vey**-guhl]
verb def: to entice; lure; ensnare by flattery or artful talk. (***)
   synonyms: entice, allure, beguile, blandish, butter up
   antonyms: disenchant, disgust, turn off
   Jack *inveigled* Susan to exercise every night.

42. Postpone [pohst-**pohn**]
verb def: to put off to a later time.
   synonyms: defer, delay, hold over,
   antonyms: carry out, continue, do, expedite
   Lucy was forced to *postpone* her departure until next week due to inclement weather.

TOEFL iBT/ TOEIC WORDS (Day 4)

43. Vigilant [vij-uh-luh-nt]
    adj def: keenly watchful to detect danger. (**)
        synonyms: acute, alert, anxious, aware
        antonyms: careless, impulsive, indiscreet, negligent
    Air traffic controllers must be *vigilant* in order to ensure that planes do not collide with one another.

44. Menace [men-is]
    noun def: something that threatens to cause harm.
        synonyms: danger, annoyance, caution, hazard
        antonyms: aid, assistance, help
    Air pollution is a *menace* to health.

45. Disregard [dis-ri-**gahrd**]
    verb def: to ignore; pay no attention; leave out of consideration.
        synonyms: ignoring, apathy, contempt, disdain, disesteem
        antonyms: attention, esteem, honor, note, regard, respect
    Carl *disregarded* a notice written by a landlord.

46. Supplicate [**suhp**-li-keyt]
    verb def: to pray humbly. (***)
        synonyms: appeal, beg, beseech, desire
    The bishop *supplicated* his parish to help the victims of the earthquake.

47. Contradict [kon-truh-**dikt**]
    verb def: to assert the contrary or opposite of.
        synonyms: belie, challenge, confront, contravene, controvert
        antonyms: accept, agree, approve, concede, confirm
    His way of life *contradicts* his stated principles.

48. Impede [im-**peed**]
    verb def: to retard in movement. (**)
        synonyms: obstruct, hinder, check, clog, close off
        antonyms: advance, aid, assist, facilitate
    Soldiers were unable to *impede* the enemy's advance due to a lack of ammunitions.

49. Exterminate [ik-**stur**-muh-neyt]
    verb def: to get rid of by destroying.
        synonyms: abolish, annihilate, destroy, decimate

TOEFL iBT/ TOEIC WORDS (Day 4)

antonyms: bear, create

Jennifer *exterminated* flies by smashing with a stick.

50. Trait [treyt]

noun def: a distinguish characteristic or quality. (**)

synonyms: affection, attribute, cast, character, custom

Sam seemed to have a *trait* of ready wit.

TOEFL iBT/ TOEIC WORDS (Day 4)

> *This book is an awesome resource for TOEFL iBT/ TOEIC test-takers. In it, they will find excellent advice on how to ace the test as well as a complete review of all the terms, many different types of listening and speaking questions, and realistic writing prompts. As a current college student in America, I recommend this book to anyone planning to take the TOEFL iBT/ TOEIC!*

Jin Park
Pre-Med, Rutgers University, NJ, USA

Drill 4

1. The word **endeavor** is closest in meaning to

    A) offspring
    B) amounts
    C) exertion
    D) torment

2. The word **allocation** is the closest in meaning to

    A) mode
    B) apportionment
    C) luster
    D) stuff

3. The word **aggressive** is closest in meaning to

    A) ferocious
    B) audacious
    C) stunning
    D) unassailable

4. The word **delay** is closest in meaning to

    A) bloat
    B) inveigle
    C) postpone
    D) jeopardize

5. The word **intimidation** is closest in meaning to

    A) vigilance
    B) menace
    C) derision
    D) disregard

Drill 4

6. The word **hinder** is closest in meaning to

    A) caution
    B) supplicate
    C) contradict
    D) impede

7. The word **procreate** is closest in meaning to

    A) array
    B) banal
    C) generate
    D) integrate

8. The word **exhibit** is closest in meaning to

    A) show
    B) deem
    C) exemplify
    D) flourish

9. The word **mitigate** is closest in meaning to

    A) hinder
    B) ignite
    C) migrate
    D) lessen

10. The word **encompass** is closest in meaning to

    A) overcome
    B) prevail
    C) surround
    D) ruthless

Drill 4

11. The word **plague** is closest in meaning to

    A) spread
    B) squander
    C) transit
    D) unify

12. The word **adversary** is closest in meaning to

    A) vex
    B) withstand
    C) opponent
    D) adjacent

13. The word **divert** is closest in meaning to

    A) boost
    B) classify
    C) discard
    D) change

14. The word **squander** is closest in meaning to

    A) extol
    B) waste
    C) incite
    D) luster

15. The word **dwindle** is closest in meaning to

    A) meticulous
    B) pity
    C) rapid
    D) decrease

Drill 4

16. The word **vain** is closest in meaning to

    A) insolent
    B) useless
    C) monarchy
    D) nourish

17. The word **adequate** is closest in meaning to

    A) enough
    B) nomadic
    C) overcome
    D) prompt

18. The word **fertile** is closest in meaning to

    A) plaster
    B) requisite
    C) abundant
    D) sequence

19. The word **inseminate** is closest in meaning to

    A) satiate
    B) tremor
    C) ubiquitous
    D) instill

20. The word **trait** is closest in meaning to

    A) character
    B) upswing
    C) weave
    D) void

1. C 2. B 3. A 4. C 5. B 6. D 7. C 8. A 9. D 10. C
11. A 12. C 13. D 14. B 15. D 16. B 17. A 18. C 19. D 20. A

TOEFL iBT/ TOEIC WORDS (Day 5)

1. Dispose [dih-**spohz**]
  verb def: give a tendency or inclination to.
      synonyms: actuate, adapt, adjust, arrange
      antonyms: discourage, disorder, displace
    His temperament *disposed* him to argue readily with people.

2. Replenish [ri-**plen**-ish]
  verb def: to make full or complete again. (**)
      synonyms: stock, furnish, make up, provide
      antonyms: deplete, use up, waste
    Rebecca went to the supermarket in order to *replenish* her stock of food in preparation for the winter.

3. Regulate [**reg**-yuh-leyt]
  verb def: to control or directly by a rule.
      synonyms: manage, organize, adapt, adjust, administer
      antonyms: disorganize, mismanage
    It was extremely difficult for Angela to *regulate* her eating behavior.

4. Dehydration [dee-hahy-**drey**-shuhn]
  noun def: to dry completely; to remove water.
      synonyms: desiccate, drain, dry, evaporate
      antonyms: moisten, wet, hydrate
    Soccer players must drink plenty of water in order not to suffer *dehydration*.

5. Facilitate [fuh-**sil**-i-teyt]
  verb def: to make easier or less difficult; help forward. (**)
      synonyms: aid, ease, expedite, forward
      antonyms: block, check, delay, detain
    The strength of the inner identities that black women forged and nurtured during slavery *facilitated* the transition to freedom.
                        — Darlene Clark Hine, *Lure and Loathing*, 1993

6. Vital [**vahyt**-l]
  adj def: pertaining to or necessary for life.
      synonyms: essential, basic, cardinal, constitute
      antonyms: inessential, insignificant, trivial
    Exercising on a daily basis is *vital* for a healthy body.

TOEFL iBT/ TOEIC WORDS (Day 5)

7. Replicate [rep-li-kit]
  verb def: to duplicate; reproduce.
    DNA *replicates* itself in the cell nucleus.

8. Release [ri-**lees**]
  verb def: to free from confinement, bondage, obligation.
      synonyms: delivery, absolution, acquittal, charge
      antonyms: check, collection, gathering, hold
    Christina has been waiting to *release* her article for publication.

9. Transport [trans-**port**]
  verb def: to carry; convey from one place to another.
      synonyms: carriage, conveyance, hauling
      antonyms: idle, remain, stay
    Trucks and buses have played major roles in *transporting* people and product.

10. Respiration [res-puh-**rey**-shuhn]
  noun def: respiring; inhalation/exhalation of air; breathing.
    The doctor regularly checks Tom's heartbeat and *respiration*.

11. Excrete [ik-**skreet**]
  verb def: to separate from an organic body.
      synonyms: discharge, defecate, ejaculate, eliminate
    Carbon dioxide is *excreted* by the cells.

12. Reverse [ri-**vurs**]
  verb def: opposite or contrary in position. (**)
      synonyms: opposite, antithesis, contradiction, contrary
      antonyms: identical, same
    John arranged the wires in *reverse* order.

13. Infectious [in-**fek**-shuhs]
  adj def: communicable by infection.
      synonyms: contagious, contaminate, corrupting, defiling
      antonyms: germless, harmless, antiseptic
    It is commonly believed that flu has an *infectious* agent.

TOEFL iBT/ TOEIC WORDS (Day 5)

14. Detect [dih-**tekt**]
   verb def: to discover or catch. (***)
   synonyms: discover, ascertain, descry, disclose
   antonyms: overlook, pass by, miss
   The doctors in the local hospital seem to have difficulties in *detecting* malignant tumors in their early stages.

15. Ingest [in-**jest**]
   verb def: to take food into the body.
   synonyms: swallow, absorb, consume, devour, digest
   Many people think that the drug is much more easily *ingested* in a liquid form than in pill form.

16. Overwhelm [oh-ver-**hwelm**]
   verb def: to overcome or overpower by superior forces.
   synonyms: flood, bury, conquer, crush, defeat, deluge
   antonyms: underwhelm, not impress
   Jennifer was *overwhelmed* by the scenery in front of her.

17. Demise [dih-**mahyz**]
   noun def: death; decease.
   synonyms: collapse, decease, dissolution, downfall
   antonyms: birth
   A decline in correct language usage is one of the hallmarks of the *demise* of a civilization.

18. Plunge [pluhnj]
   verb def: to cast or thrust forcibly.
   synonyms: descend, dive, duck, fall
   antonyms: ascend, increase, rise
   Jack *plunged* a dagger into his heart.

19. Absorb [ab-**sawrb**]
   verb def: involve the full attention of. (*)
   synonyms: comprehend, digest, follow, grasp
   antonyms: misunderstand, not get
   Nicolas was so *absorbed* in a book that he did not hear his son's voice.

TOEFL iBT/ TOEIC WORDS (Day 5)

20. Daze [deyz]
    verb def: to overwhelm; dazzle.
        synonyms: addle, amaze, astonish, astound, befuddle
    Jane was *dazed* by the splendor of palace standing in front of her.

21. Presume [pri-**zoom**]
    verb def: take for granted; assume; suppose.
        synonyms: assume, concede, conjecture, consider
        antonyms: disbelieve
    The judge *presumed* innocence until there was proof of guilt.

22. Annoy [uh-**noi**]
    verb def: to bother; to irritate. (**)
        synonyms: irritate, agitate, abrade, badger
        antonyms: aid, gratify, please, soothe
    Brad continuously *annoyed* Jessica because he hated her so much.

23. Debris [duh-**bree**]
    noun def: the remains of anything broken down.
        synonyms: litter, waste, dregs
        antonyms: cleanliness, neatness, purify
    The villagers saw their houses reduced to *debris* after an air raid.

24. Eradicate [ih-**rad**-i-keyt]
    verb def: to remove; to destroy completely. (***)
        synonyms: abolish, annihilate, demolish
        antonyms: aid, assist, bear, create
    Many doctors and researchers spent numerous hours *eradicating* smallpox through the world.

25. Beneficial [beh-uh-**fish**-uhl]
    adj def: conferring benefit; helpful.
        synonyms: benign, constructive, gainful, healthful
        antonyms: harmful, hurting, unfortunate
    The *beneficial* effect of sunshine must not be ignored by anyone under any circumstance.

26. Burgeon [**bur**-juhn]
    verb def: to grow or develop quickly. (**)
    Many people were surprised that Tony *burgeoned* into a fine artist.

TOEFL iBT/ TOEIC WORDS (Day 5)

27. Pedagogue [**ped**-uh-gog]
  noun def: educator; schoolteacher.
  Most of the students have known Dr. Schmidt as a *pedagogue*.

28. Disintegrate [dis-**in**-tuh-greyt]
  verb def: to separate into parts.
    synonyms: fall apart, atomize, break up
    antonyms: combine, meld, unite
  The old book has gradually been *disintegrating* with age.

29. Delinquency [dih-**ling**-kwuhn-see]
  noun def: failure in or neglect of duty or obligation. (***)
    synonyms: crime, default, dereliction, failure
    antonyms: good behavior
  A corrupted officer has been charged with contributing to the *delinquency* of a minor.

30. Ethnic [**eth**-nik]
  adj def: sharing a common and distinctive culture. (**)
    synonyms: racial, culture, indigenous, native
  There is a huge *ethnic* Chinese town in San Francisco.

31. Ramification [ram-uh-fi-**key**-shuhn]
  noun def: a related or derived subject, problem.
    synonyms: branch, breaking, complication, division
    antonyms: cause
  The new traffic laws proved to have many *ramifications* unnoticed by the lawmakers.

32. Emerge [ih-**murj**]
  verb def: to come forth into view or notion. (*)
    synonyms: appear, arrive, come forth, dawn
    antonyms: disappear, fade, leave
  Martinez has *emerged* as a leading contender in this professional field.

33. Subsequent [**suhb**-si-kwuhnt]
  adj def: occurring or coming later or after.
    synonyms: after, consecutive, consequent, following
    antonyms: antecedent, earlier, former, previous

TOEFL iBT/ TOEIC WORDS (Day 5)

Her *subsequent* account of her ordeal, "The Upstairs Room" (1972), was a young adult tour de force, winning a Newberry Honor and other awards. Compared with Anne Frank's "Diary of a Young Girl," it is sparer and sterner.
—Leslie Garis, *New York Times Book Review*, 22 Feb. 2009

34. Bias [bahy-uhs]
noun def: a particular tendency or inclination; prejudice.
synonyms: bent, bigotry, disposition, flash, inclination
antonyms: fairness, impartiality, justness
Sarah has strong feelings against people who have racial *bias*.

35. Transform [trans-**fawrm**]
verb def: to change into another substance.
synonyms: change, alter, communicate, convert
antonyms: leave alone, presence, stagnate
The old building was *transformed* into an art gallery.

36. Consequent [**kon**-si-kwent]
adj def: following as an effect or result.
synonyms: consistent, ensuing, resultant, intelligent
antonyms: beginning, causal, commencing
It is generally acknowledged that a fall in price will be *consequent* to a rise in production.

37. Conceive [kuhn-**seev**]
verb def: to form; hold; imagine. (**)
synonyms: accept, appreciate, apprehend, assume
antonyms: misunderstand, not believe
Jack *conceived* of this idea ten years ago.

38. Evolve [ih-**volv**]
verb def: to develop by a process of evolution.
synonyms: advance, disclose, educe, elaborate, emerge
antonyms: decrease, halt, stop
According to recently released studies, the human species *evolved* from an ancestor who was probably arboreal.

TOEFL iBT/ TOEIC WORDS (Day 5)

39. Akin [uh-**kin**]
　adj　def: related. (***)
　　　synonyms: affiliated, alike, analogous
　　　antonyms: alien, disconnected
　　　They are emotionally but not intellectually *akin*.

40. Paramount [**par**-uh-mount]
　adj　def: chief; supreme; preeminent. (***)
　　　synonyms: principal, ascendant, capital, cardinal
　　　antonyms: inferior, last, least, less, lowest
　　　It is of *paramount* importance that we make it back to camp before the storm hits, or we will freeze to death.

41. Conceptualize [kuhn-**sep**-choo-uh-lahyz]
　verb　def: to form into a concept; make a concept of.
　　　synonyms: develop a thought, visualize, gestate
　　　Even though Paul described the plan to me in detail, I found difficulty in *conceptualizing* it.

42. Scarcity [**skair**-si-tee]
　noun　def: insufficiency or shortness of supply. (**)
　　　The *scarcity* of decent libraries is surprising to everyone.

43. Differentiate [dif-uh-**ren**-shee-yet]
　verb　def: to form or mark differently from other such things.
　　　synonyms: comprehend, contrast, demarcate, discern
　　　antonyms: associate, confuse, connect, group
　　　It was amazingly difficult to *differentiate* the twins.

44. Congest [kuhn-**gest**]
　verb　def: to fill to excess; overcrowd.
　　　The park was so *congested* that people were unable to move.

45. Affluent [**af**-loo-uh nt]
　adj　def: having an abundance of wealth. (***)
　　　synonyms: wealthy, loaded, opulent
　　　antonyms: destitute, impoverished, needy
　　　An *affluent* woman, Irene was capable of giving large sums of money to charity.

TOEFL iBT/ TOEIC WORDS (Day 5)

The store catered to a mostly *affluent* clientele that was relatively price insensitive, so we could afford to pay our suppliers a premium for the very best fish. The shop also developed a significant wholesale business, and soon the great and the good of London gastronomy were flocking to our door.

— Frances Percival, *Saveur*, March 2008

46. Tranquil [trang-kwil]
  adj def: free from commotion or tumult. (**)
        synonyms: agreeable, amicable, at ease, balmy
        antonyms: chaotic, loud, noisy
    Twilight in the forest is a *tranquil* time to take a walk.

47. Sustain [suh-steyn]
  verb def: to maintain; support or hold up from below.
        synonyms: keep up, maintain, approve, befriend
        antonyms: discontinue, halt, stop
    The judge *sustained* the lawyer's objection.

48. Periphery [puh-rif-uh-ree]
  noun def: the edge or boundary; outskirt.
        synonyms: border, circuit, circumference
        antonyms: center
    The preliminary research of the subject did not take Tom beyond the *periphery* of his problem.

49. Municipal [myoo-nis-uh-puhl]
  adj def: pertaining to a town or city or its local government.
        synonyms: borough, city, civic, community
        antonyms: country, suburban
    Brad did not have any intention to participate in a *municipal* election.

50. Serenity [suh-ren-i-ty]
  noun def: the state of quality of being serene, calm. (***)
        synonyms: calmness, peacefulness, composure
        antonyms: agitation, disruption, excitement
    Lynette's meditation helps her to achieve true *serenity*.

Drill 5

1. The word **detect** is closest in meaning to

    A) daze
    B) spot
    C) presume
    D) annoy

2. The word **dispose** is closest in meaning to

    A) depose
    B) abrasive
    C) disconcert
    D) refute

3. The word **replenish** is closest in meaning to

    A) stun
    B) withstand
    C) to make full
    D) tranquil

4. The word **duplicate** is closest in meaning to

    A) copy
    B) acrimonious
    C) elate
    D) impartial

5. The word **debris** is closest in meaning to

    A) wastes
    B) verdant
    C) spurious
    D) prudent

Drill 5

6. The word **ingest** is closest in meaning to?

    A) supplicate
    B) absorb
    C) fractious
    D) consolation

7. The word **presume** is closest in meaning to

    A) thrive
    B) adjacent
    C) clasp
    D) assume

8. The word **partially** is closest in meaning to

    A) specifically
    B) passively
    C) sensibly
    D) fractionally

9. The word **alleviating** is closest in meaning to

    A) mitigating
    B) parroting
    C) discountenancing
    D) condensing

10. The word **paramount** is closest in meaning to

    A) patchy
    B) continual
    C) supreme
    D) pinpoint

Drill 5

11. The word **periphery** is closest in meaning to

    A) capricious
    B) exculpate
    C) boundary
    D) espouse

12. The word **serenity** is closest in meaning to

    A) descend
    B) calmness
    C) foster
    D) hefty

13. The word **ramification** is closest in meaning to

    A) branch
    B) hibernate
    C) pedagogic
    D) backdrop

14. The word **congest** is closest in meaning to

    A) linger
    B) enthrall
    C) anarchy
    D) crowd

15. The word **transition** is closest in meaning to

    A) change
    B) enmity
    C) subsequent
    D) utilize

Drill 5

16. The word **vital** is closest in meaning to

    A) vigilance
    B) essential
    C) usurp
    D) nimble

17. The word **excrete** is closest in meaning to

    A) nadir
    B) misgiving
    C) malady
    D) separate

18. The word **demise** is closest in meaning to

    A) mellow
    B) nostalgic
    C) end
    D) juvenile

19. The word **eradicate** is closest in meaning to

    A) get rid of
    B) fracture
    C) allocation
    D) exert

20. The word **burgeon** is closest in meaning to

    A) elaborate
    B) initiate
    C) abate
    D) bigot

1. B 2. A 3. C 4. A 5. A 6. B 7. D 8. D 9. A 10. C
11. C 12. B 13. A 14. D 15. A 16. B 17. D 18. C 19. A 20. B

TOEFL iBT/ TOEIC WORDS (Day 6)

1. Converse [kuhn-**vurs**]
    verb def: to talk informally with another
        synonyms: chat, commune, confer
        antonyms: be quiet, be silent
        Jason and Jenny often *converse* in Spanish at home.

2. Facile [**fas**-il]
    adj def: moving, acting with ease. (***)
        synonyms: accomplished, adept, adroit, apparent, articulate
        antonyms: arduous, complicated, difficult
        But in the less balmy days of their marriage and the final years of his life, Lennon produced (with Yoko's help) shallow, *facile* recordings that cannibalized his early work.
                —Francine Prose, *The Lives of the Muses*, 2002

3. Multifarious [muhl-tuh-**fair**-ee-uhs]
    adj def: numerous; various; diverse. (**)
        synonyms: assorted, divers, multiple
        antonyms: homogeneous
        Dr. Franklin immersed himself in *multifarious* interests and activities.

4. Egalitarian [ih-gal-**tair**-ee-uhn]
    noun def: asserting, resulting from, or characterized by belief in the equality of all people.
        In modern society, not many people adhere to *egalitarian* belief.

5. Kinship [**kin**-ship]
    noun def: the state or fact of being kin; family relationship.
        synonyms: affinity, blood, clan, folk
        Catherine was beginning to show a strong *kinship* with her teammates.

6. Congregate [**kahn**-gri-geyt]
    verb def: to come together; assemble. (*)
        synonyms: assemble, besiege, collect, concentrate, congress
        antonyms: divide, scatter, separate
        People began to *congregate* in the hotel lobby.

TOEFL iBT/ TOEIC WORDS (Day 6)

7. Domestic [duh-**mes**-tik]
    adj def: pertaining to the home; the household affairs.
        synonyms: household
        antonyms: business, industrial, office
    In a successful marriage, responsibility for *domestic* chores is distributed equally among husband, wife, and children.

8. Intermittent [in-ter-**mit**-nt]
    adj def: stopping or ceasing. (***)
        synonyms: irregular, sporadic, arrested, checked
        antonyms: continual, perpetual
    The flow of traffic was *intermittent* on the highway, but the commuters were thankful that it hadn't stopped completely.

9. Primordial [prahy-**mawr**-dee-uhl]
    adj def: constituting a beginning; giving origin.
        synonyms: basic, early, fundamental, prehistoric
    Many scientists claimed that all life on earth came from *primordial* ooze.

10. Norm [nawrm]
    noun def: standard; model. (**)
        synonyms: average, barometer, gauge, median
        antonyms: end, exception, extreme
    Having two cars in one family is the *norm* in the United States of America.

11. Dispute [dih-**spyoot**]
    verb def: to engage in argument.
        synonyms: altercate, brawl, broil, conflict
        antonyms: agree
    The source of the book written by Nicolas has been *disputed* for the past several years.

12. Mediate [**mee**-dee-eyt]
    verb def: To act as an intermediary between parties in a dispute. (**)
        synonyms: arbitrate, conciliate, intercede, interfere
        antonyms: argue, contend, disagree, fight
    The primary task of Michael was to *mediate* between parties by reconciliation.

TOEFL iBT/ TOEIC WORDS (Day 6)

13. Underlying [uhn-der-lahy-ing]
  adj def: lying or situated beneath.
    synonyms: basic, bottom, cardinal, concealed
    antonyms: secondary
    It is easy to tell the *underlying* difference between democracy and dictatorship.

14. Reinforce [ree-in-fawrs]
  verb def: to strengthen with some added piece.
    synonyms: strengthen, augment, boost, build up
    antonyms: subtract, take away, undermine
    The general sent out additional military supplies to *reinforce* the troops in Germany.

15. Homogeneous [hah-moh-gee-nee-uhs]
  adj def: corresponding in structure because of a common group. (**)
    synonyms: comparable, akin, alike, cognate
    antonyms: different, discrete, dissimilar, varied
    In their natural state, mountains of this type are almost entirely covered by dense forest. The wooded landscape is very uniform, lacking in contrast, and any disturbance of the *homogeneous* green blanket is very obvious ...
        — John Crowley, *Focus on Geography*, Winter 2007

16. Parochial [puh-roh-kee-uhl]
  adj def: pertaining to a parish or parishes. (***)
    synonyms: narrow, restricted, biased
    antonyms: broad, liberal, unrestricted
    It was obvious that Victor's *parochial* mentality would clash with Ivonne's liberal open-mindedness.

17. Tenable [ten-uh-buhl]
  adj def: capable of being held, maintained, or defended, as against attack. (**)
    synonyms: defendable, plausible, credible, reliable
    antonyms: unbelievable, untenable
    Greg burned down his own house so that his ex-wife could not live in it, a scarcely *tenable* action in light of the fact that this also left his children homeless.

TOEFL iBT/ TOEIC WORDS (Day 6)

18. Scarce [skairs]
adj def: insufficient to satisfy the needs of.
    synonyms: insufficient, infrequent, scant
    antonyms: abundant, plentiful, sufficient
Meat, butter, and milk turned out to be extremely *scarce* during the war.

19. Mingle [**ming**-guhl]
verb def: to mix with. (*)
    synonyms: admix, alloy, coalesce, commingle
    antonyms: disjoin
Jessica firmly refused to *mingle* with her classmates.

20. Detrimental [de-truh-**men**-tl]
adj def: harmful or damaging. (****)
    synonyms: adverse, baleful, deleterious
    antonyms: assisting, beneficial, helpful, profitable
It is generally acknowledged that smoking cigarettes can be *detrimental* to your health.

In context, the word "corruption" summarized the opinion (set forth in some of the books mentioned in the review) that, as a general matter, the growing financial dependence of the medical profession on the pharmaceutical industry is profoundly *detrimental* to sound public, medical, and scientific policy.
                  — *New York Review of Books*, 12 Feb. 2009

21. Coherent [koh-**heer**-uhnt]
adj def: to stick together; united; hold. (**)
    synonyms: articulate, comprehensible, consistent, identified
    antonyms: disorganized, incomprehensible, irrational
Dr. Lee gave a *coherent* explanation about the fundamental concept of the computer program he invented.

TOEFL iBT/ TOEIC WORDS (Day 6)

22. Aggregate [**ag**-ri-geyt]
  adj def: formed by adding materials together. (***)
    synonyms: accumulated, added, amassed, collected
    antonyms: individual, part, particular
  There were to be thirty-seven playgrounds, twenty schools. There were to be a hundred and thirty-three miles of street, paved with an inch and a half of No. 2 macadam on an *aggregate* base.
                              — Joan Didion, *New Yorker*, 26 July 1993

23. Conflict [kuhn-**flikt**]
  verb def: to come into collision; disagreement.
    synonyms: competition
    antonyms: agreement, calm, concord
  My TOEFL iBT and TOEIC classes *conflicted* with going to the concert.

24. Discord [**dis**-kawrd]
  noun def: lack of concord or harmony between persons. (*)
    synonyms: cacophony, clamor, dissonance, harshness
    antonyms: harmoniousness
  The city used to be considered as a scene of racial intolerance and *discord*.

25. Circumvent [sur-kuh m-**vent**]
  verb def: to go around; bypass. (***)
    synonyms: avoid, beguile, detour
    antonyms: face head on, deal with directly
  We *circumvented* the problem by using a different program.

  Los Angeles was the beachhead for the sushi invasion, attracting many Japanese chefs eager to make their fortunes and to *circumvent* the grueling 10-year apprenticeship required in their homeland.
                      — Jay McInerney, *New York Times Book Review*, 10 June 2007

26. Invoke [in-**voke**]
  verb def: to call for with earnest desire. (**)
    synonyms: appeal to, beg, beseech, conjure
    Gilbert tried to *invoke* his memory to justify what he had done.

TOEFL iBT/ TOEIC WORDS (Day 6)

27. Retribution [re-truh-**byoo**-shuhn]
noun def: requital according to merits.
    synonyms: compensation, punishment, reckoning
    antonyms: forgiveness, pardon, sympathy
People in James's town were torn apart by gang violence and *retribution*.

28. Monopoly [muh-**nop**-uh-lee]
noun def: exclusive possession or control of something.
    synonyms: oligarchy, proprietorship, syndicates
    antonyms: distribution, sharing
The government finally passed laws that hinder any companies from maintaining *monopolies* in a free market.

29. Subsidiary [suh-**sid**-ee-er-ee]
adj def: serving to assist or supplement. (***)
    synonyms: secondary, accessory, assisting
    antonyms: chief, important, necessary
The information service may be conducted by the information utility itself, by a *subsidiary* service, or by one or more of the subscribers.

30. Patriarch [**pey**-tree-ahrk]
noun def: male head of a family or tribal line. (**)
    synonyms: chief, founder, head, senior
    antonyms: matriarch
As the *patriarch* of the family, grandfather made all the important decisions.

31. Dogmatic [dawg-**mat**-ik]
adj def: asserting opinions in a doctrinaire or arrogant manner; opinionated. (**)
    synonyms: arbitrary, arrogant, dictatorial
    antonyms: amenable, flexible, indecisive, manageable, skeptical
What we are being treated to, clearly, is an extended set of variations on that most ancient of all intellectual chestnuts, the infinite capacity of the professorial mind for the *dogmatic* and ludicrous misinterpretation of evidence regarding past civilizations.
        — Peter Green, *New Republic*, 20 Mar. 2000

TOEFL iBT/ TOEIC WORDS (Day 6)

32. Supernatural [soo-per-**nach**-er-uhl]
  adj def: preternatural.
    synonyms: abnormal, mysterious, celestial
    antonyms: earthly, existent, genuine, natural
    The horror story was filled with *supernatural* events.

33. Scheme [skeem]
  noun def: plan; design; program of action to be followed.
    synonyms: arrangement, blueprint, codification, design
    The company's pension *scheme* turned out to be successful.

34. Transmit [trans-**mit**]
  verb def: to pass or spread to another. (***)
    synonyms: dispatch, disseminate, consign, diffuse
    antonyms: get, receive, take
    The mother *transmitted* her red hair to her children.

35. Primogeniture [prahy-muh-**jen**-i-cher]
  noun def: the state or fact of being the firstborn of children of the same
    parents, thus deserving to inherit their estate from them. (***)
    The majority of people in ancient society had a strong tendency to believe
    in *primogeniture*.

36. Validate [**val**-i-deyt]
  verb def: to confirm; legalize; give official sanction.
    synonyms: approve, authorize, certify, confirm, constitute
    antonyms: refuse, reject, veto
    Time *validated* our suspicions.

37. Forestall [fohr-**stawl**]
  verb def: to stop, prevent, hinder by action in advance. (***)
    In order to *forestall* a riot, the government deployed police.

38. Reciprocate [ri-**sip**-ruh-keyt]
  verb def: to make a return or interchange. (****)
    synonyms: exchange, equal, banter, equivalent, interchange
    antonyms: deny, refuse
    Individuals who have received a dedication ... are expected to *reciprocate*
    with a gift, perhaps placing a few folded notes of money into the hat when
    they give it back.

TOEFL iBT/ TOEIC WORDS (Day 6)

— A. L. Kennedy, *On Bullfighting*, 1999

39. Impose [im-**pose**]
　　verb def: to lay on or set.
　　　　synonyms: appoint, burden, charge, command, compel
　　　　The mayor decided to *impose* a variety of taxes on tourists.

40. Punitive [**pyoo**-ni-tiv]
　　adj def: inflicting, involving, or aiming at punishment.
　　　　synonyms: castigating, correctional
　　　　antonyms: beneficial, rewarding
　　　　The federal government made a determination to take *punitive* action
　　　　against the companies that had polluted air and water.

41. Friction [**frik**-shuhn]
　　noun def: dissension or conflict between people.
　　　　synonyms: animosity, antagonism, conflict, discontent
　　　　antonyms: agreement, harmony, peace
　　　　The primary role of oil in an engine is to reduce *friction*.

42. Stratify [**strat**-uh-fahy]
　　verb def: to classify by placing into layers. (**)
　　　　Several countries in the world *stratified* their people into class.

43. Predisposed [pree-di-**spohz**]
　　verb def: to give an inclination or tendency to beforehand.
　　　　synonyms: amenable, biased, eager
　　　　antonyms: disagreeing, disinclined, unwilling
　　　　Genetic factors may *predispose* human beings to certain metabolic diseases.

44. Animosity [an-uh-**mos**-i-tee]
　　noun def: a feeling of strong dislike, ill will
　　　　synonyms: acrimony, animus, antipathy, bitterness
　　　　antonyms: good will, love
　　　　The deep-rooted *animosity* between them made it difficult for the cousins to
　　　　work together.

45. Judicial [joo-**dish**-uhl]
　　adj def: giving or seeking judgment.
　　　　synonyms: legal, administrative, discriminating, equitable

After her father passed away, Jane's family had a *judicial* duel over lands.

46. Implement [im-pluh-muhnt]
verb def: to put into effect according to. (**)
  synonyms: achieve, actualize, bring about, carry out, complete
  antonyms: cancel, cease, delay, halt
Plans were drawn up to *implement* a state of emergency.

47. Augment [awg-ment]
verb def: to make larger; enlarge. (***)
  synonyms: aggrandize, amplify, boost, build, compound
  antonyms: decrease, degrade
Paul *augmented* his salary with overtime hours as much as possible.

... a former member of Brunet's team, Jean-Renaud Boisserie of Berkeley, is in the Middle Awash seeking to *augment* the animal fossil record—particularly that of hippopotamuses.
— Rex Dalton, *Nature*, 5 Jan. 2006

48. Apparatus [ap-uh-rat-uhs]
noun def: a group or combination of instruments or machinery.
  synonyms: device, contraption, appliance
She accidentally fell off a gymnastics *apparatus* and broke her arm.

49. Dedicate [ded-i-keyt]
verb def: to devote wholly and earnestly.
  synonyms: donate, address, allot, apply
  antonyms: misuse, steal, take, misapply
Dr. Chen *dedicated* his life to the development of ESL education in America.

50. Intricate [in-tri-kit]
verb def: having many interrelated parts. (***)
  synonyms: abstruse, baroque, complex, fancy
  antonyms: direct, methodical, simple
Herbert is very good at manipulating an *intricate* machine.

Drill 6

1. The word **facile** is closest in meaning to

    A) feudal
    B) simple
    C) ripe
    D) vile

2. The word **congregation** is closest in meaning to

    A) burden
    B) collection
    C) heed
    D) caption

3. The word **intermittent** is closest in meaning to

    A) unrivaled
    B) analogous
    C) occasional
    D) anonymous

4. The word **intervene** is closest in meaning to

    A) betray
    B) predicate
    C) accuse
    D) mediate

5. The word **kinship** is closest in meaning to

    A) validation
    B) monopoly
    C) relatives
    D) primordial

Drill 6

6. The word **primordial** is closest in meaning to

    A) arresting
    B) hinder
    C) gather
    D) principal

7. The word **norm** is closest in meaning to

    A) intricate
    B) judicial
    C) mingle
    D) standard

8. The word **dispute** is closest in meaning to

    A) argue
    B) scheme
    C) monopoly
    D) wherein

9. The word **parochial** is closest in meaning to

    A) transmit
    B) mediate
    C) narrow
    D) outing

10. The word **circumvent** is closest in meaning to

    A) retreat
    B) detour
    C) convert
    D) fulfill

Drill 6

11. The word **underlying** is closest in meaning to

    A) basis
    B) tribe
    C) dissolve
    D) duel

12. The word **coherent** is closest in meaning to?

    A) regulate
    B) stun
    C) sticking together
    D) torment

13. The word **invoke** is closest in meaning to

    A) unbiased
    B) ask for
    C) thrive
    D) undaunted

14. The word **retribution** is closest in meaning to

    A) validation
    B) agility
    C) fluctuation
    D) compensation

15. The word **reciprocate** is closest in meaning to

    A) fertile
    B) mutual
    C) futile
    D) implacable

Drill 6

16. The word **augment** is closest in meaning to

    A) increase
    B) brink
    C) abandon
    D) beneficial

17. The word **friction** is closest in meaning to

    A) bleak
    B) conjecture
    C) abrasion
    D) domestic

18. The word **forestall** is closest in meaning to

    A) delve
    B) enrich
    C) fissure
    D) stop

19. The word **dogmatic** is closest in meaning to

    A) forecast
    B) dictatorial
    C) hostile
    D) itinerant

20. The word **monopoly** is closest in meaning to

    A) insulate
    B) juvenile
    C) exclusive
    D) lethal

1. B 2. B 3. C 4. D 5. C 6. D 7. D 8. A 9. C 10. B
11. A 12 .C 13. B 14. D 15. B 16. A 17. C 18. D 19. B 20. C

TOEFL iBT/ TOEIC WORDS (Day 7)

1. Hegemony [hi-**jem**-uh-nee]
    noun def: leadership or dominant influence.
        synonyms: domination, authority, command, power
    … the very concept of "scientific truth" can only represent a social construction invented by scientists (whether consciously or not) as a device to justify their *hegemony* over the study of nature.
        — Stephen Jay Gould, *Science*, 14 Jan. 2000

2. Prowess [prou-**is**]
    noun def: exceptional valor, bravery, or ability. (*)
        synonyms: adeptness, aptitude, attainment, deftness
        antonyms: inability, weakness
    Dennis showed his *prowess* as a public speaker.

3. Reign [reyn]
    noun def: royal rule or authority. (**)
        synonyms: ascendancy, control, dynasty, empire
        antonyms: serve, submit
    King George was considered as a popular ruler throughout his *reign*.

4. Disjointed [dis-**join**-tid]
    adj def: having the joints or connections separated.
        synonyms: loose, disconnected, aimless, confused
        antonyms: coherent, contiguous, jointed, ordered
    There are many different *disjointed* societies in the world.

5. Surrender [suh-**ren**-der]
    verb def: to yield possession or power.
        synonyms: abandon, abdicate, capitulate, give up
        antonyms: fight, win
    Kenny did not have any intention to *surrender* himself to a life of hardship.

6. Endow [en-**dou**]
    verb def: to provide with a permanent fund or source of income. (**)
        synonyms: accord, award, back, confer, empower
        antonyms: receive, take
    The money Dickens donated to the hospital was used to *endow* a new wing of the hospital.

TOEFL iBT/ TOEIC WORDS (Day 7)

7. Hostile [hos-tl]
  adj def: characterized of an enemy. (***)
    synonyms: adverse, alien, allergic, bellicose, competitive
    antonyms: agreeable, gentle, kind
  Justine had a *hostile* relationship with her colleagues.

  Dugoni, a lawyer who coauthored a nonfiction book about an Idaho worker brain-damaged in 1996 by cyanide fumes, opens his debut novel with a wrongful death attorney in San Francisco, David Sloane, about to make his closing remarks defending a corporation in a similar case. Sloane, who has won 14 cases in a row, hates his arrogant client and must face an obviously *hostile* jury.
    — *Publishers Weekly*, 9 Jan. 2006

8. Divine [dih-vahyn]
  noun def: pertaining to a god.
    synonyms: almighty, angelic, blissful, celestial
  Among all the competitors, Paul appeared to have the most *divine* tenor voice.

9. Fend [fend]
  verb def: to provide or earn a living
    synonyms: bulwark, cover, dodge, guard, oppose, parry
    antonyms: surrender, yield
  Susan and Brian were forced to *fend* for themselves.

10. Preoccupied [pree-ok-yuh-pahyd]
  adj def: completely engrossed in thought; absorbed. (***)
    synonyms: absent, absorbed, asleep, bemused
    antonyms: observant, thoughtful, unoccupied
  Tina was too *preoccupied* with her worries to enjoy the delicious meal.

11. Revenue [rev-uhn-yoo]
  noun def: the income of a government from taxation or customs.
    synonyms: annuity, credit, fund, gain
    antonyms: debt, payment
  The local company has been trying to find another source of *revenue* in order to avoid bankruptcy.

TOEFL iBT/ TOEIC WORDS (Day 7)

12. Commodity [kuh-**mod**-i-tee]
noun def: an article of trade or commerce.
    synonyms: merchandise, possession, asset, chattel
    Oil has been regarded as a *commodity* in high demand.

13. Accumulate [uh-**kyoo**-myuh-leyt]
verb def: to pile up into a heap. (**)
    synonyms: accrue, acquire, add to, aggregate, amalgamate
    antonyms: disperse, dissipate, dwindle, lessen
    It is hard to believe that Lynn's debt appeared to keep on *accumulating*.

14. Pursue [per-**soo**]
verb def: to follow in order to overtake, capture.
    synonyms: chase, attend, badger, bait
    antonyms: retreat, run away
    Having graduated from college, William decided to go to Moscow in order to *pursue* higher education.

15. Reputation [rep-yuh-**tey**-shuhn]
noun def: the estimation in which a person or thing is held.
    synonyms: account, approval, credit
    Alex ruined his *reputation* by constantly making terrible mistakes.

16. Patron [**pey**-truhn]
noun def: a person who is a customer, client.
    synonyms: advocate, backer, champion, defender
    antonyms: detractor, enemy, opponent
    Many libraries offer a free on-line service where a *patron* can log on to a site and download books for free for a two-week period.

17. Elicit [ih-**lis**-it]
verb def: to draw or bring out or forth. (***)
    synonyms: educe, evoke, bring out, cause
    antonyms: cover, hide, keep
    Clara attempted to *elicit* a response with several penetrating questions.

TOEFL iBT/ TOEIC WORDS (Day 7)

18. Patronage [**pey**-truh-nij]
   noun def: financial support or business provided.
   synonyms: aegis, aid, support, auspices, grant
   antonyms: antagonism, detraction, opposition
   The university relies more on the *patronage* of its wealthy graduates to expand its fund than on tuition paid by its enrolled students.

19. Circumspect [**sur**-kuhm-spekt]
   adj def: watchful and discreet; cautious; prudent. (***)
   synonyms: cautious, discreet, cagey, calculating
   antonyms: audacious, bold, careless, indiscreet
   The detective was *circumspect* in investigating charges of child abuses.

20. Enlighten [en-**lahyt**-n]
   verb def: to give intellectual or spiritual light to; instruct. (***)
   synonyms: acquaint, advise, direct, edify
   antonyms: bewilder, confound, confuse, delude
   Dr. Smith hoped that the result of his research could *enlighten* his colleagues.

21. Diplomatic [dip-luh-**mat**-ik]
   adj def: skilled at dealing with sensitive matters or people.
   synonyms: politic, adept, arch, artful, astute
   antonyms: artless, impolite, rude, tactless
   It is not easy for any two nations to restore their full *diplomatic* relations.

22. Negotiate [ni-**goh**-shee-eyt]
   verb def: to deal or bargain with another.
   synonyms: accommodate, adjust, agree, arbitrate
   Stephen appeared to be extremely good at *negotiating* a business deal.

23. Stave off [steyv awf]
   verb def: to prevent; to keep from breaking in upon or crushing.
   Victor was unable to *stave off* bankruptcy.

TOEFL iBT/ TOEIC WORDS (Day 7)

24. Annex [an-neks]
   noun def: attachment; appendage; addition. (*)
       synonyms: adjoin, append, affix, associate
       antonyms: detach, leave off, leave out
   The emergence room is in the *annex* of the main building.

25. Cornerstone [kawr-ner-stohn]
   noun def: something that is essential or basic.
       synonyms: anchor, base, essential, keystone
   It is commonly believed that the *cornerstone* of democracy is a free speech.

26. Hieroglyphic [hahy-er-uh-glif-ik]
   adj def: designating or pertaining to a pictographic script.
   The stone Reese found was inscribed with *hieroglyphic* symbols.

27. Comprehensive [kom-pri-hen-siv]
   adj def: of large scope; covering or involving much.
       synonyms: inclusive, absolute, compendious
       antonyms: exclusive, particular, incomprehensive
   John spent numerous hours on a *comprehensive* study of world affairs.

28. Secular [sek-yuh-ler]
   adj def: pertaining to worldly things. (*****)
       synonyms: civil, earthly, lay, material, profane
       antonyms: godly, holy, religious
   Although his favorite book was the Bible, the archbishop also read *secular* works such as mysteries.

Bloomberg, by contrast, would be the most pro-immigration, pro-free trade, pro-Wall Street candidate in the race. The third-party candidate he would most resemble is John Anderson, the fiscally responsible, culturally liberal Republican who ran as an Independent in 1980. Anderson won 7% of the vote, mostly among the young, educated and *secular*. But today those people are partisan Democrats.

— Peter Beinart, *TIME*, 11 Feb. 2008

TOEFL iBT/ TOEIC WORDS (Day 7)

29. Prodigy [prod-i-gee]
noun def: a person, especially a child or young person having extraordinary talent or ability. (***)
synonyms: brain, genius, marvel, mastermind
Mozart was a musical *prodigy* at the age of four.

30. Sufficient [suh-**fish**-uhnt]
adj def: adequate for the purpose. (**)
synonyms: enough, adequate, acceptable, ample, commensurate
antonyms: deficient, inadequate, insufficient, lacking, poor
Dubois did not have *sufficient* funds to go back to school.

31. Spur [spur]
verb def: to goad, impel, or urge.
synonyms: incite, prompt, arouse, awaken, animate
antonyms: disapprove, discourage, dissuade
The reward *spurred* them to work harder.

32. Sophisticated [suh-**fis**-ti-key-tid]
adj def: complex or intricate as a system.
synonyms: refined, complicated, cultured
antonyms: naïve, uncultured, unrefined
Jenny was unable to deal with *sophisticated* electronic control systems.

33. Rupture [ruhp-cher]
noun def: the act of breaking or bursting.
synonyms: break, split, breach, burst
antonyms: closing, closure
The purpose of all that focused power is brutally obvious: to break bones and *rupture* tissue.

34. Defection [dih-**fek**-shuhn]
noun def: desertion from allegiance, loyalty, duty.
synonyms: abandonment, deficiency, dereliction, desertion
antonyms: joining
His *defection* to East Germany was regarded as treasonable.

TOEFL iBT/ TOEIC WORDS (Day 7)

35. Overthrow [oh-ver-**throh**]
verb def: to throw; knock down; overturn; topple.
    synonyms: defeat, destroy, abolish, bring down, ruin
    antonyms: give in, surrender, yield
The heavy storm *overthrew* telephone poles and trees in the street.

36. Submit [suhb-**mit**]
verb def: to give over or yield to power or authority.
    synonyms: comply, endure, abide, accede, acknowledge
    antonyms: disobey, fight, resist
Martin Luther would not *submit* to the pope's demand that he recant.

37. Bizarre [bih-**zahr**]
adj def: weird; not normal.
    synonyms: comical, curious, eccentric, grotesque
    antonyms: normal, reasonable, usual
Jessica showed up in a *bizarre* outfit at the party.

38. Inimical [ih-**nim**-i-kuhl]
adj def: adverse in tendency or effect. (**)
    synonyms: antagonistic, contrary, adverse, antipathetic
    antonyms: friendly, hospitable, kind
An increasing number of case studies show that living in inclement weather has an *inimical* effect on mental health.

39. Aesthetic [es-**thet**-ik]
adj def: pertaining to a sense of the beautiful. (***)
    synonyms: artful, artistic, creative, esthetic
    antonyms: displeasing, ugly, unattractive
There must be pragmatic and *aesthetic* reasons for planting trees on the street.

40. Explicit [ik-**splis**-it]
adj def: described in realistic detail, definite; unequivocal. (**)
    synonyms: specific, absolute, accurate, clear
    antonyms: ambiguous, confused, equivocal
The owners of the house left a list of *explicit* instructions detailing their house-sitters' duties.

TOEFL iBT/ TOEIC WORDS (Day 7)

From closer restrictions on sexually *explicit* writing came the success, in the mid-19th century, of the novelist George Thompson, who combined graphically violent scenes set in urban dystopias with coy peekaboo references to sex.
— Susan Dominus, *New York Times Book Review* 5 Apr. 2009

41. Amass [uh-**mas**]
verb def: to gather for oneself. (*)
synonyms: gather, aggregate, assemble, collect
antonyms: disturb, disperse, dissipate, divide
Jacob *amassed* his photos for his memoirs.

42. Emergent [ih-**mur**-juhnt]
adj def: coming into view, notice, or existence. (**)
synonyms: appearing, budding, coming, developing
antonyms: declining, dependent
Busing students to correct imbalances in the racial makeup of schools was necessary as result of housing patterns established in the 1940s and 1950s and was an *emergent* problem in the 1960s and 1970s.

43. Fractious [**frak**-shuhs]
adj def: irritable; peevish, quarrelsome. (***)
synonyms: awkward, captious, crabby, disorderly, fretful
antonyms: agreeable, complaisant, happy
The *fractious* crowd began to grow extremely violent.

44. Stipend [**stahy**-pend]
noun def: scholarship or fellowship allowance granted to a student. (**)
synonyms: allowance, award, fee
Dr. Pinker received a tiny amount of *stipend* from the university he was working for.

45. Accommodate [uh-**kom**-uh-deyt]
verb def: to do a kindness or a favor for.
synonyms: board, contain, domicile, furnish
antonyms: turn away, turn out
Michael sometimes *accommodated* his friends with money they desperately needed.

TOEFL iBT/ TOEIC WORDS (Day 7)

46. Severe [suh-**veer**]
  adj def: harsh; unnecessarily extreme. (*)
    synonyms: astringent, austere, biting, caustic
    antonyms: amenable, compromising, friendly
  A *severe* snowstorm prevented Peter from reaching the top of the mountain before the sunset.

47. Pledge [plej]
  noun def: a solemn promise or agreement.
    synonyms: assurance, covenant, oath, vow
    antonyms: break
  The president made a solemn *pledge* not to wage war.

48. Inexplicable [in-**ek**-spli-kuh-buhl]
  adj def: unable to explain.
    synonyms: baffling, enigmatic, indescribable, inscrutable
    antonyms: comprehensible, explainable, intelligible
  Charles had a series of seemingly *inexplicable* accidents.

49. Excavate [**eks**-kuh-veyt]
  verb def: to dig out; scoop out; expose. (***)
    synonyms: dig up, burrow, delve, hollow
    antonyms: fill
  The ground was *excavated* for a foundation.

50. Petrify [**pe**-truh-fahy]
  verb def: to convert into stone. (***)
    synonyms: calcify, fossilize, harden, solidify
    antonyms: melt, soften
  Steve appeared to be *petrified* with fear.

❝ *As CEO of Wall Street English Institute Korea, I have spent numerous hours examining and analyzing published TOEFL iBT/ TOEIC word books on the market. Unlike other vocab books, Mastering Core TOEFL iBT/ TOEIC Words with William Shin provides test-takers with not only newly updated TOEFL iBT/ TOEIC words but also comprehensive example sentences that are able to help students to hone their reading proficiencies. Needless to say, this book is what TOEFL iBT and TOEIC students have been waiting for.* ❞

JooSeog Suh
CEO of Wall Street English Institute Korea, Seoul Korea

Drill 7

1. The word **submission** is closest in meaning to

    A) rapture
    B) defection
    C) overthrow
    D) yield

2. The word **hostile** is closest in meaning to

    A) bizarre
    B) inimical
    C) aesthetic
    D) explicit

3. The word **commodity** is closest in meaning to

    A) attention
    B) locale
    C) item
    D) assembly

4. The word **exceptional** is closest in meaning to

    A) coherent
    B) emergent
    C) fractious
    D) extraordinary

5. The word **prowess** is closest in meaning to

    A) valor
    B) agile
    C) confine
    D) imprudent

Drill 7

6. The word **reign** is closest in meaning to

    A) inveigle
    B) kinship
    C) govern
    D) amass

7. The word **disjoint** is closest in meaning to

    A) absorb
    B) tolerance
    C) conceive
    D) separate

8. The word **surrender** is closest in meaning to

    A) encroach
    B) give up
    C) hinder
    D) judicial

9. The word **divine** is closest in meaning to

    A) goddess
    B) ingest
    C) mingle
    D) plague

10. The word **endow** is closest in meaning to

    A) procreate
    B) sustain
    C) provide
    D) tranquil

Drill 7

11. The word **accumulate** is closest in meaning to

    A) preoccupied
    B) replenish
    C) transmit
    D) pile up

12. The word **fertile** is closest in meaning to

    A) futile
    B) prosper
    C) adequate
    D) bias

13. The word **pursue** is closest in meaning to

    A) cluster
    B) domestic
    C) seek
    D) ethereal

14. The word **patron** is closest in meaning to

    A) client
    B) ethnic
    C) facile
    D) hostile

15. The word **elicit** is closest in meaning to

    A) integrate
    B) clarify
    C) migrate
    D) niche

Drill 7

16. The word **severe** is closest in meaning to

    A) lunacy
    B) magnify
    C) reinforce
    D) harsh

17. The word **stipend** is closest in meaning to

    A) ordain
    B) primary
    C) salary
    D) rapid

18. The word **explicit** is closest in meaning to

    A) ravage
    B) clarify
    C) spawn
    D) thrust

19. The word **inimical** is closest in meaning to

    A) spiteful
    B) tenuous
    C) unleash
    D) voluble

20. The word **spur** is closest in meaning to

    A) vague
    B) wrest
    C) stimulate
    D) lien

1. D 2. B 3. C 4. D 5. A 6. C 7. D 8. B 9. A 10. C
11. D 12. B 13. C 14. A 15. B 16. D 17. C 18. B 19. A 20. C

TOEFL iBT/ TOEIC WORDS (Day 8)

1. Assumption [uh-**suhmp**-shuhn]
   noun def: something taken for granted; a supposition.
   synonyms: acceptance, conjecture, assuming
   antonyms: doubt, unexpected
   Many scientific *assumptions* about Pluto seem to be wrong to John.

2. Extinction [ik-**stingk**-shuhn]
   noun def: the fact or condition of being extinguished.
   synonyms: annihilation, death, destruction, elimination
   Scientists have never proved the primary reasons for the *extinction* of the dinosaurs.

3. Correlation [kawr-uh-**ley**-shuhn]
   noun def: mutual relationship of two or more things.
   synonyms: equivalence, analogue, complement, correspondence
   antonyms: difference, disassociation
   An increasing number of doctors claim that there must be a direct *correlation* between smoking and lung cancer.

4. Acknowledge [ak-**nol**-ij]
   verb def: to admit to be real or true. (**)
   synonyms: accede, acquiesce, agree
   antonyms: forswear, ignore, refusal
   Paula *acknowledged* that improving test scores was impossible because she needed two jobs to support her parents.

5. Abrupt [uh-**bruhpt**]
   adj def: sudden; unexpected.
   synonyms: blunt, brusque, crusty, curt
   antonyms: calm, kind, nice
   A severe thunderstorm caused an *abrupt* power failure.

6. Substantial [suhb-**stan**-shuhl]
   adj def: of ample or considerable amount. (***)
   synonyms: important, ample, abundant, big
   antonyms: insignificant, little, minor
   Jefferson left a *substantial* amount of money not for his children but for charity; however, no one who knew him was surprised.

TOEFL iBT/ TOEIC WORDS (Day 8)

7. Verify [**ver**-uh-fahy]
   verb def: to prove the truth of, as by evidence or testimony.
        synonyms: confirm, validate, add up, attest, check
        antonyms: discredit, disprove, invalidate
        Tim spent many hours gathering information about the accident he was involved in to *verify* that he didn't do anything wrong.

8. Presumption [pri-**zuhmp**-shuhn]
   noun def: a ground or reason for presuming or believing.
        synonyms: anticipation, assumption, basis, chance
        The trial was unfair from the beginning because there was no *presumption* of innocence.

9. Vanish [**van**-ish]
   verb def: to disappear from sight; become invisible. (**)
        synonyms: disappear, dissolve, evanesce, evaporate
        antonyms: appear, arrive, come
        The frost immediately *vanished* when the sun came out.

10. Proponent [pruh-**poh**-nuhnt]
   noun def: a person who argues in favor of something. (***)
        synonyms: advocate, backer, champion, defender, exponent
        antonyms: enemy, foe, opponent
        Sarah has been known as a long-time *proponent* of preserving wild animals.

11. Unravel [uhn-**rav**-uhl]
   verb def: to free from complication or difficulty. (***)
        Laura tried to take every possible step to *unravel* the financial difficulty she was facing.

12. Enigma [uh-**nig**-muh]
   noun def: a puzzling or inexplicable occurrence or situation. (**)
        synonyms: bewilderment, conundrum, crux, puzzle
        Despite the *enigma* of the singularity, the big bang theory is unquestionably one of the most successful ideas in the history of science.
                              — Tom Yulsman, *Astronomy*, September 1999

TOEFL iBT/ TOEIC WORDS (Day 8)

13. Spew [spyoo]
   verb def: eject from the stomach through the mouth; vomit.
   synonyms: bring up, cascade, disgorge, eject
   The angry sergeant *spewed* his charges at the soldiers standing in front of him.

14. Erupt [ih-**ruhpt**]
   verb def: to burst forth; break out.
   synonyms: appear, blow up, break, burst, discharge, emit
   It was fortunate that Jenny saw molten lava *erupting* from the top of the volcano.

15. Cessation [se-**sey**-shuhn]
   noun def: a temporary or complete stop. (**)
   synonyms: abeyance, arrest, cease, cut off
   antonyms: beginning, commencement, starts
   The *cessation* of the snowstorm was a huge relief.

16. Decline [dih-**klahyn**]
   verb def: to withhold or deny consent to do so.
   synonyms: to lessen, abate, decay, degenerate
   antonyms: improve, increase, rise
   The police *declined* comment on the issue that many people are really interested in.

17. Catastrophe [kuh-**tas**-truh-fee]
   noun def: a sudden or widespread disaster or misfortune. (**)
   synonyms: calamity, accident, affliction, cataclysm
   antonyms: benefit, miracle, happiness, wonder
   The play was so poor that our whole evening turned out to be a *catastrophe*.

18. Postulate [**pos**-chuh-leyt]
   verb def: to ask; demand; claim. (***)
   synonyms: advance, affirm, assert
   antonyms: calculate
   The scientists have *postulated* the existence of water on the planet.

TOEFL iBT/ TOEIC WORDS (Day 8)

19. Extraterrestrial [ek-struh-tuh-**res**-tree-uhl]
  adj def: existing outside of the earth.
   A great number of people have begun to believe that there must be *extraterrestrial* beings in the universe.

20. Elucidate [ih-**loo**-si-deyt]
  verb def: to make lucid or clear. (*)
   synonyms: annotate, clarify, clear, demonstrate
   antonyms: confuse, distract, make, ambiguous
   The teacher *elucidated* the reason she had failed the student to his upset parents.

21. Explicate [**ek**-spli-keyt]
  verb def: to make plain or clear; explain. (**)
   synonyms: clarify, expand, amplify, construe
   antonyms: cloud, complicate, mystify
   Drew did his best to *explicate* what happened to his phone recently purchased for him by his mother.

22. Impact [**im**-pakt]
  noun def: the striking of one thing against another.
   synonyms: blow, bounce, clash
   The *impact* of the colliding cars broke the windshield.

23. Devastate [**dev**-uh-steyt]
  verb def: to destroy; lay waste; render desolate.
   synonyms: demolish, depreciate, despoil
   antonyms: enrich, help, build
   The invaders *devastated* the city with no mercy.

24. Hypothesis [hahy-**poth**-uh-sis]
  noun def: proposition; guess; assumption.
   synonyms: theory, assignment, axiom, basis
   antonyms: calculation, proof, realty, truth
   The results of the experiment did not support the *hypothesis* that he had introduced to his fellow scientists two weeks ago.

TOEFL iBT/ TOEIC WORDS (Day 8)

25. Inhibit [in-**hib**-it]
verb def: to restrain; hinder; arrest. (**)
synonyms: arrest, avert, cramp, curb
antonyms: aid, allow, approve, free, assist
The threat of being held in contempt of court *inhibited* the defendant from continuing his outbursts.

26. Integral [**in**-ti-gruhl]
adj def: pertaining to, or belonging as a part of the whole.
synonyms: component, constitute, essential, fundamental
antonyms: extrinsic, secondary, unnecessary
The point Carl made during his speech was *integral* to his plan.

27. Comprise [kuhm-**prahyz**]
verb def: to consist of; be composed of; include.
synonyms: constitute, contain, encompass
antonyms: except, exclude, fail
The Soviet Union *comprised* many different socialist countries.

28. Ruinous [**roo**-uh-nuhs]
adj def: fallen into ruin.
synonyms: annihilate, baleful, baneful, catastrophic
antonyms: assisting, beneficial, helpful
The house has fallen into a *ruinous* state.

29. Diminish [dih-**min**-ish]
verb def: to decrease; cause to seem smaller; to lessen.
synonyms: abate, attenuate, close, contract, curtail
antonyms: develop, enlarge, expand
A contagious disease suddenly *diminished* the morale of the army.

30. Foliage [**foh**-lee-ij]
noun def: the leaves of a plant; leafage. (**)
synonyms: leaves, greenness, growth
Margolis enjoyed walking through the thick green *foliage* of the jungle.

31. Herbivore [**hur**-buh-vawr]
noun def: an animal that eats grass.
There are a variety of *herbivores* living in Africa.

TOEFL iBT/ TOEIC WORDS (Day 8)

32. Carnivore [**kahr**-nuh-vawr]
   noun def: an animal that eats flesh.
   We will probe the edges of our universe with a gusto that only a satisfied *carnivore* can muster.

33. Atmosphere [**at**-muhs-feer]
   noun def: the gaseous envelope surrounding the earth.
      synonyms: pressure, air, envelope, climate
   The meteor burned up as it entered the Earth's *atmosphere*.

34. Alter [**awl**-ter]
   verb def: to make different in some particular; to change. (**)
      synonyms: adapt, adjust, change, convert, diversity
      antonyms: continue, keep, maintain, preserve
   Alice never attempted to *alter* her plan that she had established for her life.

35. Flaw [flaw]
   noun def: a feature that mars the perfection of something; defect.
      synonyms: blemish, defect, failing, foible
      antonyms: perfection, strength
   Elaine found that the plan made by Mr. Ford contained a lot of crucial *flaws*.

36. Deliberate [dih-**lib**-er-it]
   verb def: to carefully weigh or consider; to study. (***)
      synonyms: careful, cautious, conscious, considered
      antonyms: indeterminate, unintentional, unwitting
   John and Douglas *deliberated* for three more days before reaching a final decision.

37. Accurate [**ak**-yer-it]
   adj def: to free from errors or defect.
      synonyms: precise, authentic, careful, correct
      antonyms: careless, faulty, inaccurate, lax
   Max spent many hours in order to make an *accurate* decision on the project.

TOEFL iBT/ TOEIC WORDS (Day 8)

38. Conjecture [kuhn-**jek**-cher]
   noun def: theory without sufficient evidence for proof. (***)
      synonyms: speculation, assumption, conclusion, guess, hypothesis
      antonyms: fact, proof, reality, truth
      The actor refused to comment, forcing gossip columnists to print *conjecture* on his love life.

39. Impervious [im-**pur**-vee-uhs]
   adj def: not permitting of passage; impenetrable. (***)
      synonyms: hermetic, immune, impassive, impenetrable
      antonyms: exposed, open, responsive
      … Berlin struck me, above all, as *impervious* to any political reactions whatever
         — Stephen Spender, *New York Times Magazine*, 30 Oct.1977

40. Unbridled [uhn-**brahyd**-ld]
   adj def: free from restraint. (***)
      The crowd was swept with *unbridled* enthusiasm.

41. Avid [**av**-id]
   adj def: enthusiastic; ardent; keen. (**)
      synonyms: avaricious, desirous, devoted
      antonyms: dispassionate, indifferent, unenthusiastic
      Many modern people seem to be *avid* admirers of thriller movies.

42. Chaotic [key-**ot**-ik]
   adj def: completely confused or disordered.
      synonyms: anarchic, deranged, disordered
      antonyms: calm, harmonized
      The room was filled with a *chaotic* mass of books and research papers.

43. Ubiquitous [yoo-**bik**-wi-tuhs]
   adj def: existing everywhere; omnipresent.
      synonyms: all-over, omnipresent, universal
      antonyms: rare, scarce
      Hot dogs are the ideal road trip food — inexpensive, portable, *ubiquitous*.
         — Paul Lucas, *Saveur*, June/July 2008

TOEFL iBT/ TOEIC WORDS (Day 8)

44. Wrangle [rang-guhl]
　　verb def: to argue or dispute, especially in a noisy or angry manner.
　　　　synonyms: altercation, battle, bickering, contest, brawl
　　　　antonyms: agreement, peace
　　Mark decided not to *wrangle* with the drunks at the end of the bar.

45. Rebut [ri-buht]
　　verb def: to refute by evidence or argument. (***)
　　　　synonyms: controvert, defeat, deny, discomfit, disprove
　　　　antonyms: agree, approve, back down, concede
　　The moderator was careful to allow sufficient time for callers to *rebut* claims made by her guest speakers.

46. Parody [par-uh-dee]
　　noun def: a humorous or satirical imitation.
　　　　synonyms: burlesque, caricature, cartoon
　　　　antonyms: reality, truth
　　Everybody loved about his hilarious *parody* of Hamlet's soliloquy.

47. Malady [mal-uh-dee]
　　noun def: any disorder or disease of the body. (*)
　　　　synonyms: ache, affliction, ailment
　　Elizabeth visited the doctor many times, but he could not identify her mysterious *malady*.

48. Decay [dih-key]
　　verb def: to become decomposed; rot; to decline.
　　　　synonyms: atrophy, blight, consumption, decadence, decline
　　　　antonyms: development, flourish, germination
　　An increasing number of people have come to realize that the fundamental morals of our society are *decaying*.

49. Specimen [spes-uh-muhn]
　　noun def: a part or an individual taken as exemplifying a whole mass or number.
　　　　synonyms: examples, sample, exhibit
　　The church is a magnificent *specimen* of baroque architecture.

TOEFL iBT/ TOEIC WORDS (Day 8)

---

50. Gauge [geyj]
    verb def: to determine the exact dimension, capacity.
        synonyms: barometer, check, criterion, degree
        antonyms: estimate, guess
        The broadest *gauge* of the economy — the gross domestic product, adjusted for inflation — has risen a little more than 4% since the recovery began.
                — Alfred L. Malabre, Jr. *Wall Street Journal*, 26 July 1993

Drill 8

1. The word **inexplicable** is closest in meaning to

    A) impervious
    B) unexplainable
    C) unbridle
    D) inconsequential

2. The word **abrupt** is closest in meaning to

    A) avid
    B) chaotic
    C) sharp
    D) ubiquitous

3. The word **unravel** is closest in meaning to

    A) figure out
    B) wrangle
    C) cede
    D) bring about

4. The word **flaw** is closest in meaning to

    A) shortcoming
    B) parody
    C) proposition
    D) malady

5. The word **excavate** is closest in meaning to

    A) dig out
    B) flee
    C) hibernate
    D) inclement

Drill 8

6. The word **petrify** is closest in meaning to

    A) ignite
    B) harden
    C) mingle
    D) negotiate

7. The word **substantial** is closest in meaning to

    A) ordain
    B) prevail
    C) considerable
    D) rapid

8. The word **vanish** is closest in meaning to

    A) retreat
    B) suppress
    C) thrive
    D) disappear

9. The word **enigma** is closest in meaning to

    A) transit
    B) riddle
    C) vigilance
    D) wrangle

10. The word **proponent** is closest in meaning to

    A) kinship
    B) judicial
    C) supporter
    D) menace

Drill 8

11. The word **cessation** is closest in meaning to

    A) yield
    B) malady
    C) niche
    D) overcome

12. The word **spew** is closest in meaning to

    A) prevail
    B) restrict
    C) spawn
    D) eject

13. The word **decline** is closest in meaning to

    A) sustain
    B) transmit
    C) reject
    D) viable

14. The word **devastate** is closest in meaning to

    A) vital
    B) destroy
    C) avert
    D) coax

15. The word **inhibit** is closest in meaning to

    A) stop
    B) ample
    C) burgeon
    D) clasp

Drill 8

16. The word **decay** is closest in meaning to

    A) liberate
    B) modify
    C) decline
    D) meek

17. The word **rebut** is closest in meaning to

    A) motif
    B) deny
    C) heal
    D) fleet

18. The word **chaotic** is closest in meaning to

    A) forestall
    B) emerge
    C) defection
    D) disorder

19. The word **avid** is closest in meaning to

    A) destitute
    B) compress
    C) greed
    D) cohesive

20. The word **unbridled** is closest in meaning to

    A) unrestrained
    B) coalesce
    C) bizarre
    D) benign

1. B 2. C 3. A 4. A 5. A 6. B 7. C 8. D 9. B 10. C
11. A 12. D 13. C 14. B 15. A 16. C 17. B 18. D 19 .C 20. A

TOEFL iBT/ TOEIC WORDS (Day 9)

1. Ascertain [as-er-**teyn**]
    verb def: to find out definitely; learn with certainty or assurance. (**)
        synonyms: check, determine, confirm, establish
    We look at digital media—images, audio and video—and we try to *ascertain* whether or not they've been manipulated. We use mathematical and computational techniques to detect alterations in them.
        — Claudia Dreifus, *New York Times*, 2 Oct. 2007

2. Chronological [krah-nuh-**lah**-juh-kuhl]
    adj def: arranged in the order of time.
        synonyms: classified, dated, historical
    Jean's studies appear to be displayed in *chronological* order.

3. Speculative [**spek**-yuh-ley-tiv]
    adj def: contemplation; conjecture; abstract reasoning. (***)
        synonyms: theoretical, abstract, analytical, assumed, conceptual
    A *speculative* approach is not solid enough to prove any theories existing in a scientific field.

4. Artifact [**ahr**-tuh-fakt]
    noun def: handmade object, as a tool, or remains of one. (**)
    A variety of *artifacts* were found at an archaeological excavation.

5. Deteriorate [dih-**teer**-ee-uh-reyt]
    verb def: to worsen or become inferior in character, quality, value. (**)
        synonyms: adulterate, alloy, break, corrode, crumble
        antonyms: build, construct, develop, improve
    Some case studies show that smoking fewer than five cigarettes a day does not *deteriorate* lung health seriously.

6. Capsize [**kap**-sahyz]
    verb def: to turn bottom up; overturn.
        synonyms: overturn, invert, upset
    Jefferson happened to find that many people in the street tried to *capsize* the bus to save the passengers.

TOEFL iBT/ TOEIC WORDS (Day 9)

7. Spontaneous [spon-**tey**-nee-uhs]
    adj def: arising out of or resulting from a natural impulse or tendency.
        synonyms: casual, impetuous, improvised
        antonyms: deliberate, intended, planned
        His *spontaneous* remark shocked everyone in the conference because he was known as an extremely considerate scholar.

8. Degenerate [dih-**jen**-uh-reyt]
    verb def: to fall below a normal or desirable level. (***)
        synonyms: base, debauched, decadent, decayed
        antonyms: moral, upright, virtuous
        The morale of the soldiers *degenerated,* and they were unable to fight against their enemies continuously.

9. Acquire [uh-**kwahy**-r]
    verb def: to come into possession or ownership of. (**)
        synonyms: access, achieve, amass, annex
        antonyms: fall, forfeit, forgo, lose
        Acquiring English skills is becoming more and more important because English is regarded as the primary language for conducting business.

10. Magnify [**mag**-nuh-fahy]
    verb def: to make more exciting; intensify; dramatizing.
        synonyms: enlarge, aggrandize, amplify, augment
        antonyms: decrease, diminish, lessen, weaken
        The playwright *magnified* the conflict to get her point across.

11. Advent [**ad**-vent]
    noun def: a coming into place, view, or being; arrival. (***)
        synonyms: appearance, approach, arrival, coming
        antonyms: departure, end
        New Yorkers have a strong tendency to welcome the *advent* of the holiday season.

12. Device [dih-**vahys**]
    noun def: a thing made for a particular purpose; an invention.
        synonyms: instrument, accessory, agent, apparatus
        Tom attempted to find a store that carried many different electrical *devices.*

TOEFL iBT/ TOEIC WORDS (Day 9)

13. Accumulate [uh-kyoo-myuh-leyt]
verb def: to gather or collect gradually. (**)
- synonyms: accrue, acquire, add to, aggregate, amalgamate
- antonyms: disperse, dissipate, dwindle, lessen

Accumulated snow in the driveway forced Paul to go to his office by bus.

14. Decipher [dih-sahy-fer]
verb def: to make out the meaning of.
- synonyms: analyze, construe, decode
- antonyms: code, encode, scramble

Even though an archeologist spent many hours *deciphering* the hieroglyphics, he was unable to determine their meaning as a whole.

15. Successive [suhk-ses-iv]
adj def: following in order or in uninterrupted sequence.
- synonyms: alternating, consecutive, ensuing, next

Esther made the honor roll for three *successive* school terms.

16. Deduce [dih-doos]
verb def: to derive as a conclusion from something known. (*)
- synonyms: add up, analyze, assume, cogitate, collect

Based on the evidence, the police officer *deduced* that the painter had done it.

17. Inference [in-fer-uhns]
noun def: the act or process of inferring. (***)
- synonyms: conclusion, deduction, assumption, conjecture

In spite of the fact that there are virtually no controlled clinical trials examining the effects of obesity in people, we can make some *inferences* from animal research.
— Patrick Johnson, *Skeptical Inquirer*, September/October 2005

18. Sequence [see-kwuhns]
noun def: the following of one thing after another.
- synonyms: series, order, array, classification, consecution

It is easy to find any book in the library because there is a list of books in alphabetical *sequence*.

TOEFL iBT/ TOEIC WORDS (Day 9)

19. Fossil [fos-uhl]
noun def: any remains, impression, or trace.
   synonyms: deposit, impression, reconstruction
   The enormous size of dinosaur was verified by numerous *fossils* found in many places.

20. Compress [kuhm-pres]
verb def: to condense, press together.
   synonyms: compact, condense, abridge, abstract, bind
   antonyms: blow up, expand, increase, loosen
   A science book *compresses* a lot of information about human reproduction.

21. Thrust [thruhst]
verb def: to push forcibly; shove
   synonyms: boost, drive, impulsion, jump, lunge
   antonyms: pull
   Jeffrey *thrust* a dollar bill into the waiter's hand in a very impolite way.

22. Extensive [ik-sten-siv]
adj def: of great extent; wide; broad; far-reaching. (**)
   synonyms: broad, capacious, commodious, comprehensive
   antonyms: limited, narrow, restricted, short
   Dr. Scott had an *extensive* knowledge of astronomy.

23. Contrast [kahn-trast]
noun def: a person or thing that is strikingly unlike or different.
   synonyms: comparison, contradiction, converse, disparity
   antonyms: agreement, conformity, copy, equality
   The weather here is a welcome *contrast* to what we are having back home.

24. Daunt [dawnt]
verb def: to overcome with fear; intimidate. (***)
   synonyms: frighten, alarm, appall, baffle
   antonyms: aid, assist, embolden, encourage
   Ortiz has been *daunted* by a lot of work still to be done by May.

TOEFL iBT/ TOEIC WORDS (Day 9)

25. Ensnare [en-snair]
   verb def: to capture in; involve in.
   synonyms: capture, deceive, decoy, embroil
   antonyms: free, let go, liberate, release
   The police successfully *ensnared* the burglars who stole a considerable amount of money from a local bank.

26. Futile [fyoot-l]
   adj def: incapable of producing any result; ineffective. (****)
   synonyms: hopeless, pointless, abortive, barren, delusive
   antonyms: fruitful, hopeful, productive, profitable
   Fight it and you will only suffer: resistance is *futile*.

   In a digitized land of national ID cards, dropping out will be impossible, and dreaming about it will be *futile*.
   — Walter Kirn, *Atlantic*, May 2002

27. Cease [sees]
   verb def: to stop; discontinue; come to an end. (***)
   synonyms: stop, conclude, close, culminate
   antonyms: begin, commence, continue, go
   Olga begged her colleagues to *cease* their quarreling.

28. Nomadic [noh-mad-ik]
   adj def: roaming about from place to place aimlessly. (***)
   synonyms: itinerant, drifting, migrant, pastoral
   antonyms: native, settled
   The *nomadic* tribe travels from place to place, searching for grasslands for their herds.

29. Sedentary [sed-n-tar-ee]
   adj def: characterized by or requiring a sitting position. (****)
   synonyms: motionless, lazy, settled, sluggish
   antonyms: activated, energetic, mobile
   Gonzales always prefers to have a *sedentary* position because he had a car accident when he was a child.

TOEFL iBT/ TOEIC WORDS (Day 9)

30. Agrarian [uh-**grair**-ee-uhn]
  adj def: rural; agricultural.
      synonyms: peasant, rural, rustic, undomesticated
      The town Robert was born and raised in was founded in 1820 as an *agrarian* community.

31. Tribe [trahyb]
  noun def: a local division of aboriginal people.
      synonyms: blood, kin, lineage
      There were many competing Native American *tribes* in the plains states.

32. Monarchy [**mon**-er-kee]
  noun def: a state or nation in which the supreme power is actually or nominally lodged in a monarchy.
      In the 14th century, most of Europe was ruled by different *monarchies*.

33. Swath [swoth]
  noun def: a strip, belt, or long, narrow extent of anything.
      Mark cut a *swath* through the field with his scythe.

34. Nourish [**nur**-ish]
  verb def: to sustain with food or nutriment.
      synonyms: comfort, foster, furnish, nurse
      antonyms: abandon, deprive, neglect
      Dwight had long *nourished* the plants in his backyard garden.

35. Insulate [**in**-suh-leyt]
  verb def: to separate with a material that prevents or reduces leakage. (*)
      synonyms: protect, coat, isolate, seclude
      It was extremely difficult for Nicky to *insulate* herself from painful experiences.

36. Geometric [jeo-uh-**me**-trik]
  adj def: employing simple rectilinear or curvilinear lines.
      An architect decorated the walls of the castle with a *geometric* pattern.

37. Unadulterated [uhn-uh-**duhl**-tuh-rey-tid]
  adj def: not diluted or made impure. (***)
      synonyms: immaculate, sanitary, spotless
      Alex has just found that this experiment requires an *unadulterated* solution.

TOEFL iBT/ TOEIC WORDS (Day 9)

38. Subordinate [suh-**bawr**-dn-it]
   adj def: placed in or belonging to a lower order. (**)
   synonyms: supplementary, ancillary
   antonyms: chief, important, major, necessary
   About two-thirds of the way through, this nonsense comes to life for fifteen minutes when the point of view shifts to that of a *subordinate* character, an aging thug (well played by Laurence Fishburne) who is employed by the casino to spot card counters.
   — Richard Alleva, *Commonweal*, May 9, 2008

39. Scatter [**skat**-er]
   verb def: to throw loosely about. (*)
   synonyms: disperse, broadcast, cast, diffuse, disband
   antonyms: collect, gather
   The police *scattered* a crowd gathering in front of the government building.

40. Unanimous [yoo-**nan**-uh-muhs]
   adj def: characterized by or showing complete agreement. (**)
   synonyms: accepted, accordant, agreed, asserting
   antonyms: split
   In spite of all this, there has been near *unanimous* consent among climate scientists about the problem of global warming.

41. Enroot [en-**root**]
   verb def: to attach or place securely; implant deeply.
   The Williams have shown a deeply *enrooted* tradition of respect for the elderly.

42. Plague [pleyg]
   noun def: an epidemic disease that is caused by a bacterium. (***)
   synonyms: affliction, contagion, curse, epidemic
   antonyms: advantage, good fortune
   God regarded a *plague* of war and desolation as a direct punishment.

43. Tempestuous [tem-**pes**-choo-uhs]
   adj def: characterized by or subject to tempests.
   synonyms: wild, stormy, agitated, boisterous, coarse
   antonyms: calm, gentle, mild, moderate
   A number of historians believe that the 1960s were the most *tempestuous* decades in recent American history.

TOEFL iBT/ TOEIC WORDS (Day 9)

44. Upheaval [uhp-**hee**-vuhl]
   noun def: strong or violent change or disturbance.
        synonyms: cataclysm, catastrophe, commotion, convulsion
        antonyms: stagnation
        The island was created by an *upheaval* of the ocean floor.

45. Tenuous [**ten**-yoo-uhs]
   adj def: having little substance. (**)
        synonyms: weak, thin, airy, attenuate, delicate
        antonyms: healthy, significant, stable, strong
        Sveta gave a rather *tenuous* account of his past life.

46. Liaison [lee-ey-**zawn**]
   noun def: a person who initiates contact or connection.
        synonyms: communication, connection, contact
        Olivia acts as a *liaison* between the owner of the factory and the employees.

47. Delineate [dih-**lin**-ee-eyt]
   verb def: describe in detail; outline. (***)
        synonyms: depict, draw, figure, lay out
        In his speech, Martin *delineated* his plan with great care.

48. Distinct [dih-**stingkt**]
   adj def: clear; distinguished as not being the same; not identical.
        synonyms: apparent, obvious, express
        antonyms: ambiguous, fuzzy, indistinct
        The outline became less and less *distinct* as the light faded.

49. Consistent [kuhn-**sis**-tuhnt]
   adj def: agreeing; accordant; compatible.
        synonyms: dependable, even, invariable, logical
        antonyms: erratic, incongruous, inconstant
        Martin made a *consistent* effort to improve his spoken English capability by communicating with people in English as often as possible.

50. Obligate [ob-li-geyt]
   verb def: to bind or oblige morally or legally. (**)
        synonyms: astrict, constrain, indebt, restrict
        antonyms: let off
        Maria decided to *obligate* herself to run two miles three times a week in order to get her body into good shape.

Drill 9

1. The word **trap** is closest in meaning to

    A) daunt
    B) ensnare
    C) verify
    D) confine

2. The word **succession** is closest in meaning to

    A) string
    B) disturbance
    C) magnitude
    D) detriment

3. The word **sharply** is closest in meaning to

    A) oddly
    B) carefully
    C) markedly
    D) mostly

4. The word **deteriorate** is closest in meaning to

    A) classify
    B) worsen
    C) accumulate
    D) inference

5. The word **decay** is closest in meaning to

    A) accurate
    B) artifact
    C) fossil
    D) rotten

Drill 9

6. The word **acquire** is closest in meaning to

   A) obtain
   B) matter
   C) magnify
   D) clarify

7. The word **advent** is closest in meaning to

   A) cluster
   B) appearance
   C) ignite
   D) descend

8. The word **accumulate** is closest in meaning to

   A) extend
   B) linger
   C) pile up
   D) suppress

9. The word **decipher** is closest in meaning to

   A) coax
   B) erode
   C) inclement
   D) decode

10. The word **ascertain** is closest in meaning to

    A) confirm
    B) conceive
    C) embellish
    D) luster

Drill 9

11. The word **gauge** is closest in meaning to

　　A) inhabit
　　B) determine
　　C) spawn
　　D) utilize

12. The word **deduce** is closest in meaning to

　　A) compress
　　B) assume
　　C) hostile
　　D) wrangle

13. The word **thrust** is the closest in meaning to

　　A) cease
　　B) hinder
　　C) propel
　　D) deter

14. The word **magnitude** is closest in meaning to

　　A) cohere
　　B) facile
　　C) judicial
　　D) extent

15. The word **verify** is closest in meaning to

　　A) confirm
　　B) flee
　　C) ingest
　　D) integral

Drill 9

16. The word **obligate** is closest in meaning to

    A) barren
    B) annex
    C) avert
    D) force

17. The word **tenuous** is closest in meaning to

    A) apprehensive
    B) burden
    C) thin
    D) commodity

18. The word **delineate** is closest in meaning to

    A) caliber
    B) describe in detail
    C) discard
    D) assort

19. The word **plague** is closest in meaning to

    A) epidemic
    B) cease
    C) circumvent
    D) diplomatic

20. The word **insulate** is closest in meaning to

    A) deter
    B) cover
    C) emerge
    D) friction

1. D 2. A 3. C 4. B 5. D 6. A 7. B 8. C 9. D 10. A
11. B 12. B 13. C 14. D 15. A 16. D 17. C 18. B 19. A 20. B

TOEFL iBT/ TOEIC WORDS (Day 10)

1. Subdue [suhb-doo]
   verb def: to overcome and bring into subjection. (***)
       synonyms: bear down, conquer, defeat
       antonyms: arouse, incite, release, rouse
   Mark attempted to *subdue* the intruder who had broken into his house.

2. Prosper [pros-per]
   verb def: to be successful or fortunate in financial respects.
       synonyms: enriched, benefit, bloom
       antonyms: fall, lose
   Jacob has no doubt that his real estate business will *prosper*.

3. Incarnate [in-kahr-nit]
   verb def: embodied in flesh, especially a human. (***)
       synonyms: embodied, externalized, human, manifested
   Dr. Han has long been considered as a man who *incarnates* wisdom and passion.

4. Apex [ey-peks]
   noun def: the tip or point; summit; vertex. (**)
       synonyms: acme, apogee, climax, crest, crown
       antonyms: nadir
   Becoming CEO of the company he had been working for more than 20 years was the *apex* of his career.

5. Aspect [as-pekt]
   noun def: the way in which a thing may be viewed.
       synonyms: appearance, attitude, condition, facet
       antonyms: whole
   The *aspects* Stephen has been thinking about made him interested in the project in a way he'd never anticipated.

6. Swell [swell]
   verb def: to grow in bulk; to increase abnormally.
       synonyms: billow, crescendo, growth, ripple
       antonyms: decline, decrease
   The weird sound began to *swell* in her room.

TOEFL iBT/ TOEIC WORDS (Day 10)

7. Superficial [soo-per-**fish**-uhl]
  adj def: shallow; not profound or thorough. (*)
      synonyms: apparent, casual, cursory, desultory
      antonyms: analytical, careful, deep, detailed
    Although Nathan studied for the chemistry exam for the past several days, he was able to make only a *superficial* improvement on the test.

8. Insolent [**in**-suh-luhnt]
  adj def: boldly rude; disrespectful. (****)
      synonyms: abusive, arrogant, brazen, contemptuous
      antonyms: cowardly, humble, modest, polite
    … the tempos were all-out fast and the tone was flat-out *insolent*. To some, rock-and-roll was as threatening as Communism and desegregation.
                — Margo Jefferson, *New York Times*, 26 Oct. 1994

9. Bigot [**big**-uht]
  noun def: a person who is utterly intolerant of any differing creed. (***)
      synonyms: chauvinist, diehard, doctrinaire, dogmatic
      antonyms: humanitarian, liberal, tolerate
    "It's scandalous," he said, in the tones once used by Colonel Blimp, Britain's best-loved *bigot*, who adorned the pages of the *Evening Standard* throughout the 1930s.
                — Nicholas Fraser, *Harper's*, September 1996

10. Impulsive [im-**puhl**-siv]
  adj def: the influence of a particular feeling.
      synonyms: abrupt, emotional, instinctive, precipitate
      antonyms: cautious, heedful, considerable, thoughtful
    There seem to be many people who make *impulsive* decisions they later seriously regret.

11. Faction [**fak**-shuhn]
  noun def: a group or clique within a large group, party
      synonyms: bunch, cabal, camp, caucus, circle, clan
      antonyms: total, whole
    A group of people slowly divided into several *factions*.

TOEFL iBT/ TOEIC WORDS (Day 10)

12. Tribute [trib-yoot]
verb def: a gift; testimonial; compliment.
  synonyms: accolade, acknowledgement, appreciation, citation, commendation antonyms: accusation, blame, criticism
Many people in NYC tied yellow ribbons to their cars as a *tribute* to the soldiers at war.

13. Convulse [kuhn-vuhls]
verb def: to agitate; to shake violently.
  synonyms: disturb, agitate, shake up, unsettle
World War Two *convulsed* many countries in the world.

14. Advocate [ad-vuh-keyt]
verb def: to speak or write in favor of.
  synonyms: apostle, backer, champion, counsel, defender
  antonyms: antagonist, assailant, enemy
The government did not seem to *advocate* high salaries for teachers.

15. Bandit [ban-dit]
noun def: robber; outlaw.
  synonyms: brigand, criminal, crook, desperado
  antonyms: law, police
An increasing number of people once believed that the investors in this company made out like *bandits*.

16. Summit [suhm-it]
noun def: the highest point or part.
  synonyms: acme, apex, apogee, climax
  antonyms: base, bottom, nadir
Earning a doctoral degree was once the *summit* of William's ambition.

17. Lessen [les-uhn]
verb def: to decrease; calm; reduce. (**)
  synonyms: lower, reduce, abate, abridge, attenuate
  antonyms: enlarge, extend, increase, rise
Many medical studies show that taking Vitamin C on a daily basis *lessens* the risk of heart attack.

TOEFL iBT/ TOEIC WORDS (Day 10)

18. Secularize [**sek**-yuh-luh-rahyz]
verb def: to make separate from religious connection. (**)
Peter made a solid determination to *secularize* himself and not associate with any religious groups.

19. Turmoil [**tur**-moil]
noun def: a state of great commotion or confusion. (***)
    synonyms: tumult, agitation, disquiet.
    antonyms: quiet, harmony, order
Many college students unpleasantly face financial *turmoil* after they graduate from universities.

20. Sacred [**sey**-krid]
adj def: devoted; dedicated to deity. (*)
    synonyms: holy, blessed, angelic, cherished, divine
    antonyms: profane, irreligious
Thomas has written more than six *sacred* books in his life.

21. Devour [dih-**vour**]
verb def: to swallow or eat up hungrily, voraciously, or ravenously. (***)
    synonyms: swallow, consume, absorb
    antonyms: abstain, pick
Tim has a strong tendency to *devour* everything on his plate.

22. Modify [**mod**-uh-fahy]
verb def: to change somewhat in form.
    synonyms: adapt, adjust, convert, mutate
    antonyms: stagnate
Ortiz was forced to *modify* his original plan because of inclement weather.

23. Extract [ik-**strakt**]
verb def: to get; pull; draw out.
The police office finally *extracted* substantial evidence from the suspect.

24. Lucrative [**loo**-kruh-tiv]
adj def: profitable; moneymaking; remunerative.
    synonyms: fruitful, good, worthwhile
    antonyms: poorly paid, unprofitable
Tim established his one *lucrative* business when he was a high school student.

TOEFL iBT/ TOEIC WORDS (Day 10)

25. Affix [uh-**fiks**]
   verb def: to fasten; join; attach.
   synonyms: to add, annex, append, bind
   antonyms: detach, loosen, let go
   Ray *affixed* additional information and chapters to the book to look better.

26. Extort [ik-**stawrt**]
   verb def: to obtain from a person by force.
   synonyms: cheat, bleed, bully, clip, coerce
   The president's ex-lover *extorted* a cushy job from him, threatening to reveal their affair if he did not do as she wished.

27. Dissolve [dih-**zolv**]
   verb def: to break up.
   synonyms: fuse, render, soften, thaw
   antonyms: coagulate, solidify, unmixed
   Andrew always *dissolves* a spoon of sugar into the coffee.

28. Digestive [dih-**jes**-tiv]
   adj def: having the function of digesting food.
   Otis has been suffering from *digestive* problems for a long time.

29. Expiate [**ek**-spee-eyt]
   verb def: to atone for; make amends or reparation for. (****)
   synonyms: absolve, amend, appease, compensate
   The president's apology to the survivors of the notorious Tuskegee experiments was his attempt to *expiate* the nation's guilt over their mistreatment.

30. Belabor [bih-**ley**-ber]
   verb def: to assail persistently; to insist repeatedly or harp on. (***)
   I understand completely; you do not need to *belabor* the point.

31. Fatal [**feyt**-l]
   adj def: causing or capable of causing death; mortal.
   synonyms: baleful, baneful, catastrophic, disastrous
   antonyms: nourishing, vital, wholesome
   Scott made a *fatal* miscalculation, taking the curve at too high a speed.

TOEFL iBT/ TOEIC WORDS (Day 10)

32. Infest [in-**fest**]
    verb def: to spread in a troublesome manner.
        synonyms: abound, annoy, assail, beset
        The house appeared to be heavily *infested* with termites.

33. Malevolent [muh-**lev**-uh-luhnt]
    adj def: wishing evil or harm to another. (****)
        synonyms: spiteful, dirty, hostile, lousy
        antonyms: amiable, harmless, kind
    There was no acknowledgment of the effects of cycle upon cycle of *malevolent* defeat, of the injury of seeing one generation rise above the cusp of poverty only to be indignantly crushed, of the impact of repeating tsunamis of violence ...
        — Douglas A. Blackmon, *Slavery by Another Name*, 2008

34. Wrest [rest]
    verb def: to turn; twist; pull, or force by a violent twist.
        Christine *wrested* a small but sharp knife from her only child.

35. Unleash [uhn-**leesh**]
    verb def: to release; to set free.
        Mr. Ford immediately *unleashed* his dog to protect himself from a burglar.

36. Render [**ren**-der]
    verb def: to furnish; provide; exhibit; show. (**)
        synonyms: deliver, distribute impart
        antonyms: remove, take
    Mr. Smith encountered a car accident and stopped his car to *render* aid.

37. Wither [**with**-er]
    verb def: to shrivel; fade; decay. (***)
        synonyms: atrophy, blight, collapse, constrict
        antonyms: bloom, grow
    Students' interest in playing games with their friends dramatically *withered* because they had many more-important things to do.

TOEFL iBT/ TOEIC WORDS (Day 10)

38. Brink [bringk]
    noun def: verge; extreme edge. (*)
        synonyms: border, boundary, fringe
        antonyms: center, interior, middle
    The company Alex had been running for the last 20 years was on the *brink* of bankruptcy.

39. Demise [dih-**mahyz**]
    noun def: death; decease; obsolete.
        synonyms: death, annihilation, decease, departure
        antonyms: birth
    The failure to conquer a rebellion led to the *demise* of the empire.

40. Behemoth [bih-**hee**-muhth]
    noun def: huge; gigantic. (**)
    In the morning, Otis found that a *behemoth* truck was blocking his car.

41. Weaken [**wee**-kuhn]
    verb def: to make weak.
        synonyms: abate, adulterate, break up, crumble
        antonyms: build up, strengthen
    His lack of exercise and practice *weakens* his performance.

42. Burst [burst]
    verb def: to break, to appear suddenly.
        synonyms: access, barrage, blowout, breach
    Mark was surprised to observe that the sun had *burst* through the clouds.

43. Ravage [**rav**-ij]
    verb def: to work havoc, ruin, damage.
        synonyms: consume, destroy, crush
        antonyms: aid, assist, help, protect
    A hurricane literally *ravaged* a small village.

44. Span [span]
    verb def: a distance, amount, piece, etc.
        synonyms: compass, extent, length
    Jacob has had many different bad memories that *span* more than 15 years.

TOEFL iBT/ TOEIC WORDS (Day 10)

45. Odor [oh-der]
  noun def: scent; smell; fragrance. (**)
  A skunk living near my house frequently spread a strong and unpleasant *odor*.

46. Vary [vair-ee]
  verb def: to differ; change; alter. (**)
   synonyms: alter, assort, change, convert
   antonyms: remain, stay
  The result of medication *varies* depending on users' health.

47. Benign [bih-nahyn]
  noun def: having a kindly disposition; not harmful (***)
   synonyms: amiable, beneficent, complaisant, congenial
   antonyms: hateful, hostile, hurtful
  Bill was relieved to find out that the tumor was *benign* and he did not have cancer after all.

  ... substituting such *benign* power sources as the hybrid, the fuel cell, and the electric motor in place of ... the internal-combustion engine.
  — Brock Yates, *Car and Driver*, May 2000

48. Disparate [dis-per-it]
  adj def: lacking similarity or equality; unequal; different. (****)
   synonyms: contrary, contrasting, discordant, dissimilar
   antonyms: alike, equal, like, same
  Although the twins appear to be identical physically, their personalities are quite *disparate*.

  First during the nineteen-seventies, but with increasing momentum during the eighties, a loose community of physics researchers had begun to postulate that the *disparate* small particles that we learned about in high-school science class—electrons, for instance—were actually the varied vibrations of tiny open and closed looped strings.
  — Benjamin Wallace-Wells, *New Yorker*, 21 July 2008

TOEFL iBT/ TOEIC WORDS (Day 10)

49. Clarify [klar-uh-fahy]
   verb def: to make clear; to free from ambiguity.
        synonyms: analyze, elucidate, delineate, illustrate
        antonyms: confuse, muddle
        The president provided a couple of additional examples to *clarify* his stance on the issue.

50. Clemency [klem-uhn-see]
   noun def: an act that is kind or merciful in disposition
        synonyms: forgiveness; fairness
        antonyms: harsh, severe, violent
        The governor granted *clemency* to the convicted criminal.

Drill 10

1. The word **fundamental** is closest in meaning to

    A) superficial
    B) swelling
    C) basic
    D) overwhelming

2. The word **unanimous** is closest in meaning to

    A) subdue
    B) united
    C) expanse
    D) trigger

3. The word **upheaval** is closest in meaning to

    A) apex
    B) liaison
    C) obligate
    D) convulsion

4. The word **apex** is closest in meaning to

    A) empire
    B) advocate
    C) summit
    D) tribal

5. The word **lessen** is closest in meaning to

    A) bandit
    B) reduce
    C) factious
    D) subdue

Drill 10

6. The word **distinction** is closest in meaning to

    A) disparity
    B) proliferate
    C) ravage
    D) dispute

7. The word **fatal** is closest in meaning to

    A) benign
    B) span
    C) mortal
    D) descent

8. The word **severe** is closest in meaning to

    A) clement
    B) savage
    C) erupt
    D) inhibit

9. The word **modify** is closest in meaning to

    A) derive
    B) requisite
    C) malevolent
    D) alter

10. The word **verge** is closest in meaning to

    A) extort
    B) distinguish
    C) brink
    D) render

Drill 10

11. The word **wither** is closest in meaning to

    A) desiccate
    B) devour
    C) fatal
    D) magnify

12. The word **affix** is closest in meaning to

    A) diameter
    B) attach
    C) graceful
    D) emphasize

13. The word **scatter** is closest in meaning to

    A) consistent
    B) adulterate
    C) spread
    D) obligate

14. The word **delineate** is closest in meaning to

    A) advocate
    B) utilitarian
    C) tribute
    D) describe in detail

15. The word **prosper** is closest in meaning to

    A) affluent
    B) enroot
    C) sedentary
    D) agrarian

Drill 10

16. The word **clemency** is closest in meaning to?

    A) fractious
    B) mercy
    C) endow
    D) expulsion

17. The word **odor** is closest in meaning to

    A) abrupt
    B) buttress
    C) scent
    D) corrode

18. The word **ravage** is closest in meaning to

    A) cleave
    B) dwell
    C) exert
    D) ruinous

19. The word **malevolent** is closest in meaning to

    A) fractious
    B) ill-will
    C) heal
    D) inevitable

20. The word **expiate** is closest in meaning to

    A) amend
    B) keen
    C) lubricate
    D) molten

1. C 2. B 3. D 4. C 5. B 6. A 7. C 8. B 9. D 10. C
11. A 12. B 13. C 14. D 15. A 16. B 17. C 18. D 19. B 20. A

TOEFL iBT/ TOEIC WORDS (Day 11)

1. Demographic [dem-uh-**graf**-ik]
   adj def: pertaining to demography; social statistic of a human population.
   The *demographic* information provided by Census Bureau shows that the population of the word actually has decreased since 2007.

2. Impetus [**im**-pi-tuhs]
   noun def: a moving force, impulse. (***)
         synonyms: catalyst, goad, incentive
         antonyms: block, check, hindrance
   The discovery of a huge cave located in Africa has given serious *impetus* to further research.

   In a revealing comment, Mr. Updike says an *impetus* for *Rabbit, Run* was the "threatening" success of Jack Kerouac's *On the Road*, the signature book of the 1950s Beat Generation, and its frenetic search for sensation.
   — Dennis Farney, *Wall Street Journal*, 16 Sept. 1992

3. Feasible [**fee**-zuh-buhl]
   adj def: capable of being done, effected. (****)
         synonyms: achievable, appropriate
         antonyms: impossible, inconceivable, unpractical
   The government has been attempting to find a *feasible* way to create new jobs.

   Egyptian hieroglyphics ... are also usually assumed to be the product of independent invention, but the alternative interpretation of idea diffusion is more *feasible* than in the case of Chinese writing.
   — Jared M. Diamond, *Guns, Germs, and Steel*, 1997

4. Conventional [kuhn-**ven**-shuh-nl]
   adj def: adhering to accepted standards.
         synonyms: accustomed, commonplace, current, customary
         antonyms: abnormal, exotic, foreign, irregular
   The committee decided to pass a bill that prevents countries from selling their *conventional* weapons to other countries.

5. Staple [**stey**-puhl]
   noun def: principal raw material; necessary item of food. (*)
         synonyms: chief, essential, important, main
   In Asia rice has been a *staple* for a long time.

TOEFL iBT/ TOEIC WORDS (Day 11)

6. Detract [dih-**trakt**]
  verb def: to take away a part, as from quality, value. (**)
    synonyms: belittle, blister, cheapen, decrease
    antonyms: add to, increase, optimize
    It is generally accepted that small errors do not *detract* from true value of the book.

7. Tantalize [**tan**-tl-ahyz]
  verb def: to torment by teasing with. (***)
    synonyms: provoke, tease, badger, baffle
    antonyms: disenchant, repulse, turn off
    Melissa was *tantalized* by the possibilities of improving her test scores in three months.

8. Aspirant [uh-**spahyr**-uhnt]
  noun def: a person who wishes or dreams.
    synonyms: applicant, candidate, competitor
    The *aspirants* for foundation grants had yet to prove themselves.

9. Prudent [**prood**-nt]
  adj def: wise; judicious in practical affairs. (**)
    synonyms: advisable, wary, careful, cautious
    antonyms: careless, imprudent, unwise
    An endless war is not always the most moral or the most *prudent* course of action.
                                                — Richard A. Posner, *New Republic*, 2 Sept. 2002

10. Tremendous [trih-**men**-duhs]
  adj def: extraordinarily great in size
    synonyms: huge, overwhelming, amazing, appalling
    antonyms: insignificant, little, small, unimportant
    Olga has made a *tremendous* effort in order to enhance her TOEFL iBT score on the test she is going to take at the end of this month.

11. Vicious [**vish**-uhs]
  adj def: addicted to or characterized by vice; grossly immoral.
    synonyms: abhorrent, atrocious, contaminated, cruel
    antonyms: gentle, good, nice, right
    Brian was victimized by *vicious* gossip before he entered college.

TOEFL iBT/ TOEIC WORDS (Day 11)

12. Saturate [**sach**-uh-reyt]
  verb def: to cause to unite with the greatest possible amount. (**)
   synonyms: bathe, douche, imbue, immerse
   antonyms: dehydrate, dry
   Jimmy first realized that the town he has been living is *saturated* with charm.

13. Decompose [dee-kuhm-**pohz**]
  verb def: to separate into constituent parts.
   synonyms: decay, disintegrate, dissolve, fester, molder
   antonyms: combine, develop, grow, improve
   The bacteria and fungi rapidly *decomposed* a dead animal on the road.

14. Precipitate [pri-**sip**-i-teyt]
  verb def: to hasten the occurrence of. (***)
   synonyms: hurry, speed, accelerate, advance
   antonyms: check, slow, wait
   The financial difficulty John was facing was *precipitated* by the additional costs he had to take care of.

   When Achilles is informed by his mother, the sea-goddess Thetis, that vanquishing Hector on the battlefield will *precipitate* his own demise, he unhesitatingly opts for the gusto.
   — Mark Leyner, *TIME*, 13 Nov. 2000

15. Inert [in-**urt**]
  adj def: having no inherent power of action. (****)
   synonyms: apathetic, asleep, dead, dull, idle
   antonyms: active, alive, animated, lively
   "Get up, you lazybones," Tina cried to Tony, who lay in bed *inert*.

16. Lethal [**lee**-thuhl]
  adj def: harmful; made to cause death; deadly.
   synonyms: baleful, dangerous, destructive
   antonyms: beneficial, harmless, helpful
   The detective found that Thomas was murdered by *lethal* injection.

TOEFL iBT/ TOEIC WORDS (Day 11)

17. Predominate [pri-**dom**-uh-neyt]
   verb def: to be the stronger or leading element or force. (**)
      synonyms: command, dominate, domineer, overrule
      Michael Jordan *predominated* the NBA for approximately two decades.

18. Inevitable [in-**ev**-i-tuh-buhl]
   adj def: unavoidable (***)
      synonyms: assured, compulsory, decided, decreed
      antonyms: avoidable, doubtful, escapable
   The *inevitable* car accident led Jason to be hospitalized for more than three months.

   The captain of archers fidgeted and coughed and rolled his eyes at his men, as if such cupidity and dishonor were an *inevitable* but minor aspect of the human predicament ...
      — Michael Chabon, *New York Times Magazine*, 6 May 2007

19. Prevalent [**prev**-uh-luhnt]
   adj def: widespread; in general use or acceptance.
      synonyms: current, accustomed, general, established
      antonyms: isolated, limited, uncommon
      Wearing jeans is still *prevalent* among teenagers.

20. Harness [**hahr**-nis]
   noun def: the combination of straps, bands, and other parts forming the working gear.
      synonyms: belt, equipment, tackle, trappings
      Jeff and Jill worked in *harness* on their last job.

21. Erect [ih-**rekt**]
   verb def: upright in position or posture.
      synonyms: arrest, cocked, elevated, firm
      antonyms: prone, prostrate
      In the morning Paul found that someone had *erected* a telegraph pole in front of his house.

TOEFL iBT/ TOEIC WORDS (Day 11)

22. Disperse [dih-**spurs**]
    verb def: to drive or send off in various directions. (**)
        synonyms: banish, scatter, diffuse, circulate
        antonyms: arrange, assemble, garner
        As soon as the movie ended, the audience *dispersed* quickly.

23. Traverse [**trav**-ers]
    verb def: to pass or move over.
        synonyms: bisect, bridge, cover, cross
        A group of mountaineers were forced to *traverse* the north face of the mountain standing right in front of them.

24. Oscillate [**os**-uh-leyt]
    verb def: to swing or move back and forth between two points. (**)
        synonyms: dangle, flicker, fluctuate
        antonyms: remain, stay
        The fan *oscillated*, cooling down both sides of the room

25. Pivot [**piv**-uht]
    noun def: the end of a shaft or arbor.
        synonyms: center, focal, point
        antonyms: exterior, outside
        Stars orbit the *pivot* point at the center of galaxies, planets in turn orbit stars, and moons in turn orbit planets.

26. Hamper [**ham**-per]
    verb def: to hold back; hinder; impede.
        synonyms: baffle, balk, block
        antonyms: aid, allow, assist
        Jessica's concentration on studying biology in class was unfortunately *hampered* by her classmates.

27. Corrode [kuh-**rohd**]
    verb def: to eat or wear away. (**)
        synonyms: canker, consume, corrupt, destroy
        antonyms: aid, build, help
        It is a fact that liquid may *corrode* any type of steel.

TOEFL iBT/ TOEIC WORDS (Day 11)

28. Pound [pound]
   verb def: to strike repeatedly with great force.
        synonyms: belabor, hammer, palpable, pestle
        Jessica *pounds* her favorite doll when she really gets angry.

29. Undertake [uhn-der-teyk]
   verb def: to take upon oneself.
        synonyms: attempt, commence, commit
        antonyms: abstain, forego, forget
        The researchers *undertook* several experimental studies to prove their theory.

30. Worthwhile [**wurth**-hwahy]
   adj def: being worth the time or effort spent.
        synonyms: helpful, constructive, excellent, gainful
        antonyms: unhelpful, valueless, worthless
        Anderson was very careful, for he always checked out whether the book he was going to read was a *worthwhile* book.

31. Portend [pawr-**tend**]
   verb def: to indicate in advance. (***)
        synonyms: foreshadow, augur, bode, forebode
        It is commonly acknowledged that laziness *portends* an unsuccessful future.

32. Vague [veyg]
   adj def: not clear or explicitly stated. (*****)
        synonyms: ambiguous, bewildering, cloudy, dim
        antonyms: certain, clear, definite
        The instructions Paul invented were too *vague* for students to follow correctly.

> When my three years of military service ended, I looked around for some way to get to spend time in rural Vietnam as a civilian. The driving force was still primarily intellectual curiosity, along with a desire to improve my language ability in a non-Western language and some *vague* idea of doing folkloristic or literary studies in the future.
> — Neil L. Jamieson, *Understanding Vietnam*, (1993) 1995

TOEFL iBT/ TOEIC WORDS (Day 11)

33. Improvident [im-**prov**-i-duhnt]
adj def: incautious; unwary; lacking foresight. (**)
synonyms: careless, spendthrift, heedless, imprudent
antonyms: careful, misery, thrift
When she was young, Dr. Martinez was well known for her *improvident* shopping habit.

34. Synchronous [**sing**-kruh-nuhs]
adj def: tending to occur at the same time, while not displaying any causal connection.
synonyms: adjust, agree, attune, integrate
The initial purpose and ultimate goals are *synchronous* with surrounding needs.

35. Vigorous [**vig**-er-uhs]
adj def: full or characterized by vigor.
synonyms: energetic, active, dynamic, effective
antonyms: idle, impudent, lethargic
Victor made a *vigorous* effort to enhance his French language proficiency.

36. Dormant [**dawr**-muhnt]
adj def: lying asleep; in a state of rest.
synonyms: abeyant, comatose, fallow, hibernating
antonyms: active, lively
There are a lot of *dormant* volcanoes in the world.

37. Incipient [in-**sip**-ee-uhnt]
adj def: beginning to exist or appear. (***)
synonyms: basic, commencing, elementary
antonyms: developed, grown, mature
The development of the project Dr. Max had undertaken turned out to be in its *incipient* stages.

38. Juvenile [**joo**-vuh-nl]
adj def: suitable or intended for young people.
synonyms: childish, adolescent, boyish, callow
antonyms: adult, mature
Kent is well known as a prolific writer, for he has written more than 20 *juvenile* books.

TOEFL iBT/ TOEIC WORDS (Day 11)

39. Meddlesome [med-l-suhm]
   adj def: given to meddling; interfere. (***)
      synonyms: busy, impeding, hindering, meddling
      antonyms: avoiding, dodging, ignorant
   Kelly did not have a choice but to live with Jessica, who was a *meddlesome* girl, because Jessica promised to help with Kelly's chemistry exams during this semester.

40. Unwonted [uhn-wawn-tid]
   adj def: not customary or usual; rare. (***)
   Bill was extremely surprised by a neighbor, Tom, who showed *unwonted* kindness in the morning.

41. Voluble [vol-yuh-buhl]
   adj def: characterized by a ready and continuous flow of words. (**)
      synonyms: talkative, articulate, bigmouthed, chattering
   Tim came to realize that Tiffany was actually a *voluble* person, not taciturn at all.

42. Sequential [si-kwen-shuhl]
   adj def: characterized by regular sequence of parts.
      synonyms: consecutive, continuous, following, incessant
      antonyms: inconsecutive
   Phillip spent many hours putting his index cards in *sequential* order.

43. Upswing [uhp-swing]
   noun def: an upward swing or movement.
   As soon as Jeff woke up in the morning, he noticed an *upswing* in the stock market.

44. Combustion [kuhm-buhs-chuhn]
   noun def: tumult; violent excitement.
      synonyms: agitation, disturbance, flaming, ignition
   Implementing more powerful *combustion* in a car does not always result in better engine performance.

TOEFL iBT/ TOEIC WORDS (Day 11)

45. Stationary [stey-shuh-ner-ee]
adj def: standing still; not moving. (****)
   synonyms: anchored, immobile, inert, moored
   antonyms: moving, restless, unfixed
In order to lose weight, Olga rides a *stationary* bicycle twenty minutes on a daily basis.

Einstein imagined a beam of light piercing the elevator. If the elevator were rising relative to the source of light, the beam would enter at a certain height on one side of the elevator and appear to curve on its way to a lower height on the opposite wall. Einstein then imagined that the elevator were *stationary* on the surface of the earth. Since he postulated that the two circumstances are the same, Einstein concluded that the same effect would have to hold true for both. In other words, gravity must bend light.
— *Smithsonian*, June 2005

46. Grudge [gruhj]
noun def: a feeling or ill will or resentment.
   synonyms: animosity, animus, antipathy, aversion, bitterness
   antonyms: favor, forgiveness, good will
Ashley held a strong *grudge* against a former opponent.

47. Replace [ri-pleys]
verb def: to assume the former role, position.
   synonyms: alter, change, mend, oust
   antonyms: leave alone
The CEO of the company decided to hire Jefferson to *replace* the current manager.

48. Ensure [en-shoor]
verb def: to secure; to guarantee.
   synonyms: make secure, arrange, assure, certify, confirm
Brian examined every single detail of the finished product in order to *ensure* the high quality of the product.

TOEFL iBT/ TOEIC WORDS (Day 11)

49. Compromise [kom-pruh-mahyz]
    noun def: a settlement of differences by mutual concession. (***)
        synonyms: accommodation, accord, adjustment, compact
        antonyms: contest, controversy, difference, dispute
    Stephen had no intention of tolerating artistic *compromise*.

"You can't always come up with the optimal solution, but you can usually come up with a better solution," he [Barack Obama] said over lunch one afternoon. "A good *compromise*, a good piece of legislation, is like a good sentence."
            — William Finnegan, *New Yorker*, 31 May 2004

50. Tedious [tee-dee-uhs]
    adj def: marked by tedium; lengthiness, and boredom. (****)
        synonyms: monotonous, annoying, arid, banal, bromide
        antonyms: entertaining, exciting, interesting
    Thomas immediately regretted attending a *tedious* conference held in school. Writing a new spreadsheet or word-processing program these days is a *tedious* process, like building a skyscraper out of toothpicks.
            — Jeff Goodell, *Rolling Stone*, 16 June 1994

TOEFL iBT/ TOEIC WORDS (Day 11)

> *Vocabulary in TOEFL iBT/ TOEIC is like bullets in a gun-fight; the number of bullets may let you last longer but the wrong kind of bullets will only weigh you down. In this sense, Mr. Shin's book hits two birds with one stone because the quantity is in synergistic effect with the quality of the words, as they have been selected solely for their frequent appearances in recent actual TOEFL iBT/ TOEIC tests. What sets this book apart from the rest is not only this calculated efficiency but also the reinforcement of the meaning of a word by including synonyms and antonyms, for the best way to know a word is not through its definition in other words but through somewhat ineffable abstraction of its essence, elicited from its derivatives such as synonyms and antonyms. I am sure this book will be an invaluable addition to the armory of any TOEFL iBT/ TOEIC student.*

Harrison Cho
TOEFL iBT and SAT Critical Reading Instructor
RECAS Academy, NJ, USA

Drill 11

1. The word **impetus** is closest in meaning to

    A) result
    B) stimulus
    C) transition
    D) upheaval

2. The word **simultaneous** is closest in meaning to

    A) tedious
    B) vigorous
    C) synchronous
    D) avid

3. The word **inert** is closest in meaning to

    A) dormant
    B) agile
    C) replace
    D) implement

4. The word **unwonted** is closest in meaning to

    A) valuable
    B) thrive
    C) unaccustomed
    D) penetrate

5. The word **conventional** is closest in meaning to

    A) oppose
    B) ensue
    C) oscillate
    D) traditional

Drill 11

6. The word **staple** is closest in meaning to

    A) necessary
    B) utilize
    C) vertical
    D) wrangle

7. The word **precipitous** is closest in meaning to

    A) traverse
    B) haste
    C) amass
    D) coax

8. The word **saturated** is closest in meaning to

    A) demographic
    B) tantalize
    C) soaked
    D) prevalent

9. The word **tremendous** is closest in meaning to

    A) affluent
    B) boost
    C) huge
    D) harness

10. The word **ramification** is closest in meaning to

    A) branch
    B) incite
    C) judicial
    D) meticulous

Drill 11

11. The word **meddlesome** is closest in meaning to

    A) mitigate
    B) hamper
    C) aggregate
    D) forestall

12. The word **voluble** is closest in meaning to

    A) animosity
    B) regulate
    C) supplicate
    D) fluent

13. The word **corrode** is closest in meaning to

    A) eaten
    B) secular
    C) thrive
    D) boast

14. The word **portend** is closest in meaning to

    A) unravel
    B) perceive
    C) presage
    D) postulate

15. The word **tedious** is closest in meaning to

    A) boredom
    B) pledge
    C) aesthetic
    D) bigot

16. The word **impetus** is closest in meaning to

    A) mingle
    B) overwhelm
    C) stimulate
    D) prosper

17. The word **feasible** is closest in meaning to

    A) plaster
    B) rear
    C) sedentary
    D) possible

18. The word **tantalize** is closest in meaning to

    A) swath
    B) provoke
    C) thrust
    D) tribute

19. The word **prudent** is closest in meaning to

    A) careful
    B) traverse
    C) unleash
    D) vigilance

20. The word **inevitable** is closest in meaning to

    A) vanish
    B) unable to avoid
    C) weary
    D) zenith

1. B 2. C 3. A 4. C 5. D 6. A 7. B 8. C 9. C 10. A
11. B 12. D 13. A 14. C 15. A 16. C 17. D 18. B 19. A 20. B

TOEFL iBT/ TOEIC WORDS (Day 12)

1. Hierarchical [hahy-uh-**rahr**-ki-kuhl]
  adj def: belong to, or characteristic of a hierarchy. (**)
    Professor Otis, conducting Psychology 101, gave us a reading homework, a *hierarchical* organization chart.

2. Supervise [**soo**-per-vahyz]
  verb def: to oversee during execution or performance.
    synonyms: manage, administer, conduct, keep an eye on
    antonyms: serve
    Jonathan is in charge of *supervising* more than fifty subordinates working in his department.

3. Triumph [**trahy**-uhmf]
  noun def: a significant success.
    synonyms: celebration, elation, exultance, exultation
    antonyms: sadness, sorrow, unhappiness
    Jacob felt a huge *triumph* when he was awarded a scholarship from the university.

4. Peripheral [puh-**rif**-er-uhl]
  adj def: relatively irrelevant. (***)
    synonyms: exterior, external, incidental, minor
    antonyms: central, crucial, internal
    The general was not surprised to find out that there was only *peripheral* resistance by the enemy.

    Denis saw in his *peripheral* vision that a car was trying to pass him.

5. Precise [pri-**sahys**]
  adj def: strictly stated, defined.
    synonyms: exact, accurate, absolute, categorical, correct
    antonyms: ambiguous, false, imprecise, inexact
    Martinez appears to be extremely *precise* in dealing with the problems that her clients complain about.

6. Reverberate [ri-**vur**-buh-reyt]
  verb def: to echo; resound; reflect. (**)
    synonyms: echo, rebound, resound
    The classical music William was listening to nicely *reverberated* through the room.

7. Offshoot [awf-shoot]
noun def: a branch; descendant; scion; stem.

synonyms: development, product, adjunct, appendage, branch
antonyms: origin, source

The business that Max had founded several years ago had begun as an *offshoot* of an established home-appliances industry.

8. Rear [reer]
verb def: to take care of; support; raise.

synonyms: breed, bring up, care for, cultivate
antonyms: abandon, neglect

Jefferson has *reared* five different fine horses in his barn since he retired from the company.

9. Astound [uh-stound]
verb def: to overwhelm with amazement. (*)

synonyms: amaze, bewilder, confound, daze, dumbfound
antonyms: bore, dull

The way Tom handled a difficult situation literally *astounded* many people who had known him for a long time.

10. Weary [weer-ee]
verb def: to cause fatigue. (***)

synonyms: bored, discontented, disgusted, drooping
antonyms: activate, energetic, fresh

Driving two hours without a rest *wearied* Grace quickly.

I would remember the potential for return, all things circling as they do, into something like fullness, small moments of completion that weave together, like Penelope's cloth, doing and undoing themselves by turns, an unfinished pattern that guides a *weary* traveler home ...

— Paul Sorrell, *Parabola*, May 2000

TOEFL iBT/ TOEIC WORDS (Day 12)

11. Rescind [ri-sind]
   verb def: to abrogate; annul; revoke; repeal. (****)
   It is really unfortunate that the university decided to *rescind* the project of building more classrooms due to a lack of money.

   But Maria convinced Leverich that she had the authority to *rescind* the executor's decision to appoint him as biographer.
   — John Lahr, *New Yorker*, 19 Dec. 1994

12. Retool [ree-tool]
   verb def: to replace; rearrange; reorganize.
   The CEO of the company made a crucial determination to *retool* the organization of his company.

13. Cleave [kleev]
   verb def: to adhere; stick to; cling.
      synonyms: divide, split, carve, hew
      antonyms: join, unite
   It is amazing that Brian always *cleaves* to his principles no matter what situation he faces.

14. Facet [fas-it]
   noun def: phase; aspect. (*)
      synonyms: angle, appearance, character, feature
   Michael carefully examined every *facet* of the procedure before he proceeded.

15. Caliber [kal-uh-ber]
   noun def: diameter of something.
      synonyms: ability, capability, distinction, endowment
   James was impressed by the high *caliber* of the piano performance.

16. Infrastructure [in-fruh-struhk-cher]
   noun def: the basic, underlying framework or features.
      synonyms: base, framework, groundwork, support
   The government invested more money in order to enhance the country's *infrastructure*.

TOEFL iBT/ TOEIC WORDS (Day 12)

17. Indignant [in-**dig**-nuhnt]
 adj def: expressing strong displeasure. (***)
  synonyms: acrimonious, annoyed, bugged
  antonyms: gleeful, happy, pleased
 Everybody seemed to hate Robert because of his *indignant* behavior.

 Melville was so struck by the drama of the Essex (deliberately battered by an *indignant* and maddened whale, which at last brained itself by sinking the ship) that he used it as the end of *Moby-Dick*.
  —Paul Theroux, *New York Times Book Review*, 11 June 2000

18. Meek [meek]
 adj def: humbly patient or docile. (***)
  synonyms: shy, compliant, lenient, manageable
  antonyms: bold, brave, emboldened, impertinent
 Now, Tom appears to be very difficult to deal with, but he used to be a very *meek* child.

19. Emergence [ih-**mur**-juhns]
 noun def: the act or process of emerging.
  synonyms: issue, evolution, appearance, development
 The *emergence* of the Internet totally changed the way people communicate.

20. Anatomy [uh-**nat**-uh-mee]
 noun def: the science dealing with the structure of animals.
  synonyms: dissection, examination, investigation
 Medical students are required to take a class on *Anatomy*.

21. Glean [gleen]
 verb def: to gather slowly and laboriously. (***)
  synonyms: collect, accumulate, amass, ascertain, cull
 Bob spent many hours *gleaning* information about his ancestors from Dutch.

22. Torso [**tawr**-soh]
 noun def: the trunk of the human body.
 Charles does exercise three times a week in the morning so as to strengthen his *torso*.

TOEFL iBT/ TOEIC WORDS (Day 12)

23. Demonstrate [dem-uhn-streyt]
  verb def: to make evident or established by arguments.
          synonyms: display, show, authenticate, determine
          antonyms: conceal, hide
    Dr. Stephen provided and *demonstrated* many different case studies in order to prove his theory.

24. Keen [keen]
  adj def: finely sharpened.
          synonyms: enthusiastic, anxious, ardent, avid
          antonyms: reluctant, uninterested
    Victoria appeared to be *keen* on learning to play the piano when she was a child.

25. Sagacious [suh-gey-shuhs]
  adj def: acuteness of mental discernment. (***)
          synonyms: judicious, acute, apt, astute
          antonyms: careless, foolish, ignorant
    Jason happened to encounter Dr. Phillip, who is known as a young but *sagacious* scientist.

    ... the winner is praised for his *sagacious* grasp of the hopes and anxieties of the public, the loser is excoriated for the many and obvious blunders that derailed his candidacy ...
        — Hendrik Hertzberg, *New Yorker*, 18 Dec. 2000

26. Adorn [uh-dawrn]
  verb def: to decorate or to add beauty.
          synonyms: array, embellish, furbish, garnish
          antonyms: damage, deform, hurt
    Rebecca *adorned* her room with a variety of flowers.

27. Scrupulous [skroo-pyuh-luhs]
  adj def: having a strict regard for what one considers right. (****)
          synonyms: conscientious, critical, exact, fastidious
          antonyms: careless, negligent
    Scrupulous attention is required to understand the fundamental concept of the work.

TOEFL iBT/ TOEIC WORDS (Day 12)

While many assume that a conservative reading of the Constitution will lead inevitably to a conservative interpretation, Amar has argued, in scholarly articles and in a previous book, "The Bill of Rights," that paying *scrupulous* attention to the text, history and structure of the Constitution often reveals support for liberal outcomes.

— James Ryerson, *New York Times Book Review*, Nov 6. 2005

28. Scrutiny [skroot-n-ee]

noun def: a searching examination or investigation. (***)
synonyms: inquiry, analysis, audit, inspection
The speculation a group of scientists made is based on a *scrutiny* of the results of the case studies.

29. Decease [dih-sees]

noun def: the act of dying; departure from life; death.
synonyms: death, dysfunction, demise
antonyms: birth
Otis came to know that his father had a tremendous amount of debt at the time of his *decease*.

30. Unitary [yoo-ni-tar-ee]

adj def: pertaining to the use of units.
When he did research, Dr. Schmidt applied a *unitary* method.

31. Meticulous [muh-tik-yuh-luhs]

adj def: detailed; accurate; conscientious. (***)
synonyms: accurate, cautious, fastidious, fussy, heedful
antonyms: careless, messy, sloppy
Unlike his friends, Scott seemed to be extremely *meticulous* about every duty he was in charge of.

Always *meticulous* about his appearance in the past, he had become dirty and unkempt, with straggly hair, stained clothes, and patches of silver stubble on his chin.

— Minette Walters, *Fox Evil*, 2002

TOEFL iBT/ TOEIC WORDS (Day 12)

32. Perspective [per-**spek**-tiv]
   adj def: a visible scene.
   synonyms: view, outlook, aspect, attitude
   David, a realtor, was immediately concerned about a *perspective* on the main axis of an estate.

33. Perceive [per-**seev**]
   verb def: to become aware of; know.
   synonyms: notice, apprehend, descry, discern
   antonyms: miss, neglect, overlook
   Unfortunately Jonathan was unable to *perceive* a financial difficulty he was facing.

34. Regardless [ri-**gahrd**-lis]
   adv def: having or showing no regard.
   synonyms: heedless, unconcerned, blind, coarse, careless
   antonyms: attentive, heedful
   Mr. Ford made a decision *regardless* of the possible negative consequences.

35. Diminutive [dih-**min**-yuh-tiv]
   adj def: small; little; tiny.
   Alex accidentally encountered a *diminutive* snake descending from a tree.

36. Vivid [**viv**-id]
   adj def: full of life; lively; animated.
   synonyms: intense, powerful, active, animated, brilliant
   antonyms: dull, weak
   John was able to recall his dream in *vivid* detail.

37. Inexorable [in-**ek**-ser-uh-buhl]
   adj def: unyielding; unalterable; relentless (**)
   The lemmings began their *inexorable* march to the edge of the cliff.

38. Stagger [**stag**-er]
   verb def: to walk or move unsteadily.
   synonyms: falter, halt, shake
   Henry had no choice but to make a determination after *staggering* momentarily.

TOEFL iBT/ TOEIC WORDS (Day 12)

39. Travesty [**trav**-uh-stee]
  noun def: an artistic burlesque of a serious work. (***)
    synonyms: spoof, caricature, distortion, farce
    antonyms: seriousness, solemnity
  The Picasso forgery was a *travesty* of the original work.

40. Comprehensive [kom-pri-**hen**-siv]
  adj def: of large scope; covering or involving.
    synonyms: absolute, embracing, complete, comprising
    antonyms: exclusive, specific, particular
  In the conference, George showed a *comprehensive* knowledge of world affairs.

41. Savory [**sey**-vuh-ree]
  adj def: agreeable in taste or smell. (***)
    synonyms: pleasing, decent, aromatic, exquisite
    antonyms: bland, distasteful, offensive, unappetizing
  Jennifer prepared a variety of *savory* foods for the guest she invited.

42. Filmy [**fil**-mee]
  adj def: thin; light; fine; gauzy. (**)
  Jane regretted putting a *filmy* curtain up because it did not block bright sunlight.

43. Limb [lim]
  noun def: a part or member of an animal body distinct from the head and trunk.
    synonyms: leg, arm, wing, branch
  The soldier has used an artificial *limb* since he lost one of his arms.

44. Novice [**nov**-is]
  noun def: a person who is new to the circumstance. (**)
    synonyms: beginner, amateur, apprentice, colt
    antonyms: expert, professional
  Thomas Jefferson was once considered as a *novice* in politics.

45. Mature [muh-**toor**]
  adj def: ripe; fully aged; fully developed.
  Tim was so *mature* that his parents decided to let him live alone as soon as he entered college.

TOEFL iBT/ TOEIC WORDS (Day 12)

46. Commemorate [kuh-**mem**-uh-reyt]
　　verb def: to serve as a memorial or reminder of.
　　　　synonyms: admire, celebrate, immortalize, perpetuate
　　　　antonyms: dishonor, forget, neglect
　　It is well known that the monument *commemorates* the signing of the Declaration of Independence.

47. Milestone [**mahyl**-stohn]
　　noun def: a significant stage or event.
　　　　synonyms: achievement, breakthrough
　　Becoming tenured at a college was a *milestone* of Dr. Tang's teaching career.

48. Pragmatic [prag-**mat**-ik]
　　adj def: of pertaining to a practical point. (***)
　　　　synonyms: sensible, practical, efficient, logical
　　　　antonyms: idealistic, unreasonable
　　No politicians have had a *pragmatic* solution to the issues deriving from the decline in the economy.

　　… their *pragmatic* successors like Benjamin Franklin were concerned with lightning's … power but not its thrilling scenic value.
　　　　　　　　— John Updike, *New York Review of Books*, 15 Aug. 2007

49. Tirade [**tahy**-reyd]
　　noun def: a prolonged outburst of bitter, outspoken denunciation.
　　　　synonyms: abuse, berating, censure, condemnation, diatribe
　　　　antonyms: calm, harmony, peace
　　He went into a *tirade* about the failures of the government.

50. Bisect [bahy-**sekt**]
　　verb def: to cut or divide into two equal sections.
　　　　synonyms: cleave, divide, bifurcate, intersect
　　　　antonyms: combine, join
　　Tom accidentally found the spot where the railroad tracks *bisect* the highway.

TOEFL iBT/ TOEIC WORDS (Day 12)

❝ This TOEFL iBT/ TOEIC word book by William Shin is the perfect book for those who are seeking to learn English as a second language on an advanced level. All of the words included in this book are essential for usage in both professional and everyday settings. The words are very practically defined, making the definitions easy for the reader to retain. A common problem with vocabulary books is the ambiguity contained in the definitions and sentences, but TOEFL iBT and TOEIC use clear language that is easy to understand and perceive. The drills do a quick yet efficient job in testing the student in order to ensure he or she has thoroughly learned the true meaning of the words in the previous section. This book has all the key words for success in mastering the English language today, and I would recommend it to anyone who is aiming for this goal. ❞

Lisa S Ryoo
Academies @ Englewood High School, NJ, USA
Pharmacy (Ernest Mario School of Pharmacy),
Rutgers University, NJ, USA

Drill 12

1. The word **implement** is closest in meaning to

    A) fulfill
    B) rescind
    C) preoccupied
    D) withstand

2. The word **tedious** is closest in meaning to

    A) base
    B) pursue
    C) tiresome
    D) annex

3. The word **sagacity** is closest in meaning to

    A) travesty
    B) endurance
    C) attentive
    D) wisdom

4. The word **vivid** is closest in meaning to

    A) assumption
    B) graphic
    C) periphery
    D) undertake

5. The word **underlying** is closest in meaning to

    A) base
    B) triumph
    C) abrupt
    D) proclaim

Drill 12

6. The word **periphery** is closest in meaning to

    A) offshoot
    B) flourish
    C) boundary
    D) prowess

7. The word **rescind** is closest in meaning to

    A) retool
    B) cancel
    C) astound
    D) weary

8. The word **cleave** is closest in meaning to

    A) plunge
    B) postpone
    C) split
    D) affluent

9. The word **indignant** is closest in meaning to

    A) angry
    B) pity
    C) meek
    D) assumption

10. The word **emergence** is closest in meaning to

    A) scrutinize
    B) meticulous
    C) accommodate
    D) appearance

Drill 12

11. The word **render** sic closest in meaning to?

    A) keen
    B) furnish
    C) clasp
    D) grid

12. The word **delineate** is closest in meaning to

    A) evolve
    B) distort
    C) describe in detail
    D) alter

13. The word **perceive** is closest in meaning to

    A) endure
    B) regardless
    C) eradicate
    D) aware

14. The word **adorn** is closest in meaning to

    A) decorate
    B) cease
    C) pity
    D) stratify

15. The word **confine** is closest in meaning to

    A) corrode
    B) limit
    C) stagger
    D) negotiate

Drill 12

16. The word **pragmatic** is closest in meaning to

    A) wane
    B) validate
    C) valor
    D) realistic

17. The word **novice** is closest in meaning to

    A) unitary
    B) tedious
    C) beginner
    D) supplicate

18. The word **savory** is closest in meaning to

    A) scant
    B) tasteful
    C) respiration
    D) recede

19. The word **inexorable** is closest in meaning to

    A) no mercy
    B) ramification
    C) robust
    D) parody

20. The word **scrutiny** is closest in meaning to?

    A) plague
    B) oscillate
    C) examination
    D) nostalgic

1. A 2. C 3. D 4. B 5. A 6. C 7. B 8. C 9. A 10. D
11. B 12. C 13. D 14. A 15. B 16. D 17. C 18. B 19. A 20. C

TOEFL iBT/ TOEIC WORDS (Day 13)

1. Parsimonious [pahr-suh-**moh**-nee-uhs]
adj def: characterized by frugality or stinginess. (***)
    synonyms: avaricious, greedy, liberal, miserly, penurious
    antonyms: generous, lavish
    Jefferson was extremely *parsimonious* in his personal expenses.

    A society that is *parsimonious* in its personal charity (in terms of both time and money) will require more government welfare.
                            — William J. Bennett, *The Death of Outrage*, 1998

2. Superstitious [soo-per-**stish**-uhs]
adj def: pertaining to or connected with superstition.
    John was regarded as *superstitious* because no one saw him taking an exam without wearing having a ring handed down from his late father.

3. Motif [moh-**teef**]
noun def: dominant idea or feature.
    synonyms: concept, design, idea, pattern, structure
    Jason was searching the "weeping" *motif* in the Bible.

4. Enhance [en-**hans**]
verb def: to raise to a higher degree; intensify; magnify.
    synonyms: add to, adorn, aggrandize, amplify, augment
    antonyms: decrease, fix, lower
    Paul decided to expose himself to an English environment in which he might have a better chance to *enhance* his spoken English proficiency.

5. Versatile [**vur**-suh-tl]
adj def: capable of or adapted for turning easily from one to another. (****)
    synonyms: adjustable, flexible, adroit
    antonyms: inflexible, limited, unadjustable
    Otis is a *versatile* musician, able to play three different instruments.

    Horses stand apart because of their *versatile* roles in human society, which came to include dairy production, transportation, haulage, plowing, sports, warfare, religion, and status.
                            — Sandra L. Olsen, *Natural History*, May 2008

TOEFL iBT/ TOEIC WORDS (Day 13)

6. Patriotic [pey-tree-**ot**-ik]
   adj def: expressing or inspired by patriotism. (**)
        After 9.11 took place in NYC, a *patriotic* spirit swept the United States of America.

7. Eager [**ee**-ger]
   verb def: keen or sharp in desire or feeling; impatiently longing.
        synonyms: anxious, agog, ambitious, avid
        antonyms: apathetic, disinterested, uneager
        David was *eager* to improve his test score because he wanted to apply for admission to the university he desired.

8. Incorporate [in-**kawr**-puh-reyt]
   verb def: to form into a legal corporation; to draw diverse elements together to use in conjunction with each other
        synonyms: include, combine, assimilate, associate
        antonyms: divide, drop, exclude, separate
        Dr. Schnider *incorporated* many different teaching methods and approaches into his teaching style.

9. Embrace [em-**breys**]
   verb def: to take or receive gladly. (*)
        synonyms: bear, clasp, clinch, clutch, fondle
        antonyms: release, let go
        Bob never failed to *embrace* the opportunity given to him.

10. Exotic [ex-**ot**-ik]
   adj def: not native; foreign. (**)
        synonyms: alien, alluring, bizarre, colorful
        antonyms: familiar, normal, ordinary, usual
        Everyone in the classroom was surprised to see Dr. Craig wearing *exotic* attire.

11. Embroidery [em-**broi**-duh-ree]
   noun def: ornamental designs in threads of silk.
        Unlike other girls, Helen was eager to learn *embroidery* from her mother.

TOEFL iBT/ TOEIC WORDS (Day 13)

12. Kaleidoscope [kuh-**lahy**-duh-skohp]
   noun def: a continually shifting pattern, scene, or the like.
   > The skyscrapers in Manhattan were sometimes *kaleidoscopes* of changing colors.

13. Artisan [**ahr**-tuh-zuhn]
   noun def: a person skilled in an applied art
   > There was a lot of marvelous furniture made by famous *artisans*.

14. Burden [**bur**-dn]
   noun def: obligation; to load heavily. (**)
   > synonyms: affliction, anxiety, care, charge, concern, duty
   > antonyms: aid, help, relief
   > Martinez came to realize that he was under the *burden* of too many responsibilities.

15. Affect [uh-**fekt**]
   verb def: to act on; to impress the mind.
   > synonyms: influence, alter, disturb, impinge
   > The charity activity positively *affected* Brian.

16. Refine [ri-**fahyn**]
   verb def: to purify; bring to a fine state.
   > synonyms: purify, clarify, distill, filter
   > antonyms: corrupt, dirty, pollute
   > Olga *refined* her writing skills by practicing writing three short stories every night.

17. Intimate [**in**-tuh-mit]
   adj def: close personal in relationship; very private.
   > synonyms: affectionate, cherished, cozy, confidential
   > antonyms: cool, formal, incompatible
   > Jenny and Jessica have maintained an *intimate* friendship since they were children.

18. Evaporate [ih-**vap**-uh-reyt]
   verb def: to change from a liquid to solid state.
   > synonyms: disappear, vanish, fade, give off
   > antonyms: dampen, soak, wet
   > The sun *evaporates* the dew in the morning.

TOEFL iBT/ TOEIC WORDS (Day 13)

19. Contempt [kuhn-**tempt**]
   noun def: the feeling with which a person regards anything considered mean. (***)
   synonyms: disdain, antipathy, aversion, defiance, derision
   antonyms: admiration, affection, approval, endorsement
   The teacher showed deep *contempt* for her students who misbehaved in class.

   There, in the tall grass and the jungle, many would fall and the rest would return home to endure the sullen *contempt* of their fellow citizens, all to no purpose.
   — A. J. Bacevich, *Commonweal*, 12 Sept. 1997

20. Affordable [uh-**fohr**-duh-buhl]
   adj def: believed to be within one's financial means.
   There seemed to be not many *affordable* houses left on the market for the couple.

21. Opulence [**op**-yuh-luhns]
   noun def: wealth; rich; abundance. (**)
   synonyms: wealth, abundance, affluence, excess
   Mr. Green had been known for financial *opulence* before his company went bankrupt.

22. Ambiguous [am-**big**-yoo-uhs]
   adj def: open to or having several possible meanings. (***)
   synonyms: cryptic, doubtful, dubious, enigmatic
   antonyms: clear, definite, explicit
   In modern society, many people believe that women appear to be in an *ambiguous* position.

   Greater familiarity with this artist makes one's assessment of him more tentative rather than less. His best pictures exude a hypersensitive, *ambiguous* aura of grace.
   — Peter Schjeldahl, *New Yorker*, 10 Mar. 2003

TOEFL iBT/ TOEIC WORDS (Day 13)

23. Erratic [ih-**rat**-ik]
  adj def: having no certain or definite course. (***)
    synonyms: unpredictable, wandering, aberrant, abnormal
    antonyms: certain, consistent, definite
    Erratic winds deterred Jim from reaching the top of the mountain.

  My sinker has been my most *erratic* pitch. And when your foundation pitch is lacking, you have to go to other pitches. My sinker has been in and out, but mostly out.
    — Orel Hershiser, in *New York Times*, 9 May 1999

24. Colonial [kuh-**loh**-nee-uhl]
  adj def: concerning or pertaining to a colony.
    synonyms: dependent, dominion, frontier, pioneer
    antonyms: modern, new
    France used to have a huge *colonial* power and strict diplomatic policy.

25. Immediate [ih-**mee**-dee-it]
  adj def: occurring or accomplished without delay.
    synonyms: actual, critical, current, existing, extant
    antonyms: eventually, never, later
    The email sent from the university that Jeff did not plan to apply to attracted his *immediate* attention.

26. Encumber [en-**kuhm**-ber]
  verb def: to block up or fill with what is obstructive. (**)
    synonyms: charge, clog, cramp, embarrass, hamper
    antonyms: aid, assist, help
    Lack of financial support *encumbered* Brian from pursuing higher education.

27. Aspire [uh-**spahyr**]
  verb def: to long for, aim, seek ambitiously
    synonyms: crave, desire, hacker, pursue, seek
    Since she was a child, Jenny has *aspired* to become a psychologist.

28. Exemplum [ig-**zem**-pluhm]
  noun def: an anecdote that illustrates a moral point. (**)
    Most children in modern society seem to love reading an *exemplum* of heroism.

TOEFL iBT/ TOEIC WORDS (Day 13)

29. Acclaim [uh-**kleym**]
   verb def: to welcome or salute with sounds of joy.
        synonyms: acclamation, acknowledgement, applause, approbation
        antonyms: criticism, disapproval, jeering
        After her acting in the movie, critics immediately *acclaimed* Jessica's exceptional performance.

30. Tout [tout]
   verb def: to solicit support for importunately. (***)
        synonyms: acclaim, boost, herald, laud
        antonyms: conceal, hide
        The company is running advertisements *touting* the drug's effectiveness.

31. Nostalgia [nuh-**stal**-juh]
   noun def: a wistful desire to return in thought.
        synonyms: homesickness, longing, reminiscence
        When he visited NYU, which he had attended, Jack was filled with *nostalgia* for his college life.

32. Impinge [im-**pinj**]
   verb def: make an impression; have an effect or impact. (**)
        synonyms: trespass, affect, disturb, influence
        antonyms: avoid, dodge
        Human activities simply *impinge* in too many ways on the well-being of animal populations.

33. Evoke [ih-**vohk**]
   verb def: to call up or produce. (***)
        synonyms: induce, stimulate, arouse, awaken, conjure
        antonyms: halt, quiet, repress, silence
        When he tries to remember something, Frank shakes his head up and down to *evoke* a memory.

        His photographs *evoke* the isolation and solitude of the desert.

TOEFL iBT/ TOEIC WORDS (Day 13)

34. Vibrant [vahy-bruhnt]
    adj def: vibrating so as to produce sound.
        synonyms: alive, colorful, active, animated, energetic
        antonyms: dull, pale
        Many young people prefer to live in Manhattan because of its *vibrant* life styles.

35. Renown [ri-noun]
    noun def: widespread and high repute; fame.
        synonyms: fame, acclaim, celebrity, eminence
        antonyms: anonymity, obscurity, unimportance
        His discovery brought Dr. Sheen international *renown*.

36. Endow [en-dou]
    verb def: to provide with permanent fund or source of income.
        synonyms: accord, award, bequeath, bestow
        antonyms: receive, take
        Jenny always thinks that she is not *endowed* with any academic ability.

37. Quintessence [kwin-tes-uhns]
    noun def: the most perfect embodiment of something. (***)
        synonyms: essence, core, epitome, gist
        antonyms: extra
        Benjamin strongly believed that spending time helping people is the *quintessence* of charity.

        The Parthenon in Greece was considered the *quintessence* of the perfectly proportioned building.

38. Tenet [ten-it]
    noun def: opinion; principle; dogma; doctrine especially one held as true. (***)
        synonyms: assumption, conception, credo, creed
        It is virtually impossible for students to follow the *tenets* introduced by the school administrators.

39. Affirm [uh-furm]
    verb def: to confirm; state positively; maintain.
        synonyms: assert, attest, aver, avow, certify
        antonyms: deny, negate, nullify, veto
        No one can *affirm* that paintings in the museums are genuine.

TOEFL iBT/ TOEIC WORDS (Day 13)

40. Intuitive [in-**too**-ih-tiv]
    adj def: capable of being perceived.
        synonyms: immediate, inherent, innate, natural
        antonyms: calculate, mediated, taught
        It is amazing that Jenson has an *intuitive* knowledge of psychology.

41. Articulate [ahr-**tik**-yuh-lit]
    adj def: uttered cleanly in distinct syllables. (***)
        synonyms: coherent, definite, distinct, eloquent, fluent
        antonyms: unclear, unintelligible
        She is such an *articulate* defender of labor that unions are among her strongest supporters.

42. Potential [puh-**ten**-shuhl]
    adj def: possible as opposed to actual. (***)
        synonyms: promising, abeyant, budding, conceivable
        antonyms: helpless, impossible, lacking
        There seems to be no *potential* candidate for the 45th President of the United States.

43. Urge [urj]
    verb def: push or force along; impel.
        synonyms: appetite, compulsion, craving, drive
        antonyms: dislike, hate
        Rosemary *urged* her students to concentrate on their studies.

44. Deference [**def**-er-uhns]
    noun def: respect; repute; submission to judgment. (****)
        synonyms: obedience, compliance, capitulation, condescension
        antonyms: disobedience, impoliteness
        All the members of the faculty at a local community college treated one another with huge *deference*.

    Deference to leaders and intolerance toward outsiders (and toward "enemies within") are hallmarks of tribalism ...
        — Benjamin R. Barber, *Atlantic*, March 1992

TOEFL iBT/ TOEIC WORDS (Day 13)

45. Destitute [des-ti-toot]
adj def: without means of subsistence. (***)
  synonyms: bankrupt, bereft, deficient, depleted
  antonyms: lucky, prosperous, rich, secure
  During the Great Depression, many American people were *destitute*.

46. Mythos [mith-os]
noun def: the underlying system of belief.
  The superhero *mythos* has long been ingrained in children in the U.S.

47. Sacred [sey-krid]
adj def: devoted or dedicated to a deity. (**)
  synonyms: holy, blessed, angelic, cherished, divine
  antonyms: profane, ungodly
  Marco always spends time reading a *sacred* book no mater how busy he is.

48. Heal [heel]
verb def: to restore; make healthy.
  synonyms: cure, recover, alleviate, attend
  antonyms: harm, hurt, injure
  After he broke up with his girlfriend, Martinez came to realize that he needed some time to *heal*.

49. Infuse [in-fyooz]
verb def: to introduce; cause to penetrate.
  synonyms: introduce, soak, animate, imbue, impart
  The principal decided to *infuse* innovative teaching methods into the existing curriculum.

50. Reverence [rev-er-uhns]
noun def: a feeling or attitude of deep respect. (***)
  synonyms: admiration, adoration, approval, awe
  antonyms: disdain, disregard, disrespect
  A number of American people show a tremendous *reverence* to Dr. Martin Luther King, Jr.

The national pickle dish, kimchi, is held in such *reverence* that Seoul boasts a museum devoted entirely to its 160 different varieties.
— *The Encyclopedia of Herbs, Spices, & Flavorings*, 1992

TOEFL iBT/ TOEIC WORDS (Day 13)

"*Upon reviewing this TOEFL iBT/ TOEIC vocabulary book, I felt that the definitions were flawless, as is with many other books. Example sentences, which contained the vocabulary words in context, were straightforward. Personally, I felt that the pronunciations that were written for the words were aimed towards Asian students that have strong d, sh, j/g pronunciations.*

The Drill pages seemed helpful to students as well, aiming at synonyms instead of literal definitions, covering more vocabulary words.

All in all, a pretty straightforward book, written for ease of students to learn more words quickly.

Nicely written!"

Josh Kim
Computer Science Engineering (EECS)
University of Michigan — Ann Arbor College of Engineering, MI, USA

Drill 13

1. The word **malleability** is closest in meaning to

    A) adaptability
    B) dependability
    C) contemptibility
    D) affordability

2. The word **undertaking** is closest in meaning to

    A) opulence
    B) task
    C) earmark
    D) ambiguity

3. The word **mature** is closest in meaning to

    A) elaborate
    B) affluent
    C) ripe
    D) multistage

4. The word **pragmatic** is closest in meaning to

    A) astound
    B) realistic
    C) debris
    D) erect

5. The word **motif** is closest in meaning to

    A) ethnic
    B) foster
    C) adapt
    D) theme

Drill 13

6. The word **surpassed** is closest in meaning to

    A) flee
    B) facilitate
    C) exceeded
    D) glean

7. The word **integrate** is closest in meaning to

    A) elicit
    B) combine
    C) enhance
    D) constrict

8. The word **lingering** is closest in meaning to

    A) delay
    B) devise
    C) endow
    D) impinge

9. The word **burgeon** is closest in meaning to

    A) enlighten
    B) awe
    C) distinct
    D) initiate

10. The word **deference** is closest in meaning to

    A) forge
    B) colonial
    C) respect
    D) affirm

Drill 13

11. The word **evoke** is closest in meaning to

    A) potential
    B) call up
    C) humanize
    D) ignite

12. The word **articulate** is closest in meaning to

    A) viable
    B) clear
    C) proverbial
    D) acclaim

13. The word **nostalgia** is closest in meaning to

    A) reflect
    B) infuse
    C) homesickness
    D) sacred

14. The word **destitute** is closest in meaning to

    A) fertile
    B) healing
    C) inspire
    D) poverty

15. The word **spontaneous** is closest in meaning to

    A) simultaneous
    B) filmy
    C) endow
    D) retain

Drill 13

16. The word **reverence** is closest in meaning to

    A) avid
    B) bigot
    C) respect
    D) consistent

17. The word **sacred** is closest in meaning to

    A) clement
    B) blessed
    C) deliberate
    D) hone

18. The word **heal** is closest in meaning to

    A) harbor
    B) incite
    C) latent
    D) cure

19. The word **tenet** is closest in meaning to

    A) lunacy
    B) doctrine
    C) meticulous
    D) opulence

20. The word **tout** is closest in meaning to

    A) praise
    B) onerous
    C) pivot
    D) revenue

1. A 2. B 3. C 4. B 5. D 6. C 7. B 8. A 9. D 10. C
11. B 12. B 13. C 14. D 15. A 16. C 17. B 18. D 19. B 20. A

TOEFL iBT/ TOEIC WORDS (Day 14)

1. Exponential [ek-spoh-**nen**-shuhl]
    adj def: extreme rapid increase. (***)
        During the current economic decline, gas prices have increased at an *exponential* rate.

2. Intertwine [in-ter-**twahyn**]
    verb def: to become mutually involved. (**)
        synonyms: associate, blend, connect, convoluted
        When Rebecca told stories to her friends, she tried to *intertwine* the present and past.

3. Urbanize [**ur**-buh-nahyz]
    verb def: to cause to take on urban characteristics.
        One challenge in many rural areas is the inability to maintain transit service and funding as areas rapidly *urbanize*.

4. Spectacular [spek-**tak**-yuh-ler]
    adj def: given to an impressive display.
        synonyms: wonderful, astonishing, astounding, dazzling, dramatic
        antonyms: normal, ordinary, regular
        Julie enjoyed watching a *spectacular* movie on TV last night with her boyfriend.

5. Reverberate [ri-**vur**-buh-reyt]
    verb def: to reecho; resound.
        synonyms: echo, react, rebound
        The piano concerto Lynn was playing *reverberated* through the concert hall.

6. Catalyst [**kat**-l-ist]
    noun def: an agent that speeds significant change. (**)
        synonyms: agitator, enzyme, goad, impetus, impulse
        antonyms: block, blockage, prevent
        The government served as the *catalyst* that helped transform social unrest into revolution.

TOEFL iBT/ TOEIC WORDS (Day 14)

7. Potent [poht-nt]
   adj def: powerful; mighty; cogent; persuasive. (***)
        synonyms: almighty, commanding, cogent
        antonyms: disabled, fragile, helpless, impotent
        Placebo injections are more effective than placebo pills, but neither is as *potent* as sham surgery.

8. Weave [weev]
   verb def: to form by interlacing threads, yarns, strands.
        synonyms: braid, build, careen, compose
        antonyms: divide, separate
        The yarn *wove* into a beautiful fabric.

9. Toil [toil]
   noun def: hard and continuous work.
        synonyms: drudgery, effort, exertion, industry
        antonyms: enlightenment, fun, pastime
        The farmer rested from the backbreaking *toil* of putting in fences.

10. Coincide [koh-in-sahyde]
   verb def: to occupy the same place in space or time.
        synonyms: accompany, accord, acquiesce, agree, befall
        It is surprising that Jason's vocation always *coincides* with his avocation.

11. Reliable [ri-lahy-uh-buhl]
   adj def: believable; dependable in achievement.
        synonyms: trustworthy, candid, careful, certain, constant
        antonyms: deceptive, irresponsible
        Paul was not a *reliable* student because he forgot to do his homework assignment several times.

12. Outbound [out-bound]
   adj def: outward bound.
        Due to inclement weather, most of the airlines cancelled *outbound* flights.

13. Outskirts [out-skurts]
   noun def: outlying district or region.
        Mr. Johnson spent more of his life residing on the *outskirts* of town.

TOEFL iBT/ TOEIC WORDS (Day 14)

14. Lure [loor]
noun def: anything that attracts, allures, or entices. (***)
synonyms: bait, appeal, bribe, camouflage, decoy
antonyms: deterrent, warning
The promise of easy money is always the *lure* for some people to take up a life of crime

15. Churn [churn]
verb def: to agitate with violence
The hurricane winds began to *churn* the sea.

16. Disseminate [dih-**seem**-uh-neyt]
verb def: to spread out; scatter widely. (****)
synonyms: circulate, diffuse, disperse, promulgate
antonyms: collect, gather
The role of broadcasting is to *disseminate* information people need to know.

He told me that as Commanding General [General David Petraeus] he believes he should not only direct battlefield action but also *disseminate* a few easy-to-grasp concepts about the war's prosecution, which subordinate officers could then interpret on their own.
— Steve Coll, *New Yorker*, 8 Sept. 2008

17. Illuminate [ih-**loo**-muh-neyt]
verb def: to brighten with light.
synonyms: fire, highlight, ignite
antonyms: cloud, darken, obscure
A smile *illuminated* her face.

18. Explore [ik-**splawr**]
verb def: to traverse or range over; look into closely.
synonyms: analyze, burrow, delve into, examine, inspect
The government dispatched a group of scientists to *explore* the unknown territory.

TOEFL iBT/ TOEIC WORDS (Day 14)

19. Tinker [ting-ker]
   verb def: to busy oneself with a thing without useful result. (*)
        synonyms: fiddle with, doodle, fix, mess, monkey
        antonyms: leave alone
        Otis did not have any intention to *tinker* with that broken clock because he was too busy to do so.

20. Usurp [yoo-surp]
   verb def: to seize and hold without legal right. (**)
        synonyms: annex, arrogate, assume, commandeer
        antonyms: give in, relinquish, surrender
        The author was shocked to find out that the publisher he had been co-working with tried to *usurp* a copyright of his recently released book.

21. Ascend [uh-send]
   verb def: to move; climb; go upward. (***)
        synonyms: arise, climb, escalate, mount
        antonyms: decline, descend, lower
        Severe snowstorms hindered Jeff from his effort to *ascend* to the top of the mountain.

22. Predecessor [pred-uh-ses-er]
   noun def: a person who precedes another in an office.
        synonyms: forebear, foregoer, forerunner, precursor, previous
        antonyms: derivative, descendant, successor
        The new sculpture in the park was much better designed and more beautiful than its *predecessor*.

23. Commend [kuh-mend]
   verb def: to mention or praise as worthy of confidence.
        synonyms: recommend, acclaim, accredit, advocate, applaud
        antonyms: censure, criticize, disapprove, rebuke
        Col. Scott *commended* one of his soldiers, Lyon, for bravery.

TOEFL iBT/ TOEIC WORDS (Day 14)

24. Quaint [kweynt]
  adj def: having an old-fashioned attractiveness. (****)
      synonyms: bizarre, curious, droll, eccentric, erratic
      antonyms: common, conventional, regular
      William encountered an old, *quaint* house standing in the middle of town.

  A lot can change in 25 years, and Yountville has gone from an also-ran on the Napa food-and-wine tourism scene to the focus of activity. The *quaint* bed and breakfasts of yesterday have been replaced by upscale hotels and inns, and the village has become a mecca for top chefs.
  — Tim Fish, *Wine Spectator*, 15 June 2008

25. Mutinous [**myoot**-u-hns]
  adj def: disposed to, engaged in mutiny. (*)
      synonyms: rebellious, contumacious, defiant, disloyal, disobedient
      The chief of police decided to stop people from gathering in front of the park because it appeared to be a *mutinous* threat.

26. Influx [**in**-fluhks]
  noun def: a coming in.
      synonyms: arrival, convergence, entrance, incursion
      The university is preparing for a large *influx* of new students this fall.

27. Dubious [**doo**-bee-uhs]
  adj def: doubtful; marked by or occasioning doubt. (***)
      synonyms: arguable, chancy, debatable, diffident, disputable
      antonyms: certain, definite, positive, reliable
      Jenny made a *dubious* claim that someone stole her wallet yesterday in spite of the fact that she was unable to provide physical evidence to prove it.

  The recent rumbles and ruptures in the financial markets are finally making people reassess the *dubious* systems of credit that have arisen in the past few years.
  — William Safire, *New York Times Magazine*, 19 Aug. 2007

TOEFL iBT/ TOEIC WORDS (Day 14)

28. Crave [kreyv]
   verb def: to long for; want greatly.
      synonyms: hunger, long for, yearn for
      antonyms: abjure, dislike, hate
      Sophia was so needy that she always *craved* attention.

29. Proprietor [pruh-**prahy**-i-ter]
   noun def: the owner of a business establishment.
      synonyms: holder, owner, possessor
      Brad finally became a *proprietor* by establishing his own company.

30. Teem [teem]
   verb def: to abound or swarm; bring forth; produce. (**)
      synonyms: abound, bustle, crawl, prolific
      antonyms: lack, need, want
      Rapid industrialization in the late 1800s centralized business into urban centers suddenly dense with *teeming* masses of rural people attracted by the economic booms of the time.

31. Conundrum [kuh-**nuhn**-druhm]
   noun def: a riddle; enigma; puzzle. (****)
      There are many *conundrums* that still cannot be solved by modern science and high technology.

      … giving parents a wealth of educational options sometimes presents a familiar inner-city *conundrum*: What if all your choices are bad ones?
      — Katherine Boo, *New Yorker*, 9 Apr. 2001

32. Lunacy [**loo**-nuh-see]
   noun def: insanity; mental disorder.
      synonyms: aberration, absurdity, alienation, distraction
      antonyms: sanity
      Her plan to travel around world with no money was sheer *lunacy*.

33. Buttress [**buh**-tris]
   noun def: any external prop or support to steady a structure. (**)
      synonyms: abutment, column, mainstay, prop, shore
      antonyms: let down, weaken
      It is commonly acknowledged that mothers are always the *buttresses* of families.

TOEFL iBT/ TOEIC WORDS (Day 14)

34. Genuine [jen-yoo-in]
   adj def: origin; authentic.
        Craig was descended from a *genuine* Celt people.

35. Intrinsic [in-trin-sik]
   adj def: belonging to a thing by its very nature. (***)
        synonyms: innate, inborn, congenital
        antonyms: accidental, acquired, extrinsic
        Since the *intrinsic* value of gold is getting higher, the price of a college ring is dramatically rising.

        He is the ideal courtier. His nobility is *intrinsic*, and so he can drape himself in this purple cloak of tasteful modernity, make a cocktail of past and present, the cream of both.
                      — Noah Charney, *The Art Thief*, 2007

36. Abut [uh-buht]
   verb def: to be adjacent; touch or joint. (**)
        synonyms: adjoin, neighbor
        The house John lives in *abuts* a street.

37. Redundant [ri-duhn-duhnt]
   adj def: characterized by verbosity or unnecessary repetition. (****)
        synonyms: bombastic, diffuse, extra, extravagant, inessential
        antonyms: concise, essential, single, singular
        Clark was in charge of editing my book and removing any *redundant* information.

        The drone had originally been designed to go places the Blackbird could not, but it had become *redundant* on discovery of the fact that there was nowhere the SR-71 could not go in safety ...
                      — Tom Clancy, *The Cardinal of the Kremlin*, 1989

38. Testament [tes-tuh-muhnt]
   noun def: a covenant, especially between God and humans.
        synonyms: tribute, colloquy, confirmation
        That this fundamental idea is still widely used is a *testament* to the brilliance of its design.

TOEFL iBT/ TOEIC WORDS (Day 14)

39. Compromise [**kom**-pruh-mahyz]
    noun def: a settlement of difference by mutual concession.
        synonyms: accommodation, accord, adjustment, bargain, compact
        antonyms: contest, controversy, difference, dispute
        The split-level is a *compromise* between a ranch house and a multistoried house.

40. Tendency [**ten**-duhn-see]
    noun def: a natural or prevailing disposition.
        Jim seems to have a strong *tendency* to enhance his spoken English proficiency.

41. Smother [**smuhth**-er]
    verb def: to suffocate; stifle; extinguish.
        When she saw fire on the stove, Tina *smothered* it with a pillow.

42. Edifice [**ed**-uh-fis]
    noun def: a building, especially one of large size or imposing appearance. (*)
        synonyms: structure, building, erection, house
        The mansion Jason visited last week was a magnificent *edifice* with a domed ceiling.

43. Intact [in-**takt**]
    adj def: remaining uninjured, sound, or whole; untouched. (***)
        synonyms: entire, flawless, indiscrete, perfect
        antonyms: broken, defective, harmed, hurt
        It is surprising that many ancient artifacts survived the Second World War *intact*.

44. Contraption [kuhn-**trap**-shuhn]
    noun def: gadget; device; contrivance.
        A great number of people were getting curious about how the *contraption* he invented worked.

45. Inconceivable [in-kuhn-**see**-vuh-buhl]
    adj def: unimaginable; unthinkable; unbelievable; incredible. (***)
        Being unable to complete his business project might cause Douglas an *inconceivable* amount of damage to his future career.

TOEFL iBT/ TOEIC WORDS (Day 14)

46. Astonish [uh-**ston**-ish]
   verb def: to fill with sudden and overpowering surprise.
       synonyms: amaze, astound, bewilder, boggle, confound
       antonyms: bore, calm, expect
   Martinez was *astonished* by the dinner prepared by his wife, Elizabeth because, as far as he knew, she did not know how to cook.

47. Solemn [**sol**-uhm]
   noun def: grave; sober; mirthless. (*****)
       synonyms: dignified, brooding, deliberate, earnest
       antonyms: frivolous, funny, light
   The groom in a wedding ceremony made a *solemn* promise to love his wife for the rest of his life no matter how hard it was.

   The women running the office where I was given immunizations and completed more paperwork said they had a young friend back in the District who would love my British accent. They were going to call her this very instant, they teased, and then I'd have a companion for the evening. They also talked in more *solemn* tones about all the brave men and women who came through the base and then shipped off to Iraq.
                         — Willem Marx, *Harper's*, September 2006

48. August [aw-**guhst**]
   adj def: inspiring reverence or admiration; of supreme dignity. (**)
       synonyms: brilliant, eminent, exalted, glorified, high-minded
       antonyms: undignified
   Vincent spent the whole evening watching an *august* performance of a religious drama on TV.

49. Splendid [**splen**-did]
   adj def: gorgeous; magnificent; sumptuous.
   It is completely bizarre that Otis appeared to have a *splendid* time with Jessica because he hated her so much.

TOEFL iBT/ TOEIC WORDS (Day 14)

50. Inception [in-**sep**-shuhn]
 noun def: beginning; initial. (***)
   synonyms: birth, commencement, dawn, derivation, outset
   antonyms: conclusion, end, finish

   The computer program Mr. Clark was about to purchase might be able to assist him at every stage he needed to get through from *inception* to completion.

   He has led the development of commercial human spaceflight and the space tourism industry since its *inception*.

TOEFL iBT/ TOEIC WORDS (Day 14)

❝ *To understand and excel in any language requires mastery and skill with vocabulary. Having recently published an excellent SAT study book, William H. Shin has again created another vocabulary workbook for students striving to score high on the TOEFL iBT/ TOEIC. He has tailored his new book specifically for the TOEFL iBT/ TOEIC student. Although many of these students adopted English as their second or perhaps even third language, they will be relieved to hear that utilizing William H. Shin's study aid, with on-point pronunciation techniques and an approach that dissects the words from all angles, will allow them to easily learn the words that appear on the test. This book will help students not only to succeed on the TOEFL iBT/ TOEIC but will equip them with a powerful vocabulary that will guide their quest of mastering the English language.* ❞

Sooho Yun
Finance, NYU Stern School of Business, NY, USA

Drill 14

1. The word **novel** is closest in meaning to

    A) marked
    B) solemn
    C) tetchy
    D) innovative

2. The word **redundant** is closest in meaning to

    A) fruitful
    B) unnecessary
    C) august
    D) inconceivable

3. The word **genuine** is closest in meaning to

    A) bona fide
    B) splendid
    C) inceptive
    D) manageable

4. The word **taken out** is closest in meaning to

    A) scrutinize
    B) removed
    C) scraped
    D) invigorate

5. The word **potent** is closest in meaning to

    A) might
    B) commendable
    C) quaint
    D) mutinous

Drill 14

6. The word **consciousness** is closest in meaning to

   A) awareness
   B) conference
   C) dubiety
   D) craving

7. The word **exponential** is closest in meaning to

   A) astound
   B) integrate
   C) dramatic
   D) extol

8. The word **intertwine** is closest in meaning to

   A) alter
   B) to wind together
   C) elicit
   D) nourish

9. The word **reverberate** is closest in meaning to

   A) coincide
   B) acclaim
   C) re-echo
   D) glean

10. The word **requisite** is closest in meaning to

    A) exert
    B) burgeon
    C) enlighten
    D) necessary

Drill 14

11. The word **vast** is closest in meaning to

    A) apex
    B) huge
    C) ignition
    D) refine

12. The word **dissemination** is closest in meaning to

    A) spread out
    B) eradicate
    C) affirm
    D) inert

13. The word **illuminate** is closest in meaning to

    A) arresting
    B) ruffle
    C) clarify
    D) scrutinize

14. The word **tinkering** is closest in meaning to

    A) migrate
    B) unskillful
    C) profound
    D) inadvertent

15. The word **ascend** is closest in meaning to

    A) move up
    B) advent
    C) insulate
    D) meek

Drill 14

16. The word **inception** is closest in meaning to

    A) ramification
    B) sedentary
    C) beginning
    D) voluble

17. The word **august** is closest in meaning to

    A) superficial
    B) dignified
    C) tremendous
    D) void

18. The word **intact** is closest in meaning to

    A) meddlesome
    B) threaten
    C) unravel
    D) untouched

19. The word **abut** is closest in meaning to

    A) variegate
    B) acclaim
    C) next to
    D) behemoth

20. The word **intrinsic** is closest in meaning to

    A) innate
    B) bigot
    C) conjecture
    D) commodity

1. D 2. B 3. A 4. B 5. A 6. A 7. C 8. B 9. C 10. D
11. B 12. A 13. C 14. B 15. A 16. C 17. B 18. D 19. C 20. A

TOEFL iBT/ TOEIC WORDS (Day 15)

1. Muffle [muhf-uhl]
   verb def: to wrap with something to deaden or prevent sound.
       synonyms: suppress, conceal, dampen, decrease
       antonyms: let loose, tell
       Due to unusually cold weather, Jenny *muffled* up her children before they went to school.

2. Scrutinize [skroot-n-ahyz]
   verb def: to exam or analyze in detail. (**)
       synonyms: analyze, canvass, consider, contemplate, dissect
       Olga *scrutinized* all her employees because she believed that the success of her business depended mainly on her employees.

3. Invigorate [in-vig-uh-reyt]
   verb def: to give vigor; to fill with life and energy. (***)
       synonyms: activate, animate, energize, enliven, excite
       antonyms: bore, depress, dishearten, dull
       The government decided to bring factories located in China back to America in order to *invigorate* the home country economy.

4. Vapid [vap-id]
   adj def: lacking or having lost life, sharpness, or flavor.
       synonyms: flat, dull, boring, dead, inane, insipid
       antonyms: lively, pungent, sharp, spicy, strong
       Kenneth found his blind date to be *vapid* and boring and couldn't wait to get away from her.

5. Complement [kom-pluh-muhnt]
   noun def: something that completes or makes perfect.
       synonyms: addition, aggregate, augmentation, capacity, completion
       Many American people believe that a good wine is a *complement* to a decent meal.

6. Phonograph [foh-nuh-graf]
   noun def: any sound producing machine using records.
       In 1877, Thomas Edison invented the "talking *phonograph*."

TOEFL iBT/ TOEIC WORDS (Day 15)

7. Elaborate [in-**lab**-er-it]
    adj def: great care; nicety; detail; complicated. (***)
        synonyms: busy, careful, complete, decorated, elegant
        antonyms: general, normal, plain, regular, simple
        Jin made an *elaborate* preparations for the test to earn a high-enough score to apply to the university she desired to attend.

        Jumping spiders, the largest family of spiders, have excellent eyesight and perform *elaborate* courtship and threat displays, often characterized by ritualized body postures and leg waving.
                      — Simon Pollard, *Natural History*, March 1995

8. Bustle [**buhs**-uhl]
    noun def: a great show of energy.
        synonyms: clamor, excite, tumult, turmoil
        antonyms: laziness, relaxation
        The *bustle* of the crowd made Andrea remember how much she hated Christmas shopping.

9. Ensue [en-**soo**]
    verb def: to follow in order; come afterward.
        synonyms: appear, arise, come after, follow
        antonyms: antecede, precede
        In the *ensuing days*, the wounded soldier slowly regained his strength.

10. Oblige [uh-**blahyj**]
    verb def: to require or constrain by law.
        synonyms: bind, coerce, command, compel
        antonyms: let off
        Ms. Kennedy *obliged* her students to pay attention in her geology class.

11. Breakthrough [**breyk**-throo]
    noun def: any significant or sudden advance.
        synonyms: advance, progress, boost, discovery
        antonyms: step back
        The invention of the jet engine was a crucial *breakthrough* in air transportation.

TOEFL iBT/ TOEIC WORDS (Day 15)

12. Mar [mahr]
    verb def: to damage or spoil to a certain extent. (***)
        synonyms: blemish, blight, bruise, deface
        antonyms: aid, heal, help
        The psychologist *marred* his reputation by lying about his research paper to his colleagues.

13. Grimy [**grahy**-mee]
    adj def: covered with grime; dirty.
        synonyms: besmirched, dingy, filthy, grubby, messy
        antonyms: clean, pure, sterile
        This mirror is so *grimy* that Amy can barely see her reflection in it.

14. Aid [eyd]
    verb def: to provide support or relief to
        synonyms: advice, advocacy, alleviation, assist, attention
        antonyms: hindrance, impediment, obstruction
        Bill donated two million dollars to *aid* students who were unable to continue to study due to financial difficulties.

15. Amplify [**am**-pluh-fahy]
    verb def: to make larger, or greater; to enlarge.
        synonyms: add, augment, build, depart, elaborate, enlarge
        antonyms: abridge, compress, condense, contract
        The chef used a variety of seasons and spices to *amplify* the flavor of the food.

16. Condense [kuhn-**dens**]
    verb def: to make more dense or compact. (*)
        synonyms: abridge, coagulate, compact, constrict
        antonyms: enlarge, expand, lengthen
        In order to *condense* the milk, Paula was cooking it slowly.

17. Fidelity [fi-**del**-i-tee]
    noun def: strict observance of promises, duties. (****)
        synonyms: allegiance, ardor, constancy
        antonyms: disloyalty, infidelity
        The speech appeared to be transcribed with great *fidelity*.

TOEFL iBT/ TOEIC WORDS (Day 15)

Yet as Reardon emphasizes early on, *fidelity* to facts was never the point. The same dinner with friends could appear over and over in Fisher's published work, rejiggered each time to make a different point.
— Laura Shapiro, *New York Times Book Review*, 12 Dec. 2004

18. Usher [uhsh-er]
verb def: to lead; introduce.
Victor *ushered* Kelly to her seat.

19. Disdain [dis-deyn]
verb def: to look upon or treat with contempt. (**)
synonyms: antipathy, arrogance, aversion
antonyms: admiration, esteem, favor, like, praise
Jerry immediately *disdained* a business proposal since it showed a lack of consistency.

20. Impel [im-pel]
verb def: to drive; urge forward; incite.
synonyms: prompt, incite, actuate, boost, compel
antonyms: delay, dissuade, repressed, slow
His interest in ESL education *impelled* him to spend the rest of his teaching career in China.

21. Stupefy [stoo-puh-fahy]
verb def: to overwhelm with amazement; astound; astonish.
Jeffrey was *stupefied* by the fact that Jeremy graduated from high school at the age of sixteen.

22. Burlesque [ber-lesk]
noun def: any ludicrous parody or grotesque caricature.
synonyms: farcical, comic, ludicrous, mock
Many stage performers started their career in *burlesque*.

23. Hone [hohn]
verb def: to sharpen on a hone. (**)
synonyms: sharpen, grind, whet, improve
Mr. Park spent numerous hours *honing* his spoken English proficiency.

TOEFL iBT/ TOEIC WORDS (Day 15)

24. Experiment [ik-**sper**-uh-muhnt]
    noun def: test; trial or tentative procedure.
        synonyms: agreement, analysis, assay, attempt
        The product Carl introduced to the world was the result of long *experiment*.

25. Pioneer [pahy-uh-**neer**]
    noun def: a person who is first or among the earliest
        synonyms: frontier, forefather, precursor
        antonyms: following, last, late
        In the 19th century, the *pioneers* settled the Western United States.

26. Grandiose [**gran**-dee-ohs]
    adj def: more complicated or elaborate than necessary. (**)
        synonyms: pompous, august, bombastic, cosmic, imposing
        antonyms: calm, moderate, small, unpretentious
        The Mayor has a *grandiose* project to rebuild five more bridges in the next seven years.

27. Pseudonym [**sood**-n-im]
    noun def: a fictitious name used by an author; pen name.
        synonyms: incognito, nickname, pen name
        A large numbers of authors turned out to be using *pseudonyms* when they introduced their books to readers.

28. Portray [pawr-**trey**]
    verb def: to depict graphically.
        synonyms: character, copy, delineate, draw
        In the movie, the protagonist *portrayed* General MacArthur vividly and realistically.

29. Hypnosis [hip-**noh**-sis]
    noun def: artificially induced trance state resembling sleep.
        Hypnosis helped Steve to describe the terrible accident he'd had in detail.

30. Ethereal [ih-**theer**-ee-uhl]
    adj def: heavenly; celestial; upper regions of space. (***)
        A poetic imagination enabled Judy to be able to create an *ethereal* world.

TOEFL iBT/ TOEIC WORDS (Day 15)

31. Aperture [ap-er-cher]
    noun def: an opening, as a hole, crack, or gap.
        synonyms: break, breach, chasm, cleft, gap, gash
        Tina and Jessica found an *aperture* that led them to a huge and endless cave.

32. Pigment [pig-muhnt]
    noun def: a coloring matter or substance.
        synonyms: colorant, dye, paint, tint
        antonyms: colorlessness
        In order to save money, Tricia purchased a poor quality of paper that didn't accept *pigment* well.

33. Attire [uh-**tahy**-r]
    noun def: dress; array; adornment for special occasion.
        synonyms: costume, dress, garments, gear
        The restaurant Lyon visited required all customers to wear formal *attire*.

34. Translucent [trans-**loo**-suhnt]
    adj def: permitting light to pass through. (**)
        synonyms: crystal, diaphanous, limpid, lucent
        antonyms: cloudy, opaque
        Maxim provided us with a *translucent* explanation about the project he was about to undertake.

35. Apparition [ap-uh-**rish**-uhn]
    noun def: a supernatural appearance of a person.
        synonyms: delusion, haunt, phantom
        antonyms: animated, being
        There seem to be the surprising *apparitions* of cowboys in New York City.

36. Embolden [em-**bohl**-duhn]
    verb def: to make bold; encourage.
        synonyms: boost, buoy, clear, energize
        His good performance on the latest English examination *emboldened* Bryant to practice speaking English more consistently.

TOEFL iBT/ TOEIC WORDS (Day 15)

37. Undaunted [uhn-**dawn**-tid]
    adj def: undiminished in courage or valor; not giving way to fear. (***)
        synonyms: audacious, brave, fearless, intrepid
        antonyms: cowardly, shrinking
        Stephen was *undaunted* in spite of the fact that his opponents absolutely outnumbered him.

38. Swift [swift]
    adj def: moving or capable of moving with great speed.
        synonyms: abrupt, hasty, headstrong, nimble
        antonyms: delayed, slow, sluggish
        Scott was known as a *swift* runner when he was in high school.

39. Persuade [per-**sweyd**]
    verb def: to convince; prevail; induce to believe.
        synonyms: allure, convince, assure, entice
        antonyms: discourage, dissuade, hinder, prevent, repress
        Rosaline always tried to *persuade* Harry to quit smoking, but it turned out to be unsuccessful.

40. Garner [**gahr**-ner]
    verb def: to gather; earn; acquire; get. (*)
        synonyms: amass, assemble, cull, deposit
        antonyms: disperse, dissipate, divide, separate
        Lisa *garnered* crucial evidence, which proved that the suspect committed the crime.

41. Compatriot [kuhm-**pey**-tree-uht]
    noun def: a native or inhabitant of one's own country.
        Linda was honored to meet the famous actor and his theater *compatriots*.

42. Coalesce [koh-uh-**les**]
    verb def: to grow together into one body. (***)
        synonyms: blend, adhere, amalgamate, associate
        antonyms: divide, separate
        People with different point of views *coalesce* into opposing factions.

TOEFL iBT/ TOEIC WORDS (Day 15)

43. Deport [dih-**pawrt**]
verb def: to expel; banish; kick out.
    synonyms: banish, dismiss, disparate, exile, expel
    antonyms: allow, permit, stay
    According to the law, the US *deports* its criminals who do not have US citizenship.

44. Detach [dih-**tach**]
verb def: to unfasten; separate; disengage.
    synonyms: disconnect, disassemble, disengage
    antonyms: attach, combine, connect, couple
    It is impossible for students to *detach* themselves from the enormous pressure brought on by taking tests.

45. Hazard [**haz**-erd]
noun def: danger, risk, or peril.
    synonyms: danger, imperilment, jeopardy
    antonyms: protection, safeguard, safety
    The security job Tom was about to start seemed full of *hazards*.

46. Extant [**ek**-stuhnt]
adj def: existing; not destroyed.
    synonyms: actual, alive, current, existent
    antonyms: dead, extinct, gone
    There is no *extant* copy of a certain Super Bowl television broadcast; nobody bothered to keep the tapes.

47. Boisterous [**boi**-ster-uhs]
adj def: rough; noisy; rowdy. (****)
    synonyms: disorderly, effervescent, impetuous, loud, rambunctious
    antonyms: calm, quiet, restrained, silent
    At 3:00 in the morning, Benjamin suddenly woke up due to the sound of *boisterous* laughter.

    The crowd was young and *boisterous*, the cheeseburgers were juicy and perfectly charred, and the place was always packed.
    — Jonathan Black, *Saveur*, October 2007

48. Onerous [on-er-uhs]

adj def: burdensome; oppressive; troublesome; causing hardship. (*****)
 synonyms: difficult, arduous, austere, cumbersome, distressing
 antonyms: common, easy, light, trivial
 A great number of people complained about *onerous* taxes imposed by the government.

 Then everyone was asked, how fairly did you act?, from "extremely unfairly" (1) to "extremely fairly" (7). Next they watched someone else make the assignments, and judged that person's ethics. Selflessness was a virtual no-show: 87 out of 94 people opted for the easy task and gave the next guy the *onerous* one.
 — Sharon Begley, *Newsweek*, 23 June 2008

49. Skeptic [skep-tic]

noun def: a person who maintains a doubting attitude.
 synonyms: agnostic, atheist, cynic, dissenter
 antonyms: believer, devotee, disciple
 Nicholas strongly believed in his teacher, but Doug was still a *skeptic*.

50. Aqueduct [ak-wi-duhk]

noun def: conduit or artificial channel for conducting water.
 synonyms: canal, conduit, water passage
 The ancient Romans used *aqueducts* to carry water to distant villages.

TOEFL iBT/ TOEIC WORDS (Day 15)

"*English vocabulary is challenging to learn for those whose first language is not English. After my undergraduate study, I also had a difficult time finding a proper and effective vocabulary book to get a high score in TOEFL iBT/ TOEIC, which is required to get an admission from the most prestigious universities. If this book, Mastering Core TOEFL iBT/ TOEIC Words with William H. Shin, had been available at that time, I would have received a successful score for my study abroad, because this book provides not only a definition for a word not also synonyms, antonyms, and an example sentence for better understanding of the individual words. Therefore, I strongly recommend this book for students who want successful results in TOEFL iBT.*"

Dr. Gyungse Park, Ph.D.
Associate Professor
The Department of Chemistry College of Science and Technology
Kunsan National University, Korea

Drill 15

1. The word **crave** is closest in meaning to

    A) disdained
    B) longed for
    C) recognized
    D) hung to

2. The word **obliging** is closest in meaning to

    A) absolving
    B) impelling
    C) stupefying
    D) illuminating

3. The word **inspire** is closest in meaning to

    A) motivate
    B) recall
    C) deport
    D) detach

4. The word **risky** is closest in meaning to

    A) undaunted
    B) haphazard
    C) rash
    D) extant

5. The word **exaggerate** is closest in meaning to

    A) condense
    B) avert
    C) overstate
    D) comprehend

Drill 15

6. The word **breakthrough** is closest in meaning to

    A) plunge
    B) agitate
    C) embellish
    D) innovative

7. The word **amplify** is closest in meaning to

    A) enlarge
    B) coax
    C) infest
    D) novice

8. The word **mar** is closest in meaning to

    A) garner
    B) damage
    C) astonish
    D) benign

9. The word **aid** is closest in meaning to

    A) ample
    B) prevail
    C) assist
    D) prevail

10. The word **fidelity** is closest in meaning to

    A) adversary
    B) boost
    C) prompt
    D) loyalty

Drill 15

11. The word **pioneer** is closest in meaning to

    A) traverse
    B) forefather
    C) wrest
    D) glean

12. The word **spur** is closest in meaning to

    A) adapt
    B) exemplify
    C) stimulate
    D) torso

13. The word **swift** is closest in meaning to

    A) hefty
    B) enrich
    C) impose
    D) moving fast.

14. The word **aperture** is closest in meaning to

    A) hole
    B) cohere
    C) novice
    D) requisite

15. The word **grandiose** is closest in meaning to

    A) grand
    B) avert
    C) cornerstone
    D) entice

Drill 15

16. The word **skeptic** is closest in meaning to

    A) tedious
    B) cynic
    C) cease
    D) detrimental

17. The word **onerous** is closest in meaning to

    A) decay
    B) elicit
    C) futile
    D) burdensome

18. The word **boisterous** is closest in meaning to

    A) foliage
    B) garnish
    C) noisy
    D) ingest

19. The word **detach** is closest in meaning to

    A) disconnect
    B) haul
    C) ignite
    D) impetuous

20. The word **impel** is closest in meaning to

    A) impact
    B) drive
    C) allure
    D) abate

1. B 2. B 3. A 4. B 5. C 6. D 7. A 8. B 9. C 10. D
11. B 12. C 13. D 14. A 15. A 16. B 17. D 18. C 19. A 20. B

TOEFL iBT/ TOEIC WORDS (Day 16)

1. **Authorize** [aw-thuh-rahyz]
   verb def: to give authority; formally sanction; to empower.
       synonyms: accredit, bless, empower, enable, entitle
       antonyms: deny, reject
   Phillip had permission to *authorize* the wire transfer of the funds from the US to Seoul, Korea.

2. **Enormous** [in-**nawr**-muhs]
   adj def: greatly exceeding the common size. (**)
       synonyms: colossal, excessive, gigantic, gross
       antonyms: insignificant, little, minute
   Jacob decided not to undertake a business project introduced by one of his colleagues due to the *enormous* costs involved.

3. **Preeminent** [pree-**em**-uh-nuhnt]
   adj def: eminent above or before others; superior.
       synonyms: capital, chief, consummate, dominant, foremost
       antonyms: inferior, low, unimportant, unknown
   Dr. Craig appeared to be extremely *preeminent* in his profession.

4. **Impact** [**im**-pakt]
   noun def: the striking of one thing against another; forceful contact.
       synonyms: collision, bounce, brunt, buffet, clash
   His chronic smoking habit had a detrimental *impact* on his health.

5. **Prophecy** [**prof**-uh-see]
   noun def: foretelling or prediction of what is to come. (***)
       synonyms: prediction, augury, cast, divination, forecast
   Jessica had an innate gift of *prophecy* because she frequently knew what is going to happen.

6. **Haul** [hawl]
   verb def: to pull; draw with force; move by force.
       synonyms: carry, convey, draw, elevate
   Anthony *hauled* his car away from the junkyard.

TOEFL iBT/ TOEIC WORDS (Day 16)

7. Surge [surj]
   verb def: a strong, swelling, wavelike volume or body of something.
   synonyms: rush, breaker, deluge, efflux, flood, rise
   When a fire alarm went off, the people in the building immediately *surged* toward the fire exit.

8. Plethora [**pleth**-er-uh]
   noun def: overabundance; excess. (***)
   synonyms: deluge, flood, overflow, profusion
   antonyms: few, lack, little, scarcity
   Fortunately, Otis found information he needed for his research project through a *plethora* of books in the library.

   There has been a *plethora* of plays in recent years whose claim to modernity is based on indicated rather than felt emotion.
   — Arthur Miller, *Harper's*, March 1999

9. Staple [**stey**-puhl]
   noun def: a principal raw material or commodity.
   synonyms: chief, essential, fundamental, important
   antonyms: auxiliary, extra
   The two countries maintain some of the highest barriers to an imported food *staple* in the world.

10. Commodity [kuh-**mahd**-i-tee]
   noun def: an article of trade or commerce.
   synonyms: article, asset, belonging, produce
   In Africa, there is always a lack of agricultural *commodities* like grain and corn for people.

11. Novelty [**nov**-uhl-tee]
   noun def: state or quality of being novel, new, or unique.
   synonyms: freshness, innovation, modernity, newfangled
   His sarcastic witticisms had ceased being an entertaining *novelty*.

12. Dwell [dwell]
   verb def: to live; reside as a permanent resident.
   synonyms: abide, bunk, continue, establish
   Paula had a chance to *dwell* with a farm family while pursuing higher education in Germany.

TOEFL iBT/ TOEIC WORDS (Day 16)

13. Disapprove [dis-uh-**proov**]
  verb def: to condemn in opinion. (***)
    synonyms: blame, chastise, criticize, damn, decry
    antonyms: agree, approve, endorse, like
    John decided to marry Kelly even though his parents *disapproved* of his decision to marry her.

14. Vacillate [**vas**-uh-leyt]
  verb def: to waver in mind or opinion; be indecisive
    synonyms: attenuate, irresolute, dither, hedge
    antonyms: remain, stay
    Brian had *vacillated* for so many hours that the vice-president of the company made the decision instead.

15. Foremost [**fawr**-mohst]
  adj def: first in place, rank.
    synonyms: chief, initial
    antonyms: inferior, last, least, secondary
    Dr. Johnson was known as the *foremost* surgeon.

16. Admonition [ad-muh-**nish**-uhn]
  noun def: advice; caution; gentle reproof. (**)
    synonyms: advice, apprise, counsel
    When Jacob was in college, his academic advisor always gave him words of advice and *admonition*.

17. Camouflage [**kam**-uh-flahzh]
  verb def: the act, means, or result of obscuring things.
    synonyms: disguise, blind, concealment, cover
    antonyms: reveal, show, uncover
    Drab plumage provides the bird with *camouflage* against predators

18. Retrogress [re-truh-**gres**]
  verb def: to move backward.
    Since the CEO of the company passed away, the quality of the products has continue to *retrogress*.

TOEFL iBT/ TOEIC WORDS (Day 16)

19. Subterranean [subh-tuh-**rey**-nee-uhn]
   noun def: hidden; underground.
   > The Soviet Union built a number of *subterranean* bunkers that could withstand even an atomic blast.

20. Increment [**in**-kruh-muhnt]
   noun def: something added or gained in portions that are identical.
   > synonyms: accession, accretion, addition
   > antonyms: decrease, loss
   > Nicky has a strong tendency to add to his savings account in *increments* of $250.

   > They increased the dosage of the drug in small *increments* over a period of several weeks.

21. Reverse [ri-**vurs**]
   noun def: opposite or contrary in position.
   > synonyms: opposite, contradiction, contrary, adversity
   > antonyms: progress, success
   > Stephen always found something on the *reverse* side of a fabric when he was shopping in a department store.

22. Itinerant [ahy-**tin**-er-uhnt]
   adj def: traveling from place to place, especially on a circuit. (**)
   > synonyms: ambulant, floating, migratory, moving
   > antonyms: permanent, settled
   > Andrew's *itinerant* habits led him to travel around the word.

   > Portraits by *itinerant* artists vivify a genre that was scuttled by the invention of photography.

23. Granary [**grey**-nuh-ree]
   noun def: storehouse; repository.
   > When Elena visited her grandmother, she found many different *granaries* in the village.

TOEFL iBT/ TOEIC WORDS (Day 16)

24. Contemporary [kuhn-**tem**-puh-rer-ee]
   adj def: existing, occurring, or living at the same time. (***)
        synonyms: current, instant, newfangled
        It is generally believed that Newton's discovery of calculus was *contemporary* with that of Leibniz.

        Run by a local, the home store mingles *contemporary* furniture and retro accents with original artwork and bold pottery.

25. Diversion [dih-**vur**-zhuhn]
   noun def: the act of diverting or turning aside. (**)
        synonyms: aberration, alteration, deflection, departure
        antonyms: confirming, staying
        Cycling turned out to be one of his favorite *diversions*.

26. Disparate [**dis**-per-it]
   adj def: distinct in kind; essentially different. (****)
        synonyms: odd; different; contrary; discordant
        antonyms: alike, equal, like, similar
        Jason and I had totally *disparate* opinions about parenting children.

        First during the nineteen-seventies, but with increasing momentum during the eighties, a loose community of physics researchers had begun to postulate that the *disparate* small particles that we learned about in high-school science class—electrons, for instance—were actually the varied vibrations of tiny open and closed looped strings.
        — Benjamin Wallace-Wells, *New Yorker*, 21 July 2008

27. Occupy [**ok**-yuh-pahy]
   verb def: to take or fill up
        synonyms: busy, engage, engross
        antonyms: be lazy, idle
        Alana always *occupied* her children with watching cartoons on TV while she was cooking dinner.

TOEFL iBT/ TOEIC WORDS (Day 16)

28. Remnant [**rem**-nuhnt]
  noun def: a remaining, usually small, part; quantity. (***)
  synonyms: balance, dregs, dross, excess, fragment
  antonyms: whole
  A manager of the store was forced to decide that any *remnants* would go on sale tomorrow.

29. Flippant [**flip**-uhnt]
  adj def: shallow or lacking in seriousness.
  synonyms: breezy, disrespectful, flip, glib, impertinent
  antonyms: courteous, respectful, reverent
  The audience was shocked by his *flippant* remarks about patriotism.

30. Cohesive [koh-**hee**-siv]
  adj def: well organized; unified.
  Nicholson does not have a lot of friends but maintains a *cohesive* relationship with the ones he does have.

31. Employ [em-**ploi**]
  verb def: to hire or engage the services of.
  synonyms: apply, bestow, exercise, exert
  antonyms: ignore, misuse, shun
  My teacher *employed* different and effective teaching methods to help us understand better what we learned in class.

32. Affinity [uh-**fin**-i-tee]
  noun def: a natural liking for or attraction to a person, thing, or idea. (***)
  synonyms: affection, attraction, closeness
  antonyms: dislike, hatred
  It is surprising that there has always been a strong *affinity* between Carl and Jean.

  Jefferson's personal debts continued to mount ... . His addiction to French wine, like his *affinity* for French ideas, never came to grips with the more mundane realities.
  — Joseph J. Ellis, *American Heritage*, May/June 1993

TOEFL iBT/ TOEIC WORDS (Day 16)

33. Arid [**ar**-id]
   adj def: being without moisture; extremely dry. (*)
   synonyms: dry, barren, desert
   antonyms: damp, humid, moist
   The employees were getting tired of listening to an *arid* speech about responsibility given by the employer.

34. Discriminate [dih-**skrim**-uh-neyt]
   verb def: to show prejudice; bigot; partial; separate. (**)
   synonyms: assess. collate, compare, contrast, difference
   antonyms: confuse, mix up
   The pianist appeared to have an innate capability of *discriminating* between minute variations in tone.

35. Depict [dih-**pikt**]
   verb def: to represent or characterize in words.
   synonyms: design, detail, illustrate, image
   The painting vividly *depicted* the scenery of wilderness Jessica once visited.

36. Bedeck [bih-**dek**]
   verb def: to decorate; adorn, especially in a showy or gaudy manner. (***)
   The house Lynn planned to purchase was *bedecked* with a Persian handmade rug in the middle of the living room.

37. Inexplicable [in-**ek**-spli-kuh-buhl]
   adj def: beyond compression or explanation.
   She finally showed an *inexplicable* desire for the diamond ring she saw two weeks ago.

38. Scant [skant]
   adj def: barely sufficient in amount or quantity. (**)
   The Police finally gave up accusing Tom of fraud because they had found *scant* evidence.

   Even still, the *scant* evidence that exists for pretend play in non-human apes is fairly consistent.

TOEFL iBT/ TOEIC WORDS (Day 16)

39. Displace [dis-**pleys**]
    verb def: to move; remove from normal place; replace; supplant.
        synonyms: change, derange, dislocate, dislodge
        antonyms: leave
        Destroying trees and forests will *displace* a number of wild animals.

40. Paucity [**paw**-si-tee]
    noun def: smallness of quantity; scarcity. (***)
        synonyms: lack, scarcity, dearth, famine
        antonyms: abundance, affluence, plenty
        Jeremy had a *paucity* of answers for the problems he was facing.

41. Relic [**rel**-ik]
    noun def: a surviving memorial of something past.
        My grandmother tried to keep every item around her because she wanted to remember when she was young through the *relics*.

42. Obstacle [**ob**-stuh-kuhl]
    noun def: something that obstructs or hinders.
        synonyms: impediment, barrier, block, bump
        antonyms: advantage, assurance, blessing
        Jennifer attempted to overcome her *obstacles* to communicating in English.

43. Primary [**prahy**-mer-ee]
    noun def: the first or highest in rank.
        The *primary* function of secondary school is to educate students.

44. Irrespective [ir-i-**spek**-tiv]
    adj def: without regard to something else.
        Jefferson should study English every day *irrespective* of my wishes.

45. Collapse [kuh-**laps**]
    verb def: to fall or cave in; crumble suddenly. (**)
        synonyms: downfall, bankruptcy, cataclysm
        antonyms: increase, rise, success
        An earthquake *collapsed* many buildings in this town.

TOEFL iBT/ TOEIC WORDS (Day 16)

46. Obscure [uhb-**skyoor**]
   adj def: unclear to the understanding; hard to perceive. (***)
      synonyms: ambiguous, abstruse, complicated, doubtful, vague
      antonyms: apparent, explicit, obvious, perceptible
      His explanation about the book was so *obscure* that no one in the classroom understood him.

47. Affiliate [uh-**fil**-ee-eyt]
   verb def: to bring into close association.
      synonyms: branch, offshoot, partner, sibling
      Dr. Schmidt never *affiliated* himself with any political party.

48. Bevy [**bev**-ee]
   noun def: swarm; band; bunch; cluster. (**)
      There was a *bevy* of boisterous students gathering in front of the classroom.

49. Abandon [uh-**ban**-duhn]
   verb def: to leave completely and finally; forsake.
      synonyms: desert, give up, forsake
      antonyms: restraint, self-restraint
      The captain of the ship ordered his crew and passengers to *abandon* ship.

50. Brew [broo]
   verb def: to concoct; mix; cook.
      synonyms: blend, broth, compound
      Many people began to visit a local restaurant more frequently because it *brews* its own ginger ale and root beer.

TOEFL iBT/ TOEIC WORDS (Day 16)

❝ *This book, which contains the must-have 1650 words for preparation to pass the TOEFL iBT/ TOEIC test, is well laid out, with good examples through the format of daily study for 33 days. Sample sentences are very clear and brief, so foreign students who may lack familiarity with American culture can still learn words without difficulty in understanding the context. The author illustrates a very effective and time-saving study format based on his extensive experience in teaching SAT English. As a result, the book has become quite intuitive and self-explanatory for readers. I, a non-native English speaker, wish there had been such a book long time ago, and I strongly recommend it.* ❞

Dr. Hoonbae Jeon, M.D, FACS
Associate Professor of Surgery
Surgical Director, Liver Transplant Program
Director, Transplant Surgery Fellowship
University of Illinois at Chicago
Division of Transplant (MC958), Department of Surgery

Drill 16

1. The word **preeminent** is closest in meaning to

    A) foremost
    B) ambition
    C) exposition
    D) vacillation

2. The word **collapse** is closest in meaning to

    A) swell
    B) breakdown
    C) enigmatic
    D) convenient

3. The word **paucity** is closest in meaning to

    A) spur
    B) staples
    C) lack
    D) exponent

4. The word **displace** is closest in meaning to

    A) remove
    B) annoy
    C) flee
    D) rigid

5. The word **onerous** is closest in meaning to

    A) foster
    B) troublesome
    C) astonish
    D) extol

Drill 16

6. The word **haul** is closest in meaning to

    A) plethora
    B) apex
    C) confine
    D) pull

7. The word **enormous** is closest in meaning to

    A) keen
    B) myriad
    C) huge
    D) lure

8. The word **dwell** is closest in meaning to

    A) agile
    B) reside
    C) commodity
    D) impact

9. The word **itinerant** is closest in meaning to

    A) travel
    B) bedeck
    C) slippery
    D) precipitation

10. The word **contemporary** is closest in meaning to

    A) annex
    B) modern
    C) exert
    D) patron

Drill 16

11. The word **disparate** is closest in meaning to

    A) crave
    B) astound
    C) different
    D) pity

12. The word **arid** is closest in meaning to

    A) complement
    B) defection
    C) eager
    D) dry

13. The word **regardless of** is closest in meaning to

    A) irrespective
    B) in keeping with
    C) for the sake of
    D) in terms of

14. The word **demise** is closest in meaning to

    A) overtone
    B) fall
    C) affiliation
    D) bevy

15. The word **scatter** is closest in meaning to

    A) disperse
    B) overthrow
    C) perceive
    D) seethe

Drill 16

16. The word **affiliate** is closest in meaning to

    A) ethereal
    B) association
    C) facile
    D) hone

17. The word **scant** is closest in meaning to

    A) hub
    B) mature
    C) oscillate
    D) lack

18. The word **cohesive** is closest in meaning to

    A) abrasive
    B) seethe
    C) integrate
    D) pity

19. The word **remnant** is closest in meaning to

    A) prophecy
    B) leftover
    C) retool
    D) swath

20. The word **admonition** is closest in meaning to

    A) advice
    B) subdue
    C) tedious
    D) aggregate

1. A 2. B 3. C 4. A 5. B 6. D 7. C 8. B 9. A 10. B
11. C 12. D 13. A 14. B 15. A 16. B 17. D 18. C 19. B 20. A

TOEFL iBT/ TOEIC WORDS (Day 17)

1. Enact [en-**akt**]
    verb def: to make into an act or statute. (**)
        synonyms: achieve, execute, perform
        antonyms: fail, repeal, stop
    Congress will *enact* effective and appropriate laws for the problems.

2. Formulate [**fawr**-myuh-leyt]
    verb def: to express in precise form; state definitely.
        synonyms: plan, codify, compose, concoct
    Unfortunately, the scientist had unexpected difficulties in *formulating* his new scientific theory.

    The committee will outline a situation and ask you to *formulate* a plan that deals with the problem.

3. Substitute [**suhb**-sti-toot]
    adj def: a person or thing acting or serving in place of another.
        synonyms: additional, alternate, another, artificial, backup
        antonyms: permanent
    Most of the schools have several *substitute* teachers in case that its regular teachers are unable to come to teach their students.

4. Revitalize [ree-**vahyt-uh**-lhyz]
    verb def: to give new life to; to give new vitality.
    The mayor decided to invest a considerable amount of money to *revitalize* the city.

5. Nadir [**ney**-der]
    noun def: point of great adversity or despair. (***)
        synonyms: base, bottom, floor
    It is generally believed that The Great Depression was the *nadir* of despair of the 1930s.

    Nantucket reached its *nadir* in the post-Civil War period. The whaling industry had become moribund, many New Englanders had been lured to California by the discovery of gold, and the island population dropped from ten thousand in 1830 to scarcely more than three thousand in 1880.
                      — David H. Wood, *Antiques*, August 1995

TOEFL iBT/ TOEIC WORDS (Day 17)

6. Crest [krest]
noun def: the highest point or level; climax; summit.
    synonyms: acme, apex, apogee, climax
    antonyms: nadir, bottom
    As soon as Chris reached to the *crest* of the mountain, it began to thunder.

7. Hub [hubb]
noun def: a focus of activity; commerce; transportation. (*)
    synonyms: core, focus, heart
    antonyms: exterior, outside
    In high school, Alice had been known as the *hub* of all the activity.

8. Impend [im-pend]
verb def: to be imminent; be about to happen.
    He was so pessimistic that he strongly believed that some disaster always seemed to be *impending*.

9. Decent [dee-sent]
adj def: respectable; worthy. (**)
    synonyms: approved, chaste, clean, comely
    antonyms: inappropriate, indecent, poor, unsuitable
    Thomas was a *decent* man who never hesitated to help people in need.

10. Conjure [kon-jer]
verb def: to call or bring into existence by or as if by magic. (***)
    synonyms: adjure, beg, beseech, brace, crave
    antonyms: disquiet, turn off
    Reading the author's description, John *conjured* up a vision of a utopia beyond belief.

    The cotton candy *conjured* up the image of the fair grounds he used to visit as a child in Arthur's mind.

11. Abuse [uh-byooz]
verb def: to use wrongly or improperly.
    synonyms: corruption, crime, delinquency, desecration
    antonyms: aid, help, preservation
    As far as I know, Brian is not the person who *abuses* his authority.

TOEFL iBT/ TOEIC WORDS (Day 17)

12. Annual [**an**-yoo-uhl]
   adj def: pertaining to a year.
   synonyms: anniversary, once a year
   It was unfortunate that Robert did not earn enough *annual* income to support his family.

13. Halt [hawlt]
   verb def: to stop; cease temporarily.
   synonyms: arrest, break, close, cut off
   antonyms: continuation, endurance, go
   Brian and his colleagues have decided to *halt* operations during contract negotiations.

14. Predominate [pri-**dom**-uh-neyt]
   verb def: to surpass others in authority.
   synonyms: command, domineer, govern
   Senator Kennedy *predominated* in the political scene.

15. Deluge [**del**-yooj]
   noun def: flood; inundation. (**)
   Tony was extremely happy because he received a *deluge* of offers.

   The popular actor was *deluged* with fan mail.

16. Quandary [**kwon**-duh-ree]
   noun def: a state of perplexity or uncertainty. (*****)
   synonyms: bewilderment, bind, corner, difficult, dilemma
   antonyms: advantage, certainty, solution
   Many immigrant people were in a *quandary* about whether they would be able to reside in America.

   Williams's *quandary* is not unlike that faced by other urban executives who have had to wrestle with a deeply rooted power structure. The problem is especially acute for African-American mayors. They are expected to serve as sentries, protecting their cities' black communities and staving off so-called white encroachment.
   — Jonetta Rose Barras, *Washington Post*, 15 June 2003

TOEFL iBT/ TOEIC WORDS (Day 17)

17. Reshape [ree-**sheyp**]
   verb def: to shape again into different form.
      Dr. Pinker was forced to *reshape* his book cover to meet the requirements of the publisher.

18. Vanish [**van**-ish]
   verb def: to disappear from sight. (**)
      synonyms: become invisible, clear, dissolve, evanesce
      antonyms: appear, arrive, come
      The ice in front of my house suddenly *vanished* when the sun came out.

19. Indigenous [in-**dij**-uh-nuhs]
   adj def: originating in and characteristic of a particular region. (***)
      synonyms: native, inborn, aboriginal
      antonyms: alien, foreign
      There are many different types of *indigenous* people in Southern Africa.

      Viking invaders quickly subdued the *indigenous* population, known as the Picts.
                              — Jared M. Diamond, *Collapse*, 2005

20. Withstand [with-**stand**]
   verb def: to stand in opposition to; resist.
      synonyms: confront, contest, cope, cross
      antonyms: surrender, yield
      The troops successfully *withstood* numerous attacks from the enemy.

21. Hew [hyoo]
   verb def: to make; shape; smooth.
      Once he has finished his homework, Andy began to *hew* a statue from marble.

22. Hereditary [huh-**red**-i-ter-ee]
   adj def: inherited; transmitted at birth.
      synonyms: ancestral, bequeathed, genetic, inborn
      antonyms: acquire
      Prior to these experiments, protein was believed to hold our *hereditary* destiny.

TOEFL iBT/ TOEIC WORDS (Day 17)

23. Descendant [dih-**sen**-duhnt]
    adj def: offspring; scion; kin.
        synonyms: brood, child, heir, issue, offshoot
        antonyms: ascendant, predecessor
        His theory might be a *descendant* branch of the Quantum Theory.

24. Oversee [oh-ver-**see**]
    verb def: to direct; supervise. (**)
        Helen was responsible for *overseeing* the construction crew.

25. Vast [vast]
    adj def: immense; huge; ample.
        Jean found out that the store in a shopping mall would be having a *vast* sale tomorrow.

26. Inscribe [in-**skrahyb**]
    verb def: to write; print; engrave.
        The TOEFL iBT/ TOEIC reference books being sold in a local bookstore were *inscribed* with the author's signature.

27. Overlap [oh-ver-**lap**]
    verb def: to cover and extend beyond.
        synonyms: flap, overrun, project, protrude
        antonyms: divide, separate
        The ends of the tablecloth *overlap* the table.

28. Appraise [uh-**preyz**]
    verb def: to determine the worth of.
        synonyms: assay, assess, audit, calculate
        Before Jeff bought the house, he hired an expert to *appraise* it.

29. Valor [**val**-er]
    noun def: boldness or determination in facing great danger. (****)
        synonyms: bravery, boldness, courage, determination
        antonyms: cowardice
        Since he started serving his country, the General has received many medals for *valor*.

TOEFL iBT/ TOEIC WORDS (Day 17)

30. Intimate [**in**-tuh-mit]
   adj def: very private; closely personal.
        synonyms: friendly, devotee, affectionate, close, cozy
        antonyms: cool, formal, incompatible
        Jessica and Jennifer have had a long-term *intimate* friendship.

31. Compatible [kuhm-**pat**-uh-buhl]
   adj def: able to exist together with someone else.
        synonyms: accordant, adaptable, congenial, congruent, consistent
        antonyms: antagonistic, antipathy, disagreeable, inharmonious
        The printer Jenny purchased yesterday was not *compatible* with most personal computers.

32. Pathetic [puh-**thet**-ik]
   adj def: miserably or contemptibly inadequate. (***)
        synonyms: sad, miserable, deplorable, distressing
        antonyms: cheerful, happy, useful, worthwhile
        Unfortunately, Max got only a *pathetic* 1% interest in return for his five-month investment.

        The spectacle seen in the theater of the news presented the American President as a failed suppliant instead of a conquering hero—an ailing and *pathetic* figure dismissed with the smile of pity and the gift of some sweet candies shaped as miniature sculptures of the President's two dogs.
                      — Lewis H. Lapham, *Harper's*, March 1992

33. Apprehensive [ap-ri-**hen**-siv]
   adj def: having negative awareness. (**)
        synonyms: afraid, concerned, disquiet, doubtful
        antonyms: calm, undoubting, unfearful, unwonted
        Stephen seemed to be *apprehensive* of all his options.

34. Timorous [**tim**-er-uhs]
   adj def: full of fear; indicating fear: timid.
        The *timorous* dog cowered in the corner.

TOEFL iBT/ TOEIC WORDS (Day 17)

35. Insurmountable [in-ser-**moun**-tuh-buhl]
    adj def: incapable of being passed over or overcome. (***)
        synonyms: hopeless, impassable, impregnable, inaccessible
        antonyms: attainable, beatable
        Timothy faced several *insurmountable* obstacles that caused him to give up on the project.

        There are problems to be solved, but they probably aren't *insurmountable*.

36. Soar [sawr]
    verb def: to rise or ascend to a height.
        synonyms: arise, ascend, aspire, glide
        antonyms: land
        Liz happened to see a couple of eagles *soaring* into the sky.

37. Hover [**huhv**-er]
    verb def: to hang fluttering or suspended in the air.
        synonyms: drift, flicker, flutter, linger
        antonyms: rest, settle
        In order to help to capture a burglar, a police helicopter kept *hovering* over the building.

38. Swift [swift]
    adj def: quick; prompt; fast.
        You cannot cheat him because he is too *swift*.

39. Bridle [**brahyd**-l]
    noun def: anything that restrains or curbs. (**)
        synonyms: check, control, deterrent, halter, leash
        antonyms: let go, release, set free
        Jefferson's common sense turned out to be a *bridle* to his quick temper.

40. Aloft [uh-**lawft**]
    prep def: on or at the top of.
        synonyms: overhead, above
        antonyms: below, under
        Many different flags are flying *aloft* the building.

TOEFL iBT/ TOEIC WORDS (Day 17)

41. Simulate [**sim**-yuh-leyt]
   verb def: to make a pretense of.
        synonyms: affect, ape, assume, bluff, borrow
        antonyms: be real
        The scientists used a model to *simulate* the effect of an earthquake.

42. Assort [uh-**sawrt**]
   verb def: to distribute; arrange; classify.
        Entomologists spent many hours *assorting* captured butterflies according to geographic origin.

43. Momentum [moh-**men**-tuhm]
   noun def: force; impetus; speed of movement.
        synonyms: impetus, push, drive, energy
        The movie director lost his career *momentum* after two consecutive unsuccessful films.

44. Prohibit [proh-**hib**-it]
   verb def: to forbid by authority or law.
        synonyms: stop, prevent, hinder, constrain
        antonyms: allow, favor, permit, push
        Tina's mother *prohibited* her daughter from going out with Kevin, who had recently gotten laid off.

45. Invariable [in-**vair**-ee-uh-buhl]
   adj def: static; constant; not changing. (***)
        Jay has had an *invariable* bad habit, which is smoking.

46. Contagious [kuhn-**tey**-juhs]
   adj def: tending to spread from person to person.
        synonyms: endemic, epidemic, infectious, pestiferous
        antonyms: noncommunicable
        In ancient times, many different unknown *contagious* diseases killed a number of innocent people.

47. Insuperable [in-**soo**-per-uh-buhl]
   adj def: incapable of being overcome; insurmountable. (***)
        synonyms: impassable, insurmountable
        The university was forced to close down a laboratory because of *insuperable* financial difficulties.

TOEFL iBT/ TOEIC WORDS (Day 17)

48. Incredulous [in-**krej**-uh-luhs]
   adj def: disinclined or indisposed to believe; skeptical. (**)
        synonyms: distrustful, doubtful, dubious, hesitant
        antonyms: convinced, credulous
        Mr. Ford listened to Jenny's detailed explanation with an *incredulous* smile.

        "Afraid not." I made an expression to show that I was as *incredulous* about this as he was.
                          — Bill Bryson, *I'm a Stranger Here Myself*, 1999

49. Ignite [ig-**nahyt**]
   verb def: to set on fire; to kindle.
        synonyms: burn, fire, inflame, kindle
        antonyms: extinguish, put out
        The cigarette butt thrown by an unknown pedestrian *ignited* the fire.

50. Propulsion [pruh-**puhl**-shuhn]
   noun def: a means of propelling force; impulse.
        synonyms: drive, effort, energy, impulse
        Sailboats use winds as their primary source of *propulsion*.

> ❝ *Living as an international student, I am required to take the TOEFL iBT/ TOEIC exam. After studying with this amazing book by my teacher, Mr. Shin, I have been able to increase my skills tremendously. It is truly a well-thought-out and profound book. I would certainly recommend it to everyone trying to increase his/her score.* ❞

BonKyu Ku
Korea International School, Pangyo Campus, Korea

TOEFL iBT/ TOEIC WORDS (Day 17)

❝*I have no doubt that this book is the most effective TOEFL iBT/ TOEIC preparation source I have ever come across. Unlike other TOEFL iBT/ TOEIC word books,* Mastering Core TOEFL iBT/ TOEIC Words with William Shin *provides students with synonyms, antonyms, tailored example sentences, and driils that enable them not only to boost their TOEFL iBT/ TOEIC test scores but also to expand and enrich their knowledge of standard written English proficiency. By studying the Mr .Shin's book on a daily basis, I am confident that students will be able to reach their ideal TOEFL iBT/ TOEIC test scores successfully.*❞

Dr. Heejin Kim, Ph.D.
Professor and Head of Department of Music in Piano Performance
Sang Myung University, Seoul Korea

Drill 17

1. The word **height** is closest in meaning to

    A) nadir
    B) crest
    C) flank
    D) hub

2. The word **imminent** is closest in meaning to

    A) impending
    B) strong
    C) preeminent
    D) decent

3. The word **overtake** is closest in meaning to

    A) conjure
    B) abuse
    C) catch
    D) safeguard

4. The word **efficient** is closest in meaning to

    A) annual
    B) close
    C) successful
    D) bare

5. The word **withstand** is closest in meaning to

    A) forge
    B) deepen
    C) resist
    D) appraise

Drill 17

6. The word **haphazard** is closest in meaning to

    A) valorous
    B) unplanned
    C) simplistic
    D) makeshift

7. The word **disparate** is closest in meaning to

    A) united
    B) different
    C) intimate
    D) compatible

8. The word **immeasurable** is closest in meaning to

    A) pathetic
    B) apprehensive
    C) vast
    D) timid

9. The word **meticulous** is closest in meaning to

    A) incredulous
    B) classic
    C) elementary
    D) scrupulous

10. The word **comprise** is closest in meaning to

    A) consist
    B) unwanted
    C) ferrous
    D) smelt

11. The word **flourish** is closest in meaning to

    A) impose
    B) prosper
    C) collapse
    D) accelerate

12. The word **indigenous** is closest in meaning to

    A) vanish
    B) mortar
    C) native
    D) hew

13. The word **complement** is closest in meaning to

    A) vast
    B) companion
    C) exert
    D) proponent

14. The word **oversee** is closest in meaning to

    A) overlap
    B) speculate
    C) theorize
    D) watch

15. The word **assort** is closest in meaning to

    A) classify
    B) determine
    C) prohibit
    D) emerge

Drill 17

16. The word **ignite** is closest in meaning to

    A) attenuate
    B) inveigle
    C) kindle
    D) clement

17. The word **incredulous** is closest in meaning to

    A) impetus
    B) constitute
    C) internecine
    D) skeptical

18. The word **insuperable** is closest in meaning to

    A) circumspect
    B) insurmountable
    C) respectable
    D) variable

19. The word **simulate** is closest in meaning to

    A) ascend
    B) pretend
    C) haul
    D) bevy

20. The word **swift** is closest in meaning to

    A) quick
    B) perish
    C) herald
    D) abet

1. B 2. A 3. C 4. C 5. C 6. B 7. B 8. C 9. D 10. A
11. B 12. C 13. B 14. D 15. A 16. C 17. D 18. B 19. B 20. A

TOEFL iBT/ TOEIC WORDS (Day 18)

1. Interact [in-ter-**akt**]
   verb def: to communicate; collaborate; cooperate. (***)
        synonyms: collaborate, combine, connect, contact
        antonyms: not speak
        Jeremy and Stephanie didn't seem to *interact* with each other frequently.

2. Symbiosis [sim-bee-**oh**-sis]
   noun def: the living together of two dissimilar organisms. (**)
        The bird lives in *symbiosis* with the hippopotamus.

        Benjamin's evidence for nitrite-producing tongue bugs is drawn from rats, but he's confident that a similar *symbiosis* exists in humans.

3. Prolong [pruh-**lawng**]
   verb def: to lengthen out in time.
        synonyms: extend, carry on, continue, delay
        antonyms: abbreviate, shorten
        The economic recession turned out to be *prolonging* high interest rates.

4. Vest [vest]
   verb def: to invest with something, as powers.
        synonyms: empower, endow, furnish, bestow
        antonyms: disapprove
        The local factory decided to *vest* its employees with full benefits in the pension plan.

5. Perish [**per**-ish]
   verb def: to die; be destroyed through violence.
        synonyms: die, decline, decay, cease, check
        antonyms: give birth, revive
        The civilization suddenly *perished* for an unknown reason.

6. Mutual [**myoo**-choo-uhl]
   adj def: having the same relation each toward the other.
        synonyms: shared, common, bilateral, conjoint
        antonyms: detached, distract, separate, unshared
        Jeff and Paul have long considered Michael their *mutual* enemy.

TOEFL iBT/ TOEIC WORDS (Day 18)

7. Indispensable [in-di-**spen**-suh-buhl]
   adj def: necessary; requisite; essential. (***)
        Rice has been known as an *indispensable* provision since ancient times.

8. Hygiene [**hahy**-jeen]
   noun def: a condition or practice conducive to the preservation of health, such as cleanliness.
        synonyms: public health, regimen
        Poor sanitation and *hygiene* caused many people to get sick.

9. Harbor [**hahr**-ber]
   verb def: to give shelter; to offer refuge to.
        synonyms: anchorage, arm, cove, dock
        antonyms: eject, let out, uncover
        Not many countries in the world attempted to *harbor* refugees who escaped from their country.

10. Entail [en-**teyl**]
   verb def: to require; result in.
        synonyms: bring about, call for, cause, demand
        It is firmly believed that success *entails* ceaseless effort and strong spirit.

11. Liberate [**lib**-uh-reyt]
   verb def: to set free; to disengage; to discharge.
        Finally the police succeeded in *liberating* the hostages from their captors.

12. Irreparable [ih-**rep**-er-uh-buhl]
   adj def: incorrigible; incurable of being rectified. (***)
        synonyms: broken, cureless, destroyed, hopeless
        antonyms: flexible, reparable
        The damage to their relationship was *irreparable*.

        The solution is something that will control the insects without doing *irreparable* harm to other plants and animals.

13. Deteriorate [dih-**teer**-ee-uh-teyt]
   verb def: to worsen; aggravate; decay; degenerate. (***)
        Being unable to quit smoking *deteriorates* people's health.

TOEFL iBT/ TOEIC WORDS (Day 18)

14. Intestine [in-**tes**-tin]
   noun def: the digestive tract in mammals
       The doctor found some blockage in John's lower *intestine*.

15. Cardinal [**kahr**-dihn-l]
   noun def: a high ecclesiastical official of the Roman Catholic Church. (*)
       synonyms: central, chief, essential,
       antonyms: minor, insignificant, negligible
       The Pope made a determination to appoint two new *cardinals* last year.

16. Acknowledge [ak-**nol**-ij]
   verb def: to admit recognition or realization. (**)
       synonyms: accede, accept, approve, attest
       antonyms: forswear, ignore, refuse, renounce
       Many students appeared to *acknowledge* the authority of student council.

17. Repercussion [ree-per-**kuhsh**-uhn]
   noun def: an effect or result, often indirect or remote.
       synonyms: echo, effect, impact, influence
       antonyms: cause
       The *repercussions* of the quarrel between Kelly and Lincoln was widespread.

18. Biosphere [**bahy**-uh-sfeer]
   noun def: the part of the earth's crust where life exists; ecosystem.
       The definition of *biosphere* is the part of the world in which life can exist.

19. Abate [uh-**beyt**]
   verb def: to deduct; subtract; reduce; diminish. (**)
       Taking an aspirin helped Paul *abate* his back pain.

       As the hurricane force *abated,* the windspeed, dropped and the sea became calm.

20. Persecute [**pur**-si-kyoot]
   verb def: to pursue with harassing or oppressive treatment.
       synonyms: wrong, torment, afflict, aggrieve, annoy
       antonyms: comfort, commend, console
       The dictator made a ceaseless effort to find and *persecute* those who fought against his regime established in 1993.

TOEFL iBT/ TOEIC WORDS (Day 18)

21. Subsidize [**suhb**-si-dahyz]
   verb def: to furnish; aid; help.
   synonyms: contribute, endow, finance, promote
   The government finally set up a plan to *subsidize* housing for low-income families.

22. Accommodate [uh-**kom**-uh-deyt]
   verb def: to provide suitably; supply.
   synonyms: furnish, hold, house
   antonyms: turn away, turn out
   Alex is a person who normally *accommodates* his friends with large sums of money.

23. Inaugurate [in-**aw**-gyuh-reyt]
   verb def: to make a formal beginning of. (**)
   synonyms: initiate, commence, begin, introduce
   antonyms: adjourn, close, end, stop
   It is firmly believed that World War Two *inaugurated* the era of nuclear power.

24. Antecede [an-tuh-**seed**]
   verb def: to go before; in time, order, rank.
   The Italian art *anteceded* Raphael and other masters of high Renaissance.

25. Lieu [loo]
   noun def: place; stead
   idiom: in lieu of
   Jennifer gave Jack an IOU in *lieu* of cash.

26. Feast [feest]
   noun def: celebration; a sumptuous entertainment.
   synonyms: banquet, carnival, carousal
   The people in this town have a *feast* in honor of their patron saint.

27. Surplus [**sur**-pluhs]
   noun def: something that remains above what is needed. (**)
   synonyms: extra, excess, leftover, odd, remaining
   antonyms: essential, lacking, necessary
   My boss was an extremely fair person, for he always divided any *surplus* equally with his employees.

TOEFL iBT/ TOEIC WORDS (Day 18)

28. Implicit [im-**plis**-it]
    adj def: implied rather than expressly stated.
        synonyms: accurate, certain, complete, constant
        antonyms: explicit, specific
    The lawyer seemed to have an *implicit* trust in his client's honesty.

29. Robust [roh-**buhst**]
    adj def: suited to or requiring bodily strength or endurance. (****)
        synonyms: strong, healthy, hardy, brawny, flourishing, hefty
        antonyms: flabby, infirm, weak
    Joseph has always been a *robust* drinker and dancer since he graduated from high school.

    If Singapore, just seven miles to the north with its glittering skyline and *robust* economy, is Southeast Asia's Cinderella, Batam is her dark sister.
        — Peter Gwin, *National Geographic*, October 2007

30. Unparalleled [uhn-**par**-uh-leld]
    adj def: consummate; matchless; exceptional; peerless. (**)
    Martinez shows an *unparalleled* athletic ability.

31. Bequeath [blh-**kweath**]
    verb def: to hand down; pass on; dispose of.
        synonyms: bestow, commit, devise, endow
        antonyms: take
    Barbara made a solid determination to *bequeath* her business to her nephew, for she firmly believed that he was smart and intelligent enough to continue to run the business successfully.

32. Purge [purj]
    verb def: to rid; clear; free. (**)
        synonyms: abolition, catharsis, clarification
        antonyms: holding, keeping, maintenance
    The CEO of a company had no choice but to *purge* high-ranking employees following the merger.

TOEFL iBT/ TOEIC WORDS (Day 18)

33. Cumbersome [kuhm-ber-suhm]
   adj def: burdensome; troublesome. (***)
   synonyms: clumsy, awkward, clunky, leaden
   antonyms: graceful
   The project Tony was about to undertake appeared to be *cumbersome* and time consuming.

   Squad members, already decked out in *cumbersome* chemical suits, put on masks and rubber gloves.
   — Ray Wilkinson, *Newsweek*, 11 Mar. 1991

34. Catharsis [kuh-thahr-sis]
   noun def: purging; cleansing; purifying. (****)
   The companionship of domesticated pets can sometimes lead to a *catharsis* for mentally disturbed patients.

   She has learned to have her *catharsis*, take a deep breath and move on. ... she does not dwell on the negative anymore.
   — Selena Roberts, *New York Times*, 24 June 2001

35. Ban [ban]
   verb def: to stop; prevent; prohibit; forbid.
   The tyrant strictly *banned* any newspaper articles that attempted to criticize his regime.

36. Rampant [ram-puhnt]
   adj def: aggressive; boisterous; excessive. (***)
   The mayor finally took serious action to stop *rampant* crime that destroyed the city environment in which people enjoy their lives.

37. Amble [am-buhl]
   verb def: stroll; saunter.
   Mari used to be in the habit of *ambling* around the town.

38. Unbiased [uhn-bahy-uhst]
   adj def: fair; impartial; aloof; disinterested.
   Many people thought that Alex didn't offer an *unbiased* judgment of the pianist's performance.

TOEFL iBT/ TOEIC WORDS (Day 18)

39. Astute [uh-**stoot**]
    adj def: discernment; keen; sagacious. (***)
        The *astute* observation made by Mr. Ford didn't surprise anyone who knew him.

        We thought they were not very intellectually *astute*, but we didn't really understand how political a lot of what they were doing was.
                — Ben Wallace-Wells, *Rolling Stone*, 15 Nov. 2007

40. Erudite [**er**-yoo-dahyt]
    adj def: learned; scholarly. (****)
        Although his follow students thought him *erudite*, Paul knew he would have to spend many hours in serious study before he could consider himself a scholar.

        He wasn't bashful about showing himself to be feverishly *erudite*, ... terminally droll, and a wizard phrasemaker.
                — Susan Sontag, *New Yorker*, 18 & 25 June 2001

41. Illicit [ih-**lis**-it]
    adj def: unlicensed; unlawful. (**)
        The police chief found that there were a great number of *illicit* activities made engaged in by local gangsters.

        The mafia is heavily involved in *illicit* activities such as prostitution and drugs.

42. Remorse [ri-**mawrs**]
    noun def: deep and painful regret for wrongdoing; compunction.
        synonyms: anguish, attrition, compassion, compunction
        antonyms: happiness, satisfaction, remorselessness
        John was willing to forgive what Tim had done to him if Tim showed any sign of *remorse*.

43. Vain [veyn]
    adj def: arrogant; boastful; haughty. (***)
        Unlike other ordinary women, Jane seems to be very *vain* about her appearance.

TOEFL iBT/ TOEIC WORDS (Day 18)

For a half a century, scholars have searched in *vain* for the source of the jade that the early civilizations of the Americas prized above all else and fashioned into precious objects of worship, trade and adornment.
— William J. Broad, *New York Times*, 22 May 2002

44. Residue [rez-i-doo]
noun def: remainder; remnant.
A bunch of greasy *residue* from the hamburgers covered the grill in the kitchen.

45. Startle [stahr-tl]
verb def: to disturb; agitate.
The sudden lightning *startled* everyone in the house.

46. Drastic [dras-tik]
adj def: severe; extreme.
A majority of people were surprised that the government offered a *drastic* tax reduction for low-income people.

47. Attribute [uh-trib-yoot]
verb def: to regard as resulting from a specified cause.
synonyms: aspect, character, facet, mark
Jennifer *attributed* her bad temper to ill health.

48. Presume [pri-zoom]
verb def: assume; suppose. (**)
I *presume* that you must be exhausted after you drive for four hours.

49. Dissimilar [dih-sim-uh-ler]
adj def: unlike; different.
The watch Jean purchased yesterday was quite *dissimilar* to the watch Jessica is about to buy.

50. Postulate [pos-chuh-leyt]
verb def: to assert; demand; claim. (***)
synonyms: advance, affirm, assume
antonyms: calculate
One of the *postulates* the true agnostic rejects is the assumption that it is even possible for us to know whether God exists.

Drill 18

1. The word **perish** is closest in meaning to

    A) cohere
    B) expire
    C) abate
    D) endeavor

2. The word **harbor** is closest in meaning to

    A) persecute
    B) subsidize
    C) accommodate
    D) inaugurate

3. The word **entail** is closest in meaning to

    A) oversee
    B) involve
    C) retail
    D) antecede

4. The word **irreparable** is closest in meaning to

    A) springy
    B) curable
    C) unbeatable
    D) lethal

5. The word **equitable** is closest in meaning to

    A) ambling
    B) unbiased
    C) astute
    D) erudite

Drill 18

6. The word **sole** is closest in meaning to

    A) collective
    B) illicit
    C) only
    D) remorseful

7. The word **implicit** is closest in meaning to

    A) latent
    B) archaic
    C) vain
    D) showy

8. The word **diverse** is closest in meaning to

    A) subtle
    B) wary
    C) consistent
    D) multifold

9. The word **tendency** is closest in meaning to

    A) consensus
    B) complement
    C) inclination
    D) remedy

10. The word **hygiene** is closest in meaning to

    A) interaction
    B) cleanliness
    C) absorb
    D) divergent

Drill 18

11. The word **entail** is closest in meaning to

    A) independent
    B) vest
    C) sever
    D) necessitate

12. The word **replicate** is closest in meaning to

    A) intestine
    B) potential
    C) copy
    D) cardinal

13. The word **surplus** is closest in meaning to

    A) exceed
    B) purge
    C) reassert
    D) cumbersome

14. The word **indigenous** is closest in meaning to

    A) bid
    B) native
    C) decease
    D) implicit

15. The word **unparalleled** is closest in meaning to

    A) unequalled
    B) extravagance
    C) explicit
    D) alliance

Drill 18

16. The word **presume** is closest in meaning to

    A) array
    B) assume
    C) mar
    D) ossify

17. The word **illicit** is closest in meaning to

    A) convulse
    B) bleak
    C) entice
    D) unlawful

18. The word **erudite** is closest in meaning to

    A) astonish
    B) bias
    C) scholar
    D) hefty

19. The word **residue** is closest in meaning to

    A) leftover
    B) aesthetic
    C) confine
    D) mutate

20. The word **rampant** is closest in meaning to

    A) acknowledge
    B) aggressive
    C) ingest
    D) prompt

1. B 2. C 3. B 4. D 5. B 6. C 7. A 8. D 9. C 10. B
11. D 12. C 13. A 14. B 15. A 16. B 17. D 18. C 19. A 20. B

TOEFL iBT/ TOEIC WORDS (Day 19)

1. Regardless [ri-**gahrd**-lis]
adv def: having or showing no regard; unmindful.
   synonyms: indifferent, unconcerned, careless, coarse
   antonyms: concerned, heedful
   They had to finish their jobs *regardless* of the cost.

2. Ponder [**pon**-der]
verb def: to consider deeply; meditate.
   synonyms: appraise, brood, cogitate, contemplate, deliberate
   antonyms: forget, ignore, neglect
   Peter asked David to *ponder* his next words carefully.

3. Subtle [**suht**-l]
adj def: delicate; mysterious. (***)
   synonyms: deep, ethereal, exquisite, faint
   antonyms: hard, harsh, noisy, unsubtle
   Joseph seemed to have problems in understanding the *subtle* relationship between two given words.

   Although artists and patrons in Venice still sought images of ideal figures, they insisted that this imagery be rooted in a more *subtle* and insightful interpretation of human life and character.
   — Andrew Butterfield, *New York Review of Books*, 16 July 2009

4. Consensus [kuhn-**sen**-suhs]
noun def: majority of opinion.
   synonyms: agree, accord, concurrence, consent
   The *consensus* of the group was that they should meet twice a month.

5. Incline [in-**klahyn**]
verb def: to have a mental tendency or preference.
   synonyms: tendency, preference, prefer, prejudice
   Paul's attitudes did not *incline* Elaine to help Tom.

6. Blunt [bluhnt]
adj def: abrupt in address or manner; ill-timed.
   synonyms: dull, edgeless, insensitive, obtuse, pointless
   antonyms: needled, pointed, sharp
   His isolation has made him *blunt* about other people's feelings.

TOEFL iBT/ TOEIC WORDS (Day 19)

7. Adjust [uh-**juhst**]
   verb def: to accustom; alter; arrange; adapt
   Many English learners spend more hours studying spoken English to *adjust* to the business environment.

8. Preliminary [pri-**lim**-uh-ner-ee]
   adj def: leading up to the main point.
   synonyms: basic, elementary, fundamental, inductive
   antonyms: closing, final
   The *preliminary* medical examination showed that Paul needs regular exercise to lose weight.

9. Concur [kuhn-**kur**]
   verb def: to accord in opinion. (**)
   synonyms: agree, approve, acquiesce, assent
   antonyms: argue, disapprove, dispute, object
   Otis didn't seem to *concur* with the statement his opponent made the other day.

   In Washington, Robert B. Zoellick, president of the World Bank, *concurs* that only a multinational solution can really work.
   — Peter Gumbel, *Time*, 20 Oct. 2008

10. Aberrant [uh-**ber**-uhnt]
   adj def: departing from the right, normal, or usual. (***)
   synonyms: abnormal, atypical, bizarre, deviant, different
   antonyms: normal, same, true
   This winter, it hasn't snowed as much as it usually snows because of an *aberrant* weather pattern.

   The stones, silvered in the moon's *aberrant* light, shone like spectral tombs, and the figures, which Dalgliesh knew were Helena, Lettie and the Bostocks, became discarnate shapes disappearing into the darkness.
   — P.D. James, *The Private Patient*, 2008

11. Symptom [**simp**-tuhm]
   noun def: phenomenon; sign; indication.
   synonyms: evidence, expression, index, note
   The doctor discovered that Dubois has *symptoms* of an inner tumor.

TOEFL iBT/ TOEIC WORDS (Day 19)

12. Align [uh-**lahyn**]
   verb def: to arrange in a straight line.
        synonyms: adjust, coordinate, even, order
        antonyms: divide, mess up, separate
        He tried to *align* two holes to put a bolt through them.

13. Afflict [uh-**flikt**]
   verb def: to distress with mental or bodily pain. (**)
        synonyms: agonize, annoy, beset, bother, burden, distress
        antonyms: aid, comfort, help
        Susan has been *afflicted* with arthritis since the age of forty.

14. Decisive [dih-**sahy**-siv]
   adj def: having the power or quality of deciding.
        synonyms: definite, absolute, assured, certain
        antonyms: indecisive, indefinite, procrastinating
        General Anderson was known as *decisive* in manner.

15. Elastic [ih-**las**-tik]
   adj def: capable of returning to its original length.
        synonyms: pliant, flexible, adaptable
        antonyms: rigid, stiff, tense
        When on vacation, Phillip loved the *elastic* daily sightseeing plan offered by the travel agent.

16. Voluble [**vol**-yuh-buhl]
   adj def: characterized by a ready and continuous flow of words. (***)
        synonyms: fluent, glib, talkative, articulate, chatty
        Andy was so *voluble* that many people who knew him showed a lot of respect to him.

17. Insufficient [in-suh-**fish**-uhnt]
   adj def: lacking in what is necessary or required. (**)
        synonyms: bereft, defective, deficient, devoid, destitute
        antonyms: adequate, ample, enough, sufficient
        Peter thought that he generated enough money, but it turned out to be *insufficient*.

TOEFL iBT/ TOEIC WORDS (Day 19)

18. Crisp [krisp]
   adj def: hard but easily breakable.
       synonyms: brittle, crumbly, crusty, firm, fresh
       antonyms: flexible, limp, soft
   Brian put on the most *crisp* shirt and tie to impress an interviewer.

19. Quench [kwench]
   verb def: to slake; satisfy; allay (thirst, desires, passion, etc.) (**)
   Drinking a gallon of fountain water *quenched* June's thirst.

20. Manacle [**man**-uh-kuhl]
   verb def: shackle for the hand.
       synonyms: handcuff, fetter, bond, bracelet, chain
   Tim found himself *manacled* by his inhibitions.

21. Elate [ih-**leyt**]
   verb def: to make very happy or proud. (**)
       synonyms: cheer, exhilarate, encourage
   The winning of the national football championship *elated* the people living in the city.

22. Wane [weyn]
   verb def: to decrease in strength; intensity. (***)
       synonyms: diminish, abate, atrophy, decline, ebb
       antonyms: grow, increase, raise
   Her enthusiasm to pursue higher education in the US is slowly *waning* because of financial difficulties.

23. Celestial [suh-**les**-chuhl]
   adj def: pertaining to the sky or visible heaven. (**)
       synonyms: heavenly, divine, eternal, angelic
       antonyms: earthy, hellish, infernal, mortal
   Sun, moon, and stars are *celestial* bodies.

24. Proximity [prok-**sim**-i-tee]
   noun def: nearness in place, order, occurrence or relation.
       synonyms: adjacency, closeness, concurrence, contiguity
       antonyms: distance, remoteness
   The *proximity* of the curtains to the fireplace was a cause of concern for the fire department inspector.

TOEFL iBT/ TOEIC WORDS (Day 19)

25. Prominent [prom-uh-nuhnt]
  adj def: standing out so as to be seen easily.
    synonyms: important, conspicuous, standing out, embossed
    antonyms: depressed, invisible, obscured
    When she was five years old, Lynn became *prominent* in the music industry.

26. Spate [speyt]
  noun def: sudden; almost overwhelming, outpouring. (**)
    synonyms: deluge, flood, foment, flurry
    There was a *spate* of articles on the Theory of Relativity in the 1980s.

27. Conducive [kuhn-doo-siv]
  adj def: tending to produce, contributive.
    synonyms: helpful, leading, promotive
    antonyms: adverse, discouraging, hindering, unfavorable
    Eating good food must be *conducive* to maintaining good health.

28. Prerequisite [pri-rek-wuh-zit]
  noun def: something required beforehand. (****)
    synonyms: necessary, essential, expedient, imperative, mandatory
    antonyms: optional, unnecessary, voluntary
    A visa is still a *prerequisite* for traveling in many countries.

  Future greatness does not always inspire popularity. Coolness, in the high-school or hip sense of the word, is not a *prerequisite* for leadership.
  — Evan Thomas, *Newsweek*, 2 Aug. 2004

29. Optical [op-ti-kuhl]
  adj def: pertaining to the sense of sight.
    In the desert, many people usually suffer from an *optical* illusion that fools them.

30. Stalk [stawk]
  verb def: to pursue or approach prey, quarry.
    Timothy was very angry about the fact that Tina had been *stalking* him for a week.

TOEFL iBT/ TOEIC WORDS (Day 19)

31. Allude [uh-**lood**]
verb def: to refer to casually or indirectly. (***)
The doctor *alluded* to some health problems without showing any concrete evidence to his patient.

As *alluded* to previously, the entire universe may actually exist in a higher-dimensional space.
— Clifford A. Pickover, *Surfing Through Hyperspace*, 1999

32. Parch [pahrch]
verb def: to make extremely, excessively dry. (*)
synonyms: blister, brown, dehydrate, desiccate
antonyms: dampen, moisten, wet
Exercising without stopping for three hours had *parched* his throat.

33. Premature [pree-muh-**choor**]
noun def: occurring, coming or done too soon.
synonyms: unfledged; unripe; inopportune, unripe
antonyms: backward, delayed, mature, overdue
Medical studies show that too much exposure to the sun might cause *premature* aging of the skin.

34. Recurrent [ri-**kur**-uhnt]
adj def: occurring repeatedly.
synonyms: continued, cyclical, frequent, chain
antonyms: halted, infrequent, permanent
Thomas seemed to have *recurrent* problems with the brand-new car he purchased two weeks ago.

35. Amplify [**am**-pluh-fahy]
verb def: to make larger; stronger; extend.
synonyms: add, augment, boost, deepen, develop
antonyms: abridge, compress, condense, contact
The preacher focused on *amplifying* the importance of brotherly love.

36. Detonate [**det**-n-yet]
verb def: to explode with suddenness and violence.
synonyms: blast, fulminate, burst, discharge
The soldier *detonated* the bomb that could be heard from all directions.

TOEFL iBT/ TOEIC WORDS (Day 19)

37. Obtuse [uhb-**toos**]
   adj def: not quick or alert in perception. (**)

   synonyms: dull, insensitive, opaque, insensitive
   antonyms: bright, intelligent, smart
   Brad was so *obtuse* that he didn't understand what Kelly told him.

   Murdoch's art, like all good art, is highly structured and controlled—a house neat and clean enough to satisfy the most morally *obtuse* of her upper-class British characters.
   — Martha C. Nussbaum, *New Republic*, 31 Dec. 2001 & 7 Jan. 2002

38. Conviction [kuhn-**vik**-shuhn]
   noun def: a fixed or firm belief.

   synonyms: confidence, creed, doctrine, dogma, faith
   John held deep *convictions* about his religious beliefs.

39. Piquant [**pee**-kuhnt]
   adj def: sharp in taste or flavor. (***)

   synonyms: poignant, provocative, pungent, provocative
   antonyms: bland, dull
   The fried fish was heavily seasoned with a *piquant* sauce.

40. Contradict [kon-truh-**dikt**]
   verb def: to oppose; to speak against.

   synonyms: belie, confront, contravene, controvert
   antonyms: accept, agree, approve, concede
   It is obvious that many politicians *contradict* the promises they make during election campaign.

41. Doom [doom]
   noun def: fate or destiny, especially adverse fate.

   synonyms: annihilation, calamity, cataclysm, catastrophe, conclusion
   The author decided to fill his book with a series of gloom and *doom*.

42. Barren [**bar**-uhn]
   adj def: incapable of producing offspring.

   synonyms: unfruitful, unproductive, empty, fallow, fruitless
   antonyms: developing, fecund, fertile
   Not many wild animals might be able to survive in this *barren* area.

TOEFL iBT/ TOEIC WORDS (Day 19)

43. Probe [prohb]
   noun def: to search into or examine thoroughly.
   synonyms: delving, decision, inquest, inquiry, exploration
   The *probe* recently conducted by the CIA has provided much of substantial evidence.

44. Lubricate [**loo**-bri-keyt]
   verb def: to make slippery; smooth.
   synonyms: anoint, cream, grease, lube
   antonyms: dry
   Engine oil was invented to be used to *lubricate* the engine of any type of vehicle.

45. Pristine [**pris**-teen]
   adj def: having its original purity; uncorrupted or unsullied.
   synonyms: clean, primeval, early, first, immaculate, intact
   A *pristine* white shirt worn by Sheldon in the morning surprised everyone in the office.

46. Discard [dih-**skahrd**]
   verb def: to cast aside or dispose; to get rid of. (**)
   synonyms: abandon, abdicate, abjure, banish, cancel
   antonyms: embrace, keep, retain
   They *discarded* a pile of tires in the junkyard.

47. Content [kon-**tent**]
   adj def: satisfied with what one is or has.
   synonyms: appease, complacent, contented, gratified
   antonyms: discontent, upset, needy
   Completing her education at NYU made Michelle feel *content* in many different ways.

48. Fallacy [**fal**-uh-see]
   noun def: a deceptive, misleading, or false notion. (***)
   synonyms: aberration, ambiguity, artifice, bias
   antonyms: certainty, evidence, honesty
   It is a common *fallacy* that girls are good at learning foreign languages.

TOEFL iBT/ TOEIC WORDS (Day 19)

49. Fade [feyd]
    verb def: to lose brightness or vividness of color.
        synonyms: blanch, bleach, discolor, dull
        antonyms: sharpen, strengthen
    His shirt *faded* in color after repeated washings.

50. Disprove [dis-**proov**]
    verb def: to prove to be false or wrong. (**)
        synonyms: belie, confound, confute, contradict, controvert
        antonyms: credit, prove, validate
    Magellan's circumnavigation of the world *disproved* any related notions that the earth is flat.

> ❝ I love the fact that the words in the book are simply defined, without the fancy embellishments of explaining the root of the word and elaborate sentences. It reads easier than a dictionary and the drills are concise — although I think it'd be a good idea to group similar words together to make it easier to remember and distinguish the small differences between meanings. ❞

Michelle Shin
Psychology and English double major,
Boston University, MA, USA

TOEFL iBT/ TOEIC WORDS (Day 19)

❝*This book,* Mastering Core TOEFL iBT/ TOEIC Words with William H. Shin, *is impressive. It has some sophisticated information about the words that makes them easier to remember. For example, synonyms and antonyms are included for each word, and I can associate the new word with words that I already know. Moreover, one point that differentiates this vocab book from others is the author's delicacy. He makes it easier for the students to pronounce the word by highlighting the major accent, using the phonetic alphabet, and using asterisks to draw attention to the words frequently appearing on the tests so that students can pay careful attention to those particular words. Overall, the book is easier to read too; you can see all about the word in a compact space. I hope you buy this book and step into the world of TOEFL iBT/ TOEIC.*❞

Jungwook Kang
Korea International School, Pangyo Campus, Korea

Drill 19

1. The word **erratic** is closest in meaning to

    A) sweeping
    B) insufficient
    C) crisp
    D) inconsistent

2. The **exacerbate** is closest in meaning to

    A) worsen
    B) quench
    C) manacle
    D) elate

3. The word **virtually** is closest in meaning to

    A) objectively
    B) nearly
    C) equitably
    D) recurrently

4. The word **glare** is closest in meaning to

    A) flame
    B) amplification
    C) elucidation
    D) detonation

5. The word **fancy** is closest in meaning to

    A) conviction
    B) imagination
    C) piquancy
    D) distrust

Drill 19

6. The word **hazardous** is closest in meaning to

    A) doomful
    B) weak
    C) dangerous
    D) mysterious

7. The word **obscure** is closest in meaning to

    A) detective
    B) kaput
    C) dissect
    D) unclear

8. The word **repercussion** is closest in meaning to

    A) echo
    B) substantial
    C) indicate
    D) reveal

9. The word **regulate** is closest in meaning to

    A) adjust
    B) control
    C) detect
    D) discard

10. The word **disprove** is closest in meaning to?

    A) deviate
    B) nausea
    C) refute
    D) magnify

Drill 19

11. The word **wane** is closest in meaning to

    A) increase
    B) harbor
    C) allude
    D) decrease

12. The word **prerequisite** is closest in meaning to

    A) conducive
    B) necessary
    C) dormant
    D) inspiration

13. The word **fertile** is closest in meaning to

    A) parch
    B) plethora
    C) productive
    D) hostile

14. The word **inspect** is closest in meaning to

    A) wax
    B) proximity
    C) spate
    D) exam

15. The word **allude** is closest in meaning to

    A) imply
    B) stalk
    C) spur
    D) prominent

Drill 19

16. The word **fallacy** is closest in meaning to

    A) ample
    B) deception
    C) hew
    D) unleash

17. The word **discard** is closest in meaning to

    A) arid
    B) condense
    C) vivid
    D) desert

18. The word **pristine** is closest in meaning to

    A) purity
    B) efficient
    C) scatter
    D) compliment

19. The word **barren** is closest in meaning to

    A) prominent
    B) unproductive
    C) outset
    D) adept

20. The word **piquant** is closest in meaning to

    A) flourish
    B) destitute
    C) stimulating
    D) agitate

1. D 2. A 3. B 4. A 5. B 6. C 7. D 8. A 9. B 10. C
11. D 12. B 13. C 14. D 15. A 16. B 17. D 18. A 19. B 20. C

TOEFL iBT/ TOEIC WORDS (Day 20)

1. Manifest [**man**-uh-fest]
 adj def: readily perceived by the eye or the intellect. (****)
   synonyms: apparent, obvious, bold, conspicuous
   antonyms: ambiguous, concealed, obscure
   The evidence the police provided to the court *manifested* the guilt of the defendant.

   The argument, for all of its *manifest* inadequacies ... captured the national imagination and shaped subsequent religious discourse. It provided avocabulary, an explanation, and a new set of boundaries for the restructured American religion that had by then been developing for half a century.
   — Jonathan D. Sarna, *American Judaism*, 2004

2. Immaculate [ih-**mak**-yuh-lit]
 adj def: free from spot or stain. (**)
   synonyms: unspoiled, errorless, exquisite, bright
   antonyms: dirty, filthy, foul, unclean
   The superintendent put a lot of effort into keeping the white carpet on the floor *immaculate*.

   After I cleaned my apartment for hours, it was finally *immaculate*.

3. Mellow [**mel**-oh]
 adj def: full-flavored from ripeness. (***)
   synonyms: aged, cultured, developed
   antonyms: hard, immature, sour, tart
   Mr. Anderson was an extremely strict and demanding instructor, but, ironically, he *mellowed* toward the end of his teaching career.

4. Tinge [tinj]
 noun def: to impart a trace or sight degree of some color to.
   synonyms: cast, colorant, dye, hue, pigment
   antonyms: white
   Jennifer wore a light-blue dress *tinged* with gray.

5. Diffract [dih-**frakt**]
 verb def: to break up or bend by fraction.
   Light is *diffracted* when it passes through a prism.

TOEFL iBT/ TOEIC WORDS (Day 20)

6. Complimentary [kom-pluh-**men**-tuh-ree]
   adj def: given free as a gift of courtesy.
        synonyms: adulatory, flattering, appreciative, eulogistic
        antonyms: blaming, censuring, insulting, disparaging
        The hotel Nicole stayed at for a couple of days offered her two *complimentary* movie tickets.

7. Murky [**mur**-kee]
   adj def: obscure or thick with mist. (**)
        synonyms: dark, gloomy, cheerless, dingy
        antonyms: bright, clear, light, luminous
        It should be no surprise that there are a number of politicians with *murky* pasts.

8. Inhospitable [in-**hos**-pi-tuh-buhl]
   adj def: not inclined to, or characterized by, hospitality.
        synonyms: brusque, rude, ungenerous
        antonyms: friendly, kind
        The business proposal he submitted to his boss received some *inhospitable* feedback.

9. Unerring [uhn-**ur**-ing]
   adj def: not missing the mark. (*)
        synonyms: accurate, certain, faultless, certain
        antonyms: erring, imperfect, inaccurate
        Brandon appears to have an *unerring* instinct for learning foreign languages.

10. Parameter [puh-**ram**-i-ter]
   noun def: characteristic or factor; aspect.
        synonyms: limit, boundary, guidelines, constraint
        The equilateral diplomatic relationship between countries is based on the *parameters* of their foreign policy.

11. Cognizance [**kog**-nuh-zuhns]
   noun def: awareness; realization; knowledge; notice.
        The perfect understanding of the theory Dr. Phil introduced was beyond most of his colleagues' *cognizance*.

TOEFL iBT/ TOEIC WORDS (Day 20)

12. Grueling [groo-uh-ling]
   adj def: trying or exhausting. (***)
   synonyms: exhausting, tiresome, arduous, brutal
   antonyms: easy, facile
   It is hard to understand that quite a few self-trained runners participate in the *grueling* Boston Marathon in spite of the fact that they don't have serious intentions of winning it.

13. Compulsion [kuhm-puhl-shuhn]
   noun def: the act of compelling; constraint.
   synonyms: coercion, constraint, compelling, duress
   antonyms: freedom, free will, independence
   The police force might be able to stop some types of illegal transactions without using *compulsion*.

14. Inadequate [in-ad-i-kwit]
   adj def: not enough; inept; unsuitable. (**)
   The supplies turned out to be *inadequate* to meet our needs.

   It was a case of weak science reaching for a premature conclusion from insufficient data and an *inadequate* experiment.

15. Preponderance [pri-pon-der-uhns]
   noun def: the fact or quality of being preponderant. (***)
   synonyms: supremacy, ascendancy, bulk, command
   antonyms: inferiority
   Throughout world history, no nation except Rome enjoyed overwhelming military *preponderance*.

16. Arduous [ahr-joo-uhs]
   adj def: requiring great exertion; laborious. (****)
   synonyms: burdensome, formidable, grueling, harsh
   antonyms: easy, facile, motivating
   Since he came to the U.S to study, Tino has gone through a long and *arduous* college life.

TOEFL iBT/ TOEIC WORDS (Day 20)

Traveling for several days by train, stagecoach and horseback, they would reach Mariposa Grove, a stand of some 200 ancient giant sequoias, where they would rest before embarking on an *arduous* descent via 26 switchbacks into the valley.

— Tony Perrottet, *Smithsonian*, July 2008

17. Susceptible [suh-**sep**-tuh-buhl]
adj def: capable of being affected emotionally. (***)
  synonyms: naïve, vulnerable, affected, gullible
  antonyms: resistant, resisting, unsusceptible
Natalie is enormously *susceptible* to cold weather because of her chronic rheumatism.

Researchers at the University of South Carolina say that a chemical found abundantly in red wine, apples and onions helps protect against influenza, especially after a rigorous respiratory workout, when the body is more *susceptible* to infection.

— Kim Marcus *et al.*, *Wine Spectator*, 31 May 2009

18. Rampant [**ram**-puhnt]
adj def: violent in action or spirit; raging. (**)
  synonyms: aggressive, boisterous, blustering
The chief of police promised to make a serious effort to stop to the *rampant* crime that was destroying the city.

19. Threshold [**thresh**-ohld]
noun def: opening; beginning; entrance.
Working at Morgan Stanley once he had graduated from Wharton Business School at University of Pennsylvania was the *threshold* of his new career.

20. Taxing [**tak**-sing]
adj def: wearingly burdensome.
  synonyms: burdensome, demanding, enervating, exacting
  antonyms: easy, untroubling
It took Jason numerous hours to complete a very *taxing* workload.

21. Solstice [**sol**-stis]
noun def: a furthest or culminating point; a turning point. (**)
Many people do not recognize the winter *solstice* time.

TOEFL iBT/ TOEIC WORDS (Day 20)

The winter *solstice*, by contrast, is the first day of winter and the shortest day of the year.

22. Benighted [bih-**nahy**-tid]
adj def: intellectually or morally ignorant.
Ben scoffed at the crowd, as he believed it consisted entirely of *benighted* individuals.

23. Fickle [**fik**-uhl]
adj def: likely to change due to caprice.
  synonyms: capricious, coquettish, faithless, frivolous
  antonyms: aware, cognizant, consistent, reliable
Mike got tired of the *fickle* weather in NYC.

24. Brunt [bruhnt]
adj def: the main force or impact, as of an attack.
  synonyms: burden, force, impact, pressure
The *brunt* of responsibility for the project had fallen on Tom's shoulders.

25. Jaunt [jawnt]
noun def: a short journey. (*)
  synonyms: expedition, adventure, amble
While waiting for my car to be fixed, I took a photo *jaunt* around the city.

26. Latent [**leyt**-nt]
adj def: present but not visible.
  synonyms: abeyant, covert, contained, concealed, inactive
  antonyms: active, apparent, clear, live
Tom seems to have a *latent* ability to learn foreign languages.

27. Toilsome [**toil**-suhm]
adj def: characterized by or involving toil. (***)
  synonyms: arduous, laborious, onerous, strenuous
David was faced with the *toilsome* task of repairing the broken windows.

The model of a disciplined artist dedicated to a *toilsome* art practice, she has ardent followers.

TOEFL iBT/ TOEIC WORDS (Day 20)

28. Commodious [kuh-**moh**-dee-uhs]
    adj def: spacious; convenient; roomy.
        The couple finally found a house that provided several *commodious* closets they desperately needed.

29. Receding [ri-**seed**-ing]
    adj def: drawing back; retreating; withdrawing.
        Dr. Smith was really getting concerned about his *receding* hairline.

30. Abrasion [uh-**brey**-zhuhn]
    noun def: a scraped spot or area.
        synonyms: chafe, injury, chafing, erosion
        Fortunately, Brian walked away from the plane crash with only minor *abrasions*.

31. Chaos [**key**-os]
    noun def: a state of utter confusion or disorder.
        synonyms: anarchy, clutter, disarray, discord
        antonyms: calm, harmony, normality, order
        The loss of electricity caused *chaos* throughout the city.

32. Stagnate [**stag**-neyt]
    verb def: to cease to run or flow. (***)
        synonyms: constipate, decay, decline, fester
        antonyms: grow, strengthen
        The show began to *stagnate* right after the leading lady left.

    Dead legs and non-recirculated plumbing lines that allow hot water to *stagnate* also provide areas for growth of the organism.

33. Fracture [**frak**-cher]
    noun def: the breaking of a bone, cartilage.
        synonyms: break, breach, split, rupture, disunity
        Jennifer suffered a wrist *fracture* when she fell on the ice.

34. Fissure [**fish**-er]
    noun def: narrow opening produced by cleavage or separation.
        synonyms: gap, cleavage, cleft
        Jeffrey accidentally fell into a deep *fissure* while trying to find artifacts in the desert.

TOEFL iBT/ TOEIC WORDS (Day 20)

35. Erode [ih-**rohd**]
    verb def: to eat into; destroy by slow consumption.
        synonyms: abrade, bite, consume, corrode, crumble
        It is commonly believed that battery acid *erodes* the engine.

36. Enhance [en-**hans**]
    verb def: to raise to a higher degree.
        synonyms: improve, raise, intensify
        antonyms: decrease, fix, lower
        Muhammad *enhanced* his spoken English proficiency by practicing communicating in English with his co-workers on a daily basis.

37. Sever [**sev**-er]
    verb def: to cut or separate from the whole. (**)
        synonyms: bisect, carve, cleave, detach, disconnect
        antonyms: combine, join, unite
        Her leg was *severed* in a car accident when she was a child.

38. Vestige [**ves**-tij]
    noun def: mark; trace; visible evidence of something that is no longer present.
        synonyms: glimmer, relic, remains, remnant
        These superstitions are *vestiges* of an ancient religion.

39. Implacable [im-**plak**-uh-buhl]
    adj def: not to be appeased; mollified, or pacified.
        synonyms: inexorable, not mollified, adamant, dogged.
        antonyms: merciless, cruel, grim, pitiless
        Jeff appeared to have an *implacable* competition with his academic rival, Joshua.

40. Infringe [in-**frinj**]
    verb def: to commit a breach or infraction. (***)
        synonyms: encroach, trespass, violate, breach
        antonyms: violate, borrow, break, impose
        Bartorli was required to appear in court because he *infringed* a traffic violation when he was on his way to Chicago.

TOEFL iBT/ TOEIC WORDS (Day 20)

41. Percolate [pur-kuh-leyt]
   verb def: to permeate; pass through; filter; penetrate
        When Jason turned on the switch, the coffee maker on the table immediately started to *percolate*.

42. Velocity [vuh-los-i-tee]
   noun def: rapidity of motion or operation.
        synonyms: acceleration, celerity, dispatch
        It is extremely difficult to measure the *velocity* of sound without using special equipment.

43. Veneer [vuh-neer]
   noun def: a thin layer of wood or other material.
        synonyms: pretense, front, appearance, coating
        antonyms: reality
        Joe walked into the house, where he found a wall with a stone *veneer*.

44. Infinitesimal [in-fin-i-tes-uh-muhl]
   adj def: extremely small. (**)
        synonyms: atomic, inconsiderable, little
        antonyms: big, huge, large
        Alex thinks he looks like Jean Simmons, but I can find only *infinitesimal* similarities.

45. Entitle [en-tahyt-l]
   verb def: to give a title or right.
        synonyms: denominate, designate, dub, style
        The student ID card *entitled* Claudia to a discount for purchasing any books in the university bookstore.

46. Qualm [kwahm]
   noun def: an uneasy feeling; misgiving. (****)
        synonyms: agitation, anxiety, apprehension, compunction, conscience
        antonyms: approval, comfort, contentedness
        Longoria has been experiencing *qualms* about the success of the venture.

        They accept the market's complexity without *qualms*, yet insist the complexity of biological phenomena requires a designer.

TOEFL iBT/ TOEIC WORDS (Day 20)

47. Desolate [des-uh-lit]
  adj def: barren; treeless; gloomy.
    There were many unknown, *desolate* islands many years ago.

48. Irrigate [ir-i-geyt]
  verb def: to supply water by artificial means.
    synonyms: spray, soak, flood
    When Tina's face came into contact with the harmful chemical substance, she immediately *irrigated* her eyes with fresh water.

49. Contour [kon-toor]
  verb def: the outline of a figure or body.
    synonyms: mold, shape, build
    A number of cars provide seats that are *contoured* to comfort.

50. Tandem [tan-duhm]
  noun def: a group of two or more arranged one behind the other or used or acting in conjunction.
    The team has a *tandem* of talented guards.

    Some things may have simply evolved in *tandem* with other more beneficial traits.

❝ Mr. Shin has successfully published an TOEFL iBT/ TOEIC vocabulary book that will truly have students "master core words." This concise, yet elucidative book has nearly every TOEFL iBT/ TOEIC vocab word a student would encounter on the test, as well as synonyms, antonyms, example sentences, and constructive drills. By dissecting this comprehensive book from beginning to end, it is guaranteed that students will be able to utilize their enriched vocabulary knowledge on the TOEFL iBT/ TOEIC and build an educated vocabulary. ❞

Suny Kim
Cresskill High School, NJ, USA

TOEFL iBT/ TOEIC WORDS (Day 20)

"*I strongly encourage that every TOEFL iBT/ TOEIC student give this book a thorough study. The words listed in the study guide are all words that are prevalent on the real test. Clear and concise, it will be especially useful for international students who are having trouble memorizing vocabulary in a language that is foreign to them. Each word isnot only accompanied by synonyms and antonyms, they also come equipped with pronunciations and example sentences, allowing the student to easily dissect and learn each word from every perspective possible. Additionally, there are practice questions at the end of each section, which makes it not another mundane list of words but rather an interactive implement. Make sure to pick up this book and give it a try!*"

Hyunah Yong
Textiles, RISD (Rhode Island School of Design), RI, USA

Drill 20

1. The word **rite** is closest in meaning to

    A) fad
    B) ovation
    C) flake
    D) ceremony

2. The word **exacting** is closest in meaning to

    A) talent
    B) toilsome
    C) level
    D) commodious

3. The word **emulate** is closest in meaning to

    A) copy
    B) brunt
    C) rampant
    D) converse

4. The word **entrench** is closest in meaning to

    A) congregate
    B) fracture
    C) place
    D) collapse

5. The word **itinerant** is closest in meaning to

    A) abrasion
    B) travel schedule
    C) conduit
    D) stagnate

Drill 20

6. The word **impede** is closest in meaning to

    A) ascend
    B) compels
    C) genetic
    D) barrier

7. The word **deterioration** is closest in meaning to

    A) implacability
    B) infringement
    C) degeneration
    D) chaos

8. The word **vestige** is closest in meaning to

    A) entitle
    B) trace
    C) fault
    D) qualm

9. The word **impermeable** is closest in meaning to

    A) unable to penetrate
    B) drain
    C) conduit
    D) abrasion

10. The word **fissure** is closest in meaning to

    A) cavity
    B) karat
    C) spelunk
    D) gap

Drill 20

11. The word **enhance** is closest in meaning to

    A) collapse
    B) improve
    C) worsen
    D) shorten

12. The word **sever** is closest in meaning to

    A) halt
    B) leech
    C) cut
    D) access

13. The word **desolate** is closest in meaning to

    A) bleak
    B) flat
    C) narrow
    D) exuberant

14. The word **strain** is closest in meaning to

    A) animation
    B) account
    C) repentance
    D) burden

15. The word **detrimental** is closest in meaning to

    A) harmful
    B) pointed
    C) incremental
    D) flatter

Drill 20

16. The word **desolate** is closest in meaning to

    A) linger
    B) devastated
    C) avid
    D) indignant

17. The word **qualm** is closest in meaning to

    A) doubt
    B) secular
    C) aggregate
    D) compunction

18. The word **veneer** is closest in meaning to

    A) scatter
    B) abut
    C) pretense
    D) protract

19. The word **infringe** is closest in meaning to

    A) align
    B) violate
    C) speculate
    D) congest

20. The word **stagnant** is closest in meaning to

    A) motionless
    B) articulate
    C) irreparable
    D) renounce

1. D 2. B 3. A 4. C 5. B 6. D 7. C 8. B 9. A 10. D
11. B 12. C 13. A 14. D 15. A 16. B 17. D 18. C 19. B 20. A

TOEFL iBT/ TOEIC WORDS (Day 21)

1. Delve [delv]
   verb def: to carry on intensive and thorough research.
   synonyms: burrow, examine, excavate, explore
   He has spent many hours *delving* into the issues of tax reform.

2. Hilarious [hi-**lair**-ee-uh s]
   adj def: arousing great merriment; extremely funny
   synonyms: amusing, comical, convivial, exhilarated, frolicsome, gay
   antonyms: grave, serious, somber
   She gave us a *hilarious* account of her first days as a teacher.

   Raymond is different, so well written and acted, so perfectly pitched, that even the silences, especially the silences, are *hilarious*. It makes comedy look easy.
   — James Morris, *Wilson Quarterly*, Autumn 2005

3. Intercept [in-ter-**sept**]
   verb def: to cut off; take; seize; halt.
   The enemy *intercepted* a messenger whose task was to deliver important information to headquarters.

4. Deciduous [dih-**sij**-oo-uhs]
   adj def: shedding leaves annually. (**)
   Jim was looking at the bare branches of a *deciduous* tree in front of his apartment.

5. Evaporate [ih-**vap**-uh-reyt]
   verb def: to convert into a gaseous state or vapor; to drive off.
   synonyms: concentrate, dehydrate, desiccate, disappear
   antonyms: dampen, wet
   The morning sunshine *evaporated* the dew on the grass.

6. Pore [pawr]
   verb def: to read or study with steady attention or application. (*)
   synonyms: brood, contemplate, dwell on, examine, look over
   antonyms: flip through, scan
   Stephen *pored* over the strange events of the preceding evening.

   They are not so good for devoted fans who want to *pore* over everything a group puts out.

TOEFL iBT/ TOEIC WORDS (Day 21)

7. Neutralize [noo-truh-lahyz]
   verb def: to make neutral; to make ineffective.
       The soldiers *neutralized* the attack by dividing the enemy forces.

8. Secrete [si-kreet]
   verb def: to discharge or release by the process of secretion. (***)
       synonyms: discharge, emanate, excrete, extrude
       antonyms: pour in
       Insulin is *secreted* in response to rising levels of glucose in the blood.

9. Temper [tem-per]
   verb def: to be or become tempered.
       It is common sense that troops were *tempered* in battle.

10. Bleak [bleek]
   adj def: barren, desolate, and often windswept.
       synonyms: austere, bare, blighted, bombed
       antonyms: appealing, bright, nice
       A dark and *bleak* wintry day has caused Jenny to feel gloomy.

11. Exuberant [ig-zoo-ber-uhnt]
   adj def: effusively and almost uninhibitedly. (*****)
       synonyms: abound, profuse, energetic, animated
       antonyms: depressed, discouraged, lifeless
   Everyone likes to hang out with him because he has an *exuberant* personality.

   Steven Spielberg's career has been famously schizoid. On the one hand, he has made films borne aloft by *exuberant* juvenility (the *Indiana Jones* pictures, *Jurassic Park*, and so forth); on the other hand, he has made mature films of serious intent (*The Color Purple, Schindler's List, Saving Private Ryan*). And ... there is also a third hand: he has combined those two types, most notably in *Close Encounters of the Third Kind*, in which he transmuted a fascinating science fiction film into near-theology.
                                 — Stanley Kauffmann, *New Republic*, 23 July 2001

12. Repentance [ri-pen-tns]
   noun def: deep sorrow; compunction or contrition for a past sin.
       synonyms: attrition, contriteness, grief
       antonyms: happiness

TOEFL iBT/ TOEIC WORDS (Day 21)

Many people are clearly aware that *repentance* is the very first step on the path to redemption.

13. Flatter [flat-er]
verb def: to try to please with compliments. (**)
    synonyms: adulate, blandish, cajole, charm
    antonyms: belittle, castigate, condemn
He *flattered* her by praising his academic achievement.

14. Emit [ih-mit]
verb def: to release; give forth; send out.
    synonyms: diffuse, discharge, afford, breathe
    antonyms: conceal, contain, refrain, suppress
Steve was surprised to watch black and dark smoke *emitting* from the building right across from the street.

Lasers work by trapping light in or near a material that can *emit* more photons with the same wavelength, or color.

15. Circumvent [sur-kuhm-vent]
verb def: to go around; bypass. (***)
    synonyms: fool, mislead, avoid, beguile, bilk
    antonyms: aid, allow, assist, help
Thomas always *circumvents* the real issues when confronting an unpleasant situation.

Los Angeles was the beachhead for the sushi invasion, attracting many Japanese chefs eager to make their fortunes and to *circumvent* the grueling 10-year apprenticeship required in their homeland.
    — Jay McInerney, *New York Times Book Review*, 10 June 2007

16. Deception [dih-sep-shuhn]
noun def: the state of being deceived. (**)
    synonyms: misleading, betrayal, cheat, betrayer, cheat
    antonyms: frankness, honesty, honor
After he died, his numerous *deceptions* became known.

The chronic underestimation of costs, verging on outright *deception*, has continued.

TOEFL iBT/ TOEIC WORDS (Day 21)

17. Grunt [gruhnt]
  verb def: to utter deep, guttural sounds.
    synonyms: snort, squeak, groan
    Several workers in my house were *grunting* with effort as they moved a grand piano to the living room.

18. Adjacent [uh-**jey**-suhnt]
  adj def: near; close; adjoin. (**)
    synonyms: adjoining, beside, close
    antonyms: apart, away, detached
    Harrison didn't have to work any more because he inherited two large *adjacent* buildings from his late father.

    The Harrimans owned two large *adjacent* houses on N Street, one for themselves and one for Averell Harriman's pictures.
        — Larry McMurtry, *New York Times Review of Books*, 23 Oct. 2003

19. Squirt [skwurt]
  verb def: to eject liquid; emit; flow. (***)
    Jefferson *squirted* oil on the kitchen floor while making French fries for his children.

20. Mimicry [**mim**-ik-ree]
  noun def: the act, practice, or art of mimicking.
    I suggested "*mimicry*" as a method for improving pronunciation for English as a Second Language students.

21. Trickery [**trik**-uh-ree]
  noun def: deception; joke; chicanery. (***)
    Tiffany always resorts to *trickery* when she needs something from her boyfriend.

    The ongoing collision of marketing and social networks doesn't necessarily have to involve *trickery* or deception.

TOEFL iBT/ TOEIC WORDS (Day 21)

22. Procure [proh-**kyoor**]
    verb def: to obtain or get by care; effort. (****)
        synonyms: acquire, obtain, annex, appropriate
        antonyms: give away, have, lose
        Jenny made an every effort to *procure* a ticket for a concert she had always wanted to attend.

        It was at that encounter in Pakistan that Faris was put in charge of *procuring* acetylene torches to slice suspension cables, as well as torque tools to bend portions of train track.
                — Daniel Eisenberg, *Time*, 30 June 2003

23. Manifold [**man**-uh-fohld]
    adj def: many kinds, numerous and varied.
        synonyms: abundant, copious, assorted
        antonyms: one, single, sole
        Tom found that there were *manifold* programs for social reform.

24. Nimble [**nim**-buhl]
    adj def: quick and light in movement. (**)
        synonyms: quick, dexterous, adept, agile
        antonyms: awkward, clumsy, slow, unhandy
        Brian appeared to have an innate *nimble* wit when he associated with people he didn't know.

25. Multiplicity [muhl-tuh-**plis**-tee]
    noun def: a large number; variety.
        Dr. Smith was extremely disappointed by the fact that the book he had written had a *multiplicity* of spelling errors and grammar mistakes.

26. Succumb [suh-**kuhm**]
    verb def: to give way to superior force. (***)
        synonyms: accede, bow, capitulate, cave, cease
        antonyms: conquer, create, overcome, win
        He finally *succumbed* and allowed his wife to get rid of his armchair that he had used since he was 25 years old.

TOEFL iBT/ TOEIC WORDS (Day 21)

27. Segment [seg-muhnt]
    noun def: one of the parts into which something naturally separates.
        synonyms: compartment, cut, division, portion
        One of the constituent parts into which a body, entity, or quantity is divided or marked off by is a *segment*.

28. Ample [am-puhl]
    adj def: adequate for the purpose of needs; plentiful.
        synonyms: adequate, sufficient, abundant
        antonyms: insufficient, meager, not enough
        Students have *ample* opportunities to enhance their standardized test scores.

29. Resurrect [rez-uh-rekt]
    verb def: to raise from the dead; bring back into use. (**)
        Jessica tried to *resurrect* her acting career by taking acting courses at a local university.

30. Decease [dih-sees]
    noun def: departure from life; death; to die.
        synonyms: dysfunction, demise, dissolution, reaper
        antonyms: birth
        He was really surprised that his father had many debts at the time of his *decease*.

31. Pragmatic [prag-mat-ik]
    adj def: pertaining to a practical point of view. (**)
        synonyms: sensible, efficient, logical
        antonyms: idealistic, unreasonable
        Most college students seem to have a strong tendency to take courses that provide *pragmatic* knowledge for them.

32. Niche [nich]
    noun def: an ornamental recess in a wall. (*****)
        synonyms: alcove, nook, hollow, recess
        Having spent many hours in his work, he finally found his *niche* in the business world.

TOEFL iBT/ TOEIC WORDS (Day 21)

To succeed in this new world, you have to sell yourself. You go to a brand-name college, not to imbibe the wisdom of its professors, but to make impressions and connections. You pick a *niche* that can bring attention to yourself and then develop your personal public relations efforts to let the world know who you are.
— Alan Wolfe, *New York Times Book Review*, 7 Jan. 2001

33. Bolster [bohl-ster]
verb def: to support with or as with a pillow or cushion.
  synonyms: aid, assist, help, boost, brace, buttress
  antonyms: hinder, obstruct
Microsoft clearly wants to *bolster* its Internet presence in the event that Google is correct.

34. Gnarl [nahrl]
verb def: to twist into a knotted or distorted form.
His fingers crimp and *gnarl*, turning the hand into a disfigured claw.

35. Embed [em-bed]
verb def: to fix into a surrounding mass.
  synonyms: sink, implant, bury, deposit, fasten
  antonyms: dig up
The "Excalibur" myth is about a sword *embedded* in a stone.

36. Glaze [gleyz]
verb def: to furnish or fill with glass.
  synonyms: varnish, burnish, cover
Their eyes *glazed* over as the lecture droned on.

37. Ornament [awr-nuh-muhnt]
noun def: accessory, article, or detail used to beautify the appearance.
  synonyms: accessory, adornment, art, array
Jenny put many different kinds of *ornaments* on her hair.

38. Sporadic [spuh-rad-ik]
adj def: appearing in scattered or isolated instances. (***)
  synonyms: fitful, infrequent, on-and-off
  antonyms: constant, continuous, dependable
Since he followed the diet *sporadically*, lapsing into his old bad eating habits, Mick did not lose weight.

TOEFL iBT/ TOEIC WORDS (Day 21)

The law was indeed tightened, prohibiting the employment of illegal aliens on the valid assumption that removing the magnet of jobs is necessary to stem illegal immigration. But enforcement was *sporadic* at best, and has now virtually ceased.
— Mark Krikorian, *National Review*, 26 Jan. 2004

39. Somber [som-ber]
 adj def: gloomily dark; shadowy; dimly lighted. (***)
  synonyms: bleak, cloudy, depressive, dim, dingy
  antonyms: cheerful, happy, joyful
  Everyone at the funeral was wearing dark, *somber* clothes except for the little girl in the flowered dress.

  Looking out at his audience, a *somber* mass of monks, Gregory gave Mary a new identity that would shape her image for fourteen hundred years.
— Jonathan Darman, *Newsweek*, 29 May 2006

40. Resilient [ri-zil-yuhnt]
 adj def: springing back; rebounding. (**)
  synonyms: return, rebound, recover, flexible, buoyant, elastic
  antonyms: hard, rigid, stiff
  Luckily, Roman was a *resilient* person, and was able to pick up the pieces and move on with his life after losing his business.

  The tallow tree, an ornamental species introduced by Benjamin Franklin in 1772, can quickly grow to 10 meters and is *resilient* to many pests.
— *New Scientist*, 19-25 Aug. 2006

41. Dissipate [dis-uh-peyt]
 verb def: to scatter in various directions; disperse. (****)
  synonyms: disperse, scatter, squander, spread
  antonyms: accumulate, collect, gather, hoard
  Once the sun had risen, the mist on the grass *dissipated.*

  The fog gradually *dissipated,* revealing all the ships docked in the harbor.

42. Intricate [in-tri-kit]
adj def: having many interrelated parts or facets.
    synonyms: entangle, involved, complicated
    antonyms: direct, methodical, simple, systematic
    Joseph spent all afternoon learning how to use an *intricate* machine.

43. Threaten [thret-n]
verb def: to utter a threat against; menace.
    synonyms: warn, pressure, abuse, admonish
    antonyms: alleviate, help, protect, relieve
    She *threatened* to quit if they didn't give her a raise, but no one believed her.

44. Plague [pleyg]
verb def: an epidemic disease that causes high mortality.
    synonyms: affliction, contagion, curse, epidemic, infection
    antonyms: advantage, good fortune
    The question of his academic future *plagued* him with doubt.

45. Predispose [pree-di-spohz]
verb def: to give an inclination or tendency to.
    synonyms: activate, affect, bend, bias
    antonyms: discourage, dissuade
    The evidence *predisposed* him to public censure.

46. Adverse [ad-vurs]
adj def: unfavorable or antagonistic in purpose or effect. (***)
    synonyms: opposite, confronting, unfavorable, detrimental
    antonyms: aiding, auspicious, favorable, helpful
    They cancelled the baseball game due to *adverse* weather conditions.

    The Bankruptcy Code requires that debtor's counsel be disinterested and not have an interest *adverse* to the estate.
    — *Lawyers Weekly USA*, 4 Oct. 1999

47. Misgiving [mis-giv-ing]
noun def: distrust; apprehension; a feeling a doubt. (*)
    I felt some *misgivings* about his ability to do the job.

TOEFL iBT/ TOEIC WORDS (Day 21)

48. Runoff [ruhn-awf]
   noun def: something that drains or flows off. (***)
   New and better practices can be put in place to reduce *runoff* effectively.

49. Contingent [kuhn-tin-juhnt]
   adj def: dependent for existence, occurrence.(**)
   synonyms: accidental, casual, chance, dependent, fortuitous
   antonyms: certain, definite, real, sure
   Unfortunately our plans are heavily *contingent* on the weather.

   The isolation of the capitalist classes in Germany meant that liberty as an ideal had no *contingent* link with capitalism, as had happened in Western Europe.
   — Orlando Patterson, *New Republic*, 8 Nov. 1999

50. Exterminate [ik-stur-muh-neyt]
   verb def: to destroy; get rid of; extirpate.
   synonyms: abolish, annihilate, destroy, decimate
   antonyms: bear, create
   Barbara hired people to *exterminate* insects and ants in her house.

Drill 21

1. The word **desolate** is closest in meaning to

    A) bleak
    B) flat
    C) narrow
    D) exuberant

2. The word **strain** is closest in meaning to

    A) animation
    B) account
    C) repentance
    D) burden

3. The word **detrimental** is closest in meaning to

    A) pointed
    B) harmful
    C) incremental
    D) flattering

4. The word **deception** is closest in meaning to

    A) jeopardy
    B) acquisition
    C) trickery
    D) velocity

5. The word **excavate** is closest in meaning to

    A) protect
    B) dig
    C) circle
    D) share

Drill 21

6. The word **agility** is closest in meaning to

    A) nimbleness
    B) carelessness
    C) maturity
    D) multiplicity

7. The word **segment** is closest in meaning to

    A) division
    B) notification
    C) adaptation
    D) reform

8. The word **fertilize** is closest in meaning to

    A) divert
    B) mimicry
    C) encounter
    D) produce

9. The word **distinguish** is closest in meaning to

    A) meek
    B) squirt
    C) differ
    D) halt

10. The word **profound** is closest in meaning to

    A) irrigation
    B) deep
    C) delve
    D) aesthetic

Drill 21

11. The word **exceed** is closest in meaning to

    A) surplus
    B) infrastructure
    C) intercept
    D) contour

12. The word **adjacent** is closest in meaning to

    A) grunt
    B) spawn
    C) next
    D) agile

13. The word **contingent** is closest in meaning to

    A) interrupt
    B) skeptic
    C) affect
    D) dependent

14. The word **justify** is closest in meaning to

    A) reliable
    B) appropriate
    C) confirmed
    D) revised

15. The word **secrete** is closest in meaning to

    A) emit
    B) temper
    C) pores
    D) neutralize

Drill 21

16. The word **misgiving** is close in meaning to

    A) animosity
    B) uncertainty
    C) tedium
    D) anonymity

17. The word **adverse** is closest in meaning to

    A) asymmetry
    B) discord
    C) sequence
    D) unfavorable

18. The word **plague** is closest in meaning to

    A) affix
    B) petrify
    C) disease
    D) extend

19. The word **resilient** is closest in meaning to

    A) lessen
    E) flexible
    F) depict
    G) vanquish

20. The word **sporadic** is closest in meaning to

    A) on and off
    B) abstruse
    C) elicit
    D) explicit

1. A 2. D 3. B 4. C 5. B 6. A 7. A 8. D 9. C 10. B
11. A 12. C 13. D 14. B 15. A 16. B 17. D 18. C 19. B 20. A

TOEFL iBT/ TOEIC WORDS (Day 22)

1. Sterile [ster-il]
   adj def: free from living germs or microorganisms. (**)
        synonyms: antiseptic, arid, aseptic, barren, bleak, dead
        antonyms: dirty, fruitful, productive
       My youth was getting gloomy, cold, and *sterile*.

2. Artificial [ahr-tuh-fish-uhl]
   adj def: made by human skill; produced by humans.
        synonyms: fake, imitation, bogus, counterfeit
        antonyms: genuine, natural, real
       The country's borders are *artificial* and were set with no consideration for the various ethnic groups in the region.

3. Erect [ih-rekt]
   verb def: upright in position or posture.
        synonyms: elevated, firm, perpendicular, raised
        antonyms: prone, prostrate
       It was surprising to find that a lone tree remained *erect* after the terrible tornado had passed.

4. Strive [strahyv]
   verb def: exert oneself vigorously. (*)
        synonyms: struggle, rival, conflict, aim, assay, attempt
        antonyms: forget, skip
       Anderson continued to *strive* toward his academic goals.

5. Hinge [hinj]
   verb def: to be dependent or contingent on.
        synonyms: axis, hook, juncture
       Everything *hinged* on his decision.

6. Confine [kuhn-fahyn]
   verb def: to enclose; restrict; shut; keep. (**)
        synonyms: bound, bar, constrain, detain
        antonyms: free, liberate, release
       Miranda *confined* her remarks to errors in the report.

       Most museum goers *confine* themselves to murmurs of appreciation or the occasional reverent flip of a program page.

TOEFL iBT/ TOEIC WORDS (Day 22)

7. Impend [im-pend]
  verb def: to be imminent; be about to happen.
   Jennifer felt that danger *impended*.

8. Herald [**her**-uhld]
  noun def: a person or thing that precedes or comes before.
   synonyms: frontier, pioneer, indication, signal, usher
   Mercury was the *herald* of the Roman gods.

9. Phenomenon [fi-**nom**-uh-non]
  noun def: something that is impressive or extraordinary.(***)
   synonyms: marvel, abnormality, exception
   antonyms: normality, regularity
   People have reported seeing ball lightning — a rare *phenomenon* that resembles a glowing sphere of electricity — for hundreds of years.

   For example, we talk more loudly in cars, because of a *phenomenon* known as the Lombard effect—the speaker involuntarily raises his voice to compensate for background noise.
   — John Seabrook, *New Yorker*, 23 June 2008

10. Interfere [in-ter-**feer**]
  verb def: to come into opposition.
   synonyms: meddle, intervene, baffle, balk
   antonyms: aid, assist, help
   The tribe had a strong resentment of outsiders who attempted to *interfere* with their traditional ways of doing things.

11. Monitor [**mon**-i-ter]
  noun def: a person appointed to supervise students.
   synonyms: advise, audit, check, oversee
   antonyms: forget, ignore, neglect
   John was appointed as *monitor* for the third-grade class.

12. Subtle [suht-l]
  adj def: thin; tenuous; rarified; delicate. (**)
   Their many *subtle* shades include greens, oranges, and violets blended from lots of different genetic proclivities.

TOEFL iBT/ TOEIC WORDS (Day 22)

Although artists and patrons in Venice still sought images of ideal figures, they insisted that this imagery be rooted in a more *subtle* and insightful interpretation of human life and character.
— Andrew Butterfield, *New York Review of Books*, 16 July 2009

13. Variation [var-ee-**ey**-shuhn]
noun def: the act, process, or accident of varying in condition.
synonyms: difference, alternative, displacement
antonyms: agreement, similarity
The movie begins with a somewhat irreverent *variation* on the Nativity story.

14. Provoke [pruh-**vohk**]
verb def: to anger; enrage; exasperate.
A mishap *provoked* a hearty laugh.

15. Subterranean [suhb-tuh-**rey**-nee-uhn]
noun def: hidden; underground.
The Soviet Union built many *subterranean* bunkers that supposedly could withstand even an atomic blast.

16. Void [void]
adj def: having no legal force.
synonyms: useless, ineffectual, vain
antonyms: full, occupied
An agreement is *void* if obtained by force.

17. Precursor [pri-**kur**-ser]
noun def: a person or thing that precedes. (**)
synonyms: forefather, frontier, harbinger
18th-century lyric poets like Robert Burns were *precursors* of the Romantics.

18. Proliferate [pruh-**lif**-uh-reyt]
verb def: to grow or produce by multiplication of parts. (***)
synonyms: burgeon, engender, expand, generate
antonyms: decline, decrease, fall off
Rumors about the car accident *proliferated* on the Internet.

He only had two guinea pigs initially, but they *proliferated* to such an extent that he soon had dozens.

19. Mutate [myoo-teyt]
verb def: to change; alter.
>Over time, her feelings *mutated* from hatred into love.

20. Distort [dih-stawrt]
verb def: to twist awry or out of shape.
>synonyms: deform, twist, alter, curve
>The loss of both her parents at an early age *distorted* her outlook on life.

21. Mock [mok]
verb def: to attack or treat with ridicule or contempt. (**)
>synonym: false, feigned, fraudulent, imitation, mimic, irritation
>antonyms: authentic, genuine, real
>His actions *mocked* people gathering in the convention.

22. Summit [suhm-it]
noun def: the highest point or part.
>synonyms: top, acme, apex, climax, crest
>antonyms: base, bottom, nadir
>John was determined to make it to the *summit* of Mount Everest.

23. Imminent [im-uh-nuhnt]
adj def: likely to occur at any moment; impending. (***)
>synonyms: close, coming, expectant, at hand
>antonyms: distant, doubtful, far, future
>We had to pump her up by promising her that ice cream would be her *imminent* reward for being brave and getting a shot.

>The FBI, the Department of Homeland Security, and the local authorities were momentarily stunned, and began frantically trying to prepare for what they feared were further *imminent* attacks.
>— Richard A. Clarke, *Atlantic*, January/February 2005

TOEFL iBT/ TOEIC WORDS (Day 22)

24. Precede [pri-**seed**]
  verb def: to go before.
  synonyms: antecede, antedate, anticipate
  antonyms: follow, go after
  Minutes before 10:30 p.m. in China, the stadium pulsed with the emotions that always *precede* a 100-meter final.
  — Tim Layden, *Sports Illustrated*, 25 Aug. 2008

25. Expulsion [ik-**spuhl**-shuhn]
  noun def: the act of driving out or expelling.
  synonyms: banishing, bounce, debarment, deportment
  antonyms: import, welcoming
  The prisoner's *expulsion* from society embittered him.

26. Foreshadow [fawr-**shad**-oh]
  verb def: to show or indicate beforehand. (*)
  synonyms: indicate, adumbrate, forebode, foretell
  Jennifer's early interest in airplanes *foreshadowed* her later career as a pilot.

27. Embitter [em-**bit**-er]
  verb def: to make bitter; cause to feel bitterness.
  synonyms: acerbate, aggravate, anger, annoy
  antonyms: calm, comfort, pacify
  The family refused to let their devastating collision with a drunk driver permanently *embitter* them.

28. Abnormal [ab-**nawr**-muhl]
  adj def: aberrant; atypical; deviate; bizarre; not normal.
  Kevin's *abnormal* behavior surprised all his classmates and teachers.

29. Emanate [**em**-uh-neyt]
  verb def: to flow out; issue; proceed. (**)
  synonyms: emit, arise, discharge, derive
  antonyms: take, withdraw
  While Brendan was preparing for dinner, good smells *emanated* from the kitchen.

TOEFL iBT/ TOEIC WORDS (Day 22)

30. Deform [dih-**fawrm**]
  verb def: to mar the natural form or shape.
    synonyms: mar, distort, disfigure, blemish
    antonyms: beautify, improve
    In cases where the drug was taken during pregnancy, its effects *deformed* the infants.

31. Deflate [dih-**fleyt**]
  verb def: to depress or reduce. (***)
    synonyms: collapse, decrease, depress
    antonyms: blow up, expand, inflate
    They decided to *deflate* the tires slightly to allow the truck to drive under the overpass.

32. Inflate [in-**fleyt**]
  verb def: to cause; to expand.
    synonyms: increase, aggrandize, amplify, augment
    antonyms: compress, contract, shrink
    Economists warn that rapid economic growth could *inflate* prices.

33. Tremor [**trem**-er]
  noun def: involuntary shaking of the body or limbs.
    synonyms: trembling, quivering, agitation
    antonyms: stillness
    Small *tremors* were still being felt several days after the earthquake.

34. Forecast [**fawr**-krast]
  verb def: to predict; conjecture; contrive.
    Although the economy was not getting better, many economists *forecast* lower interest rates.

35. Evacuate [ih-**vak**-yoo-yet]
  verb def: to leave empty; vacate.
    synonyms: vacate, remove, abandon, decamp
    antonyms: come in, enter, load
    The mayor decided to *evacuate* the people in the town in the path of the flood.

TOEFL iBT/ TOEIC WORDS (Day 22)

36. Pending [pen-ding]
   adj def: awaiting; forthcoming; imminent.
        She received a four-year sentence and is currently out on bail *pending* appeal.

37. Cataclysm [kat-uh-kliz-uhm]
   noun def: a sudden and violent physical action. (**)
        synonyms: calamity, cataract, catastrophe, collapse
        antonyms: happiness, miracle, wonder
        The revolution could result in a worldwide *cataclysm*.

38. Inconsistent [in-kuhn-sis-tuhnt]
   adj def: lacking in harmony between the different parts or elements.
        synonyms: odd, variance, capricious, discordant
        antonyms: consistent, consonant, regular, steady
        The summary seemed to be *inconsistent* with the previously stated facts.

39. Consecutive [kuhn-sek-yuh-tiv]
   adj def: following one another in uninterrupted succession.
        synonyms: successive, following, constant, ensuing
        antonyms: broken, discontinuous, infrequent
        The team's winning streak has lasted for seven *consecutive* games.

40. Inaccuracy [in-ak-yer-uh-see]
   noun def: something inaccurate; error.
        synonyms: error, blunder, deception, imprecision
        antonyms: accuracy, correctness, right
        Brian pointed out the *inaccuracy* of his professor's explanation about the theory.

41. Influential [in-floo-en-shuhl]
   adj def: effective; powerful; dominant.
        synonyms: affecting, controlling, dominant, affection, governing
        antonyms: unimportant, ineffective, weak
        Harrison is known as an *influential* teacher in his school.

42. Predetermine [pree-di-tur-min]
   verb def: to settle; decide in advance.
        Susan believed that God has *predetermined* her destiny.

TOEFL iBT/ TOEIC WORDS (Day 22)

43. Infiltrate [in-**fil**-treyt]
verb def: to cause to pass in.
> synonyms: enter, permeate, pass through, access
> The intelligence staff had been *infiltrated* by spies.

44. Saturate [**sach**-uh-reyt]
verb def: to imbue thoroughly or completely. (***)
> synonyms: drench, bathe, douche; imbue
> antonyms: dehydrate, dry
> Jeff *saturated* a sponge with soapy water and began to wash his car.

45. Encounter [en-**koun**-ter]
verb def: to come upon or meet with.
> synonyms: confrontation, rendezvous
> antonyms: avoidance, evasive, retreat
> Steve and John were very angry when they *encountered* each other, but they departed with big smiles.

46. Impede [im-**peed**]
verb def: to retard in movement or progress.
> synonyms: bar, block, brake, check, curb
> antonyms: advice, aid, assist, facilitate
> He claims that economic growth is being *impeded* by government regulations.

47. Stationary [**stey**-shuh-ner-ee]
adj def: standing; not moving. (****)
> synonyms: anchored, immobile, inert, motionless
> antonyms: mobile, moving, restless
> It is hard to believe that the market price has remained *stationary* for the past several weeks.

Einstein imagined a beam of light piercing the elevator. If the elevator were rising relative to the source of light, the beam would enter at a certain height on one side of the elevator and appear to curve on its way to a lower height on the opposite wall. Einstein then imagined that the elevator were *stationary* on the surface of the earth. Since he postulated that the two circumstances are the same, Einstein concluded that the same effect would have to hold true for both. In other words, gravity must bend light.

— *Smithsonian*, June 2005

TOEFL iBT/ TOEIC WORDS (Day 22)

48. Induce [in-doos]
  verb def: to lead or move by persuasion.
    synonyms: bring about, cause, produce, abet, actuate, breed
    antonyms: discourage, halt, hinder, prevent
    Tim tried to *induce* Kelly to buy a concert ticket because his girlfriend, Jennifer, was performing.

49. Discharge [dis-chahrj]
  verb def: to relieve of a charge or load.
    synonyms: setting free, acquittal, exoneration, liberation
    antonyms: hold, imprisonment, incarceration
    The doctor decided to *discharge* the patient who had been hospitalized for the last three months.

50. Ingrate [in-greyt]
  noun def: thankless person; self-seeker; bounder. (***)
    When none of the relatives thanked her for the fruitcakes she had sent them, Doris condemned them all as *ingrates*.

TOEFL iBT/ TOEIC WORDS (Day 22)

❝*As one of the former students of the author, I believe that this book is not your average TOEFL iBT/ TOEIC book. After studying the material in the book thoroughly, I felt that it was enough to prepare me for the actual test itself. Because he has a lot of experience as a teacher for the course itself, the author knows exactly what he is looking for and how to teach it to the readers. Every little detail that is in the book is there for only one reason: to teach the student better for a higher score on the exam. Overall, the book is clear, well edited, and perfect for students who are looking to learn more about the TOEFL iBT/ TOEIC test.*❞

Ye Seul Lee
Pharmacy, St. John's University, NY, USA

Drill 22

1. The word **strive** is closest in meaning to

    A) avid
    B) keen
    C) eager
    D) classify

2. The word **detect** is closest in meaning to

    A) cohesive
    B) find
    C) disparity
    D) jaunt

3. The word **debris** is closest in meaning to

    A) kinship
    B) monitor
    C) mythos
    D) remains

4. The word **hinge** is closest in meaning to

    A) joint
    B) meek
    C) nimble
    D) niche

5. The word **vast** is closest in meaning to

    A) oscillate
    B) onerous
    C) huge
    D) prevail

Drill 22

6. The word **dormant** is closest in meaning to

    A) ineffective
    B) unnoticed
    C) inactive
    D) unprovoked

7. The word **phenomenon** is closest in meaning to

    A) application
    B) emergence
    C) dissemination
    D) occurrence

8. The word **confined** is closest in meaning to

    A) prudent
    B) speculative
    C) tribute
    D) restricted

9. The word **subtle** is closest in meaning to

    A) complicated
    B) tantalize
    C) vex
    D) wane

10. The word **herald** is closest in meaning to

    A) withstand
    B) erupt
    C) initiate
    D) piety

Drill 22

11. The word **fluctuation** is closest meaning to

    A) mutation
    B) swing
    C) repetition
    D) difference

12. The word **precursor** is closest in meaning to

    A) prudent
    B) retain
    C) reliable
    D) forefather

13. The word **emanate** is closest in meaning to

    A) precede
    B) reverse
    C) emit
    D) imminent

14. The word **consecutive** is closest in meaning to

    A) renown
    B) successive
    C) abnormal
    D) tremor

15. The word **exhibit** is closest in meaning to

    A) display
    B) contain
    C) contradict
    D) absorb

Drill 22

16. The word **stationary** is closest in meaning to

    A) seethe
    B) myriad
    C) fixed
    D) portend

17. The word **saturate** is closest in meaning to

    A) halt
    B) soaked
    C) mitigate
    D) entail

18. The word **cataclysm** is closest in meaning to

    A) disaster
    B) apex
    C) internecine
    D) chaotic

19. The word **deform** is closest in meaning to

    A) august
    B) malady
    C) disfigure
    D) separate

20. The word **abnormal** is closest in meaning to?

    A) deface
    B) efficient
    C) align
    D) aberrant

1. C 2. B 3. D 4. A 5. C 6. C 7. B 8. D 9. A 10. C
11. B 12. D 13. C 14. B 15. A 16. C 17. B 18. A 19. C 20. D

TOEFL iBT/ TOEIC WORDS (Day 23)

1. Dilute [dih-**loot**]
　verb　def: to weaken; alter; diminish. (***)
　　　The power of the company's president seemed to be *diluted* by the hiring of the new CEO.

　　　Despite the prospect of *dilution*, shareholders reacted positively in after-hours trading.

2. Propulsion [pruh-**puhl**-shuhn]
　noun　def: the act or process of propelling.
　　　　synonyms: drive, force, impulse, momentum, effort
　　　Sailboats use wind as their source of *propulsion*.

3. Emission [ih-**mish**-uhn]
　noun　def: something that is emitted; discharge.
　　　　synonyms: diffusion, discharge, ejection, exhalation, issue
　　　　antonyms: concealment, containment, refrain
　　　John made a tremendous effort to reduce the *emission* of greenhouse gases.

4. Confine [kuhn-**fahyn**]
　verb　def: to enclose within bounds; limit.
　　　　synonyms: limit, restrict, enclose, enslave
　　　　antonyms: free, liberate, release
　　　She *confined* her remarks to errors in the report.

5. Impermeable [im-**pur**-mee-uh-buhl]
　adj　def: impassable; impervious. (***)
　　　　synonyms: airtight, dense, hermetic
　　　Several geologists found an *impermeable* layer of rock in the middle of the desert.

6. Delicate [**del**-i-kit]
　adj　def: fine in texture, quality.
　　　　synonyms: elegant, delightful, flimsy
　　　　antonyms: coarse, harsh, indelicate
　　　Scott showed me how to use a *delicate* instrument purchased the other day to repair my motorbike.

TOEFL iBT/ TOEIC WORDS (Day 23)

7. Intermittent [in-ter-**mit**-nt]
   adj def: stopping or ceasing for a time. (****)
   synonyms: irregular, sporadic, discontinuous
   antonyms: constant, continue
   The flow of traffic was *intermittent* on the highway, but the commuters were thankful that it hadn't stopped completely.

   Decades of *intermittent* but recurring controversies with imperial authorities, and the lodestar of the glorious Revolution, disposed Americans to continue to believe that representation existed, first and foremost, to protect the rights of their communities against the abuse of executive power.
   — Jack N. Rakove, *Original Meanings*, 1996

8. Brackish [**brak**-ish]
   adj def: salty; distasteful; unpleasant.
   The coffee in my office is often some *brackish* brew that's been sitting around for a couple of hours.

9. Extract [ik-**strakt**]
   verb def: to pull or draw out.
   synonyms: excerpt, citation, abstract
   antonyms: insertion
   Jason *extracted* a completely personal meaning from what was said.

10. Domestic [duh-**mes**-tik]
   adj def: devoted to home life.
   synonyms: household, calm, indoor
   antonyms: business, industrial, office
   In a successful marriage, *domestic* responsibilities will be shared equally.

11. Gush [guhsh]
   verb def: to flow out or issue suddenly.
   synonyms: outpour, burst, flood, cascade, flush
   Water *gushed* from the broken pipe.

12. Sustain [suh-**steyn**]
   verb def: to maintain; support; hold; bear up.
   It is obviously difficult for Paul to *sustain* a business conversation with both his customers.

TOEFL iBT/ TOEIC WORDS (Day 23)

13. Anomalous [uh-**nom**-uh-luhs]
    adj def: atypical; abnormal; bizarre. (**)
        Advanced forms of life may be *anomalous* in the universe.

14. Coincide [koh-in-**sahyd**]
    verb def: to occupy the same place in space or time.
        synonyms: accompany, accord, acquiesce
        antonyms: clash, deviate, differ, disagree
        The heaviest snowfall of the season *coincided* with the start of our weeklong ski vacation.

15. Consolidate [kuhn-**sol**-i-deyt]
    verb def: to bring together; strengthen; combine.
        synonyms: add to, amass, bind, band
        antonyms: disjoin, disperse, divide, part
        The administration hopes that such measures will *consolidate* its position.

16. Profile [**proh**-fahyl]
    noun def: the outside or contour of the human face.
        synonyms: delineation, figuration, line, portrait
        Linda did not like the way her *profile* looked, so she elected for cosmetic surgery to correct the problem.

17. Dictate [**dik**-teyt]
    verb def: to command; rule; decree; dictum.
        Dr. Smith, the president of the company, always *dictates* all business letters to his personal secretary.

18. Topography [tuh-**pog**-tuh-fee]
    noun def: the detailed mapping or charting of the features. (***)
        It is interesting that a map of the *topography* of the coastline shows a significant loss of wetlands.

19. Burrow [**bur**-oh]
    verb def: to make a hole or passage in
        synonyms: couch, den, hove, lair
        In order to move faster, we tried to *burrow* our way through the crowd.

TOEFL iBT/ TOEIC WORDS (Day 23)

20. Simultaneous [sahy-muhl-**tey**-nee-uhs]
   adj def: existing, occurring, or operating at the same time.
        synonyms: coinciding, concurrent, accompanying, synchronic
        antonyms: different, divided, preceding, separate
        Last night Lydia heard two *simultaneous* gunshots from the house where her aunt resides.

21. Segregate [**seg**-ri-geyt]
   verb def: to keep apart from another. (**)
        synonyms: separate, dissociate, disconnect
        The civil rights movement fought against practices that *segregated* blacks and whites.

22. Turbulence [**tur**-byuh-luhns]
   noun def: the quality or state of being turbulent.
        synonyms: violent disorder, commotion
        The plane Christine was on hit quite a bit of *turbulence* during her flight.

23. Impoverish [im-**pov**-er-ish]
   adj def: to reduce to poverty. (**)
        synonyms: make poor, bankrupt, deplete
        Bad farming practices *impoverished* the soil.

        Through he had more money than he could count, Bruce did nothing to help his *impoverished* relatives.

24. Nascent [**nas**-uhnt]
   adj def: beginning to exist or develop. (****)
        The advertising campaign was still in a *nascent* stage, and nothing had been finalized yet.

        In the mid-'60s, Toronto was home to Yorkville, a gathering spot for draft resisters, a petri dish for a *nascent* coffeehouse and rock scene similar to the one developing in New York's Greenwich Village.
                              — Mike Sager, *Rolling Stone*, 27 June 1996

TOEFL iBT/ TOEIC WORDS (Day 23)

25. Contend [kuhn-**tend**]
   verb def: to struggle in opposition. (**)
        synonyms: struggle, dispute, strive
        antonyms: abandon, desert, give up
        A great number of people in New York *contended* that taxes were getting too high.

26. Eminence [**em**-uh-nuhns]
   noun def: high station, rank.
        synonyms: repute, fame, celebrity
        antonyms: inferiority, unimportance
        The old citadel sits on an *eminence* with a commanding view of the city.

27. Extravagance [ik-**strav**-uh-guhns]
   noun def: unrestrained; excessive. (***)
        synonyms: indulgence, waste, absurdity, amenity
        antonyms: economy, providence, saving, thrift
        That sports car William purchased two weeks ago appeared to be an inexcusable *extravagance*.

28. Reflective [ri-**flek**-tiv]
   adj def: thoughtful; contemplative; pondering.
        Benjamin has been considered as a *reflective* person since he was in college.

29. Evolve [ih-**volv**]
   verb def: to come forth gradually.
        synonyms: develop, progress, advance
        antonyms: block, decrease, halt, stop
        Many people believed that the human species *evolved* from an ancestor that was probably arboreal.

30. Inevitable [in-**ev**-i-tuh-buhl]
   adj def: unable to be avoided; evaded. (**)
        synonyms: unalterable, certain, decreed
        antonyms: avoidable, doubtful, fortuitous, uncertain
        The *inevitable* end of human life is death.

TOEFL iBT/ TOEIC WORDS (Day 23)

31. Pathetic [puh-**thet**-ik]
adj def: causing or evoking pity, sympathetic.
    synonyms: sad, affecting, distressing, pitiful
    antonyms: cheerful, happy, useful
    In return for his investment, Greg received a *pathetic* 1% interest.

32. Extraordinary [ik-**strawr**-dn-er-ee]
adj def: beyond what is usual, ordinary, regular. (***)
    synonyms: amazing, bizarre, exceptional, incredible
    antonyms: common, customary, familiar
    No one seemed eager to replicate the last round, especially given the *extraordinary* length of time it took to complete.

A polymer based on the elastic protein that enables fleas to perform their *extraordinary* jumping feats has been synthesized. The material ... is, perhaps unsurprisingly, rubbery and highly resilient; indeed, some of its properties exceed those of a material used to make bouncy balls for the playground.
    — Rosamund Daw, *Nature*, 13 Oct. 2005

33. Affix [uh-**fiks**]
verb def: fasten; join; attach.
    He *affixed* his signature to the document in order to approve it.

34. Incentive [in-**sen**-tiv]
adj def: something that incites or tends.
    synonyms: stimulating, provocative, reward
    antonyms: block, hindrance, turn-off
    The company is offering a special low price as an added *incentive* for new customers.

35. Milieu [mil-**yoo**]
noun def: environment; atmosphere; background. (**)
    Theirs was a bohemian *milieu* in which people often played romantic musical chairs.
    — Edmund White, *New York Review of Books*, 12 Feb. 2009

TOEFL iBT/ TOEIC WORDS (Day 23)

36. Replace [ri-**pleys**]
    verb def: to assume the former role, position.
        synonyms: displace, alter, back up, change
        antonyms: leave, alone
    Electricity has *replaced* gas in lighting.

37. Adopt [uh-**dopt**]
    verb def: to choose; take; select one's own.
        synonyms: accept, affirm, approve, assent
        antonyms: disown, reject, repudiate, repulse
    Jeff was born in England, but he has *adopted* Canada as his home.

38. Geothermal [jee-oh-**thur**-muhl]
    adj def: pertaining to the internal heat of the earth.
    There are a lot of *geothermal* activities on earth.

39. Vent [vent]
    verb def: to relieve; discharge; release.
    Kenny *vented* his profound disappointment by criticizing his successor.

40. Extinct [ik-**stingkt**]
    adj def: no longer extant; desolate; extinguish.
        synonyms: abolished, asleep, bygone, deceased, defunct
        antonyms: alive, existing, extant
    A few overgrown ruins are all that remain of that once mighty but now *extinct* civilization.

41. Eddy [**ed**-ee]
    noun def: current; swirl; tide.
    The cruise Tim was on was unfortunately caught in a strong *eddy*.

42. Prospect [**pros**-pekt]
    noun def: lookout; anticipation; expectation; contemplation.
    There was no *prospect* that the two parties would reach an agreement anytime soon.

43. Lurk [lurk]
    verb def: to lie or wait in concealment. (**)
        synonyms: hide, slink, steal, creep
        antonyms: come out

TOEFL iBT/ TOEIC WORDS (Day 23)

Brian and Liana sensed that there must have been someone out there *lurking* in the shadows.

The burglar *lurked* in the bushes until Scott left the house; then he broke in.

44. Copious [koh-pee-uhs]
   adj def: large in quantity or number. (***)
         synonyms: abundant, plentiful, bountiful
         antonyms: lacking, meager, needing, poor
      She ordered a *copious* amount of food in order to feed more than one hundred guests attending the reception after the concert.

      It was no surprise that spin was more *copious* than ever during the election campaign.
                  — Michael Kinsley, *TIME*, 25 Dec. 2000–1 Jan. 2001

45. Attain [uh-teyn]
   verb def: to reach; achieve; accomplish; acquire; arrive.
         Jonathan strongly refused to let the injury keep him from *attaining* his ultimate goal of participating in the Olympics.

46. Collaborate [kuh-lab-uh-reyt]
   verb def: to work together; cooperate; collude.
         He *collaborated* with Nazis during the Second World War.

47. Comprise [kuhm-prahyz]
   verb def: to make up; consist of; add up; compass.
         Lectures *comprised* the day's activities.

48. Defiant [dih-fahy-uhnt]
   adj def: disobedient; disregardful; audacious. (**)
         Unlike his colleagues, James took a *defiant* stand on the issue introduced by the CEO of the company.

49. Radical [rad-i-kuhl]
   adj def: forming a basis or foundation.
         synonyms: fundamental, basic, cardinal, primal
         antonyms: extrinsic, nonessential, superficial
      There are some *radical* differences between the two business proposals.

50. Typify [**tip**-uh-fahy]
   verb def: to serve as a typical example of.
        synonyms: represent, characterize, embody, epitomize
        Gothic architecture is *typified* by soaring rooflines and stained glass.

Drill 23

1. The word **impermeable** is closest in meaning to

    A) avid
    B) dormant
    C) impassable
    D) adverse

2. The word **gush** is closest in meaning to

    A) ambiguous
    B) outpouring
    C) condense
    D) bevy

3. The word **anomalous** is closest in meaning to

    A) aberrant
    B) cease
    C) stable
    D) defer

4. The word **dictate** is closest in meaning to

    A) novel
    B) redundant
    C) emulate
    D) command

5. The word **simultaneous** is closest in meaning to

    A) foliage
    B) coincide
    C) constitute
    D) juvenile

Drill 23

6. The word **segregate** is closest in meaning to

    A) endow
    B) accumulate
    C) alienate
    D) fertile

7. The word **contend** is closest in meaning to

    A) ascertain
    B) plague
    C) encounter
    D) compete

8. The word **reflective** is closest in meaning to

    A) emission
    B) thoughtful
    C) acknowledge
    D) clarify

9. The word **pathetic** is closest in meaning to

    A) pitiful
    B) artifact
    C) clement
    D) caliber

10. The word **incentive** is closest in meaning to

    A) exceed
    B) allure
    C) hostile
    D) implicit

Drill 23

11. The word **replace** is closest in meaning to

    A) displace
    B) acclaim
    C) burgeon
    D) conspicuous

12. The word **lurk** is closest in meaning to

    A) precursor
    B) hide
    C) factious
    D) elaborate

13. The word **copious** is closest in meaning to

    A) brink
    B) abundant
    C) evoke
    D) intermittent

14. The word **collaborate** is closest in meaning to

    A) flatter
    B) abuse
    C) keen
    D) work together

15. The word **defiant** is closest in meaning to

    A) aloft
    B) bizarre
    C) coax
    D) disobedient

Drill 23

16. The word **prospect** is closest in meaning to

    A) profound
    B) aggregate
    C) anticipation
    D) alleviate

17. The word **adopt** is closest in meaning to

    A) circumvent
    B) select
    C) anatomy
    D) cluster

18. The word **inevitable** is closest in meaning to

    A) unavoidable
    B) uncomfortable
    C) indignant
    D) consequent

19. The word **eddy** is closest in meaning to

    A) abate
    B) swirl
    C) modify
    D) verge

20. The word **milieu** is closest in meaning to

    A) articulate
    B) boisterous
    C) atmosphere
    D) huge

1. C 2. B 3. A 4. D 5. B 6. C 7. D 8. B 9. A 10. B
11. A 12. B 13. B 14. D 15. D 16. C 17. B 18. A 19. B 20. C

TOEFL iBT/ TOEIC WORDS (Day 24)

1. Distinguish [dih-**sting**-gwish]
   verb def: to mark off as different.
     synonyms: analyze, ascertain, classify, decide, admire
     Jennifer seemed to have trouble *distinguishing* the difference between the two of them.

2. Exile [**eg**-zahyl]
   verb def: expulsion from one's native land by authoritative decree.
     synonyms: expel, banish, separate, displace
     antonyms: import, take in, welcome
     Disobeying his father will get Tom *exiled* from his family.

3. Persecute [**pur**-si-kyoot]
   verb def: to pursue with harassing or oppression.
     synonyms: oppress, outrage, pester, bother, crucify
     antonyms: comfort, commend, console
     A number of innocent people in the 14th century were *persecuted* for the fact that they believed in God.

4. Serendipitous [ser-uhn-**dip**-i-tuhs]
   adj def: come upon or found by accident. (***)
     synonyms: fortuitous, found by accident
     It is believed that there were many *serendipitous* scientific discoveries.

5. Apt [apt]
   adj def: inclined; disposed; prone.
     synonyms: applicable, suitable, apposite, correct
     antonyms: incorrect, unsuitable, disinclined
     The dog we encountered on the street was *apt* to run off if the dog owner didn't put him on a leash.

6. Adherent [ad-**heer**-uhnt]
   adj def: a person who follows or upholds a leader. (**)
     synonyms: supporter, follower, believer, advocate
     Most of the bandages on the market are originally made from mildly *adherent* fiber.

7. Nihilism [**nahy**-uh-liz-uhm]
   noun def: total rejection of established laws and institutions.
     synonyms: abnegation, anarchy, atheism, denial

antonyms: faith, obedience, optimism
After the revolution, Stalin's *nihilism* marked the continuous reign of terror.

Robert's *nihilism* expressed itself in his lack of concern with the norms of decent, moral society.

8. Dissent [dih-**sent**]
verb def: to differ in sentiment or opinion. (**)
synonyms: disagree, disapproval, conflict, difference, discord
antonyms: approval, concurrence, ratification, sanction
Two of the justices *dissented* from the majority decision.

9. Convention [kuhn-**ven**-shuhn]
noun def: agreement; compact; contract.
A *convention* has developed for expressing the names of newspapers in print in italics.

10. Illustrate [il-uh-**streyt**]
verb def: to furnish with drawings, pictures.
synonyms: demonstrate, exemplify, clarify, evince
antonyms: hide, obscure
In order to help students understand more clearly, the professor *illustrated* his lecture with stories of his own experiences in the field.

11. Surrealistic [suh-ree-uh-**lis**-tik]
adj def: characteristic of surrealism.
The *surrealistic* style of painting at first struck many people as odd.

12. Immune [ih-**myoon**]
adj def: protected from a disease. (**)
synonyms: invulnerable, exempt, insusceptible, resistant
antonyms: unguarded, vulnerable
Taking the medicine prescribed by his doctor led Paul to be *immune* to diphtheria.

TOEFL iBT/ TOEIC WORDS (Day 24)

13. Accuse [uh-kyooz]
  verb def: to charge with the fault.
    synonyms: apprehend, arraign, arrest, betray
    antonyms: absolve, exculpate, exonerate, praise
    The police *accused* the person who happened to be at the crime scene of murder.

14. Allege [uh-lej]
  verb def: to assert with proof.
    synonyms: declare, affirm, claim, assertive
    antonyms: contradict, deny, disagree
    He *alleged* that the mayor has accepted bribes.

15. Greedy [gree-dee]
  noun def: excessively or inordinately desirous of wealth.
    synonyms: avaricious, avid, covetous, gluttonous
    antonyms: abstemious, charitable, generous
    Alex has been known as a ruthless and *greedy* businessman.

16. Cherish [cher-ish]
  verb def: to hold or treat as dear.
    synonyms: admire, adore, appreciate
    antonyms: abandon, denounce, forsake, renounce
    Jason always *cherished* the experience of participating in a concert event.

17. Absurd [ab-surd]
  adj def: utterly or obviously senseless, illogical. (***)
    synonyms: foolish, inane, stupid
    antonyms: certain, logical, rational, reasonable
    In the year 2000, the election process continued for an *absurd* amount of time.

  In an era when federal judges issue rulings that in their impact often rival the lawmaking of any legislature in the land, it is increasingly *absurd* that their proceedings should remain off-limits to the same wider public scrutiny that news cameras have brought to courts in 48 states.
  — *Editor & Publisher*, 14 July 2003

TOEFL iBT/ TOEIC WORDS (Day 24)

18. Anachronism [uh-**nak**-ruh-riz-uhm]
noun def: agnosticism; absolutism. (****)

    The aged hippie used *anachronisms* like "groovy" and "far out" that had not been popular for years.

    In our modern world of pre-made, rush-rush, tightly scheduled lives, Amanda Blake Souls is an *anachronism*. At their home in coastal Maine, her family of six makes most of what they use—everything from bread and crafts to clothes and toys.
    — Jean Van't Hul, *Mothering*, March/April 2009

19. Realm [relm]
noun def: a royal domain, kingdom. (*)
    synonyms: region, sphere, domain, branch
    The king sent messengers far and wide throughout his *realm* with the proclamation.

20. Spectator [**spek**-tey-ter]
noun def: a person who looks on or watches.
    synonyms: beholder, bystander, clapper, witness
    The accident I happened to witness in the morning attracted a large crowd of *spectators*.

21. Mundane [muhn-**deyn**]
noun def: pertaining to this world or earth. (***)
    synonyms: worldly, earthly, common, ordinary
    The plot of that thriller was completely *mundane*; as usual, the film ended in a huge explosion.

    On him, a *mundane* navy blazer looked like an Armani dinner jacket; around him, a dusky locker room became the chandeliered lobby of the Savoy.
    — Curry Kirkpatrick, *ESPN*, 19 Mar. 2001

22. Outrageous [out-**rey**-juhs]
adj def: violent in action or temper.
    synonyms: abominable, atrocious, barbaric, beastly
    antonyms: delightful, good, wonderful
    At first it seemed like an *outrageous* idea, but then we realized that it wasn't so crazy after all.

TOEFL iBT/ TOEIC WORDS (Day 24)

23. Strip [strip]
   verb def: to deprive of covering.
   synonyms: deprive, take away, remove, divest
   antonyms: clothe, cover
   The owner of the building hired people to completely *strip* it of its original woodwork in order to remodel it.

24. Experiment [ik-**sper**-uh-muhnt]
   noun def: a test; trial; tentative procedure.
   synonyms: agreement, analysis, assay
   The product recently released to the market was the result of long *experiment*.

25. Innovative [**in**-uh-vey-tiv]
   adj def: tending to innovate; creative.
   synonyms: creative, avant-garde, cutting-edge
   Brady introduced an excellent solution, which was an *innovative* approach to the problem the company was facing.

26. Juxtapose [**juhk**-stuh-pohz]
   verb def: to place close together; side by side. (**)
   synonyms: bring together, connect, pair
   A display perfectly *juxtaposes* modern art with classical art.

27. Discipline [**dis**-uh-plin]
   noun def: training to act in accordance with.
   synonyms: conduct, control, cultivation, development
   antonyms: chaos, confusion, disorder
   A daily stint at the typewriter is excellent *discipline* for a writer.

28. Garner [**gahr**-ner]
   verb def: to gather or deposit in.
   synonyms: store, deposit, collect
   antonyms: disperse, dissipate
   Stanley put a ceaseless effort to *garner* a national reputation as a financial expert.

TOEFL iBT/ TOEIC WORDS (Day 24)

29. Barter [bahr-ter]
   verb def: to change in trade.
        synonyms: bargain, exchange, haggle
        Tom is *bartering* away his pride for material gain.

30. Conspicuous [kuhn-spik-yoo-uhs]
   adj def: easily seen or noticed.
        synonyms: obvious, apparent, distinct
        antonyms: concealed, hidden, imperceptible
        Marc was always *conspicuous* by his booming laughter.

31. Carnivore [kahr-nuh-vawr]
   noun def: an animal that eats flesh.
        Some marsupials are herbivores and eat only green plants, while others are *carnivores* and eat only meat.

32. Forgo [fawr-goh]
   verb def: to abstain or refrain from; do without. (**)
        synonyms: abandon, abdicate, abjure, abstain
        antonyms: continue, indulge, keep
        I think Jenny will *forgo* dessert this evening, for she is trying to lose weight.

33. Hover [huhv-er]
   verb def: to hang fluttering or suspended in the air.
        synonyms: drift, flicker, fritter, fly
        antonyms: lie, rest, settle
        Numerous economists predict that unemployment rates will be *hovering* around 25 percent.

34. Symmetry [sim-i-tree]
   noun def: the correspondence in size, form, and arrangement. (**)
        synonyms: proportion, agreement, arrangement, balance
        antonyms: asymmetry, difference, disproportion, imbalance
        The recently constructed building in front of my house turned out to have perfect *symmetry*.

35. Dehydrate [dee-hahy-dreyt]
   verb def: deprive or remove water.
        Athletes must drink lots of water in order not to get *dehydrated*.

TOEFL iBT/ TOEIC WORDS (Day 24)

36. Respiration [res-puh-**rey**-shuhn]
    noun def: the act of respiring; inhalation and exhalation of air.
        The doctor regularly checked his heart and *respiration*.

37. Expel [ik-**spel**]
    verb def: to drive or force out or away; discharge.
        synonyms: cast out, disgorge, dislodge, ejaculate
        antonyms: absorb, admit, take in
        The club may *expel* any members who do not follow the rules.

38. Ventilate [**ven**-ti-eyt]
    verb def: to provide with fresh air.
        synonyms: circulate, bring into open, advertise, circulate
        As soon as he walked into the room, Paul immediately opened the windows to *ventilate* the room.

39. Abdomen [**ab**-duh-muhn]
    noun def: belly; gut; intestines; tummy.
        Last night Liana showed us a tiny tattoo on her *abdomen*, right next to her belly button.

40. Spiral [**spahy**-ruhl]
    adj def: curling; winding; circling.
        A *spiral* staircase takes visitors up onto the top of the building, which is, he believes, one of the tallest buildings in the world.

41. Regulate [**reg**-yuh-leyt]
    verb def: to control or direct by a rule, principle.
        synonyms: adjust, direct, adapt, administer, allocate
        antonyms: deregulate, disorganize, mismanage
        It is essential that the government *regulate* how much lead may be found in our water supply.

42. Subterranean [suhb-tuh-**rey**-nee-uhn]
    adj def: hidden; underground; covered.
        Before World War Two took place, Nazis had built numerous *subterranean* bunkers that supposedly could withstand even an atomic blast.

TOEFL iBT/ TOEIC WORDS (Day 24)

43. Prone [prohn]
   adj def: having a natural inclination or tendency to something. (***)
        synonyms: prostrate, reclining, level
        antonyms: sitting, straight, upright
        He was *prone* to emotional outbursts under stress.

        Hull then corralled the rebound and shoveled the puck past the left arm and leg of the *prone* Hasek with his forehand, touching off a wild on-ice celebration.
                  — Michael Farber, *Sports Illustrated*, 28 June 1999

44. Dictate [dik-teyt]
   verb def: to command; rule; decree; code.
        The president *dictated* peace terms to a conquered enemy.

45. Configure [kuhn-**fig**-yer]
   verb def: to design; adapt to form.
        The planes are *configured* to accommodate more passengers in each row.

46. Colossal [kuh-**los**-uhl]
   adj def: extraordinarily great in size, extent, or degree.
        synonyms: huge, gigantic, enormous, immense
        antonyms: tiny, small, teeny
        The CEO of the company was surprised to find that there had been many *colossal* failures for the past ten fiscal years.

47. Concoct [kon-**kokt**]
   verb def: to prepare or make by combining ingredients.
        synonyms: devise, make up, contrive, create, contrive
        The chef *concocted* a recipe in order to enhance the quality of the dish.

48. Ritual [**rich**-oo-uhl]
   adj def: an established or prescribed procedure for a religious or other rite.
        synonyms: ceremony, tradition, custom, convention
        Many people in the Catholic church wanted to eliminate some of the *ritual* of the mass.

TOEFL iBT/ TOEIC WORDS (Day 24)

49. Equilibrium [ee-kwuh-**lib**-ree-uhm]
   noun def: a state of rest or balance. (**)
      synonyms: evenness, calm, composure, equanimity
      antonyms: imbalance, unevenness
      The pressure of the situation caused me to lose my *equilibrium*.

      We must find *equilibrium* between commercial development and conservation of our natural treasures.

50. Equivalent [ih-**kwiv**-uh-luhnt]
   adj def: equal in value, measure, force. (***)
      synonyms: same, similar, akin, analogous
      antonyms: changeable, different, obverse
      In some ways, the British prime minister is *equivalent* to our president.

"*William Shin is the #1 instructor of SAT words. Today, he debuts the new TOEFL iBT book,* Mastering Core TOEFL iBT/ TOEIC Words *with William Shin. Any foreign students who want to study in the U.S. must review this book, because, with Mr. Shin's help, they will achieve success in TOEFL iBT/ TOEIC.*"

Dr. SUNGHO YOON, Ph.D., A.M.ASCE
Research Professor
Department of Civil & Urban Engineering
Polytechnic Institute of New York University, NY, USA

TOEFL iBT/ TOEIC WORDS (Day 24)

❝ *Without memorizing core TOEFL iBT/ TOEIC words, students will struggle to attain high scores on the TOEFL iBT.* Mastering Core TOEFL iBT/ TOEIC Words with William Shin *is a collection of some of the most commonly used vocabulary words on the TOEFL iBT/ TOEIC. I strongly believe that the word book facilitates students' memorization process by providing example sentences, concise multiple-choice questions, and a review of the more complex words. Memorize the words from cover to cover, and you'll be prepared.* ❞

Haeseung Chung
Founder of Jongro M School, Seoul Korea

Drill 24

1. The word **equivalent** is closest in meaning to

    A) drain
    B) marine
    C) juvenile
    D) similar

2. The word **ritual** is closest in meaning to

    A) congregation
    B) ceremony
    C) hover
    D) cooperation

3. The word **concoct** is closest in meaning to

    A) convulsive
    B) impulsive
    C) mixed
    D) realm

4. The word **colossal** is closest in meaning to

    A) intrinsic
    B) huge
    C) offshoot
    D) explore

5. The word **distinguish** is closest in meaning to

    A) different
    B) partake
    C) contemporary
    D) spectator

Drill 24

6. The word **exile** is closest in meaning to

    A) intricate
    B) banish
    C) vanish
    D) garnish

7. The word **serendipity** is closest in meaning to

    A) acclaim
    B) illustrate
    C) disregard
    D) luck

8. The word **nihilism** is closest in meaning to

    A) surrealism
    B) preoccupied
    C) placate
    D) denial

9. The word **dissent** is closest in meaning to

    A) cherish
    B) disagree
    C) absurd
    D) anachronism

10. The word **immune** is closest in meaning to

    A) greedy
    B) abandon
    C) protect
    D) distort

Drill 24

11. The word **accuse** is closest in meaning to

    A) collaborate
    B) apprehend
    C) comprise
    D) ascendant

12. The word **absurd** is closest in meaning to

    A) foolish
    B) radical
    C) typify
    D) distinguish

13. The word **realm** is closest in meaning to

    A) domain
    B) exile
    C) persecution
    D) dedicate

14. The word **strip** is closest in meaning to

    A) adhere
    B) apt
    C) bare
    D) overarch

15. The word **juxtapose** is closest in meaning to

    A) entice
    B) swell
    C) dissent
    D) connect

Drill 24

16. The word **garner** is closest in meaning to

    A) anomalous
    B) coincide
    C) amass
    D) replenish

17. The word **conspicuous** is closest in meaning to

    A) resume
    B) obvious
    C) tremendous
    D) huge

18. The word **forgo** is closest in meaning to

    A) prevent
    B) encourage
    C) abundant
    D) sustain

19. The word **symmetry** is closest in meaning to

    A) inhibit
    B) profound
    C) balance
    D) retrieve

20. The word **dehydrate** is closest in meaning to

    A) tension
    B) hegemony
    C) preeminent
    D) desiccate

1. D 2. B 3. C 4. B 5. A 6. B 7. D 8. D 9. B 10. C
11. B 12. A 13. A 14. C 15. D 16. C 17. B 18. A 19. C 20. D

TOEFL iBT/ TOEIC WORDS (Day 25)

1. Wherein [hwer-in]
　　adv def: in what particular or respect; in which.
　　　　Wherein this document can be demonstrated to be out of compliance with current standards, that section will be considered null and void.

2. Extend [ik-**stend**]
　　verb def: to make longer; larger; aggrandize; draw out to the full length
　　　　He tried to *extend* the measuring tape as far as it goes.

3. Leeward [**lee**-werd]
　　adj def: moving toward the quarter toward which the wind blows. (**)
　　　　We turned the boat to *leeward*.

4. Discrepancy [dih-**skrep**-uhn-see]
　　noun def: the state or quality of being discrepant. (*****)
　　　　　　synonyms: discordance, disparity, difference, conflict
　　　　　　antonyms: agreement, concordance, consistency
　　　　There are certain *discrepancies* between the two versions of the story John has just completed reading.

　　　　Dr. Derman, who spent 17 years at Goldman Sachs and became managing director, was a forerunner of the many physicists and other scientists who have flooded Wall Street in recent years, moving from a world in which a *discrepancy* of a few percentage points in a measurement can mean a Nobel Prize or unending mockery to a world in which a few percent one way can land you in jail and a few percent the other way can win you your own private Caribbean island.
　　　　　　　　　　　　— Dennis Overbye, *New York Times*, 9 Mar. 2009

5. Ongoing [**on**-goh-ing]
　　adj def: continuous; evolving; growing.
　　　　Stella has made an *ongoing* effort to improve her score on the standardized test she is scheduled to take.

6. Divergence [dih-**vur**-juhns]
　　noun def: the act of diverging. (**)
　　　　　　synonyms: aberration, alteration, deflection
　　　　　　antonyms: accord, concord, convergence
　　　　Any *divergence* from the community's strict moral code was met with social ostracism.

TOEFL iBT/ TOEIC WORDS (Day 25)

7. Ostracism [**os**-truh-siz-uhm]
noun def: exclusion from social acceptance, privileges. (****)
synonyms: avoidance, boycott, exclusion, exile
Larry knew that *ostracism* would be his fate when, after he made an obnoxious comment, all the other guests at the party turned their backs to him.

Life in Japan is showing tentative signs of returning to normal, but a fresh challenge may be facing the expatriates and Japanese who left and are now trickling back to their offices: how to cope with *ostracism* and anger from their colleagues who have worked through the crisis.

8. Incur [in-**kur**]
verb def: to come into or acquire; become liable.
synonyms: acquire, arouse, catch, gain
Submitting students to the rigors of learning seemed only to *incur* the wrath of many of them ...
— Ben Marcus, *TIME*, 8 Jan. 2001

9. Symbiosis [sim-bee-**oh**-sis]
noun def: the living together of two dissimilar organisms. (***)
The rhino and the tick-eating bird live in *symbiosis*; the rhino gives the bird food in the form of ticks, and the bird rids the rhino of parasites.

The bird lives in *symbiosis* with the hippopotamus.

10. Ferment [**fur**-ment]
verb def: enzyme; agent; leaven; agitation.
It is generally believed that wine *ferments* in oak barrels.

11. Reinforce [ree-in-**fawrs**]
verb def: to strengthen with some added piece, support.
synonyms: augment, support, buttress, carry, energize
antonyms: subtract, undermine, weaken
The bad weather forecast only *reinforces* our decision to leave early tomorrow.

12. Axis [**ak**-sis]
noun def: the line about which a rotating body moves. (**)
synonyms: arbor, hinge, pivot, pole
The *Axis*, Germany, Italy, and Japan, engaged against the Allied nations in World War Two.

TOEFL iBT/ TOEIC WORDS (Day 25)

13. Gauche [gohsh]
   adj def: lacking social grace, sensitivity, or acuteness.
        synonyms: awkward, clumsy, crude, halting
        antonyms: elegant, graceful, mannerly, polished
        Their exquisite manners always make me feel *gauche*.

14. Intersperse [in-ter-**spurs**]
   verb def: to scatter; diversify; diffuse. (**)
        Timothy *interspersed* a dull speech with interesting anecdotes.

        Mushrooms were *interspersed* among the bushes and clumps of moss in the shady forest.

15. Intertwine [in-ter-**twahyn**]
   verb def: to twist; associate; connect; convolute.
        It is well known that Jefferson always tells stories in which the present and the past *intertwine*.

16. Congenial [kuhn-**jeen**-yuhl]
   adj def: agreeable; suitable; pleasing in nature or character. (***)
        synonyms: adapted, affable, compatible, consistent, cooperate
        antonyms: disagreeable, incompatible, unfriendly
        Couples with *congenial* personalities stay together longer than couples who are polar opposites.

        She moved on, leaving behind the world of politics for the more *congenial* sphere of the arts.
                — Amy Fine Collins, *Vanity Fair*, March 2001

17. Congenital [kuhn-**jen**-i-tl]
   adj def: inbred; indwelling; intrinsic; innate. (**)
        The baby was unfortunately born with several *congenital* diseases.

18. Sterile [**ster**-il]
   adj def: unproductive; clean; aseptic; bare.
        In modern society, a great number of *sterile* couples have sometimes chosen to adopt needy children.

TOEFL iBT/ TOEIC WORDS (Day 25)

19. Forage [**fawr**-ij]
 verb def: to wander or go in search. (**))
   synonyms: explore, pilfer, plunder, raid
   David suddenly went *foraging* in the attic for old mementos.

20. Intensify [in-**ten**-suh-fayh]
 verb def: to make intense or more intense.
   synonyms: strengthen, sharpen, accent, aggrandize
   antonyms: calm, lower, slow
   We could hear the wind howling outside as the storm *intensified*.

21. Etymology [et-uh-**mol**-uh-jee]
 noun def: word history; derivation; origin. (*****)
   The professor devoted himself to an ambitious study of the *etymology* of all words beginning with "E."

   Visible just beneath the entries are tantalizing glimpses of the lexicographer's craft: scouring periodicals for fresh coinages, poring over competing dictionaries in search of elusive *etymologies* and hounding writers and scholars in the service of ... "ear candy" or plain old "duh."
     — Margalit Fox, *New York Times Book Review*, 18 June 1995

22. Placebo [pluh-**see**-boh]
 noun def: fake pill; inactive drug; sugar pill.
   A lot of doctors strongly believe in a *placebo* effect.

23. Placate [**pley**-keyt]
 verb def: to appease; assuage; pacify. (***)
   The burglar tried to *placate* the snaring Doberman by saying, "Nice doggy," and offering it a treat.

   Although Rumsfeld was later thrown overboard by the Administration in an attempt to *placate* critics of the Iraq War, his military revolution was here to stay.
     — Jeremy Scahill, *Nation*, 2 Apr. 2007

TOEFL iBT/ TOEIC WORDS (Day 25)

24. Persistent [per-**sis**-tuhnt]
    adj def: persisting, especially in spite of opposition, obstacle.
        synonyms: determined, continuous, assiduous, bound, constant
        antonyms: lazy, relenting, surrendering
    Contrary to *persistent* myth, Hoover was an activist.
                — Steve Forbes, *Forbes*, 30 June 2008

25. Prescribe [pri-**skrayhb**]
    verb def: to lay down as a rule or a course of action.
        synonyms: appoint, assign, choose, command, decide, decree
    The doctor *prescribed* three months of physical therapy for Christine's leg injury.

26. Predicament [pri-**dik**-uh-muhnt]
    noun def: unpleasantly difficult, perplexing, or dangerous situation. (****)
        synonyms: deadlock, dilemma, exigency, dilemma
    Because he had spent all of his money, Bancha found himself in a miserable *predicament* when his rent bill arrived.

    The captain of archers fidgeted and coughed and rolled his eyes at his men, as if such cupidity and dishonor were an inevitable but minor aspect of the human *predicament* ...
                — Michael Chabon, *New York Times Magazine*, 6 May 2007

27. Alleviate [uh-**lee**-vee-eyt]
    verb def: to make easier to endure. (***)
        synonyms: lessen, calm, endure, mitigate, lighten
        antonyms: aggravate, heighten, increase
    The medicine will help to *alleviate* the pain.

    For decades, as you probably know, researchers have found that when you tell patients that you're giving them medicine, many report that their symptoms are *alleviated,* even if they're only taking sugar pills.
                — Daniel Zwerdling, *Gourmet*, August 2004

28. Diagnose [**dahy**-uhg-nohs]
    verb def: to analyze; determinate; distinguish; pinpoint.
    The doctor *diagnosed* the illness as influenza.

TOEFL iBT/ TOEIC WORDS (Day 25)

29. Ailment [eyl-muhnt]
noun def: ache; disease; disorder; illness.
Susan has been suffering from a chronic back *ailment* since she accidentally sprained her back.

30. Virtue [vur-choo]
noun def: moral excellence, goodness. (**)
synonyms: honor, integrity, asset, charity
antonyms: dishonor, evil, immorality, vice
He led me across the concrete floor, through a concrete warehouse, and to the concrete screening room, where he began to extol the *virtue* and beauty of his eleven-mile-long sewage interceptor.
— Frederick Kaufman, *Harper's*, February 2008

31. Concede [kuhn-seed]
verb def: to acknowledge as true. (***)
synonyms: accept, accord, admit, allow, avow
antonyms: contradict, disagree, dispute, refuse
Jessica was so persistent that Jim *conceded* at last.

… he *conceded* that with six kids, something like this was bound to happen. At least one of them had to be a bad egg.
— Markus Zusak, *The Book Thief*, 2005

32. Allot [uh-lot]
verb def: to divide; distribute; assign.
The government *allotted* the available farmland among the settlers.

33. Thereby [thair-bayh]
adv def: by that; by means of that.
Alex signed the contract, *thereby* forfeiting his right to the property inherited from his parents.

34. Dilemma [dih-lem-uh]
noun def: any difficult or perplexing situation. (***)
synonyms: crisis, Catch-22, impasse, mess, mire
antonyms: miracle, solution, wonder
They're usually too small for us to even appreciate that there's a moral *dilemma* to them.

TOEFL iBT/ TOEIC WORDS (Day 25)

When it comes to the boss, there is a real *dilemma*. You're caught between a career-limiting rejection of virtual friendship or a career-limiting access to photos of yourself glassy-eyed at a party.

— Jared Sandberg, *Wall Street Journal*, 10 July 2007

35. Undergo [uhn-der-**goh**]
   verb def: bear; encounter; endure; experience.
       The result shows that Dianne will need to *undergo* an operation.

36. Supervise [**soo**-per-vahyz]
   verb def: to oversee during execution or performance.
       synonyms: administer, conduct, inspect, direct
       The manager has *supervised* more than 20 staff personnel since he became head of the department.

37. Legitimacy [li-**jit**-uh-muh-see]
   noun def: the state or quality of being legitimate.
       The *legitimacy* of the military dictatorship was not recognized by most other nations.

38. Discretionary [dih-**skresh**-uh-ner-ee]
   adj def: subject or left to one's own discretion. (**)
       synonyms: elective, facultative, leftover, optional
       According to the *New York Times*, *discretionary* investing in houses dropped dramatically last year.

39. Tactics [**tak**-tiks]
   noun def: a plan for promoting a desired end or result.
       In order to improve their test scores, test takers must have a variety of *tactics* and specific study plans.

40. Tempt [tempt]
   verb def: to entice or allure to do something. (**)
       synonyms: attract, bait, captivate, charm, coax
       antonyms: discourage, repulse, turn off
       The book Dina was reading on the bus *tempted* her to continue to read more on the subject.

TOEFL iBT/ TOEIC WORDS (Day 25)

41. Optimistic [op-tuh-**mis**-tik]
    adj def: disposed to take a favorable view of events or conditions.
        synonyms: assured, cheerful, confident, reflecting
        antonyms: dejected, depressed, sorrowful
        Maria seemed to have a very *optimistic* attitude towards pursuing higher education in spite of the fact that she turned 45 years old.

42. Indispose [in-di-**spohz**]
    verb def: to render averse or unwilling; disincline. (**)
        The extensive exercise at the gym *indisposed* Tina for any further physical activity that day.

43. Retrospect [**re**-truh-spekt]
    verb def: to look back upon; contemplate.
        synonyms: hindsight, recollection, reconsideration
        antonyms: forethought, prophecy, prospect
        Greg frequently *retrospects* to a period in his youth.

44. Accelerate [ak-**sel**-uh-reyt]
    verb def: to increase speed; hasten; expedite.
        Many people in the United States firmly believe that cutting taxes will help to *accelerate* economic growth.

45. Malpractice [mal-**prak**-tis]
    noun def: failure of a professional person.
        synonyms: abuse, misconduct, dereliction
        Unlike other doctors, Dr. Otis didn't have *malpractice* insurance to protect himself against lawsuits.

46. Doctrine [**dok**-trin]
    noun def: opinion; principle; article of faith; attitude.
        It is said that many modern psychologists now question the *doctrines* of Sigmund Freud.

47. Consent [kuhn-**sent**]
    noun def: to permit; approve; agree; comply. (***)
        By common *consent,* Becket was appointed official delegate.

TOEFL iBT/ TOEIC WORDS (Day 25)

48. Addle [ad-l]
   verb def: confuse; muddle. (***)
        The alcohol had *addled* John's brain and left him confused.

49. Mesmerize [mez-muh-rahyz]
   verb def: to hypnotize; enthrall; magnetize.
        Running into the house, a couple discovered that the children were *mesmerized* by a television show.

50. Appease [uh-peez]
   verb def: to bring to a state of peace, quiet, ease. (****)
        synonyms: soothe, calm, quite, ease
        antonyms: aggravate, annoy, incite, irritate
   Eating everything on the dining table finally *appeased* his hunger.

But I imagine he and his siblings, who profited handsomely from the sale, have mixed emotions. They may be sad they had to sell, yet relieved that they are no longer under pressure to *appease* Wall Street's demand for growth and profits.
                              — James Laube, *Wine Spectator*, 31 Mar. 2005

TOEFL iBT/ TOEIC WORDS (Day 25)

❝ *This TOEFL iBT/ TOEIC preparatory book is filled with necessary information that really helps to ease the burden of excess studying. It is concise, yet very substantial in that it covers basically all the vocabulary words that are bound to show up on the exam. Also, the short quizzes found at the end of each section assist to drill the words again and again, which promises success and accurate memorization. This book is one of the few preparatory books that is purely convenient and not overwhelming.* ❞

Harrin Choi
Cresskill High School, NJ, USA

Drill 25

1. The word **discrepancy** is closest in meaning to

    A) affluent
    B) different
    C) hinder
    D) prevent

2. The word **ostracism** is closest in meaning to

    A) expel
    B) astound
    C) constitute
    D) juxtapose

3. The word **incur** is closest in meaning to

    A) exacerbate
    B) affiliate
    C) arouse
    D) encompass

4. The word **ferment** is closest in meaning to

    A) abandon
    B) agitate
    C) clement
    D) forage

5. The word **intertwine** is closest in meaning to

    A) abnormal
    B) bigot
    C) consequence
    D) convolute

Drill 25

6. The word **congenial** is closest in meaning to

    A) circumspect
    B) burrow
    C) agreeable
    D) investigate

7. The word **sterile** is closest in meaning to

    A) acclaim
    B) antiseptic
    C) foreshadow
    D) illiterate

8. The word **placate** is closest in meaning to

    A) calm
    B) alter
    C) conjecture
    D) impact

9. The word **predicament** is closest in meaning to

    A) difficult situation
    B) disguise
    C) incite
    D) lethal

10. The word **alleviate** is closest in meaning to

    A) affluent
    B) consent
    C) lessen
    D) emerge

Drill 25

11. The word **ailment** is closest in meaning to

    A) circulatory
    B) disorder
    C) spiracle
    D) crucial

12. The word **allot** is closest in meaning to

    A) concoct
    B) impervious
    C) subterranean
    D) divide

13. The word **dilemma** is closest in meaning to

    A) retain
    B) amass
    C) doctrine
    D) quandary

14. The word **supervise** is closest in meaning to

    A) plague
    B) pesticide
    C) oversee
    D) threaten

15. The word **tempt** is closest in meaning to

    A) allure
    B) intuitive
    C) strive
    D) debris

Drill 25

16. The word **indispose** is closest in meaning to

    A) hinged
    B) disinclined
    C) vast
    D) provoke

17. The word **retrospect** is closest in meaning to

    A) disseminate
    B) emergence
    C) occurrence
    D) consideration

18. The word **malpractice** is closest in meaning to

    A) confined
    B) erupt
    C) misconduct
    D) dormant

19. The word **consent** is closest in meaning to

    A) agree
    B) impend
    C) herald
    D) interfere

20. The word **addle** is closest in meaning to

    A) subtle
    B) confused
    C) variation
    D) classified

1. B 2. A 3. C 4. B 5. D 6. C 7. B 8. A 9. A 10. C
11. B 12. D 13. D 14. C 15. A 16. B 17. D 18. C 19. A 20.B

TOEFL iBT/ TOEIC WORDS (Day 26)

1. Incriminate [in-**krim**-uh-neyt]
verb def: to accuse of or present proof of a crime. (**)
  synonyms: accuse, allege, attack, blame
  In exchange for a reduced sentence, the thief agreed to *incriminate* his accomplice.

2. Medicament [muh-**dik**-uh-muhnt]
noun def: remedy; medicine; heal substance.
  It is not surprising that in the 19th century most of the physicians carried *medicaments* that included powerful opiates.

3. Dispense [dih-**spens**]
verb def: to deal out; distribute, disperse. (***)
  synonyms: allocate, allot, apportion, assign
  antonyms: receive, take
  Pharmacists will *dispense* medicine only to customers with a doctor's prescription.

  The primary purpose of articles in the newspaper is to *dispense* advice to millions of readers every day.

4. Reluctant [ri-**luhk**-tuhnt]
adj def: unwilling; disinclined. (**)
  synonyms: afraid, averse, backward, cautious
  antonyms: anxious, eager, ready
  Brian seemed to be *reluctant* to join the summer music camp.

  94% of the butterflies are females, and they jostle for the attention of the few males, who seem *reluctant* suitors.
  — Carl Zimmer, *Science*, 11 May 2001

5. Anticipate [an-**tis**-uh-peyt]
verb def: to realize beforehand.
  synonyms: expect, foresee, assume, divine
  antonyms: be amazed; be surprised, doubt
  They never *anticipated* a military attack from the adjacent nation.

TOEFL iBT/ TOEIC WORDS (Day 26)

6. Transparency [trans-**pair**-uhn-see]
   noun def: a seeing through. (***)
   The professor used a lot of *transparencies* and an overhead projector during her lectures in order to help students understand more clearly and vividly.

7. Instigate [**in**-sti-geyt]
   verb def: to cause by incitement.
   synonyms: influence, provoke, abet, actuate
   antonyms: halt, prevent, stop
   According to the newspaper, there has been an increased amount of violence *instigated* by gangs.

8. Respective [ri-**spek**-tiv]
   adj def: pertaining individually.
   synonyms: particular, specific, individual, personal, relevant
   antonyms: indefinite
   It was late when the concert let out, so we all went our *respective* ways.

9. Continuum [kuhn-**tin**-yu-uhm]
   noun def: continue; continual. (***)
   Most people, including his family, believed that Jefferson's motives for volunteering lie somewhere on the *continuum* between charitable and self-serving.

10. Subsistence [suhb-**sis**-tuhns]
   noun def: the state or fact of subsisting. (**)
   synonyms: provision, food, legacy, reality
   Many people are beginning to believe in the *subsistence* of a soul as a separate entity from the body.

11. Pastoral [**pas**-ter-uhl]
   adj def: having simplicity, charm, serenity.
   synonyms: agrarian, bucolic, country, idyllic
   antonyms: agitated, bustling, busy, urban
   Jonathan beautifully painted a *pastoral* scene of a flower-filled meadow.

12. Predominate [pri-**dom**-uh-neyt]
   adj def: to have numerical superiority or advantage. (**)
   synonyms: command, govern, noticeable, prevail

TOEFL iBT/ TOEIC WORDS (Day 26)

Without a doubt, blue and yellow are *predominate* colors in the painting Tom is looking at.

13. Subsist [suhb-**sist**]
verb def: to continue; exist; live; manage. (***)
It is common sense that the author's right to royalties shall *subsist* for the term of the copyright.

14. Renew [ri-**noo**]
verb def: to start over; refurbish; extend; mend.
Tom was aware that it was time to *renew* his driver's license.

15. Hence [hens]
adv def: for that reason; therefore; accordingly.
The meat in the refrigerator seemed to be very fresh and *hence* satisfactory.

16. Usher [**uhsh**-er]
verb def: to act as an usher to; lead, introduce.
synonyms: guide, bring in, conduct, escort
The attendant was waiting for us and then *ushered* us to the seats we had reserved over the phone.

17. Barter [**bahr**-ter]
verb def: to trade by exchange of commodities.
synonyms: trade, bargain, exchange, swap
Jeff had no intention to *barter* away his pride to gain money.

18. Deplete [dih-**pleet**]
verb def: to consume; exhaust; bleed; diminish. (**)
The fire appeared to *deplete* a variety of trees and flowers in the forest.

The ozone layer is gradually being *depleted* by pollution.

19. Abuse [uh-**byooz**]
verb def: to use wrongly or improperly.
synonyms: debase, misconduct, fault, wrong use
antonyms: adulation, approval, commendation
A number of politicians tend to *abuse* their authority to acquire what they want.

TOEFL iBT/ TOEIC WORDS (Day 26)

20. Holistic [hoh-**lis**-tik]
   adj def: incorporating the concept of holism in theory or practice.
   synonyms: complete, whole, aggregate, comprehensive, entire
   Eric is studying internal medicine and believes in a *holistic* approach to healing.

21. Nouveau [noo-voh]
   adj def: newly or recently created, developed, or come to prominence. (**)
   The sudden success of the firm created several *nouveau* millionaires.

22. Transcend [tran-**send**]
   verb def: to rise above or go beyond; overpass. (**)
   synonyms: go beyond, surpass, exceed, outrival
   His extensive and rich knowledge of what he is interested in made him *transcend* his friends and colleagues.

   Yoga helps Lynn to *transcend* the petty frustrations of everyday life and to achieve true spirituality.

23. Derogatory [dih-**rog**-uh-tawr-ee]
   adj def: tending to lessen the merit or reputation of. (****)
   synonyms: offensive, aspersing, belittling, calumnious
   antonyms: appreciative, complimentary, favorable
   Dr. Goldenberg was really upset about the fact that one of his colleagues made a *derogatory* remark about his recently released article.

   The aroma of wine made from Concord ... grapes is often described as "foxy," a wine term as *derogatory* as it is vague.
   —Danny May et al., *Berkshire Home Style*, March 2007

24. Trivial [**triv**-ee-uhl]
   adj def: insignificant; little value; ordinary. (***)
   Thomas must be a very generous person, for he never blamed anyone who made a *trivial* mistake.

   His later memory, untutored and unsupported by anything so *trivial* as evidence or documents, now flourished and ran wild.
   —Muriel Spark, *Curriculum Vitae*, (1992) 1993

TOEFL iBT/ TOEIC WORDS (Day 26)

25. Pecuniary [pi-**kyoo**-nee-er-ee]
   adj def: pertaining to money. (**)
        synonyms: economic, fiscal, monetary, business
        The judge recused himself from the case because he had a *pecuniary* interest in the company that was being sued.

26. Partake [pahr-**teyk**]
   verb def: to take or have a part or share.
        synonyms: receive, take, have a share, engage
        Unlike other winners, Joe was not willing to *partake* in a victory celebration.

27. Persuasive [per-**swey**-siv]
   adj def: effective; influential; convincing; credible.
        Chris made an extremely *persuasive* argument about how to decrease pollution in our town.

28. Demarcate [dih-**mahr**-keyt]
   verb def: to determine or mark off the boundaries of. (**)
        synonyms: limit, separate, detach, divide
        In order to protect his land from wild animals, he decided to *demarcate* it with high fences.

        Americans have a clear outlook on values and clearly *demarcate* between good and evil.

29. Obsolete [ob-suh-**leet**]
   adj def: no longer in use. (****)
        synonyms: ancient, antique, bygone, old-fashioned
        antonyms: current, contemporary, present
        Many people think that camera film turned to be an *obsolete* item in the modern world.

        It may not be welcome news in her home state of Pennsylvania, but chemist Cynthia Kuper could help make steel *obsolete*. Experimenting with carbon nanotubes, structures a few atoms wide but 100 times stronger and much lighter than steel, Kuper calls her work an "amusement park discovery."

        — Joanna Chung, *Newsweek*, 23 Sept. 2002

TOEFL iBT/ TOEIC WORDS (Day 26)

30. Irrevocable [ih-**rev**-uh-kuh-buhl]
    adj def: not to be revoked or recalled. (***)
        synonyms: unchangeable, established, immutable
        antonyms: alterable, changeable, reversible
        William made an *irrevocable* decision about his academic future.

        Once he had pushed the red button, the president's decision to launch a missile was *irrevocable*.

31. Perpetrate [**pur**-pi-treyt]
    verb def: to commit a crime; enact; execute. (***)
        The man was planning to *perpetrate* a robbery at the first bank.

32. Trigger [**trig**-er]
    verb def: to initiate; to precipitate.
        synonyms: activate, bring about, cause, generate
        antonyms: block, check, halt
        The collapse of the US dollar *triggered* an international fiscal crisis.

33. Recur [ri-**kur**]
    verb def: to happen again; repeat.
        Encountering Kelly on the street last week kept *recurring* in John's mind because he had been in love with her when he was in high school.

34. Plentitude [**plen**-te-tud]
    noun def: fullness or adequacy in quantity.
        synonyms: a lot, numerous, abundance
        Jason found that there seemed to be a *plentitude* of decent houses available to him on the market.

35. Predisposition [pree-dis-puh-**zish**-uhn]
    noun def: tendency; willingness; inclination.
        Common experiences are recorded and are inherited as *predispositions* to respond emotionally to certain categories of experience.

36. Propensity [pruh-**pen**-si-tee]
    noun def: inclination; tendency; weakness. (***)
        Charles used to have a strong *propensity* to drink two cans of beer before he went to bed.

TOEFL iBT/ TOEIC WORDS (Day 26)

> Other researchers are exploring how the adolescent *propensity* for uninhibited risk taking propels teens to experiment with drugs and alcohol.
> — Claudia Wallis, *TIME*, 10 May 2004

37. Interdisciplinary [in-ter-**dih**-se-ple-ner-e]
adj def: involving two or more academic subjects.
The project, which was led by two professors, covered a wide scope of *interdisciplinary* subjects such as biochemistry and genetics.

38. Incarcerate [in-**kahr**-suh-reyt]
verb def: to enclose; constrict; confine; imprison. (**)
Two men have been *incarcerated* for a crime for the last seven years.

39. Volatile [**vol**-uh-tl]
adj def: explosive; changeable; capricious. (***)
It is extremely dangerous to combine two different *volatile* chemicals into one.

> I am beginning to hear investors say that the best way to beat this *volatile* market is by trading—anxiously moving in and out of securities as the market ebbs and flows. In my view there is no surer path to the poorhouse.
> — John W. Rogers, Jr., *Forbes*, 25 May 2009

40. Fatigue [fuh-**teeg**]
noun def: weariness from bodily or mental exertion.
    synonyms: debility, dullness, enervation, annul
    antonyms: energy, freshness, spirit
Driving several hours without a stop caused James to feel *fatigue*.

41. Irritate [**ir**-i-teyt]
verb def: to upset; anger; affront; annoy.
The child's rudeness *irritated* everyone on the airplane, including the cabin crew.

42. Disprove [dis-**proov**]
verb def: to prove to be false or wrong; refute; invalidate. (**)
    synonyms: belie, break, confound, contradict, controversy
    antonyms: credit, prove, validate
Magellan's circumnavigation of the globe *disproved* any lingering notions that the earth is flat.

TOEFL iBT/ TOEIC WORDS (Day 26)

43. Mitigate [mit-i-geyt]
    verb def: to lessen in force; calm; become milder. (****)
        synonyms: abate, allay, alleviate, appease, assuage
        antonyms: aggravate, incite, increase, intensify
        Taking a pill his pain immediately *mitigated* John's pain.

    At the far end of the room is a sliding glass door, taped with an X to *mitigate* shattering. The framing is flimsy, and rattles from mortar rounds even a half-mile away.
                      — William Langewiesche, *Atlantic*, May 2005

44. Euphoria [yoo-fawr-ee-uh]
    noun def: a feeling of happiness; confidence. (***)
        synonyms: bliss, ecstasy, elation, exaltation
        The initial *euphoria* following their victory in the election has now subsided.

    Euphoria overwhelmed her when she discovered that she had scored a perfect 120 on her TOEFL iBT.

45. Encapsulate [en-kap-suh-leyt]
    verb def: to become enclosed, condense; summarize.
        synonyms: encase, box, cover, envelop
        The contaminated material should be *encapsulated* and removed.

46. Herbivorous [hur-biv-er-uhs]
    adj def: feeding on plants.
        Chimpanzees collect protein through their *herbivorous* diet on a daily basis.

47. Capitalize [kap-i-tl-ahyz]
    verb def: to take advantage of.
        synonyms: benefit, exploit, gain, subsidize
        Jefferson finally won a match by *capitalizing* on his opponent's consecutive mistakes.

48. Ample [am-puhl]
    adj def: sufficient; more than necessary.
        The SUV Jim had decided to purchase provided *ample* space for his children.

TOEFL iBT/ TOEIC WORDS (Day 26)

49. Foresight [fawr-sahyt]
  noun def: care or provision for the future. (**)
    synonyms: anticipation, discernment, circumspection
    antonyms: hindsight, ignorance, thoughtlessness
  They had the *foresight* to invest the money wisely.

50. Fabricate [fab-ri-keyt]
  verb def: to make by art or skill and labor.
    synonyms: manufacture, assemble, compose
    antonyms: break, demolish, destroy
  Timothy hired the finest craftsman in the town to *fabricate* a wristband for the watch inherited from his father.

> *Living as an international student, I am required to take the TOEFL iBT/ TOEIC exam. After studying with this amazingly written out book by my teacher Mr. Shin, I have been able to increase my skills tremendously. It is truly a well thought out and profound book. I would certainly recommend it to everyone trying to increase his/her score.*

BonKyu Ku
Korea International School, Pangyo Campus, Korea

TOEFL iBT/ TOEIC WORDS (Day 26)

❝ *I highly recommend this book for your TOEFL iBT/ TOEIC because it is great if you do not have too many hours to devote to the test. It goes straight to the points you need to know to do well in the test. Also, it is a perfect tool to get as much practice as you need before the TOEFL iBT/ TOEIC exam. I'm glad that I got the book. The book gives the idea and concept of whole steps of the exam. In conclusion, I believe that, if you are going to take the test, buy this book.* ❞

Jung Hwan Lee
Queen of Peace High School, NJ, USA

Drill 26

1. The word **incriminate** is closest in meaning to

    A) confine
    B) accuse
    C) impend
    D) unprovoked

2. The word **anticipate** is closest in meaning to

    A) expect
    B) disseminate
    C) occur
    D) erupt

3. The word **instigate** is closest in meaning to

    A) vast
    B) dormant
    C) urge
    D) herald

4. The word **continuum** is closest in meaning to

    A) interfere
    B) phenomenon
    C) monitor
    D) continuous

5. The word **pastoral** is closest in meaning to

    A) agrarian
    B) subtle
    C) variation
    D) classified

Drill 26

6. The word **subsist** is closest in meaning to

    A) mutation
    B) exist
    C) distort
    D) oscillate

7. The word **usher** is closest in meaning to

    A) proliferate
    B) guide
    C) precursor
    D) fluctuate

8. The word **barter** is closest in meaning to

    A) rim
    B) revenue
    C) exchange
    D) summit

9. The word **abuse** is closest in meaning to

    A) reverse
    B) imminent
    C) misuse
    D) precede

10. The word **derogatory** is closest in meaning to

    A) expel
    B) foreshadow
    C) abnormality
    D) belittle

Drill 26

11. The word **trivial** is closest in meaning to

    A) deform
    B) swell
    C) insignificant
    D) deflate

12. The word **pecuniary** is closest in meaning to

    A) tremor
    B) fiscal
    C) evacuate
    D) pending

13. The word **demarcate** is closest in meaning to

    A) boundary
    B) forecast
    C) cataclysmic
    D) inconsistent

14. The word **obsolete** is closest in meaning to

    A) useless
    B) consecutive
    C) division
    D) inaccuracy

15. The word **irrevocable** is closest in meaning to

    A) irrelevant
    B) static
    C) reflect
    D) unable to return

Drill 26

16. The word **recur** is closest in meaning to

    A) predicate
    B) vertical
    C) happen again
    D) infester

17. The word **propensity** is closest in meaning to

    A) permeate
    B) tendency
    C) satire
    D) encounter

18. The word **incarcerate** is closest in meaning to

    A) confine
    B) porous
    C) impede
    D) percolate

19. The word **volatile** is closest in meaning to

    A) changeable
    B) impervious
    C) stationary
    D) emission

20. The word **mitigate** is closest in meaning to

    A) induce
    B) dilute
    C) lessen
    D) intermittent

1. B 2. A 3. C 4. D 5. A 6. B 7. B 8. C 9. C 10. D
11. C 12. B 13. A 14. A 15. D 16. C 17. B 18. A 19. A 20. C

TOEFL iBT/ TOEIC WORDS (Day 27)

1. Notwithstanding [not-with-**stan**-ding]
    prep def: although; however; against; in spite of.
        Natalie decided to go to the game, doctor's orders *notwithstanding*.

2. Procure [proh-**kyoor**]
    verb def: to obtain or get by care or effort. (**)
        synonyms: acquire, obtain, annex, appropriate
        antonyms: give away, have, lose
        Amazingly, many people find ways to *procure* cheaper produce, even to live off the land with tiny plots they stake out outside the towns.

        It was at that encounter in Pakistan that Faris was put in charge of *procuring* acetylene torches to slice suspension cables, as well as torque tools to bend portions of train track.
                                        — Daniel Eisenberg, *Time*, 30 June 2003

3. Adroit [uh-**droit**]
    adj def: expert or nimble in the use of hands. (**)
        synonyms: skillful, expert, ingenious
        antonyms: awkward, clumsy, dense, inept, stupid, unskilled
        The *adroit* athlete completed even the most difficult obstacle course with ease.

        Perry had been known as an *adroit* debater before he started to work in the company as a coordinator.

4. Appeal [uh-**peel**]
    noun def: an earnest request for aid.
        synonyms: aid, request, entreaty, support
        antonyms: denial, disavowal, refusal
        Brian helped to organize an *appeal* on behalf of his classmates.

5. Enculturation [en-kuhl-chuh-**ra**-shen]
    noun def: a change, modification, or adaptation of behavior or ideas by gaining knowledge of their cultural basis. (****)
        It is generally acknowledged that the *enculturation* process occurs more frequently than in the past.

TOEFL iBT/ TOEIC WORDS (Day 27)

6. Ambivalent [am-**biv**-uh-luhnt]
   adj def: uncertainty or fluctuation. (***)
        synonyms: equivocation, doubt, confusion, dilemma
        antonyms: certainty, decisiveness
        Alexander Horowitz said that the conversion to entirely digital television broadcasts would eliminate the flicker-fusion problem, making TV-viewing more viable (but no more olfactorily interesting) for dogs — which are no doubt *ambivalent*.

7. Celestial [suh-**les**-chuhl]
   adj def: heavenly; astral; blessed; eternal.
        Tom was surprised to discover that the late afternoon sunlight gave the room a *celestial* glow.

8. Petty [**pet**-ee]
   adj def: little; not important; secondary.
        No one could have predicted that *petty* grievances would cause Natasha to cry in front of her family members.

9. Custody [**kuhs**-tuh-dee]
   noun def: keeping; guardianship; care.
        synonyms: aegis, auspicious, observation
        antonyms: freedom, liberation, liberty
        Finally, I located my car, in the *custody* of the local police.

10. Punctuality [puhngk-choo-**al**-ih-tee]
   noun def: strict observation in keeping engagements; promptness.
        Without a doubt, *punctuality* is extremely important in the modern business world.

11. Dexterity [dek-**ster**-i-tee]
   noun def: skill in using the hands or body. (****)
        synonyms: agility, cleverness, adroitness, artistry
        antonyms: awkwardness, clumsiness, inability, ineptness
        Her strength and *dexterity* in the ring and her ability to knock out the toughest of fighters won her fame and acceptance.

TOEFL iBT/ TOEIC WORDS (Day 27)

Russ Cellan, Ferguson's coach at Freeport (New York) High, and Ron Prince, his former offensive line coach at Virginia, both attribute Ferguson's *dexterity* and footwork to his extensive martial arts training ...
— Nunyo Demasio, *Sports Illustrated*, 10 Apr. 2006

12. Irreparable [ih-**rep**-er-uh-buhl]
adj def: incapable of being rectified, remedied. (***)
synonyms: irrecoverable, irredeemable, irremediable, irretrievable, irreversible antonyms: fixable, reparable,
The damage to their relationship was *irreparable*.

13. Symmetrical [si-**me**-tri-kuhl]
adj def: balanced; well-proportioned; equal. (**)
Poison ivy has asymmetrical leaves as opposed to *symmetrical* leaves.

14. Lenient [**lee**-nee-uhnt]
adj def: agreeably tolerant; permissive. (***)
synonyms: permissive, indulgent, tolerant, benign
antonyms: hard, intolerant, limiting
He has a strong tendency to be *lenient* toward beautiful women.

The judge was known for his *lenient* disposition; he rarely imposed long jail sentences on criminals.

15. Overlap [oh-ver-**lap**]
verb def: to cover; extend along; coincide; overlay.
In the United States, baseball season *overlaps* football season in September and October.

16. Parallel [**par**-uh-lel]
adj def: aligned; side-by-side; coextending.
It is not surprising that Canada and the United States appear to have many *parallel* economic interests.

17. Moderate [**mod**-er-it]
adj def: kept or keeping within reasonable or proper limits.
synonyms: calm, temperate, abstinent, bearable
antonyms: excessive, extreme, outrageous
The hotel Anne was staying in Milan offered comfortable rooms at *moderate* prices.

TOEFL iBT/ TOEIC WORDS (Day 27)

18. Respective [ri-**spek**-tiv]
  adj def: individual; particular; each.
    Jenny tried not to discuss the *respective* merits of the candidates.

19. Desertification [dih-zur-tuh-fi-**key**-shuhn]
  noun def: the process by which an area becomes a desert.
    The organization was awarded for its efforts to prevent further *desertification* in Africa.

20. Inversion [in-**vur**-zhuhn]
  noun def: the state of being inverted.
      synonyms: transportation, reversal, contradiction, conversion
      In most languages, *inversion* of two words changes the meaning of the sentence.

21. Aggravate [**ag**-ruh-veyt]
  verb def: to make worse or more severe. (***)
      synonyms: worsen, annoy, irritate, nettle
      antonyms: appease, mollify, soften
      His unwillingness to quit smoking has *aggravated* his chronic illness.

22. Thwart [thwawrt]
  verb def: to frustrate or baffle a plan or purpose. (****)
      synonyms: oppose, prevent, stop, hinder
      antonyms: aid, assist, encourage, forward
      Paul did everything to *thwart* his girlfriend from leaving for NYC.

  Thwarted in its attempt to get the food inside the box, the chimp threw it to the ground in frustration.

23. Plateau [pla-**toh**]
  noun def: a land area having a relatively level surface considerably raised.
      synonyms: elevation, upland, tableland, mesa
      The price of gas seems to have reached a *plateau*.

24. Counterfeit [**koun**-ter-fit]
  adj def: forged; not genuine; fraud.
      The FBI arrested a man suspected of illegally circulating *counterfeit* $100 bills in the United States.

TOEFL iBT/ TOEIC WORDS (Day 27)

25. Abolish [uh-**bol**-ish]
   verb def: to do away with; put an end to; annul. (**)
        synonyms: end, annul, void, abate, abrogate, dissolve
        antonyms: confirm, enact, establish, institute
        The United States of America *abolished* slavery by constitutional amendment on December 6, 1865.

26. Remand [ri-**mand**]
   verb def: to send back; remit; consign again. (***)
        The judge *remanded* the case for further consideration.

27. Evaporate [ih-**vap**-uh-reyt]
   verb def: to change from a liquid to solid state.
        synonyms: disappear, vanish, fade, give off
        antonyms: dampen, soak, wet
        The sun *evaporates* the dew in the morning.

> *Well written and organized, outstanding selection of vocabulary. If you are struggling with the reading section in the TOEFL iBT, this is your go-to book. With definitions, synonyms, antonyms, examples, and drills,* Mastering Core TOEFL iBT/ TOEIC Words with William Shin *will doubtlessly prepare you to ace the TOEFL iBT/ TOEIC!*

Claudia Dawon Oh
Harvard University, MA, USA

TOEFL iBT/ TOEIC WORDS (Day 27)

28. Unprecedented [uhn-**pres**-i-den-tid]
   adj def: without previous instance. (****)
        synonyms: exceptional, original, aberrant, abnormal
        antonyms: known, unexceptional, unremarkable
        Today businesses can measure their activities and customer relationships with *unprecedented* precision.

        … on one occasion, a president (Eisenhower) refers to himself as "conservative." Four years later, the Republican presidential nominee (Goldwater) announces that he is "a conservative." Another sixteen years later, Ronald Reagan, a self-declared conservative, is elected president by an overwhelming majority. By that time—1980—more Americans identify themselves as conservatives than as liberals. This was, and remains, a tectonic transformation, *unprecedented* in American history.
        — John Lukacs, *Harper's*, March 2008

29. Drastic [**dras**-tik]
   adj def: acting with force or violence.
        synonyms: severe, extreme, extensive, desperate, exorbitant
        antonyms: calm, collected, easy
        A newly elected mayor surprised people by proposing a *drastic* tax-reduction plan.

30. Intervene [in-ter-**veen**]
   verb def: to come between disputing people.
        synonyms: intercede, mediate, arbitrate, intercede
        antonyms: ignore, leave alone
        Nothing important *intervened* between meetings.

31. Comprehensive [kom-pri-**hen**-siv]
   adj def: of large scope; covering.
        synonyms: absolute, across, embracing, compendious, complete
        antonyms: exclusive, particular, selective, specific
        All students must take a *comprehensive* examination in order to graduate from high school.

32. Dedicate [**ded**-i-keyt]
   verb def: to allot; donate; set aside; apportion.
        Steve decided to *dedicate* the rest of his life to the development of English education in his country.

TOEFL iBT/ TOEIC WORDS (Day 27)

33. Purview [pur-vyoo]
　　noun def: the range of operation, authority, control, concern. (***)
　　　　These responses to serve the changing needs of students are by no means the sole *purview* of the for-profits.

　　　　After the true shock and awe of a campaign of massive surplus, as in the Gulf War, no regime would have risked its survival by failing to go after the terrorists within its *purview*.
　　　　　　　　　　　— Mark Helprin, *Wall Street Journal*, 17 May 2004

34. Index [in-deks]
　　noun def: a sequential arrangement of material.
　　　　synonyms: indication, basic, clue, evidence
　　　　antonyms: disarrange, disorder, disorganize
　　　　The card catalog is an *index* to the materials in the library.

35. Pictorial [pik-tawr-ee-uhl]
　　adj def: having the visual appeal or imagery of a picture; a pictorial metaphor.
　　　　The photojournalist who used to work for the *New York Times* is now planning to do a primarily *pictorial* report on the famine in Africa.

36. Commission [kuh-mish-uhn]
　　noun def: the act of doing.
　　　　synonyms: carrying out, perpetrating
　　　　Commission of a felony will produce a longer jail sentence than *commission* of a misdemeanor.

37. Onset [on-set]
　　noun def: beginning or start.
　　　　synonyms: access, encounter, inception, kickoff
　　　　antonyms: conclusion, end, finish
　　　　A number of case studies show that if you take enough vitamin C at the *onset* of a cold, you'll often recover faster.

38. Proclamation [prok-luh-mey-shuhn]
　　noun def: announcement; broadcast; declaration; decree.
　　　　Abraham Lincoln made a determination to issue a *proclamation*, which freed the slaves.

TOEFL iBT/ TOEIC WORDS (Day 27)

39. Reliance [ri-**lahy**-uhns]
  noun def: confidence or trustful dependence.
      synonyms: assurance, belief, credence
      antonyms: disbelief, independence
   Alex's *reliance* on drugs and alcohol has been a source of great distress to his family.

40. Suspicion [suh-**spish**-uhn]
  noun def: doubt; conjecture; distrust; incertitude.
      Suspicion caused Miranda to stay up all night long.

41. Tumultuous [too-**muhl**-choo-uhs]
  adj def: full of tumult or riotousness. (**)
      synonyms: confused, agitated, boisterous, fierce
      antonyms: calm, orderly, peaceful
   After the piano concert, the pianist received a *tumultuous* five-minute standing ovation.

   For someone with such a *tumultuous* inner world, the muscular choice-is-all school of moral philosophy could not be satisfactory.
                — Martha C. Nussbaum, *New Republic*, 31 Dec. 2001

42. Patriotism [**prey**-tree-uh-tiz-uhm]
  noun def: loyalty; nationalism; allegiance.
   Ironically, many people do not seem to agree with him politically, but no one has any doubt about his *patriotism*.

43. Bulk [buhlk]
  noun def: magnitude in three dimensions.
      synonyms: size, largeness, aggregate, amplitude
   Buying merchandise in *bulk* quantities allows discount stores to offer lower prices to their customers.

44. Facet [**fas**-it]
  noun def: surface; aspect; angle. (***)
   Tricia carefully examined every *facet* of the argument.

TOEFL iBT/ TOEIC WORDS (Day 27)

45. Cognition [kog-**nish**-uhn]

noun def: the act of knowing; perception.

> synonyms: apprehension, attention, awareness
> antonyms: ignorance, unawareness
> *Cognition* is a function of a certain area of the human brain.

46. Inquiry [in-**kwahy**-ree]

noun def: a seeking or request for truth, information, or knowledge.

> synonyms: analysis, audit, check, delving
> antonyms: answer, reply
> Discovered when Galileo Galilei turned the first astronomical telescope to the heavens in 1610, the Jovian system has been a focus of scientific *inquiry* ever since.
> — Chad Galts, *Brown Alumni Monthly*, November 1996

47. Pinnacle [**pin**-uh-kuhl]

noun def: the highest point, a lofty peak. (**)

> synonyms: top, crest, acme, apex
> antonyms: base, bottom, nadir
> Having completed writing his book, Dr. Chen reached the *pinnacle* of the success.

> The whole show was excellent, but the *pinnacle* was when the skater did a backwards flip.

48. Premise [**prem**-is]

noun def: hypothesis; assumption; assertion. (****)

> Unfortunately, the *premise* of this argument is wrong.

> Called behavioral ecology, it starts from the *premise* that social and environmental forces select for various behaviors that optimize people's fitness in a given environment. Different environment, different behaviors—and different human "natures."
> — Sharon Begley, *Newsweek*, 29 June 2009

TOEFL iBT/ TOEIC WORDS (Day 27)

49. Quandary [**kwahn**-duh-ree]
noun def: a state of perplexity or uncertainty. (*****)
synonyms: bewilder, dilemma, doubt, impasse
antonyms: advantage, certainty, solution
Bill found himself in a quite *quandary* when he realized that he had promised to give the job to two different applicants.

Williams's *quandary* is not unlike that faced by other urban executives who have had to wrestle with a deeply rooted power structure. The problem is especially acute for African American mayors. They are expected to serve as sentries, protecting their cities' black communities and staving off so-called white encroachment.
— Jonetta Rose Barras, *Washington Post*, 15 June 2003

50. Disproportion [dis-pruh-**pawr**-shuhn]
noun def: lack of proportion.
synonyms: imbalance, asymmetry, difference, discrepancy
antonyms: equality, evenness, balance
The salary Chris earns in the company is in *disproportion* to what people who have similar jobs earn.

Drill 27

1. The word **procure** is closest in meaning to

    A) obstruct
    B) earn
    C) emit
    D) induce

2. The word **ambivalent** is closest in meaning to

    A) uncertainty
    B) discharge
    C) dilution
    D) encounter

3. The word **celestial** is closest in meaning to

    A) porous
    B) confined
    C) heavenly
    D) impermeable

4. The word **custody** is closest in meaning to

    A) seepage
    B) intermittent
    C) guardianship
    D) effluence

5. The word **dexterity** is closest in meaning to

    A) oscillating
    B) estuarine
    C) extraction
    D) highly skilled

Drill 27

6. The word **irreparable** is closest in meaning to

    A) gush
    B) artesian
    C) domestic
    D) destroyed

7. The word **lenient** is closest in meaning to

    A) generous
    B) feasible
    C) exploit
    D) sustainable

8. The word **parallel** is closest in meaning to

    A) aligned
    B) desirable
    C) viable
    D) consolidate

9. The word **aggravate** is closest in meaning to

    A) weather
    B) worsen
    C) underlying
    D) decay

10. The word **thwart** is closest in meaning to

    A) profile
    B) dictate
    C) prevent
    D) topography

Drill 27

11. The word **counterfeit** is closest in meaning to

    A) fake
    B) burrow
    C) vigorous
    D) percolating

12. The word **abolish** is closest in meaning to

    A) divisive
    B) lessen
    C) abrogate
    D) convective

13. The word **remand** is closest in meaning to

    A) penetrate
    B) send back
    C) segregate
    D) turbulence

14. The word **intervene** is closest in meaning to

    A) intercede
    B) concern
    C) disperse
    D) advent

15. The word **comprehensive** is closest in meaning to

    A) impoverish
    B) hereditary
    C) inevitable
    D) reciprocal

Drill 27

16. The word **onset** is closest in meaning to

    A) reciprocal
    B) egalitarian
    C) beginning
    D) coincide

17. The word **tumultuous** is closest in meaning to

    A) disparate
    B) derived
    C) replete
    D) chaos

18. The word **facet** is closest in meaning to

    A) mutual
    B) nascent
    C) aspect
    D) nascent

19. The word **pinnacle** is closest in meaning to

    A) content
    B) reflective
    C) evolve
    D) top

20. The word **quandary** is closest in meaning to

    A) dilemma
    B) alluvial
    C) diverting
    D) surplus

1. B 2. A 3. C 4. C 5. D 6. D 7. A 8. A 9. B 10. C
11. A 12. C 13. B 14. A 15. D 16. C 17. D 18. C 19. D 20. A

TOEFL iBT/ TOEIC WORDS (Day 28)

1. Persistent [per-**sis**-tuhnt]
   adj def: lasting or enduring tenaciously.
        synonyms: determined, continuous, assiduous
        antonyms: lazy, surrendering, yielding
        Most high school students in the United States make a *persistent* and ceaseless effort to improve their SAT scores.

2. Endure [en-**door**]
   verb def: to hold out against; sustain without impairment.
        synonyms: abide, accustom, allow, brave, brook
        antonyms: discontinue
        Many people have *endured* great financial pressures because of the decline in the economy.

3. Manipulate [muh-**nip**-yuh-leyt]
   verb def: to manage or influence skillfully.
        synonyms: employ, feel, form, operate
        antonyms: leave alone
        When he was a little boy, Victor learned to *manipulate* a tractor because his father desperately needed his help.

4. Rupture [**ruhp**-cher]
   noun def: the act of breaking or bursting.
        synonyms: break, split, breach, cleft
        antonyms: closing, closure
        The flood caused the *rupture* of the dam in a small town.

5. Supposition [suhp-uh-**zish**-uhn]
   noun def: the act of supposing.
        synonyms: assumption, hypothesis, doubt, idea
        antonyms: fact, knowledge, proof, reality
        The *supposition* Paul made in a faculty meeting last week proved correct.

6. Hallmark [**hawl**-mahrk]
   noun def: an official mark or stamp.
        synonyms: symbol, authentication, certification, indication
        It is said that accuracy is a *hallmark* of good scholarship.

TOEFL iBT/ TOEIC WORDS (Day 28)

7. Standstill [**stand**-stil]
   noun def: the state of cessation of movement or action.
   synonyms: stop, cessation, deadlock, delay
   antonyms: advance, progress
   When he was on his way to work, Charles encountered a car accident that had brought traffic to a *standstill*.

8. Stride [strahyd]
   verb def: to walk with long steps vigorously.
   synonyms: march, parade, stalk, parade
   The teacher *strode* across the classroom toward one of her students who wasn't paying attention in her class.

9. Prejudice [**prej**-uh-dis]
   noun def: a bias, judgmental, or unfavorable opinion.
   The war against *prejudice* turned out to be never-ending.

10. Submerge [suhb-**murj**]
   verb def: to put or sink below the surface.
   synonyms: descend, immerse, inundate
   antonyms: dry, surface
   His aspirations slowly *submerged* under the necessity of making a living.

11. Float [floht]
   verb def: to rest or remain on the surface of a liquid.
   synonyms: drift, glide, hang, hover
   antonyms: drown, sink
   He found that an empty boat was *floating* down the river.

12. Shallow [**shal**-oh]
   adj def: of little depth; not deep.
   synonyms: empty, cursory, depthless, superficial
   antonyms: deep
   Taking *shallow* breaths, Jefferson resumed talking with his children.

TOEFL iBT/ TOEIC WORDS (Day 28)

13. Victim [**vik**-tim]
    noun def: a person who suffers from a destructive action.
        synonyms: casualty, dupe, fatality, gambit
        antonyms: criminal, culprit
        In NYC, there are a lot of family members of 9.11 *victims* suffering from terrible memories of their loss.

14. Snap [snap]
    verb def: to make a sudden, sharp, distinct sound.
        synonyms: ease, breeze, no problem
        antonyms: difficulty
        The boy *snapped* the wing off his toy airplane.

15. Specimen [**spes**-uh-muhn]
    noun def: a part or an individual taken as exemplifying a whole mass.
        synonyms: example, sample, case, representative
        An increasing number of architects have said that the church in a small town is a magnificent *specimen* of baroque architecture.

16. Apprehend [ap-ri-**hend**]
    verb def: to take into custody; arrest by legal warrant.
        synonyms: bag, bust, capture, collar, grab
        antonyms: lose, not catch
        The local police made a lot of effort to *apprehend* the burglars.

17. Constrict [kuhn-**strikt**]
    verb def: to draw or press in.
        synonyms: shrink, press, contract
        antonyms: expand, free, loosen, open
        The decline in the economy has *constricted* job opportunities in this country.

18. Secrete [si-**kreet**]
    verb def: to discharge, generate, or release by the process of secretion. (**)
        Insulin is *secreted* in response to rising levels of glucose in the blood.

19. Digestive [dih-**jes**-tiv]
    adj def: pertaining digestion.
        Steve regularly takes a *digestive* pill because he has had a serious stomach problem.

TOEFL iBT/ TOEIC WORDS (Day 28)

20. Antiseptic [an-tuh-**sep**-tik]
adj def: uncontaminated; antibiotic; aseptic; disinfectant.
Chefs are required to wear *antiseptic* white jackets while preparing food in the kitchen.

21. Undaunted [uhn-**dawn**-tid]
adj def: undismayed; not discouraged; not forced to.
  synonyms: brave, audacious, intrepid, fearless
  antonyms: cowardly, shrinking
Although she was outnumbered by her opponents, she seemed to be *undaunted*.

22. Salubrious [suh-**loo**-bree-uhs]
adj def: favorable to or promoting health. (***)
  synonyms: healthful, invigorating, beneficial, hygiene
Run down and sickly, Rita hoped that the fresh mountain air would have a *salubrious* effect on her health.

23. Fierce [feers]
adj def: menacingly wild, savage, or hostile.
  synonyms: angry, awful, boisterous, bold
  antonyms: calm, gentle, meek, nonviolent, peaceful
The suggestion introduced by my colleague in the conference appeared to face *fierce* opposition.

24. Boggy [**bog**-ee]
adj def: containing or full of bogs.
It is extremely difficult driving through the *boggy* terrain.

25. Scorch [skawrch]
verb def: to affect by burning.
  synonyms: burn, blacken, blister, broil
  antonyms: freeze
The collar of the shirt was yellow where the iron had *scorched* it.

TOEFL iBT/ TOEIC WORDS (Day 28)

26. Clutch [kluhch]
　verb def: to seize with or as with the hands.
　　　synonyms: catch, clasp, clinch, embrace
　　　antonyms: let go, unfasten
　　　The bird swooped down and *clutched* its prey with its claws.

27. Abhor [ab-**hawr**]
　verb def: to regard with extreme repugnance or aversion. (****)
　　　synonyms: aversion, hatred, detest, loathe, abominate
　　　antonyms: admire, approve, cherish, adore, desire
　　　We believe we know that Americans *abhor* extremes and mistrust ideology.
　　　　　　　　　　　　　　— David Frum, *Atlantic*, March 1995

　　　After she repeatedly failed to learn the Pythagorean theorem, Susan began to *abhor* geometry.

28. Dread [dred]
　verb def: to fear greatly.
　　　synonyms: awful, dire, frightful, terrible
　　　antonyms: pleasant, pleasing, wonderful
　　　Elena really *dreaded* to think that she might fail the final test.

29. Seize [seez]
　verb def: to take hold of suddenly. (**)
　　　synonyms: grab, take, appropriate, clasp
　　　antonyms: give, offer, release
　　　Seizing the moment, Chris introduced herself to the famous film director.

30. Ultimate [**uhl**-tuh-mit]
　adj def: last; further; decisive; maximum.
　　　The Gulf Coast of Florida has been called the *ultimate* vacation spot in the United States.

31. Legislative [**lej**-is-ley-tiv]
　adj def: having the function of making laws.
　　　synonyms: lawmaking, congressional, decreeing, enacting
　　　Although he was very young and even childish, he showed a lot of interest in politics and the *legislative* process.

TOEFL iBT/ TOEIC WORDS (Day 28)

32. Mechanism [mek-uh-niz-uhm]
noun def: an assembly of moving parts.
> synonyms: apparatus, appliance, components
> A variety of case studies show that humans are born with psychological *mechanisms* for dealing with a tragic loss.

33. Dissent [dih-sent]
verb def: to differ in sentiment or opinion. (**)
> synonyms: conflict, denial, difference, contention
> antonyms: approval, agreement, concurrence
> Two of the justices *dissented* from the majority decision.

34. Proponent [pruh-poh-nuhnt]
noun def: a person who puts forward a proposition.
> synonyms: advocate, backer, champion, defender
> antonyms: enemy, foe, opponent
> There were a lot of vocal *proponents* of the use of electric-powered cars.

35. Overarch [oh-ver-ahrch]
verb def: to span with or like an arch.
> A new bridge *overarches* the river that divides our city in two.

36. Ratify [rat-uh-fahy]
verb def: to confirm by expressing consent.
> synonyms: affirm, authorize, approval,
> antonyms: deny, disaffirm, disagree, renounce
> Lincoln's home state of Illinois was the first to *ratify* the 13th Amendment to the U.S. Constitution, which provided for the abolition of slavery.

37. Provision [pruh-vizh-uhn]
noun def: supplying; arrangement; foundation. (**)
> The President, of all people, should know how difficult it is to take care of basic things like, say, prescription drugs for the elderly or shelter from the storm — especially if your government places a low priority on the efficient *provision* of public services and a high priority on the care and feeding of cronies ...
>
> — Joe Klein, *Time*, 6 Feb. 2006

TOEFL iBT/ TOEIC WORDS (Day 28)

38. Prerogative [pri-**rog**-uh-tiv]
   noun def: an exclusive right. (***)
        synonyms: privilege, authority, claim, immunity
        antonyms: duty, obligation
        It is acknowledged that the royal *prerogative* exempts the king from taxation.

        That sense that the future may not last for long is often assumed to be a *prerogative* of youth, the dialectical complement of another misconception the young are noted for—the conviction that they are immortal.
                      — Thomas M. Disch, *Atlantic*, February 1992

39. Censure [**sen**-sher]
   noun def: strong or vehement expression of disapproval. (**)
        synonyms: criticize, reproach, reprimand, admonish
        antonyms: compliment, praise, endorsement, ratification
        The country faced international *censure* for its alleged involvement in the assassination.

40. Appease [uh-**peez**]
   verb def: to bring to a state of peace, quiet. (****)
        synonyms: quiet, ease, calm, contentment
        antonyms: aggravate, annoy, incite
        We all sang lullabies to try to *appease* the bawling infant.

        But I imagine he and his siblings, who profited handsomely from the sale, have mixed emotions. They may be sad they had to sell, yet relieved that they are no longer under pressure to *appease* Wall Street's demand for growth and profits.
                      — James Laube, *Wine Spectator*, 31 Mar. 2005

41. Autonomous [aw-**ton**-uh-muhs]
   adj def: independent; free; self-governing; sovereign.
        Native Americans are regarded as *autonomous* in many respects and thus not subject to a number of state and local laws.

42. Delegate [**del**-i-git]
   noun def: a person designated to act for or represent another.
        synonyms: representative, agent. ambassador
        Allison was selected as a *delegate* to the conference held in Washington D.C

TOEFL iBT/ TOEIC WORDS (Day 28)

43. Sovereign [sov-rin]
noun def: dominant; effective; absolute. (***)

The king did not take kindly to those who refused to recognize his *sovereign* power.

Ricky Martin, *sovereign* of Latin pop culture, is back.
— Raquel Cepeda, *Vibe*, May 1999

44. Veto [vee-toh]
noun def: the power or right vested in one branch of a government to cancel a decision. (**)
synonyms: refusal, ban, denial
antonyms: allow, approve, permit

The president has decided to exercise his *veto* over a new bill.

45. Amend [uh-mend]
noun def: repair of a relationship or situation.
synonyms: alter, modify, rephrase, repair
antonyms: blemish, corrupt, debase

By apologizing for being late to his boss, he made *amends* in an uncomfortable situation.

46. Desert [dih-zurt]
verb def: to leave; run away; fall. (***)

Boulet saw his longtime partner *desert* him in the midst of the storm and had his wife and daughter skip town in its aftermath.
— Mike Flaherty, *TV Guide*, 10-16 Sept. 2007

47. Innate [ih-neyt]
adj def: inherited; native; congenital. (**)

Daniel appeared to have an *innate* gift to learn to play the piano.

48. Expedient [ik-spee-dee-uhnt]
adj def: advisable; beneficial; discreet. (***)

It was considered more *expedient* to send the fruit directly to the retailer instead of though a middleman.

Marley found it *expedient* to maintain social relationships with gunmen and politicians from both political parties.
— Robert Palmer, *Rolling Stone*, 24 Feb. 1994

TOEFL iBT/ TOEIC WORDS (Day 28)

49. Extraneous [ik-**strey**-nee-uhs]
  adj def: introduced or coming from without. (***)
      synonyms: unneeded, irrelevant, accidental, extra
      antonyms: appropriate, basic, essential
    When none of the committee members acknowledged that she had even spoken, June realized that her presence at the meeting was completely *extraneous*.

    Obviously, some degree of packaging is necessary to transport and protect the products we need, but all too often manufacturers add *extraneous* wrappers over wrappers and layers of unnecessary plastic.
                          — Al Gore, *An Inconvenient Truth*, 2006

50. Introvert [**in**-truh-vurt]
  noun def: egoist; loner; narcissist; solitary; a shy person.
    Mr. Ford seemed to be an extremely *introvert* in spite of the fact that he has been known as an eloquent speaker.

> ❝ As an attorney, I know the importance of vocabulary as a building block of effective communication. This book is not only excellent for TOEFL iBT/ TOEIC preparation but will also lay a foundation for a student's life. Highly recommended. ❞
>
> ---
>
> Isabella Kim
> Attorney, Bellevue, WA, USA
> Tufts University, Suffolk University Law School

TOEFL iBT/ TOEIC WORDS (Day 28)

❝ *Once you open this book, you will be more familiar with TOEFL iBT/ TOEIC. A number of students' TOEFL iBT/ TOEIC scores have climbed significantly due to the vocabulary that they have learned in Mr. Shin's lectures. Because the vocabulary in Mr. Shin's lectures covers most of those on the SAT, it is very helpful for the students. I would be happy to recommend this book to those who are planning to take the TOEFL iBT/ TOEIC exam shortly. You will be surprised to see how much you have improved with this book.* ❞

_____

Jisu Yoo
Psychology, Indiana University Bloomington, IN, USA

Drill 28

1. The word **manipulate** is closest in meaning to

    A) advent
    B) impoverish
    C) hereditary
    D) control

2. The word **submerge** is closest in meaning to

    A) inevitable
    B) reciprocal
    C) inundate
    D) coincide

3. The word **shallow** is closest in meaning to

    A) disparate
    B) depthless
    C) derived
    D) replete

4. The word **apprehend** is closest in meaning to

    A) arrest
    B) mutual
    C) nascent
    D) contend

5. The word **secrete** is closest in meaning to

    A) eminence
    B) exotic
    C) extravagance
    D) conceal

Drill 28

6. The word **antiseptic** is closest in meaning to?

    A) manifest
    B) reflective
    C) aseptic
    D) evolve

7. The word **salubrious** is closest in meaning to

    A) fertile
    B) divert
    C) wholesome
    D) irrigate

8. The word **undaunted** is closest in meaning to

    A) alluvial
    B) brave
    C) scarce
    D) surplus

9. The word **abhor** is closest in meaning to

    A) hatred
    B) disperse
    C) catastrophic
    D) geothermal

10. The word **fierce** is closest in meaning to

    A) violent
    B) vent
    C) diminish
    D) extinct

Drill 28

11. The word **ultimate** is closest in meaning to

    A) clarity
    B) stun
    C) turbulent
    D) final

12. The word **dissent** is closest in meaning to

    A) rigid
    B) arduous
    C) disagree
    D) pathetic

13. The word **proponent** is closest in meaning to

    A) extra
    B) extreme
    C) support
    D) extraordinary

14. The word **ratify** is closest in meaning to

    A) affix
    B) approve
    C) incentive
    D) alloy

15. The word **prerogative** is closest in meaning to

    A) privilege
    B) antecedent
    C) milieu
    D) replace

Drill 28

16. The word **censure** is closest in meaning to

    A) blame
    B) adopt
    C) conceive
    D) boast

17. The word **appease** is closest in meaning to

    A) tension
    B) calm
    C) emerge
    D) assimilate

18. The word **sovereign** is closest in meaning to

    A) hegemony
    B) realm
    C) absolute power
    D) forfeit

19. The word **veto** is closest in meaning to

    A) preeminence
    B) vaunt
    C) refusal
    D) confine

20. The word **extraneous** is closest in meaning to

    A) turbulent
    B) irrelevant
    C) frigid
    D) arduous

1. D 2. C 3. B 4. A 5. D 6. C 7. C 8. B 9. A 10.A
11. D 12. C 13. C 14. B 15. A 16. A 17. B 18. C 19. C 20. B

TOEFL iBT/ TOEIC WORDS (Day 29)

1. Furnish [**fur**-nish]
　　verb　def: to provide with necessities.
　　　　　synonyms: supply, decorate, array, equip
　　　　　Mario has been depressed that he is unable to *furnish* his new rented apartment.

2. Compliance [kuhm-**playh**-uhns]
　　noun　def: the act of conforming or yielding.
　　　　　synonyms: agreement, assent, concession, conformity
　　　　　antonyms: defiance, denial, dissent, fight
　　　　　There has been a low rate of *compliance* with the new law.

3. Flaw [flaw]
　　noun　def: the feature that mars the perfection of something.
　　　　　synonyms: imperfection, blemish, defect, fault
　　　　　antonyms: fine point, perfection, strength
　　　　　Harrison found that there were a lot of different *flaws* in his plan.

4. Comparison [kuhm-**par**-uh-suhn]
　　noun　def: the act of comparing.
　　　　　synonyms: contrasting, allegory, association, collating
　　　　　The researchers spent numerous hours gathering a *comparison* of the data from the two studies.

5. Regression [ri-**gresh**-uhn]
　　noun　def: the act of going back to a previous place.
　　　　　synonyms: return, reversion, retrogression
　　　　　A group of psychologists found that the boys often undergo *regression* to really childish behavior when they are put in large groups.

6. Assemble [uh-**sem**-buhl]
　　verb　def: to come together; bring together; congregate; amass.
　　　　　synonyms: amass, bunch, collect, convoke
　　　　　antonyms: disperse, scatter
　　　　　Last night, Tino *assembled* his new bicycle in the garage.

7. Impartial [im-**pahr**-shuhl]

adj def: fair; unprejudiced; candid. (***)

1 Peter 1:17 says that God judges people's work *impartially*.

If the judge is not *impartial,* then all of her rulings are questionable.

8. Pledge [plej]

noun def: a solemn promise or agreement.

synonyms: assurance, covenant, guarantee, oath
antonyms: break

Unlike other candidates, Montgomery promised to fulfill a campaign *pledge* to cut taxes.

9. Bicameral [bahy-**kam**-er-uhl]

adj def: having two branches, chambers, or houses as legislative bodies.

Most of the countries in the word have a *bicameral* legislature.

10. Consequential [kon-si-**kwen**-shuhl]

adj def: following as an effect, result.

synonyms: significant, considerable, eventful, important
antonyms: insignificant, uneventful, unimportant

Steve Jobs made many *consequential* innovations in computer software.

11. Explicit [ik-**splis**-it]

adj def: fully and clearly expressed or demonstrated. (****)

synonyms: specific, unambiguous, accurate, absolute, certain
antonyms: ambiguous, confused, equivocal, implicit

The owners of the house left a list of *explicit* instructions detailing their house-sitters' responsibilities.

From closer restrictions on sexually *explicit* writing came the success, in the mid-19th century, of the novelist George Thompson, who combined graphically violent scenes set in urban dystopias with coy peekaboo references to sex.

— Susan Dominus, *New York Times Book Review,* 5 Apr. 2009

TOEFL iBT/ TOEIC WORDS (Day 29)

12. Adjudicate [uh-**joo**-di-keyt]
verb def: to pronounce; decree; settle; determine.
synonyms: arbitrate, decide, determine, mediate
antonyms: defer, dodge, ignore
The Board of Education will *adjudicate* when claims are made against secondary school teachers.

13. Subsequent [**suhb**-si-kwuhnt]
adj def: occurring or coming later. (**)
synonyms: after, consecutive, consequent, ensuing
antonyms: antecedent, earlier, former
Subsequent to their arrival in Chicago, they bought a new car.

Her *subsequent* account of her ordeal, "The Upstairs Room" (1972), was a young adult tour de force, winning a Newberry Honor and other awards. Compared with Anne Frank's "Diary of a Young Girl," it is sparer and sterner.
— Leslie Garis, *New York Times Book Review*, 22 Feb. 2009

14. Inalienable [in-**eyl**-yuh-nuh-buhl]
adj def: not transferable to another. (***)
synonyms: absolute, inherent, basic, entailed
antonyms: acquired, changeable, impermanent, transitory
The right to survive must be the first on any list of *inalienable* right.

15. Controversy [**kon**-truh-vur-see]
noun def: a prolonged public dispute.
synonyms: strife, argument, contention
antonyms: accord, forbearance, harmony, peace
The principal made the final decision that aroused much *controversy* among the students and teachers.

16. Inanimate [in-**an**-uh-mit]
adj def: cold; dead; defunct; dull.
"Pathetic fallacy" is the literary term for the ascription of human feelings or motives to *inanimate* natural elements.

17. Convention [kuhn-**ven**-shuhn]
noun def: an agreement, compact.
> synonyms: agreement, contract, tradition
> antonyms: disagreement, discord
> They say that school is just as important for teaching children social codes and *conventions* as for teaching math and literature.

18. Sensuous [**sen**-shoo-uhs]
adj def: pertaining to sensible objects.
> synonyms: flesh, hedonistic, luscious, lush
> antonyms: luscious, carnal
> The boom box began to produce the *sensuous* sound of jazz music that created a warm atmosphere.

19. Temperate [**tem**-per-it]
adj def: not extreme in opinion. (**)
> synonyms: calm, checked, moderate, constant
> antonyms: immoderate, stormy, violent
> Harry has been widely known as a *temperate* man since he was a college student.

20. Impermanent [im-**pur**-muh-nuhnt]
adj def: transitory; temporary; interim. (***)
> Marc's love toward Kelly turned out to be an *impermanent* fancy.

21. Pastoral [**pas**-ter-uhl]
adj def: having simplicity; charm; serenity.
> synonyms: peaceful, agrarian, bucolic, idyllic, provincial
> antonyms: agitated, bustling, busy, urban
> Tony and Miranda have enjoyed living in the house situated in a charming *pastoral* setting.

22. Intermediate [in-ter-**mee**-dee-it]
adj def: being, situated, or acting between two points.
> synonyms: middle, between, center, common
> antonyms: end, extreme
> Bob is allowed to take *intermediate* French because he already passed beginning French last semester.

TOEFL iBT/ TOEIC WORDS (Day 29)

23. Pulverize [**puhl**-vuh-rahyz]
   verb def: to reduce to dust or powder. (**)
        synonyms: abrade, atomize, bray, break
        antonyms: build, construct, create
        Kevin was a veteran standup comedian who could *pulverize* any audience in seconds.

24. Communal [kuh-**myoon**-l]
   adj def: used or shared in common by everyone.
        synonyms: common, collective, shared, conjoint
        antonyms: individual, personal, community
        The tribe lived in *communal* huts.

25. Idiosyncrasy [id-ee-uh-**sing**-kruh-see]
   noun def: a characteristic, habit, mannerism, or the like. (***)
        synonyms: affectation, bit, distinction, eccentricity, habit
        Her habit of using "like" in every sentence was just one of her *idiosyncrasies*.

        His numerous *idiosyncrasies* included a fondness for wearing bright-green shoes with mauve socks.

26. Emphasize [**em**-fuh-sahyz]
   verb def: to give emphasis to; lay stress upon.
        synonyms: stress, accent, affirm, articulate
        antonyms: depreciate, forget, ignore, undertake
        Before she went out with Drew, she *emphasized* that she had to be home early.

27. Dictum [**dik**-tuhm]
   noun def: an authoritative pronouncement; judicial assertion.
        synonyms: proverb, adage, aphorism, moral
        There are numerous *dictums* that advise people what to do and how to do it.

28. Edifice [**ed**-uh-fis]
   noun def: a building, especially one of large size.
        synonyms: erection, pile, structure
        The Metropolitan Museum in NYC is a magnificent *edifice* with a domed ceiling.

TOEFL iBT/ TOEIC WORDS (Day 29)

29. Impeccable [im-**pek**-uh-buhl]
   adj def: faultless; flawless; irreproachable. (****)
        The dress rehearsal was *impeccable*; nothing needed to be changed before the actual performance.

        Grandfather found a reason to slip in every five minutes. The empty soda cans had to be removed, the bowl of potato chips refreshed. He was sure that he moved unnoticed, like an *impeccable* waiter of the old school ...
                            — Darryl Pinckney, *High Cotton*, 1992

30. Slipshod [**slip**-shod]
   adj def: careless; untidy; slovenly.(***)
        antonyms: careful, neat, polished, well-done
        Jefferson was really surprised to find that Stephen did a *slipshod* job.

31. Ruminant [roo-muh-nuhnt]
   noun def: contemplative; meditative. (**)
        Dr. Phil had been considered as a *ruminant* scholar before he retired.

32. Duress [doo-**res**]
   noun def: compulsion by threat or force, coercion.
        synonyms: threat, hardship, bondage, confinement
        Fearing that the dean might expel him, he confessed to cheating on the test, not willingly but under *duress*.

33. Abridge [uh-**brij**]
   verb def: to shorten by omissions while retaining the basic nature of. (***)
        synonyms: abbreviate, abstract, compress, condense
        antonyms: add, enlarge, expand, extend
        The Bill of Right is designed to hinder Congress from *abridging* the rights of Americans.

        The teacher assigned an *abridged* version of *Tristram Shandy* to her class, as the original was very long.

TOEFL iBT/ TOEIC WORDS (Day 29)

34. Egregious [ih-**gree**-juhs]
adj def: extraordinary in some bad way; glaring. (***)
    synonyms: bad, outrageous, arrant, atrocious
    antonyms: arrant, capital, deplorable, extreme
It is hard to imagine how the editor could allow such an *egregious* error to appear.

… the public perception is that too many corporate executives have committed *egregious* breaches of trust by cooking the books, shading the truth, and enriching themselves with huge stock-option profits while shareholders suffered breathtaking losses.
    — John A. Byrne *et al.*, *Business Week*, 6 May 2002

35. Gullible [**guhl**-uh-buhl]
adj def: easily deceived or cheated. (*****)
    synonyms: naïve, credulous, foolish, green
    antonyms: astute, discerning, perceptive, suspicious
William was not *gullible* enough to believe something that outrageous.

The *gullible* landlord believed that Rich's story that he was only going away for a few days, despite the moving boxes that littered the apartment.

36. Gregarious [gri-**gair**-ee-uhs]
adj def: fond of the company of others; social. (****)
    synonyms: friendly, affable, convivial, cordial
    antonyms: cold, introverted, unsocial
Marc is naturally *gregarious*, a popular member of several clubs and a sought-after lunch companion.

[J.P.] Morgan was attracted to bright, self-possessed women who met him on his own ground, felt at home in society, and shared his *gregarious* instincts and sybaritic tastes.
    — Jean Strouse, *New Yorker*, 29 Mar. 1999

37. Heinous [**hey**-nuhs]
adj def: hateful; odious; abominable; reprehensible. (***)
    synonyms: abhorrent, abominate, accursed, atrocious
    antonyms: glorious, lovely, magnificent
Nobody could believe the *heinous* crime the baby-sitter had committed.

TOEFL iBT/ TOEIC WORDS (Day 29)

While admittedly the crimes rappers commit have often been more *heinous* than those committed by other entertainers, rappers seem to face more opprobrium. Though hip-hop has become mainstream, much of mass media still has antiquated ideas of rap music and rappers.

— *Vibe*, May 2001

38. Jeopardize [jep-er-dahyz]
verb def: to put in danger.
  synonyms: endanger, chance, gamble, imperil
  Andrew *jeopardized* his life every time he dived from the tower.

39. Languid [lang-gwid]
adj def: lacking in vigor or vitality. (****)
  synonyms: apathetic, comatose, enervate, indifferent
  antonyms: alert, animated, energetic, lively
  The hot, humid weather of late August can make anyone feel *languid*.

40. Lithe [lahyth]
adj def: bending readily; pliant; limber. (**)
  synonyms: flexible, graceful, slender
  antonyms: awkward, fat, stiff, thick
  The ballet dancer was almost as *lithe* as a cat.

  The dancer's movements were *lithe* and graceful, even when she was not performing.

41. Mollify [mol-uh-fahy]
verb def: to soften in feeling and temper. (***)
  synonyms: mitigate, soothe, allay, appease, diminish
  antonyms: agitate, depress, exasperate, harass
  The manager of the store decided to give the angry client a full refund to *mollify* him.

42. Nocturnal [nok-tur-nl]
adj def: nighttime; after dark; happening night.
  Travelers on the Underground Railroad escaped from slavery to the North by a series of *nocturnal* flights.

TOEFL iBT/ TOEIC WORDS (Day 29)

43. Opulent [op-yuh-luhnt]
   adj def: rich; wealthy; affluent; abundant; copious.
   The mansion of newspaper tycoon Hearst is famous for its *opulent* décor.

44. Repudiate [ri-pyoo-dee-yet]
   verb def: to reject as having no authority or binding force. (***)
      synonyms: abandon, abjure, cast off, defect
      antonyms: admit, approve
   The old woman's claim that she was Russian royalty was *repudiated* when DNA tests showed she was not related to them.

   During the Algerian war of independence, the United States had also *repudiated* France's claimed right to attack a town in neighboring Tunisia that succored Algerian guerrillas ...
   — Christopher Hitchens, *Harper's*, February 2001

45. Tenacious [tuh-ney-shuhs]
   adj def: holdng fast; retentive. (****)
      synonyms: adamant, bound, fast, determined, coherent
      antonyms: surrendering, weak, yield
   Tenacious in pursuit of her goal, she applied for the grant unsuccessfully four times before it was finally approved.

   But raw capitalism has also proved *tenacious*, evolving its own means of endlessly restimulating consumption ...
   — Nicholas Fraser, *Harper's*, November 2003

46. Unpalatable [uhn-pal-uh-tuh-buhl]
   adj def: distasteful; unpleasant. (*****)
   Although Scott agreed with the candidate on many issues, he wouldn't vote for him, because he found the candidate's position on capital punishment *unpalatable*.

47. Vivacious [vi-vey-shuhs]
   adj def: lively; spirited; active; animate. (***)
      synonyms: active, alert, cheerful, ebullient
      antonyms: boring, dispirited, dull
   She was so *vivacious* and outgoing, always ready to try something new.

TOEFL iBT/ TOEIC WORDS (Day 29)

Historically, in nations where city economies are dying and where, as well, cities are drained in service to transactions of decline, one city remains *vivacious* longest: the capital city.

— Jane Jacobs, *Cities and the Wealth of Nations*, (1984) 1985

48. Wrath [rahth]
noun def: strong, stern, or fierce anger. (**)
    synonyms: acrimony, asperity, dander, displeasure
    antonyms: happiness, love
    He denounced the criminals in a speech filled with righteous *wrath*.

That winter it rained in Los Angeles for three months straight, as if I had brought with me a terrible *wrath* that somehow agitated the atmosphere, releasing a flood of rain.

— Patrick Moore, *Tweaked*, 2006

49. Zealous [zel-uhs]
adj def: enthusiastic; ardent; avid; dedicated. (***)
    Sophie was a *zealous* supporter of the cause who never missed a rally.

I was *zealous* in my demands on my sisters for promptness in rehearsals. I was passionate, intolerant of small talk, hungry for knowledge, grabby, bossy, precocious.

— Lynn Margulis, *Curious Minds*, (2004) 2005

50. Wan [won]
adj def: showing or suggesting ill health; fatigue. (****)
    synonyms: colorless, weak, anemic, ashen
    antonyms: colorful, strong, flushed
    The sick child had a *wan* face.

Drill 29

1. The word **flaw** is closest in meaning to

    A) defect
    B) grain
    C) rigid
    D) arduous

2. The word **assemble** is closest in meaning to

    A) pathetic
    B) affixed
    C) gather
    D) incentive

3. The word **impartial** is closest in meaning to

    A) alloy
    B) brittle
    C) antecedent
    D) fair

4. The word **pledge** is closest in meaning to

    A) milieu
    B) guarantee
    C) replace
    D) adopt

5. The word **explicit** is closest in meaning to

    A) clarify
    B) conceive
    C) boast
    D) emerge

6. The word **subsequent** is closest in meaning to

   A) hegemony
   B) dominate
   C) later
   D) vaunt

7. The word **inalienable** is closest in meaning to

   A) parallel
   B) precipitate
   C) inseparable
   D) induce

8. The word **sensuous** is closest in meaning to

   A) anomalous
   B) coincide
   C) decline
   D) fleshy

9. The word **convention** is closest in meaning to

   A) tradition
   B) replenish
   C) resume
   D) profound

10. The word **temperate** is closest in meaning to

    A) migrate
    B) moderate
    C) abundant
    D) sustain

Drill 29

11. The word **idiosyncrasy** is closest in meaning to

    A) oddity
    B) inhibit
    C) ascent
    D) retrieve

12. The word **dictum** is closest in meaning to

    A) eddy
    B) swirl
    C) proverb
    D) copious

13. The word **impeccable** is closest in meaning to

    A) lurk
    B) accurate
    C) disturb
    D) integrity

14. The word **slipshod** is closest in meaning to

    A) convulsive
    B) unsophisticated
    C) impulsive
    D) careless

15. The word **abridge** is closest in meaning to

    A) shorten
    B) realm
    C) spectator
    D) partaking

Drill 29

16. The word **egregious** is closest in meaning to

    A) contemporary
    B) intrinsic
    C) notorious
    D) offshoot

17. The word **gullible** is closest in meaning to

    A) intricate
    B) banal
    C) naïve
    D) mundane

18. The word **heinous** is closest in meaning to

    A) innovative
    B) terrifying
    C) juxtapose
    D) breakthrough

19. The word **languid** is closest in meaning to

    A) garner
    B) stimulate
    C) acclaim
    D) dull

20. The word **lithe** is closest in meaning to

    A) flexible
    B) disregard
    C) illustrate
    D) immune

1. A 2. C 3. D 4. B 5. A 6. C 7. C 8. D 9. A 10. B
11. A 12. C 13. B 14. D 15. A 16. C 17. C 18. B 19. D 20. A

TOEFL iBT/ TOEIC WORDS (Day 30)

1. Berate [bih-**reyt**]
verb def: to scold; rebuke; criticize. (**)
    synonyms: castigate, censure, chew, chide
    antonyms: compliment, hail, praise
    The judge angrily *berated* the two lawyers for their unprofessional behavior in court.

2. Flagrant [**fley**-gruhnt]
adj def: shockingly noticeable or evident; obvious. (***)
    synonyms: flaunt, blatant, shame, atrocious
    antonyms: concealed, disguised, hidden, mild
    Nixon was forced to resign the presidency after a series of *flagrant* crimes against U.S. Constitution.

    His *flagrant* disregard for the rules has resulted in his dismissal from the job.

3. Guileless [**gahyle**-lis]
adj def: free from guile; sincere, honest. (**)
    synonyms: candid, frank, artless, ingenuous
    antonyms: clever, crafty, cunning, deceitful
    Deborah's *guileless* personality and complete honesty make it hard for her to survive in the harsh world of politics.

4. Haughty [**haw**-tee]
adj def: disdainfully proud; snobbish; scornfully. (***)
    synonyms: arrogant, rude, imperious, lofty
    antonyms: humble, meek, timid
    The *haughty* waiter smirked when I remarked that it was odd that a French restaurant didn't even have French fries on the menu.

    The teacher resented Sally's *haughty* attitude and gave her a D for the semester.

5. Kismet [**kiz**-mit]
noun def: fate; destiny; divine.
    Anderson always said that it was *kismet* that Cooper and Vanderbilt met at a showing of their favorite movie.

TOEFL iBT/ TOEIC WORDS (Day 30)

6. Jubilant [joo-buh-luhnt]
   adj def: showing great joy, satisfaction, or triumph.
        synonyms: happy, elated, enrapture
        antonyms: depressed, sad, sorrowful, unhappy
        We were *jubilant* after our victory in the state championships.

7. Kinetic [ki-**net**-ik]
   adj def: pertaining to motion; caused by motion.
        A *kinetic* sculpture is one that moves.

8. Lethargic [luh-**thahr**-jik]
   adj def: affected with lethargy; drowsy.
        synonyms: lazy, sluggish, apathetic, comatose
        antonyms: active, busy, energetic, vital
        You'll need to move your lure as slowly as possible to tempt the *lethargic* fish into feeding...
                — Lenny Rudow, *Boating*, December 1997

9. Malleable [**mal**-ee-uh-buhl]
   adj def: capable of being extended or shaped. (**)
        synonyms: pliable, flexible, adaptable, ductile
        antonyms: firm, rigid, stiff
        Gold is so *malleable* that it can be beaten into a thin foil.

        The brothers Warner presented a flexible, *malleable* world that defied Newton, a world of such plasticity that anything imaginable was possible.
                — Billy Collins, *Wall Street Journal*, 28–29 June 2008

10. Nebulous [**neb**-yuh-luhs]
   adj def: hazy; indistinct; cloudlike. (*)
        synonyms: ambiguous, amorphous, dim, imprecise
        antonyms: apparent, definite, obvious, plain
        During the campaign, the candidate promised to fight crime. But when reporters asked for details, his plan was *nebulous* — he could not say whether he would hire more police or support longer jail sentences.

TOEFL iBT/ TOEIC WORDS (Day 30)

11. Reminiscence [rem-uh-**nis**-uhns]
   noun def: the act or process of recalling past experience, events. (**)
        The old timer's *reminiscence* of his childhood was of a time when there were no cars.

12. Obnoxious [uhb-**nok**-shuhs]
   adj def: highly objectionable or offensive. (****)
        synonyms: repulsive, abhorrent, abominable
        antonyms: agreeable, delightful, kind
        The last time Lydia went to the movies, an *obnoxious* person sitting beside her talked loudly during the entire movie.

        Let's get right into it. The title of your book, *Why We Suck*, is pretty *obnoxious*. Are we really that bad?
        — Rachel Deahl, *Boston Globe*, 30 Nov. 2008

13. Terse [turs]
   adj def: neatly or effectively concise. (***)
        synonyms: cut, brief, brusque, compact, compendium
        antonyms: lengthy, prolix, wordy
        Her *terse* style writing was widely praised for coming directly to the point.

        Everything about him is tidy, from his *terse* wit to the flecks of gray hair that fall in precise iterations around the edges of his scalp.
        — Devin Gordon, *Newsweek*, 29 July 2002

14. Tepid [**tep**-id]
   adj def: lukewarm; cool; disinterested; dull.
        Roxanne refused to take a bath in the *tepid* water, fearing that she would catch a cold.

15. Unkempt [uhn-**kempt**]
   adj def: uncared for or neglected.
        synonyms: uncared, unpolished, rough
        antonyms: kempt, neat, tidy, trim
        Sam's long hair and wrinkled shirt seemed *unkempt* to his grandmother; she told him he looked like a bum.

TOEFL iBT/ TOEIC WORDS (Day 30)

16. Querulous [**kwer**-uh-luhs]
  adj def: full of complaints, complaining. (**)
     synonyms: gauche, bemoan, critical, carping, censorious
     antonyms: cheerful, happy, easy-going
     The nursing-home attendant needed a lot of patience to care for the three *querulous,* unpleasant residents on his floor.

17. Toady [**toh**-dee]
  noun def: obsequious; flatter; sycophant. (***)
     No one liked the office *toady*, who spent most of her time complimenting the boss on what a great job he was doing.

18. Unstinting [uhn-**stin**-ting]
  adj def: giving freely; generous.
     Eleanor Roosevelt was much admired for her *unstinting* efforts on behalf of the poor.

19. Vehement [**vee**-uh-muhnt]
  adj def: passionate; zealous; ardent; impassioned. (**)
     Susan responded to the accusation of cheating with a *vehement* denial.

  Cranes rise above the old rooftops, adding new office towers and new condominiums and new malls to a city where Jonathan Swift once issued his *vehement* bulletins.
  — Pete Hamill, *Gourmet*, April 2007

20. Writhe [rahyth]
  verb def: to twist the body about, or squirm. (**)
     synonyms: agonize, bend, distort, jerk, recoil
     antonyms: be still
     After being hit by a car, the pedestrian was *writhing* in pain.

21. Zest [zest]
  noun def: keen relish; hearty enjoyment.
     synonyms: taste, flavor, piquancy, charm, ginger, interest
     antonyms: blandness, dullness
     His humor added a certain *zest* to the performance.

TOEFL iBT/ TOEIC WORDS (Day 30)

22. Bombastic [bom-**bas**-tik]
adj def: pompous; grandiloquent; orotund.

Many people believe that old-fashioned *bombastic* political speeches don't work on television, which demands a more intimate style of communication.

23. Fervent [**fur**-vuhnt]
adj def: having or showing great warmth or intensity. (*)

synonyms: enthusiastic, ardent, blazing, devout
antonyms: apathetic, cool, dispassionate

In the days just after his religious conversion, his piety was at its most *fervent*.

24. Jeer [jeer]
verb def: to speak or shout derisively; scoff.

synonyms: heckle, banter, condemn

As the foolish political candidate stumbled through his poorly written speech, the crowd began to *jeer*.

25. Fortuitous [fawr-**too**-uh-tuhs]
adj def: happening or produced by chance or accident. (***)

synonyms: lucky, accident, fluke, casual, contingent
antonyms: calculated, deliberate, designed

Rachelle got her start in the music industry when a powerful agent happened, *fortuitously,* to attend one of her gigs.

... the intensification of competition on the job market has only exacerbated our class anxiety, as hiring seems all the more uncertain if not *fortuitous*.

— Jeffrey J. Williams, *College English*, November 2003

26. Genial [**jeen**-yuhl]
adj def: warmly and pleasantly cheerful; cordial.

synonyms: affable, agreeable, amiable, cheerful, congenial
antonyms: aloof, cool, cranky, irritable, moody

A good host welcomes all visitors in a warm and *genial* fashion.

TOEFL iBT/ TOEIC WORDS (Day 30)

27. Hypocrisy [hi-**pok**-ruh-see]
   noun def: a persistence of having a virtue character, moral.
   synonyms: deceitful, pretense, affectation, bigotry
   antonyms: sincerity, truth, forthrightness
   It is not surprising that teenagers often have a keen awareness of their parents' *hypocrisies*.

28. Mendacious [men-**dey**-shuhs]
   adj def: telling lies, especially habitually; dishonest. (****)
   synonyms: deceitful, deceptive, duplicitous, equivocating, fallacious
   antonyms: frank, sincere, truthful
   So many of her stories were *mendacious* that I decided she must be a pathological liar.

   Indeed, the racist and Malthusian elements in Darwin's work are subjects on which the new secularists are either silent, delicate, or *mendacious*.
   — Eugene McCarraher, *Commonweal*, 15 June 2007

29. Meager [**mee**-ger]
   adj def: deficient in quantity or quality. (**)
   synonyms: inadequate, barren, deficient, exiguous
   antonyms: adequate, large, liberal
   Although she's now rich and famous, Miranda, unlike other successful people, always remembers her *meager* beginnings as a child from a poor family.

30. Obese [oh-**bees**]
   adj def: corpulent; outsize; plump.
   There are a lot of *obese* people suffering from anxiety-induced overeating.

31. Ratify [**rat**-uh-fahy]
   verb def: to confirm by expressing consent; approval.
   synonyms: accredit, affirm, authorize, approve.
   antonyms: deny, disaffirm, disagree, renounce
   The Senate *ratified the* treaty after only a brief debate.

32. Raze [reyz]
   verb def: to tear down; demolish; batter; demolish.
   The developer *razed* the old school building and built a high-rise condominium complex.

TOEFL iBT/ TOEIC WORDS (Day 30)

33. Temerity [tuh-**mer**-i-tee]
   noun def: reckless; boldness; foohardiness. (****)
      Only someone who didn't understand the danger would have the *temerity* to try to climb Everest without a guide.

      He defeated giant corporations—the auto industry, big pharma—back when no one else was even trying to; he had the *temerity* to believe that fighting for safety and quality and transparency was a quintessentially American thing to do.
      — Owen Gleiberman, *Entertainment Weekly*, 16 Feb. 2007

34. Surreptitious [sur-uhp-**tish**-uhs]
   adj def: acting in a stealthy way. (***)
         synonyms: sneaky, secret, clandestine, covert
         antonyms: overboard, authorized, honest, open
      A number of FBI agents believe that the apartment houses a *surreptitious* drug-dealing business.

      The letter didn't offer up the jewels, only shadowy suggestions about their disappearance, claiming that [heiress, Carolyn] Skelly, in a *surreptitious* trading of parcels with "a man in an ankle-length tweed overcoat," had left a bag full of jewelry on the floor at J.F.K.
      — Mark Seal, *Vanity Fair*, December 2001

35. Vague [veyg]
   adj def: not clearly stated or expressed.
         synonyms: ambiguous, amorphous, bewildering, doubtful
         antonyms: certain, clear, definite, sure
      Nina felt terrified when she sensed a *vague* shape in the dark.

36. Tentative [**ten**-tuh-tiv]
   adj def: done as a trial, experiment. (**)
         synonyms: conditional, experimental, dependent
         antonyms: certain, decisive, definite, final
      A firm schedule has not been established, but the dance recital has been given a *tentative* date of January 15.

      In the winter, retirees from the Midwest fill the trailer parks. They are known with *tentative* affection as snowbirds.
      — William Langewiesche, *Atlantic*, June 1992

TOEFL iBT/ TOEIC WORDS (Day 30)

37. Withhold [with-**hohld**]
   verb def: to hold back; restrain; refrain.
        synonyms: abstain, bridle, check, conceal, constrain
        antonyms: let go, release
        She has $20 *withheld* from her paycheck every week.

38. Adulation [ah-ju-la-shen]
   noun def: extreme admiration. (****)
        Few young actors have received greater *adulation* than did Marlon Brando after his performance in *A Streetcar Named Desire*.

39. Buttress [**buh**-tris]
   noun def: support built to steady a structure.
        synonyms: brace, support, strut, abutment
        antonyms: let down, weaken
        The endorsement of the American Medical Association is a powerful *buttress* for the claims made about this new medicine.

40. Consternation [kon-ster-**ney**-shuhn]
   noun def: a sudden, alarming amazement. (*****)
        synonyms: dismay, distress, anxiety, awe
        antonyms: calm, composure, happiness, tranquility
        When a voice in the back of the church shouted out, "I know why they should not be married!" the entire gathering was thrown into *consternation*.

        The fact that the exact depth was recorded on the bottles was the source of considerable *consternation* among the admirals presiding over the Navy inquiry last week. The depth an attack sub can reach is supposed to be classified... .
                    — Karen Breslau *et al.*, *Newsweek*, 2 Apr. 2001

41. Alacrity [uh-**lak**-ri-tee]
   noun def: cheerful readiness, promptness.
        synonyms: liveliness, promptness, briskness, eagerness
        antonyms: apathy, aversion, disinclination, dullness
        Jefferson and I accepted John's invitation with *alacrity*.

TOEFL iBT/ TOEIC WORDS (Day 30)

42. Heterogeneous [het-er-uh-**jee**-nee-uhs]
    adj def: different in kind; unlike; incongruous.
        synonyms: assorted, amalgamate, composite, varied
        antonyms: identical, pure, single, uniform
        The conference was attended by a *heterogeneous* group of artists, politicians, and social climbers.

43. Jaundiced [**jawn**-dist]
    adj def: affected with or colored by or as if by jaundice.
        synonyms: tainted, prejudiced, biased, disapproving
        antonyms: clean, fresh, unbiased, unprejudiced
        She seemed to have an extremely *jaundiced* view of politics and politicians.

44. Longevity [lon-**jev**-i-tee]
    noun def: durability; endurance; long life.
        synonyms: durability, endurance, lastingness
        The *longevity* of a car's tires depends on how the car is driven.

45. Mandate [**man**-deyt]
    noun def: authority; order; check; charge.
        The new policy on gays in the military went into effect as soon as the president issued his *mandate* about it.

46. Mercurial [mer-**kyoor**-ee-uhl]
    adj def: flighty; temperamental; buoyant; capricious; changeable; volatile. (**)
        The *mercurial* personality of Robin Williams, with his many voices and styles, made him perfect for the role of the ever-changing genie in Aladdin.

47. Truncate [**truhng**-keyt]
    verb def: to shorten by cutting off a part. (**)
        synonyms: abridge, clip, crop, curtail, pare, prune
        antonyms: elongate, expand, lengthen, stretch
        Marc decided not to *truncate* a long and detailed explanation about the problems his family was facing.

48. Nonchalant [non-shuh-**lahnt**]
adj def: coolly unconcerned, indifferent, or unexcited. (****)
synonyms: airy, aloof, apathetic, calm
antonyms: intense, jumpy, nervous
Unlike the other players on the football team, who pumped their fists when their names were announced, John ran on the field with a *nonchalant* wave.

In those stories, we already find the qualities the world would come to know as "Kafkaesque": the *nonchalant* intrusion of the bizarre and horrible into everyday life, the subjection of ordinary people to an inscrutable fate.
— Adam Kirsch, *New York Times Book Review*, 4 Jan. 2009

49. Ostracize [**os**-truh-sahyz]
verb def: to exclude, banish, or expatriate from society.
synonyms: exile, avoid, deport, exclude
antonyms: embrace, welcome
His friends *ostracized* him after his father's arrest.

50. Timorous [**tim**-er-uhs]
adj def. full of fear; fearful.
synonyms: timid, fearsome
Thomas spoke with a *timorous* voice.

Drill 30

1. The word **guileless** is closest in meaning to

    A) immune
    B) greedy
    C) allege
    D) honest

2. The word **haughty** is closest in meaning to

    A) placate
    B) cherish
    C) rude
    D) absurdity

3. The word **jubilant** is closest in meaning to

    A) illustrate
    B) adapt
    C) happy
    D) convulsive

4. The word **lethargic** is closest in meaning to

    A) disease
    B) lazy
    C) juvenile
    D) prominent

5. The word **malleable** is closest in meaning to

    A) flexible
    B) conspicuous
    C) congregate
    D) carnivores

Drill 30

6. The word **obnoxious** is closest in meaning to

    A) cooperate
    B) forgo
    C) assume
    D) harmful

7. The word **terse** is closest in meaning to

    A) hover
    B) brief
    C) assume
    D) congenial

8. The word **tepid** is closest in meaning to

    A) vast
    B) sterile
    C) lukewarm
    D) monopolize

9. The word **querulous** is closest in meaning to

    A) forage
    B) complain
    C) intensify
    D) integrate

10. The word **toady** is closest in meaning to

    A) flatter
    B) intertwined
    C) intersperse
    D) colony

Drill 30

11. The word **vehement** is closest in meaning to

    A) accumulate
    B) zealous
    C) lethal
    D) equilibrium

12. The word **zest** is closest in meaning to

    A) equivalent
    B) delineate
    C) drained
    D) flavor

13. The word **fortuitous** is closest in meaning to

    A) delineate
    B) identical
    C) accidental
    D) substantial

14. The word **jeer** is closest in meaning to

    A) homeostatic
    B) wherein
    C) annual
    D) heckle

15. The word **meager** is closest in meaning to

    A) extend
    B) expulsion
    C) scanty
    D) discrepancy

Drill 30

16. The word **raze** is closest in meaning to

    A) destroy
    B) fluctuate
    C) ascend
    D) consistent

17. The word **temerity** is closest in meaning to

    A) incur
    B) consistent
    C) rashness
    D) symbiotic

18. The word **tentative** is closest in meaning to

    A) ferment
    B) conditional
    C) ingest
    D) corridor

19. The word **consternation** is closest in meaning to

    A) reinforce
    B) axis
    C) maximize
    D) dismay

20. The word **alacrity** is closest in meaning to

    A) promptness
    B) unique
    C) minute
    D) fused

1. D 2. C 3. C 4. B 5. A 6. D 7. B 8. C 9. B 10. A
11. B 12. D 13. C 14. D 15. C 16. A 17. C 18. B 19. D 20. A

TOEFL iBT/ TOEIC WORDS (Day 31)

1. Bereft [bih-**reft**]
adj def: bereaved; deprived; destitute. (**)
> Orphans sometimes grow up insecure because they are *bereft* of parental love.

> She finds the child's mother, alone, who has apparently gone into the woods just to cry. The *bereft* mother is played by Julianne Moore.
> — Stanley Kauffmann, *New Republic*, 31 Jan. 2000

2. Carping [**kahr**-ping]
adj def: characterized by fussiness or petulance. (**)
> synonyms: complaining, censorious, critical, deprecatory
> antonyms: complimentary, forgiving
> Victoria frequently met a *carping* old woman while working at a local nursery home.

> The newspaper is famous for its demanding critics, but none is harder to please than the *carping* McNamara, said to have single-handedly destroyed many acting careers.

3. Circumscribe [**sur**-kuhm-skrahyb]
verb def: to draw a line around; encircle. (**)
> synonyms: delineate, demarcate, encircle, enclose
> antonyms: free, loose, open
> Her social activities are *circumscribed* by school regulations.

4. Hedonist [**heed**-n-ist]
noun def: a person whose life is devoted to the pursuit of pleasure.
> synonyms: debauchee, epicure, gourmand, libertine
> antonyms: ascetic
> Having inherited great wealth, he chose to live the life of a *hedonist*, traveling the world in luxury.

5. Impinge [im-**pinj**]
verb def: to encroach; make an impression; strike.
> synonyms: affect, disturb, encroach, influence
> antonyms: avoid, dodge
> You have a right to do whatever you want as long as your actions don't *impinge* on the rights of others.

TOEFL iBT/ TOEIC WORDS (Day 31)

6. Liability [lahy-uh-**bil**-tee]
   noun def: responsibility; accountability; amenability
   The insurance company had a *liability* of millions of dollars after the town was destroyed by a tornado.

7. Modicum [**mod**-i-kuhm]
   noun def: atom; crumb; dash; drop. (***)
   The plan for his new business was well designed; with a *modicum* of luck, he should be successful.

8. Nurture [**nur**-cher]
   verb def: to feed and protect; support; encourage.
      synonyms: breeding, care, diet, edible
      antonyms: deprivation, ignorance, neglect
   The money given by the National Endowment for the Arts helps *nurture* local arts organizations throughout the country.

9. Notify [**noh**-tuh-fahy]
   verb def: to inform; give notice to.
      synonyms: acquaint, air, alert, announce, apprise
      antonyms: conceal, hide, suppress
   The landlord failed to *notify* the tenants of the planned demolition of the building.

10. Obsessive [uhb-**ses**-iv]
   adj def: haunted or preoccupied by an idea or feeling.
   His concern with cleanliness became so *obsessive* that he washed his hands twenty times every day.

11. Oblivious [uh-**bliv**-ee-uhs]
   adj def: unaware; ignorant; absent; abstracted. (***)
      synonyms: absent, blundering, careless, deaf, distracted
      antonyms: aware, concerned, conscious, sensitive
   Nancy was *oblivious* to the noisy squabbles of her brother and his friends.

   They were pushing and shouting and *oblivious* to anyone not in their group.
   — P. J. O'Rourke, *Rolling Stone*, 14 Nov. 1996

TOEFL iBT/ TOEIC WORDS (Day 31)

12. Portend [pawr-tend]
verb def: to indicate in advance. (**)
    synonyms: indication, augury, boding, caution
    According to folklore, a red sky at dawn *portends* a day of stormy weather.

13. Repudiate [ri-pyoo-dee-eyt]
verb def: to reject as having no authority. (***)
    synonyms: cast off, refuse, deny, reverse, revoke
    antonyms: admit, approve
    After it became known that the congressman had been a leader of the Ku Klux Klan, most politicians *repudiated* him.

    During the Algerian war of independence, the United States had also *repudiated* France's claimed right to attack a town in neighboring Tunisia that succored Algerian guerrillas ...
                — Christopher Hitchens, *Harper's*, February 2001

14. Terminate [tur-muh-neyt]
verb def: to bring to an end; put an end to.
    synonyms: stop, finish, abolish, abort, adjourn, bound
    antonyms: begin, initiate, open, start
    The nutritional-supplement company *terminated* its contract with the famous athlete.

15. Unanimous [yoo-nan-uh-muhs]
adj def: accepted; accordant; agreed; uncontested. (***)
    The city council vote to begin a recycling plan was *unanimous*.

16. Vacate [vey-keyt]
verb def: to give up possession or occupancy.
    synonyms: abandon, abrogate, annul, clear, depart
    antonyms: fill, occupy, overflow
    Alex had to *vacate* his apartment because his lease had expired.

17. Vitalize [vahyt-l-ahyz]
verb def: to give life to; make vital.
    The government's flagrant acts of injustice *vitalized* the opposition.

TOEFL iBT/ TOEIC WORDS (Day 31)

18. Consolation [kahn-suh-**ley**-shuhn]
noun def: relief; comfort; alleviation; assuagement.
Jennifer's faith was a *consolation* during his troubles.

19. Hamper [**ham**-per]
verb def: to hold back; hinder; impede.
synonyms: impede, restrict, entangle
antonyms: aid, allow, assist
The dancer's movement was *hampered* by her elaborate costume.

20. Anarchy [**an**-er-kee]
noun def: a state of society without government or law. (**)
synonyms: lawlessness, chaos, disorder, disregard
antonyms: order, rule
Several months after the Nazi government was destroyed, there was no effective government in parts of Germany, and *anarchy* ruled.

Its immigration policies in the last five years have become the envy of those in the West who see in all but the most restrictive laws the specter of terrorism and social *anarchy*.
— Caroline Moorehead, *New York Review of Books*, 16 Nov. 2006

21. Contaminate [kuhn-**tam**-uh-neyt]
verb def: to make impure or unsuitable by contact.
synonyms: adulterate, alloy, befoul, corrupt
antonyms: clean, cure, heal, purify
Chemicals dumped in a nearby forest had seeped into the soil and *contaminated* the local water supply.

22. Denigrate [**den**-i-greyt]
verb def: to speak damagingly of; criticize.
synonyms: belittle, malign, asperse, calumniate
antonyms: boost, cherish, compliment
The firm's president tried to explain his plans for improving the company without seeming to *denigrate* the work of his predecessor.

TOEFL iBT/ TOEIC WORDS (Day 31)

23. Florid [flawr-id]
    adj def: excessively ornate; showy.
        synonyms: aureate, decorative, embellished, figurative
        antonyms: unelaborated, natural, plain, undecorated
        The grand ballroom was decorated in a *florid* style.

24. Gratuitous [gruh-too-i-tuhs]
    adj def: unnecessary or unwarranted. (**)
        synonyms: unjustified
        Since her opinion was not requested, her harsh criticism of his singing seemed a *gratuitous* insult.

25. Haphazard [hap-haz-erd]
    adj def: characterized by lack of order.
        synonyms: accidental, aimless, careless, casual
        antonyms: careful, intentional, methodical, organized
        Ironically, Peter's *haphazard* artwork turned out to be fairly good.

26. Incisive [in-sahy-siv]
    adj def: intelligent; acute; clever; concise.
        Franklin settled the debate with a few *incisive* remarks that summed up the issue perfectly.

27. Negligible [neg-li-juh-buhl]
    adj def: not worth considering.
        synonyms: trifle, trivial
        antonyms: important, significant
        It is obvious from our *negligible* dropout rate that our students love our program.

28. Malevolence [muh-lev-uh-luhns]
    noun def: ill will; hatred. (**)
        Critics say that Iago, the villain in Shakespeare's *Othello*, seems to exhibit *malevolence* with no real motivation.

29. Malediction [mal-i-dik-shuhn]
    noun def: curse; anathema; damn; denunciation.
        In the fairy tale "Sleeping Beauty," the princess is trapped in a death-like sleep because of the *malediction* uttered by an angry witch.

TOEFL iBT/ TOEIC WORDS (Day 31)

30. Nonplus [non-**pluhs**]
   verb def: to render utterly perplexed. (***)
       synonyms: confuse, perplex, astonish, baffle
       antonyms: clear up, educate, enlighten
       Jenny was *nonplused* by the game of hearts and therefore lost badly.

31. Mollify [**mol**-uh-fahy]
   verb def: to soften in feeling or temper. (**)
       synonyms: pacify, soothe, abate, alleviate
       antonyms: agitate, depress, exasperate, harass
       The landlord fixed the heat, but the tenants still were not *mollified*.

32. Ominous [**om**-uh-nuhs]
   adj def: pretending evil or harm; foreboding. (***)
       synonyms: menacing, augural, baleful, baneful
       antonyms: auspicious, happy, lucky, promising
       Ominous black clouds gathered on the horizon, for a violent storm was fast approaching.

       Not many sets of initials became universally recognizable during the twentieth century, and those that did often had *ominous* overtones, from SS to KGB.
                 — Geoffrey Wheatcroft, *Atlantic*, March 2001

33. Resilient [ri-**zil**-yuhnt]
   adj def: spring back, rebounding. (*)
       synonyms: airy, flexible, buoyant, elastic
       antonyms: hard, inflexible, rigid, stiff
       A pro athlete must be *resilient,* able to lose a game and come back the next with confidence and enthusiasm.

       The tallow tree, an ornamental species introduced by Benjamin Franklin in 1772, can quickly grow to 10 meters and is *resilient* to many pests.
                 — *New Scientist*, 19-25 Aug. 2006

34. Therapeutic [ther-uh-**pyoo**-tik]
   adj def: healing; ameliorate; beneficial.
       Hot-water spas were popular in the nineteenth century among the sickly, who believed that soaking in the water had *therapeutic* effects.

TOEFL iBT/ TOEIC WORDS (Day 31)

35. Ultimate [uhl-tuh-mit]
   adj def: last; final; concluding; closing.
   The new fashions from Paris are the *ultimate* in chic.

36. Xenophobia [zen-uh-foh-bee-ah]
   noun def: an unreasonable fear or hatred of foreigners or strangers. (****)
   It is commonly thought that countries in which *xenophobia* is prevalent often have more restrictive immigration policies than countries which are more accepting of foreign influences.

37. Zealot [zel-uht]
   noun def: a person who shows zeal.
   synonyms: enthusiast, diehard, activist, fanatic
   antonyms: moderate
   The religious *zealot* had no time for those who failed to share his strongly held beliefs.

38. Writ [rit]
   noun def: command; decree; document; mandate.
   Writs are considered more legally valid than oral statements.

39. Belie [bih-lahy]
   verb def: to show to be false; contradict.
   synonyms: lie, disprove, contradict
   antonyms: attest, approve
   Julie's youthful appearance *belied* her long, distinguished career in show business.

40. Whimsical [hwim-zi-kuhl]
   adj def: given to whimsy or fanciful notion. (****)
   synonyms: playful, fanciful, amusing, caprice, erratic
   antonyms: behaving, reasonable, sensible
   He dismissed his generous gift to his college as a sentimental fancy, an old man's *whimsical* gesture.

   You can practically taste the tropics in these *whimsical* doughnuts. Ripe bananas, toasted coconut and your favorite rum transform traditional doughnuts into paradisiacal ones.
   — Janice Wald Henderson, *Chocolatier*, March 2001

TOEFL iBT/ TOEIC WORDS (Day 31)

41. Affected [uh-**fek**-tid]
   adj def: acted upon, influenced.
   > synonyms: afflicted, concerned, distressed, sympathetic, touched
   > antonyms: calm, unmoved, unperturbed
   Japanese women were taught to speak in an *affected* high-pitched voice, which was thought girlishly attractive.

42. Caustic [**kaw**-stik]
   adj def: corrosive; abrasive; acid; acerbic; erosive. (**)
   No one was safe when the satirist H.L.Mencken unleashed his *caustic* wit.

   His [Roosevelt's] *caustic* cousin, Alice Roosevelt Longworth, called him a sissy and a mama's boy.
   — Garry Wills, *Atlantic*, April 1994

43. Flamboyant [flam-**boi**-uhnt]
   adj def: strikingly bold or brilliant. (***)
   > synonyms: extravagant, theatrical, baroque
   > antonyms: calm, moderate, modest
   At *Mardi Gras*, partygoers compete to show off the most wild and *flamboyant* outfits.

   Crazy artists, or *flamboyant* ones, can be strangely comforting. We feel we understand where their visions come from; we're lulled by the symmetry of turbulent art and turbulent lives.
   — Stephen Schiff, *New Yorker*, 28 Dec. 1992–4 Jan. 1993

44. Incorrigible [in-**kawr**-i-juh-buhl]
   adj def: bad; hopeless; incurable.
   Jane is known as an *incorrigible* liar among her friends.

45. Indeterminate [in-di-**tur**-muh-nit]
   adj def: uncertain; vague; borderless.
   The college plans to enroll an *indeterminate* number of students; the size of the class will depend on the number of applicants and how many accept offers of admission.

TOEFL iBT/ TOEIC WORDS (Day 31)

46. Fraternize [frat-er-nahyz]
   verb def: to associate with; hang out; be friendly.
        Although baseball players are not supposed to *fraternize* with their opponents, players from opposing teams often chat before games.

47. Gruesome [groo-suhm]
   adj def: causing great horror.
        synonyms: horrible; awful; appalling; daunting
        antonyms: beautiful, pleasant, pretty
        The horror film was filled with *gruesome* scenes.

48. Harbinger [hahr-bin-jer]
   noun def: a person who goes ahead and makes known.
        synonyms: indication, augury, forerunner, foretoken
        The groundhog's appearance on February 2 is a *harbinger* of spring.

49. Hasty [hey-stee]
   adj def: acting or moving with speed.
        synonyms: speedy, abrupt, agile, brief
        antonyms: delayed, lazy, lingering, loitering
        Jefferson later realized that he made a *hasty* decision to quit his job.

50. Lurid [loor-id]
   adj def: gruesome; horrible; terrible; pallid; extreme.
        While the serial killer was on the loose, the newspapers were filled with *lurid* stories about his crimes.

> "This is the book that I really want to recommend to students who are planning to take the TOEFL iBT/ TOEIC test. This book was really well organized by each day and contained mostly important words that you absolutely need to know. In addition, I really enjoyed memorizing words with this book. I realized the words in this book appear in many other book,s too. As it was perfect book for me, I am sure it would be for you, too. Good luck!"

Alice Kim
Northern Valley Demarest High School, NJ, USA

TOEFL iBT/ TOEIC WORDS (Day 31)

❝ *The distinctive words that are displayed in this book go far beyond those of any other TOEFL iBT/ TOEIC books. Not only does this book contain the most common vocabulary words, but it also provides helpful exercises and drills that will inevitably boost one's score. As a former student of Mr. Shin, I strongly advise those who are preparing for the TOEFL iBT/ TOEIC exams to use this book to its maximum potential. Good luck to those who are taking the exams, and make sure to utilize the pivotal vocabulary words that are presented in this book.* ❞

Jiho Kim
Fort Lee High School, NJ, USA

Drill 31

1. The word **circumscribe** is closest in meaning to

    A) unique
    B) minute
    C) boundary
    D) pollinator

2. The word **impinge** is closest in meaning to

    A) fuse
    B) migrate
    C) metabolism
    D) encroach

3. The word **bereft** is closest in meaning to

    A) hibernate
    B) symmetry
    C) trait
    D) deprive

4. The word **nurture** is closest in meaning to

    A) edifice
    B) feed
    C) dehydrate
    D) terrestrial

5. The word **oblivious** is closest in meaning to

    A) circulatory
    B) expel
    C) forgetfulness
    D) ventilation

Drill 31

6. The word **repudiate** is closest in meaning to

    A) deny
    B) regulate
    C) prone
    D) desiccate

7. The word **terminate** is closest in meaning to

    A) end
    B) colossal
    C) inhabit
    D) impervious

8. The word **vacate** is closest in meaning to

    A) evaporate
    B) concoct
    C) abandon
    D) retain

9. The word **consolation** is closest in meaning to

    A) permanent
    B) susceptible
    C) advent
    D) relief

10. The word **denigrate** is closest in meaning to

    A) threaten
    B) belittle
    C) plague
    D) decline

Drill 31

11. The word **incisive** is closest in meaning to?

    A) acute
    B) intrinsic
    C) predisposed
    D) prolific

12. The word **malediction** is closest in meaning to

    A) adverse
    B) misgiving
    C) curse
    D) runoff

13. The word **mollify** is closest in meaning to

    A) ban
    B) employ
    C) appropriate
    D) calm

14. The word **ultimate** is closest in meaning to

    A) skeptic
    B) final
    C) effect
    D) chemical

15. The word **zealot** is closest in meaning to

    A) enthusiast
    B) erecting
    C) complement
    D) artificial

Drill 31

16. The word **whimsical** is closest in meaning to

    A) contingent
    B) caprice
    C) render
    D) exterminate

17. The word **belie** is closest in meaning to

    A) lie
    B) integrate
    C) hypothesize
    D) intuitive

18. The word **incorrigible** is closest in meaning to

    A) strive
    B) detect
    C) hopeless
    D) debris

19. The word **fraternize** is closest in meaning to

    A) hinge
    B) vast
    C) wobble
    D) associate

20. The word **lurid** is closest in meaning to

    A) inactive
    B) gruesome
    C) unprovoked
    D) dissemination

1. C 2. D 3. D 4. B 5. C 6. A 7. A 8. C 9. D 10. B
11. A 12. C 13. D 14. B 15. A 16. B 17. A 18. C 19. D 20. B

TOEFL iBT/ TOEIC WORDS (Day 32)

1. Boor [boor]
  noun def: a churlish or rude person.
  synonyms: brute, buffoon, goon, lout, oaf, peasant, vulgarian
  antonyms: charmer, exciter
  I can't invite a *boor* like him to dinner because he would offend the other guests.

2. Boisterous [**boi**-ster-uhs]
  adj def: brawling; clamorous; disorderly; impetuous. (***)
  The *boisterous* soccer fans ran riot in the street until the police restrained them.

  The crowd was young and *boisterous*, the cheeseburgers were juicy and perfectly charred, and the place was always packed.
  — Jonathan Black, *Saveur*, October 2007

3. Bravado [bruh-**vah**-doh]
  noun def: a pretentious, swaggering display of courage.
  synonyms: boastfulness, bombast, bragging, bully
  antonyms: cowardice, fear, restraint
  The coward's *bravado* quickly vanished when his captors threatened to hit him; he began to whine for mercy.

4. Insipid [in-**sip**-id]
  adj def: without distinctive interesting or stimulating qualities. (***)
  synonyms: dull, uninteresting, anemic, acrid
  antonyms: exciting, exhilarating, pleasing
  The critic claimed that the soup was *insipid,* lacking any type of spice.

  While it is fashionable to write off that decade as an *insipid* time, one long pajama party, the '50s, in sport at least, were a revolutionary age.
  — Frank Deford, *Sports Illustrated*, 27 Dec. 1999–31 Jan. 2000

5. Longevity [lon-**jev**-i-tee]
  noun def: the length or duration of life.
  synonyms: durability, endurance, long life
  The reduction in early deaths from infectious diseases is responsible for most of the increase in human *longevity* over the past two centuries.

TOEFL iBT/ TOEIC WORDS (Day 32)

6. Malinger [muh-**ling**-ger]
    verb def: to pretend illness to avoid work. (***)
        His boss suspected him of *malingering* because of his frequent absences from work.

7. Nauseous [**naw**-shuhs]
    adj def: affected with nausea.
        synonyms: disgusting, abhorrent, brackish
        antonyms: nice, pleasing, soothing
    He could have a headache, feel *nauseous*, and have pain when swallowing.

    Instead what they do is all sit together and feel really bad, and pray. Nobody does anything as *nauseous* as try to make everybody all pray together or pray aloud or anything, but you can tell what they're doing.
        — David Foster Wallace, *Rolling Stone*, 25 Oct. 2001

8. Obstinate [**ob**-stuh-nit]
    adj def: firmly or stubbornly adhering to one's purpose.
        synonyms: stubborn, determined, adamant
        antonyms: agreeable, amenable, cooperative, flexible
    Hal's mother tried to get him to eat his spinach, but he remained *obstinate*.

9. Rancorous [**rank**-kuh-rus]
    adj def: expressing bitter hostility.
        Many Americans are disgusted by recent political campaigns, which seem more *rancorous* than ever before.

10. Tranquility [trang-**kwil**-i-tee]
    noun def: quality or state of being tranquil; calmness. (***)
        synonyms: peace, quiet, composure, equanimity
        antonyms: chaos, disturbance, loudness, violence
    She moved from New York City to rural Vermont, seeking the *tranquility* of country life.

11. Utilitarian [yoo-til-i-**tair**-ee-uhn]
    adj def: practical; effective; functional.
        The design of the Model T car was simple and *utilitarian*, lacking the luxuries found in later models.

TOEFL iBT/ TOEIC WORDS (Day 32)

12. Abyss [uh-**bis**]
 noun def: a deep, immeasurable space or gulf.
  synonyms: chasm, crevasse, depth, fissure
  Looking down into the *abyss* was terrifying, for I could not see the bottom.

13. Vicarious [vahy-**kair**-ee-uhs]
 adj def: taking the place of another person or thing. (****)
  synonyms: proxy, commissioned, delegated
  Great literature broadens our minds by giving us *vicarious* participation in the lives of other people.

  I am a *vicarious* eater, often preferring a description of a meal to eating it. I hoard the Wednesday food section of the *New York Times*, savoring it as my late-night reading, finishing always with the restaurant review.
  — Anne-Marie Slaughter, *Commonweal*, 14 June 2002

14. Acrimonious [ak-ruh-**moh**-nee-uhs]
 adj def: caustic; stinging; bitter. (***)
  The election campaign became *acrimonious,* as the candidates traded insults and accusations.

  Each man came out of their *acrimonious* 200-meter showdown on July 23 with an injured hamstring and a decidedly negative vibe.
  — Tim Layden, *Sports Illustrated*, 11 Sept. 2000

15. Demure [di-**myoor**]
 adj def: characterized by shyness and modesty; reserved. (**)
  synonyms: bashful, blushing, decorous, diffident
  antonyms: aggressive, bold, extroverted, outgoing
  The *demure* heroines of Victorian fiction have given way to today's stronger, more opinionated, and more independent female characters.

  So even if you think you've moved past your reputation as The Rebel, two minutes after getting together with your more *demure* sister, you're likely to fall back into that hell-raiser role.
  — Jessica Mehalic, *Cosmopolitan*, August 2001

TOEFL iBT/ TOEIC WORDS (Day 32)

16. Frugal [froo-guhl]
adj def: economical in use or expenditure. (****)
    synonyms: abstemious, canny, chary
    antonyms: generous, lavish, spendthrift, wasteful
    With our last few dollars, we bought a *frugal* dinner: a loaf of bread and a piece of cheese.

    His meals are the *frugal* fare of the poor: tea, bread, and yogurt, a bit of cheese, vegetables.
        — Johanna McGeary, *Time* , 25 Oct. 2004

17. Germinate [jur-muh-neyt]
verb def: grow; bud; develop; generate.
    synonyms: bud, develop, generate, live, originate
    antonyms: halt, slow, stop
    Three weeks after planting, the seeds will *germinate*.

18. Laudatory [law-duh-tawr-ee]
adj def: containing or expressing praise.
    synonyms: complimentary, adulatory, approving, commendatory
    antonyms: blaming, castigating, critical
    The ads for the movie are filled with *laudatory* comments from critics.

19. Mediocrity [mee-dee-ok-ri-tee]
noun def: the state of being middling or poor in quality. (**)
    The New York Mets, who had finished in ninth place in 1968, won the world's championship in 1969, going from horrible to great in a single year and skipping *mediocrity*.

20. Mercurial [mer-kyoor-ee-uhl]
adj def: temperamental; capricious; changeable; fickle; volatile. (***)
    Quick as quicksilver to change, Jane was *mercurial* in nature and therefore erratic.

    Few moments in English history have been hungrier for the future, its *mercurial* possibilities and its hope of richness, than the spring of 1603.
        — Adam Nicolson, *God's Secretaries*, 2003

TOEFL iBT/ TOEIC WORDS (Day 32)

21. Nuance [noo-ahns]
noun def: a subtle difference or distinction in expression. (***)
synonyms: slight difference, shading, dash, degree
At first glance, Monet's paintings of water lilies all look much alike, but the more you study them, the more you appreciate the *nuances* of color and shading that distinguish them.

Between the lines of lexicographical *nuance* and quotation, Johnson was paying old debts and seeking out wisdom about himself and his adopted city, as well as compiling perhaps the greatest commonplace book in the history of mankind.
— Andrew O'Hagan, *New York Review*, 27 Apr. 2006

22. Transgress [trans-**gres**]
verb def: to violate a law, command, moral code.
There are legal consequences for companies that *transgress* the rules.

23. Pugnacious [pugh-**ney**-shuhs]
adj def: inclined to quarrel or fight readily. (***)
synonyms: belligerent, aggressive, antagonistic, brawling
antonyms: kind, nice, easy-going
The serene eight-year old used to be a *pugnacious* troublemaker in her youth, but she is softer now.

That's a bass for you: *pugnacious*, adaptable and ever ready to demonstrate that the first order of business on any given day, drought or no drought, is eating anything that it can fit its big, powerful mouth around.
— Pete Bodo, *New York Times*, 22 Oct. 1995

24. Renunciation [ri-nuhn-see-**ey**-shuhn]
noun def: an act or instance of relinquishing or repudiating something. (***)
synonyms: abandonment, rejection, abdication, abnegation
antonyms: appreciation, approval, compliment
King Edward's *renunciation* of the British throne was caused by his desire to marry an American divorcee, something he couldn't do as king.

TOEFL iBT/ TOEIC WORDS (Day 32)

25. Transient [tran-shuhnt]
adj def: not lasting, enduring, or permanent. (***)
synonyms: temporary, brief, changeable, deciduous
antonyms: enduring, lasting, permanent
Long-term visitors to this hotel pay at a different rate than *transient* guests who stay for just a day or two.

A summer in New York is actually Europe, the Sequel — city of *transient* Danes and Italians and Spaniards and French.
— Guy Trebay, *Village Voice*, 30 July 1991

26. Untenable [uhn-ten-uh-buhl]
adj def: incapable of being defended. (****)
The theory that this painting is a genuine Van Gogh became *untenable* when the artist who actually painted it came forth.

The Agriculture Department is in an *untenable* position. With the two hats that it wears—one to protect consumer health and the other to help farmers sell food—it cannot tell us to eat fewer calories. After all, fewer calories generally mean less food, which would fly in the face of the department's mandate to help farmers.
— Marian Burros, *New York Times*, 14 Aug. 2002

27. Vindicate [vin-di-keyt]
verb def: to clear, as from an accusation, imputation, suspicion. (*)
synonyms: absolve, acquit, argue, assert
antonyms: accuse, blame, convict, punish
Lincoln's Gettysburg Address was intended to *vindicate* the objectives of the Union in the Civil War.

28. Virtuoso [vur-choo-oh-soh]
noun def: a person who has special skill or knowledge.
synonyms: ace, adept, authority, maestro
antonyms: amateur, rookie
Vladimir Horowitz was one of the great piano *virtuosos* of the twentieth century.

TOEFL iBT/ TOEIC WORDS (Day 32)

29. Expunge [ik-**spuhnj**]
verb def: to strike or bolt out; erase.
    synonyms: erase, obliterate, efface, wipe out
    The censor wanted to *expunge* all parts of Joyce's *Ulysses* he thought were obscene.

30. Extricate [**ek**-stri-keyt]
verb def: to free or release from entanglement.
    synonyms: disengage, liberate, disburden, disengage
    antonyms: entangle, involve
    Jenny hasn't been able to *extricate* herself *from* her legal problems.

31. Fatal [**feyt**-l]
adj def: capable of causing death; mortal.
    synonyms: deadly, lethal, baleful, calamitous
    antonyms: healthful, nourishing, vital
    The race car driver suffered a *fatal* accident when his car hit a patch of oil on the roadway.

32. Garrulous [**gar**-uh-luhs]
adj def: excessively talkative in a rambling, roundabout manner. (***)
    synonyms: chattering, effusive, glib, gushing
    antonyms: mum, quiet, reserved, silent, still
    My *garrulous* friend often talks on the telephone for hours at a time.

    Salman grew ever more *garrulous* as the yellow liquid in the bottle went down; Baal couldn't recall when he'd last heard anyone talk up such a storm.
    — Salman Rushdie, *The Satanic Verses*, 1989

33. Glee [glee]
noun def: open delight or pleasure; exultant.
    synonyms: cheerfulness, delectation, blitheness, elation
    antonyms: discouragement, sadness, unhappiness
    The child was filled with *glee* at the sight of so many presents.

TOEFL iBT/ TOEIC WORDS (Day 32)

34. Heed [heed]
   verb def: to give careful attention to. (**)
   synonyms: care, thought, attention, caution
   antonyms: carelessness, disregard, indifference, neglect
   Steve did not *heed* his teacher in class.

   It may be possible to desensitize a cat to being petted for extended periods. ... A safer solution is to consistently limit petting time, and to *heed* the cat's cues that she's had enough.
   — *Cat Watch*, August 2008

35. Inoculate [in-**nok**-yuh-leyt]
   verb def: to affect or treat.
   synonyms: immunize, vaccinate, protect
   Pasteur found he could prevent rabies by *inoculating* patients with the virus that causes the disease.

36. Inert [in-**urt**]
   adj def: having no inherent power of action, motion. (***)
   synonyms: lifeless, apathetic, asleep, dormant, sluggish
   antonyms: active, alive, animated, mobile
   Lizards are *inert* in the heat of the desert afternoon.

37. Limber [**lim**-ber]
   adj def: characterized by ease in bending the body.
   synonyms: flexible, agile, elastic, graceful
   antonyms: rigid, straight, stiff
   The gymnast warmed up for thirty minutes so that she would be *limber* before her routine.

38. Obtrusive [uhb-**troo**-siv]
   adj def: having or showing a disposition to obtrude.
   synonyms: pushy, obvious, forward, impertinent
   antonyms: modest, shy
   Philip should sing more softly; his bass is so *obtrusive* that the other singers can barely be heard.

TOEFL iBT/ TOEIC WORDS (Day 32)

39. Pragmatism [**prag**-muh-tiz-uhm]
   noun def: character or conduct that emphasizes practicality.
        Roosevelt's approach toward the Great Depression was based on *pragmatism*: "Try something," he said. "If it doesn't work, try something else."

40. Reprehensible [rep-ri-**hen**-suh-buhl]
   adj def: deserving in reproof, rebuke, or censure.
        synonyms: shameful, amiss, blamable, censurable
        antonyms: creditable, good, kind, respectable
        Although the athlete's misdeeds were *reprehensible,* not all fans agree that he deserves to be excluded from the Baseball Hall of Fame.

41. Stoic [**stoh**-ik]
   adj def: aloof; apathetic; dispassionate; calm. (***)
        A soldier must respond to the death of his comrades in *stoic* fashion, since the fighting will not stop for his grief.

        "That would have been to dishonor him," said Carr, a notorious *stoic* who was nearly overcome by emotion in his postgame press conference. Instead, he told the Wolverines that the best way to honor Schembechler was "to play in a way that would have made him proud."
                  — Austin Murphy, *Sports Illustrated*, 27 Nov. 2006

42. Spurious [**spyoor**-ee-uhs]
   adj def: counterfeit; fake; affected; apocryphal. (****)
        The report of a burning building turned out to be *spurious,* although who created the hoax is still uncertain.

        One reiterated theme of his book is that the electoral process can be the most dangerous of delusions, tending to confer a *spurious* legitimacy on those most willing to corrupt it.
                  — Hilary Mantel, *New York Review*, 21 Sept. 2006

43. Tedium [**tee**-dee-uhm]
   noun def: the quality or state of being wearisome.
        For most people, watching the Weather Channel for 24 hours would be sheer *tedium.*

TOEFL iBT/ TOEIC WORDS (Day 32)

44. Sully [suhl-ee]
   verb def: soil; stain; blacken; blot; tarnish.
   Nixon's misdeeds as president did much to *sully* the reputation of the American government.

45. Unyielding [uhn-yeel-dihng]
   adj def: determined not to give up or change one's mind about.
   The pioneers faced the challenge of setting the frontier with *unyielding* courage.

46. Verdant [vur-dnt]
   adj def: green with vegetation; covering with growing plants.
   synonyms: blooming, flourish, grassy
   antonyms: dying
   Southern England is famous for its *verdant* countryside filled with gardens and small farms.

47. Abdicate [ab-di-keyt]
   verb def: to renounce; relinquish; give up.
   synonyms: abandon, abjure, abnegate, cede
   antonyms: assert, assume, claim, defend
   With the angry mob clamoring outside the palace, the king *abdicated* his throne and fled with his mistress.

48. Adjunct [aj-uhngkt]
   noun def: addition; help; accessory; appendage.
   An *adjunct* professor is one not given the same full-time status as other faculty members.

49. Bile [bahyle]
   noun def: ill temper; irritability. (**)
   Mr. Watkins is very harsh when he grades essays; his comments reveal his *bile* and sharp tongue.

50. Canine [key-nahyn]
   adj def: pertaining to or characteristic of dogs.
   Canine relates to dogs in the same way as feline relates to cats.

Drill 32

1. The word **boisterous** is closest in meaning to

    A) noisy
    B) confine
    C) mutate
    D) differ

2. The word **insipid** is closest in meaning to

    A) distort
    B) oscillate
    C) dull
    D) proliferate

3. The word **malign** is closest in meaning to

    A) precursor
    B) harmful
    C) fluctuate
    D) rim

4. The word **nauseous** is closest in meaning to

    A) revere
    B) summit
    C) imminent
    D) disgusting

5. The word **tranquility** is closest in meaning to

    A) calmness
    B) precede
    C) expulsion
    D) foreshadow

Drill 32

6. The word **vicarious** is closest in meaning to

    A) abnormality
    B) emanate
    C) indirect
    D) deform

7. The word **abyss** is closest in meaning to

    A) swell
    B) deep
    C) deflate
    D) tremor

8. The word **frugal** is closest in meaning to

    A) forecast
    B) economy
    C) evacuate
    D) pending

9. The word **laudatory** is closest in meaning to

    A) cataclysmic
    B) consecutive
    C) inconsistent
    D) praise

10. The word **mediocrity** is closest in meaning to

    A) divisive
    B) inaccuracy
    C) average
    D) interruption

Drill 32

11. The word **mercurial** is closest in meaning to

    A) irrelevant
    B) codependent
    C) static
    D) changeable

12. The word **renunciation** is closest in meaning to

    A) inconclusive
    B) reflecting
    C) abandon
    D) frequency

13. The word **transient** is closest in meaning to

    A) scarce
    B) unlimited
    C) temporary
    D) plentiful

14. The word **vindicate** is closest in meaning to

    A) uphold
    B) precipitate
    C) infiltrate
    D) permeate

15. The word **virtuoso** is closest in meaning to

    A) saturate
    B) maestro
    C) encounter
    D) unimpeded

Drill 32

16. The word **fatal** is closest in meaning to

    A) impervious
    B) lethal
    C) stationary
    D) viable

17. The word **garrulous** is closest in meaning to

    A) talkative
    B) extract
    C) gush
    D) artesian

18. The word **heed** is closest in meaning to

    A) carefulness
    B) domestic
    C) delicate
    D) exploit

19. The word **reprehensible** is closest in meaning to

    A) sustain
    B) consolidate
    C) shameful
    D) veneer

20. The word **tedium** is closest in meaning to

    A) weather
    B) underlying
    C) decay
    D) dullness

1. A 2. C 3. B 4. D 5. A 6. C 7. B 8. B 9. D 10. C
11. D 12. C 13. C 14. A 15. B 16. B 17. A 18. A 19. C 20. D

TOEFL iBT/ TOEIC WORDS (Day 33)

1. Arcane [ahr-**keyn**]
   adj def: known or understood by very few.
   synonyms: hidden, secret, esoteric
   antonyms: common, commonplace, normal
   Eliot's "Waste Land" is filled with *arcane* lore, including quotations in Latin, Greek, French, German, and Sanskrit.

2. Disconcert [dis-kuhn-**surt**]
   verb def: to disturb the self-possession of. (**)
   synonyms: disturb, confuse, shake, abash
   antonyms: calm, comfort, soothe
   We were *disconcerted* by the unexpected changes to the program.

3. Eclectic [ih-**klek**-tik]
   adj def: selecting or choosing from various sources. (***)
   synonyms: comprehensive, general, assorted, broad, catholic
   antonyms: narrow, particular, specific, unvaried
   The Mellon family art collection is an *eclectic* one, including works ranging from ancient Greek sculptures to modern paintings.

   All around us, fishers galumphed past. ... They carried an *eclectic* array of rods, nets, buckets and coolers.
   — Stephen C. Sautner, *New York Times*, 2 Apr. 2000.

4. Felicitous [fi-**lis**-i-tuhs]
   adj def: well-suited for the occasion. (**)
   synonyms: appropriate, suitable, apropos, apt
   antonyms: improper, inopportune, unfitting
   The sudden blossoming of the dogwood trees the morning of Matt's wedding seemed a *felicitous* sign of good luck.

5. Horrid [**hawr**-id]
   adj def: to cause horror; shockingly dreadful; abominable.
   The weather has been just *horrid*; we have had three storms in a week.

6. Inadvertent [in-uhd-**vur**-tnt]
   adj def: characterized by lack of attention. (***)
   synonyms: accidental, careless, chance, feckless
   antonyms: advertent, attentive, deliberate

TOEFL iBT/ TOEIC WORDS (Day 33)

Marc wrote his paper in such a hurry that he made many *inadvertent* errors.

7. Formidable [**fawr**-mi-duh-buhl]
adj def: causing fear, apprehension, or dread.
   synonyms: horrible, terrifying, appalling, awful
   antonyms: feeble, friendly, harmless, nice
The steep face of rock we were directed to climb was indeed *formidable*.

She was known throughout Manchester as a *formidable* woman, and being educated had only piled more formidability on top of what she had been born with.
— Edward P. Jones, *The Known World*, 2003

8. Incredulous [in-**krej**-uh-luhs]
adj def: indisposed to believe. (****)
   synonyms: distrustful, doubtful, dubious, hesitant
   antonyms: believing, convinced, credulous
I was *incredulous* about Ismael's wild fishing story about "the one that got away."

"Afraid not." I made an expression to show that I was as *incredulous* about this as he was.
— Bill Bryson, *I'm a Stranger Here Myself*, 1999

9. Vilify [**vil**-uh-fahy]
verb def: to speak ill of, defame; slander.
   synonyms: abuse, asperse, berate, calumniate, censure
   antonyms: compliment, praise
He was *vilified* in the press for his comments.

10. Munificent [myoo-**nif**-uh-suhnt]
adj def: extremely liberal in giving.
   synonyms: giving, generous, beneficent, bounteous
   antonyms: careful, greedy, mean, selfish
The billion-dollar donation to the United Nations was probably the most *munificent* act of charity in history.

TOEFL iBT/ TOEIC WORDS (Day 33)

11. Nettle [net-l]
   verb def: to annoy; irritate; provoke. (*)
   Little brothers always *nettle* their older brothers by tagging along and being bothersome.

12. Ossify [os-uh-fahy]
   verb def: to cover into or cause to harden like bone.
   synonyms: congeal, fossilize, freeze, petrify
   antonyms: melt, soften
   Martin met a young man who began to *ossify* right after college.

13. Nefarious [ni-fair-ee-uhs]
   adj def: extremely wicked or villainous. (**)
   synonyms: bad, sinful, atrocious, base, corrupt
   antonyms: good, honorable, respectable
   Nefarious deeds are never far from an evil-doer's mind.

   Moreover, those starry-eyed states inclined to perceive international relations in moral terms frequently underestimate the *nefarious* machinations of their competitors on the world political stage.
   — Richard Wolin, *New Republic*, 4 June 2001

14. Paradox [par-uh-doks]
   noun def: a false or self-contradictory proposition.
   synonyms: contradiction, puzzle, absurdity, oddity
   The *paradox* of government is that the person who most desires power is the person who least deserves it.

15. Orthodox [awr-thuh-doks]
   adj def: conforming to beliefs, attitudes, or modes.
   synonyms: accepted, traditional, acknowledge, admitted
   antonyms: heterodox, unconventional, untraditional
   She believes in the benefits of both *orthodox* medicine and alternative medicine.

16. Peddle [ped-l]
   verb def: to carry from place to place.
   synonyms: solicit, trade, vend
   Jonathan *peddled* his idea for a new movie to every executive in Hollywood.

TOEFL iBT/ TOEIC WORDS (Day 33)

17. Restitution [res-ti-**too**-shuhn]
  noun def: reparation made by giving an equivalent. (**)
      synonyms: compensation; repayment; amends; indemnification
      antonyms: fee, penalty
      Some Native American Leaders are demanding that the U.S. government make *restitution* for the lands taken from them by white settlers.

18. Surrogate [**sur**-uh-geyt]
  noun def: a person appointed to act for another; deputy.
      synonyms: substitute, alternate, backup, delegate
      antonyms: real
      When the congressman died in office, his wife was named to serve the rest of his term as a *surrogate*.

19. Solace [**sol**-is]
  noun def: comfort in sorrow, misfortune. (**)
      synonyms: peace, alleviation, assuagement
      antonyms: trouble, upset, worry
      Upset as she was by her poodle's death, Florence took *solace* in the fact that he had died happy.

      Solaced by an abundance of whisky, champagne and cigars, he always bounced back, restoring and recreating himself through intensely active immersion in one or another of his varied interests ...
              — Robert Kuttner, *New York Times Book Review*, 23 Oct. 1988

20. Transmute [trans-**myoot**]
  verb def: to change from one nature into another. (**)
      In the middle ages, the alchemists tried to discover ways to *transmute* metals such as iron into gold.

21. Arbitrary [**ahr**-bi-trer-ee]
  adj def: subject to individual will. (***)
      synonyms: whimsical, chance, capricious, erratic, random
      antonyms: circumspect, despotic, bossy, domineering
      Jessica won a prize, but not Fred, making the judges' decision seem completely *arbitrary*.

      U.S. News was revealed to have considered assigning in its next rankings an *arbitrary* SAT score to Sarah Lawrence College because the school no

TOEFL iBT/ TOEIC WORDS (Day 33)

longer collects applicants' scores.

— Julie Rawe, *Time*, 2 Apr. 2007

22. Disingenuous [dis-in-**jen**-yoo-uhs]
adj def: lacking in frankness, candor. (***)
> synonyms: insincere, artful, crooked, deceitful
> antonyms: honest, ingenuous, native
>
> When the Texas billionaire ran for president, many considered his "jest plain folks" style *disingenuous*.

23. Espouse [ih-**spouz**]
verb def: to make one's own; adopt or embrace, as a cause. (**)
> synonyms: stand up for, support, accept
> antonyms: forsake, reject
>
> No politicians in America today will openly *espouse* racism, although some behave and speak in racially prejudiced ways.

24. Evanescent [ev-uh-**nes**-uhnt]
adj def: fading away; fleeting; transient.
> As she walked by, the *evanescent* fragrance of her perfume reached me for just an instant.

25. Inarticulate [in-ahr-**tik**-yuh-lit]
adj def: lacking the ability to express oneself.
> synonyms: blurred, dumb, halting, hesitant
> antonyms: articulate, communicative
>
> A skilled athlete may be an *inarticulate* public speaker, as demonstrated by many post-game interviews.

26. Oblique [oh-**bleek**]
adj def: diverging from a given straight line or course. (****)
> synonyms: slanting, angled, askance, askew
> antonyms: direct, forthright, straightforward
>
> Usually open and friendly, Allie has been behaving in a curiously *oblique* manner lately.

Harden ... , who missed a month with a strained left *oblique* muscle, has become one of the game's most intimidating starters in just his second full big league season.

— Albert Chen, *Sports Illustrated*, 8 Aug. 2005

TOEFL iBT/ TOEIC WORDS (Day 33)

27. Polarize [**poh**-luh-rahyz]
 verb def: to divide into sharply opposing factions, political groups.
  For years, the abortion debate *polarized* the American people, with many people voicing extreme views and few trying to find a middle ground.

28. Staid [steyd]
 adj def: of settled or sedate character.
  synonyms: restrained, calm, composed, demure
  antonyms: frivolous, sporting, willing
  Everyone in the classroom was surprised by the racy joke from the usually *staid* professor.

29. Vigil [**vij**-uhl]
 noun def: watchfulness maintained for any reason.
  synonyms: watch, attention, awareness, guard
  The nurse kept her *vigil* at the bedside of the dying man.

30. Wily [**wahy**-lee]
 adj def: craft; clever; artful.
  A *wily* judge of character, Jessica takes advantage of car buyers' insecurities to sell them a bigger machine than they really need.

31. Zenith [**zee**-nith]
 noun def: the highest point or state. (**)
  synonyms: top, acme, apex, climax
  antonyms: bottom, nadir
  Many PGA golfers strongly believed that winning The Masters Tournament was the *zenith* of their golfing career.

32. Affectation [af-ek-**tey**-shuhn]
 noun def: a trait or expression characterized by artificiality.
  synonyms: air, appearance, façade, insincerity
  antonyms: naturalness, simplicity
  James once spent three months in France and has now acquired the silly *affectation* of using French phrases in casual conversation.

33. Aperture [**ap**-er-cher]
 noun def: an opening as a hole or crack.
  synonyms: breach, break, chasm, cleft
  The photograph was taken using a fast shutter speed and a large *aperture*.

TOEFL iBT/ TOEIC WORDS (Day 33)

34. Cantankerous [kan-**tang**-ker-uhs]
   adj def: disagreeable to deal with; contentious. (***)
        synonyms: difficult, captious, cranky, crusty
        antonyms: easy, happy, nice
        Contemporaries often found him aloof, standoffish, and *cantankerous* and his mannerisms and diction inscrutable.
              — Jonathan Spence, *New York Review of Books*, 22 Oct. 2009

35. Felicity [fi-**lis**-i-tee]
   noun def: the state of being happy. (**)
        synonyms: happiness, bliss, delight, ecstasy
        She was so good, she deserved nothing but *felicity* her whole life.

36. Fertile [**fur**-tl]
   adj def: capable of producing vegetation.
        synonyms: abundant, arable, bountiful, fecund
        antonyms: barren, fruitless, impotent, infertile
        This subject remains a *fertile* field for additional investigation.

37. Curtail [ker-**teyl**]
   verb def: to cut short; abridge; reduce; diminish. (***)
        Because of the military emergency, all soldiers on leaves were ordered to *curtail* their absences and return to duty.

38. Decry [dih-**krahy**]
   verb def: to denounce as faulty or worthless.
        synonyms: criticize, blame, abuse, asperse
        antonyms: applaud, compliment, exalt, laud
        Cigarette ads aimed at youngsters have led many to *decry* the marketing tactics of the tobacco industry.

39. Effrontery [ih-**fruhn**-tuh-ree]
   noun def: shameless or impudent boldness; barefaced audacity.
        synonyms: nerve, boldness, arrogance, audacity
        antonyms: modesty, shame, shyness
        The sports world was shocked when the pro basketball player had the *effrontery* to choke his head coach during a practice session.

TOEFL iBT/ TOEIC WORDS (Day 33)

40. Florid [flawr-id]
adj def: excessively ornate; showy.
> synonyms: elaborate, baroque, decorative, embellished
> antonyms: natural, plain, unornate
> The grand ballroom was decorated in a *florid* style.

41. Inexorable [in-ex-ser-uh-buhl]
adj def: not to be convinced or moved. (**)
> synonyms: cruel, pitiless, adamant, bound
> antonyms: flexible, lenient, merciful
> It is difficult to imagine how the mythic character of Oedipus could have avoided his evil destiny; his fate appears *inexorable*.

42. Liability [lahy-uh-bil-i-tee]
noun def: responsibility; accountability; amenability.
> The insurance company had a *liability* of millions of dollars after the town was destroyed by a tornado.

43. Pallid [pal-id]
adj def: pale or deficient in color.
> synonyms: pale, anemic, ashen, ashy
> The new musical offers only *pallid* entertainment: the music is lifeless, the acting is dull, and the story is absurd.

44. Pariah [puh-rahy-uh]
noun def: any person or animal that is generally despised or avoided. (*****)
> synonyms: outcast, bum, deportee, derelict
> The *pariah* dog hovered at the outskirts of the camp, begging for scraps.

> For decades, African states longed for the day when South Africa would be liberated from its status as the apartheid *pariah* and become the economic engine that would pull Africa out of its mire of poverty and underdevelopment, much as Japan did for the Pacific Rim.
> — Allister Sparks, *Wilson Quarterly*, Spring 2001

45. Aeronautic [air-uh-naw-tik]
adj def: relating to aircraft.
> The Air Force's Stealth plane is reported to be a masterpiece of *aeronautic* design.

TOEFL iBT/ TOEIC WORDS (Day 33)

46. Belated [bih-**ley**-tid]
  adj def: late; slow; behind; delayed.
    She called her mother on January 5 to offer her a *belated* "Happy New Year."

47. Delegate [**del**-i-geyt]
  verb def: to send or appoint as deputy or representative.
    synonyms: representative, agent, ambassador, appointee
    The president decided to *delegate* the vice president to represent the administration at the peace talks.

48. Egoism [**ee**-goh-iz-uhm]
  noun def: self-centeredness; assurance; boasting.
    Robert's *egoism* was so great that all he could talk about was the importance — and the brilliance — of his own opinions.

49. Foppish [**fop**-ish]
  adj def: excessively refined and fastidious in taste and manner.
    synonyms: natty, fashionable, dandified, dapper
    The *foppish* character of the 1980s wore bright-colored spats and a top hat; in the 1980s, he wore fancy suspenders and a shirt with a contrasting collar.

50. Winsome [**win**-suhm]
  adj def: sweetly or innocently charming. (**)
    synonyms: charming, alluring, appealing, delightful, attractive
    She was a bright, *winsome* gamine who could draw a smile out of anyone.

TOEFL iBT/ TOEIC WORDS (Day 33)

> *The words in this book will not only help readers prepare for a test but also enhance their language skills in everyday life and in their professional careers. They range from those used in casual conversation to those found in formal correspondence and professional documents. Strong verbal and written communication skills are a competitive edge in one's career; this book, Mastering Core TOEFL iBT/ TOEIC Words with William H. Shin, will help readers reach that goal.*

Woobin Lee, PhD
Aptina Imaging, WA, USA

Drill 33

1. The word **arcane** is closest in meaning to

    A) advent
    B) impoverish
    C) hidden
    D) hereditary

2. The word **felicitous** is closest in meaning to

    A) inevitable
    B) reciprocal
    C) appropriate
    D) egalitarian

3. The word **horrid** is closest in meaning to

    A) coincide
    B) disparate
    C) shocking
    D) derived

4. The word **incredulous** is closest in meaning to

    A) replete
    B) unbelieving
    C) mutual
    D) nascent

5. The word **munificent** is closest in meaning to

    A) generous
    B) potent
    C) eminence
    D) exotic

6. The word **nettle** is closest in meaning to

    A) extravagance
    B) manifestation
    C) upset
    D) reflective

7. The word **ossify** is closest in meaning to

    A) evolve
    B) alluvial
    C) harden
    D) diverting

8. The word **restitution** is closest in meaning to

    A) fertile
    B) compensation
    C) irrigate
    D) scarce

9. The word **surrogate** is closest in meaning to

    A) substitute
    B) surplus
    C) timber
    D) grain

10. The word **arbitrary** is closest in meaning to

    A) pathetic
    B) turbulent
    C) arduous
    D) caprice

Drill 33

11. The word **disingenuous** is closest in meaning to

    A) insincere
    B) extra
    C) affixed
    D) incentives

12. The word **espouse** is closest in meaning to

    A) frank
    B) alloy
    C) support
    D) prattle

13. The word **oblique** is closest in meaning to

    A) askance
    B) milieu
    C) antecedent
    D) replace

14. The word **staid** is closest in meaning to

    A) adopted
    B) calm
    C) conceive
    D) consideration

15. The word **vigil** is closest in meaning to

    A) complain
    B) boast
    C) monetize
    D) watchful

Drill 33

16. The word **zenith** is closest in meaning to

    A) ensue
    B) tension
    C) top
    D) emerge

17. The word **aperture** is closest in meaning to

    A) assimilate
    B) hegemony
    C) dominate
    D) hole

18. The word **felicity** is closest in meaning to

    A) realm
    B) forfeit
    C) happiness
    D) preeminence

19. The word **decry** is closest in meaning to

    A) criticize
    B) vaunt
    C) dominion
    D) confined

20. The word **florid** is closest in meaning to

    A) anomalous
    B) elaborate
    C) decline
    D) resume

1. C 2. D 3. C 4. B 5. A 6. C 7. C 8. B 9. A 10. D
11. A 12. C 13. A 14. B 15. D 16. C 17. D 18. C 19. A 20. B

Word Index

A

Abandon 217
Abate 239
Abdicate 439
Abdomen 324
Aberrant 250
Abhor 378
Abnormal 295
Abolish 364
Abrasion 268
Abridge 393
Abrupt 98
Absorb 61
Abstruse 13
Absurd 320
Abuse 224, 348
Abut 186
Abyss 432
Accelerate 339
Acclaim 171
Accommodate 91, 240
Accumulate 86, 113
Accurate 103
Accuse 320
Acknowledge 98, 239
Acquire 112
Acrimonious 432
Adapt 33
Addle 340
Adequate 46
Adherent 318
Adjacent 32, 280
Adjudicate 390
Adjunct 439
Adjust 250

Admonition 211
Adopt 311
Adorn 156
Adroit 360
Adulation 409
Advent 112
Adversary 48
Adverse 49, 285
Advocate 126
Aeronautic 451
Aesthetic 90
Affect 168
Affectation 449
Affected 423
Affiliate 217
Affinity 214
Affirm 172
Affix 128, 310
Afflict 251
Affluent 65
Affordable 169
Aggravate 363
Aggregate 75
Aggressive 48
Agile 34
Agitate 20
Agrarian 116
Aid 197
Ailment 337
Akin 65
Alacrity 409
Align 251
Allege 320
Alleviate 23, 336
Allocate 45
Allot 337

Word Index

Allude 254
Aloft 229
Alter 103
Alternate 35
Amass 91
Ambiguous 169
Ambivalent 361
Amble 242
Amend 381
Ample 46, 282, 353
Amplify 197, 254
Anarchy 419
Anachronism 321
Anatomy 155
Animosity 78
Annex 88
Annoy 62
Annual 8, 225
Anomalous 307
Antecede 240
Anticipate 346
Antiseptic 377
Aperture 200, 449
Apex 124
Apparatus 79
Apparition 200
Appeal 360
Appease 340, 380
Appraise 227
Apprehend 376
Apprehensive 228
Apt 318
Aqueduct 203
Arbitrary 447
Arcane 444
Arduous 265
Arid 215
Array 31
Arresting 7
Articulate 173

Artifact 111
Artificial 291
Artisan 168
Ascend 183
Ascertain 111
Aspect 124
Aspirant 138
Aspire 170
Assemble 388
Assort 230
Assumption 98
Astonish 188
Astonishing 31
Astound 153
Astute 243
Asymmetrical 24
Atmosphere 103
Attain 312
Attire 200
Attribute 244
Audacious 51
Augment 79
August 188
Authorize 209
Autonomous 380
Avert 37
Avid 104
Axis 333

B

Ban 242
Banal 19
Bandit 126
Barren 255
Barter 323, 348
Bedeck 215
Befuddle 10

Word Index

Behemoth 130
Belabor 128
Belated 452
Belie 422
Bemoan 38
Beneficial 62
Benighted 267
Benign 131
Bequeath 241
Berate 402
Bereft 416
Bevy 217
Bias 64
Bicameral 389
Biennial 47
Bigot 125
Bile 439
Biosphere 239
Bisect 160
Bizarre 90
Bleak 278
Bloat 51
Blunt 249
Boggy 377
Boisterous 202, 430
Bolster 283
Bombastic 406
Boor 430
Boost 8
Brackish 306
Bravado 430
Breakthrough 196
Brew 217
Bridle 229
Brink 130
Brunt 267
Bulk 367
Burden 168
Burgeon 62
Burlesque 198

Burrow 307
Burst 130
Bustle 196
Buttress 185, 409

C

Caliber 154
Camouflage 9, 211
Canine 439
Cantankerous 450
Capitalize 353
Capsize 111, 258
Cardinal 239
Carnivore 103, 323
Carping 416
Cataclysm 297
Catalyst 180
Catastrophe 100
Categorize 20
Catharsis 242
Caustic 423
Cease 115
Celestial 252, 361
Censure 380
Cessation 100
Chaos 268
Chaotic 104
Cherish 320
Cherub 24
Chronological 111
Churn 182
Circumscribe 416
Circumspect 87
Circumvent 75, 279
Clarify 132
Clasp 13
Classify 7

Word Index

Cleave 154
Clemency 132
Cluster 9
Clutch 378
Coalesce 201
Coax 13
Cognition 368
Cognizance 264
Coherent 74
Cohesive 214
Coincide 181, 307
Collaborate 312
Collapse 216
Colonial 170
Colossal 325
Combustion 144
Commemorate 160
Commend 183
Commission 366
Commodious 268
Commodity 86, 210
Communal 392
Comparison 388
Compatible 228
Compatriot 201
Complement 195
Compliance 388
Complimentary 264
Comprehensive 88, 150, 365
Compress 114
Comprise 102, 312
Compromise 146, 187
Compulsion 265
Concede 337
Conceive 64
Conceptualize 65
Concoct 325
Concur 250
Condense 197
Conducive 253

Configure 325
Confine 20, 291, 305
Conflict 75
Congest 65
Congenial 334
Congenital 334
Congregate 71
Conjecture 104
Conjure 224
Consecutive 297
Consensus 249
Consent 339
Consequent 64
Consequential 389
Consistent 118
Consolation 419
Consolidate 307
Conspicuous 25, 323
Constitute 36
Constraint 31
Constrict 376
Consternation 409
Contaminate 419
Contend 309
Contingent 286
Contradict 52
Controversy 390
Consecutive 297
Consensus 249
Consent 339
Consistent 118
Consolidate 307
Conspicuous 25
Constitute 36
Constraint 31
Constrict 376
Contagious 230
Contemporary 213
Contempt 169
Content 256

461

Word Index

Contingent 286
Continuum 347
Contour 271
Contradict 52, 255
Contraption 187
Contrast 114
Controversy 390
Conundrum 185
Convention 319, 391
Conventional 137
Converse 71
Conviction 255
Convulse 126
Copious 312
Cornerstone 88
Correlation 98
Corrode 141
Counterfeit 363
Courtship 35
Crave 185
Crest 224
Crisp 252
Cumbersome 242
Curtail 450
Custody 361

D

Daunt 114
Daze 62
Debris 62
Decay 105
Decease 157, 282
Decent 224
Deception 279
Deciduous 277
Decipher 113
Decisive 251
Decline 100
Decompose 139
Decry 450
Dedicate 79, 365
Deduce 113
Deem 26
Defection 89
Deference 173
Defiant 312
Deflate 296
Deform 296
Degenerate 112
Dehydration 59, 323
Delay 49
Delegate 380, 452
Deliberate 103
Delicate 305
Delineate 118
Delinquency 63
Deluge 37, 225
Delve 277
Demarcate 350
Demise 61, 130
Demographic 137
Demonstrate 156
Demure 432
Denigrate 419
Depict 25, 215
Deplete 348
Deport 202
Derive 22
Derogatory 349
Descend 9
Descendant 227
Desert 381
Desertification 363
Desiccate 32
Designate 46
Desolate 271
Destitute 174

Word Index

Detach 202
Detect 61
Deter 31
Deteriorate 111, 238
Detonate 254
Detract 138
Detrimental 74
Devastate 101
Device 112
Devour 127
Dexterity 361
Diagnose 336
Dictate 307, 325
Dictum 392
Differentiate 65
Diffract 263
Digestive 128, 376
Dilemma 337
Dilute 305
Diminish 102
Diminutive 158
Diplomatic 87
Disapprove 211
Discard 24, 256
Discharge 299
Discipline 322
Disconcert 444
Discord 75
Discrepancy 332
Discretionary 338
Discriminate 215
Disdain 198
Disfigure 25
Disguise 11
Disingenuous 448
Disintegrate 63
Disjointed 84
Disparate 131, 213
Dispense 346
Disperse 141

Displace 216
Dispose 59
Disproportion 369
Disprove 257, 352
Dispute 72
Disregard 52
Disseminate 182
Dissent 319, 379
Dissimilar 244
Dissipate 284
Dissolve 128
Distinct 118
Distinguish 20, 318
Distort 294
Divergence 332
Diverse 24
Diversion 213
Diversity 33
Divert 46
Divine 85
Doctrine 339
Dogmatic 76
Domestic 72, 306
Dominate 45
Doom 255
Dormant 143
Drastic 244, 365
Dread 378
Dubious 184
Duress 393
Dwell 37, 210
Dwindle 49

E

Eager 167
Eclectic 444
Eddy 311

Word Index

Edifice 187, 392
Effervescent 23
Effrontery 450
Egalitarian 71
Egoism 452
Egregious 394
Elaborate 19, 196
Elastic 251
Elate 252
Elicit 86
Elucidate 101
Emanate 295
Embed 283
Embellish 21
Embitter 295
Embolden 200
Embrace 167
Embroidery 167
Emerge 63
Emergence 155
Emergent 91
Eminence 309
Emission 305
Emit 279
Emphasize 392
Employ 214
Enact 223
Encapsulate 353
Encode 26
Encompass 47
Encounter 298
Encroach 37
Enculturation 360
Encumber 170
Endeavor 14, 45
Endemic 35
Endow 84, 172
Endure 8, 374
Engrave 22
Enhance 166, 269

Enigma 99
Enlighten 87
Enliven 13
Enormous 34, 209
Enrich 12
Enroot 117
Ensnare 115
Ensue 196
Ensure 145
Entail 238
Entice 35
Entitle 270
Entrench 21
Equatorial 7
Equilibrium 326
Equivalent 326
Eradicate 62
Erect 140, 291
Erode 7, 269
Erratic 170
Erudite 243
Erupt 100
Esoteric 20
Espouse 448
Ethereal 22, 199
Ethnic 63
Etymology 335
Euphoria 353
Evacuate 296
Evanescent 448
Evaporate 168, 277, 364
Evoke 171
Evolve 64, 309
Exacerbate 10
Exaggerate 23
Excavate 92
Exclude 12
Excrete 60
Exemplify 25
Exemplum 170

Word Index

Exert 50
Exigent 37
Exile 318
Exotic 167
Expedient 381
Expel 324
Extensive 114
Experiment 199, 322
Expiate 128
Explicate 101
Explicit 90, 389
Exploit 33
Explore 182
Exponential 180
Expose 48
Expulsion 295
Expunge 436
Extant 202
Extend 7, 332
Extensive 114
Exterminate 52, 286
Extinct 311
Extinction 98
Extol 13
Extort 128
Extract 127, 306
Extraneous 382
Extraordinary 310
Extraterrestrial 101
Extravagance 19, 309
Extricate 436
Exuberant 278

F

Fabricate 354
Facet 154, 367
Facile 71

Facilitate 59
Faction 125
Fade 257
Fallacy 256
Fatal 128, 436
Fatigue 352
Feasible 137
Feast 240
Felicitous 444
Felicity 450
Fend 85
Ferment 333
Ferocious 50
Fertile 47, 450
Fervent 406
Fickle 267
Fidelity 197
Fierce 377
Filmy 159
Fissure 268
Flagrant 402
Flamboyant 423
Flatter 279
Flaw 103, 388
Flee 11
Fleet 48
Flippant 214
Float 375
Florid 420, 451
Flourish 33
Fluctuate 10
Foible 48
Foliage 102
Foppish 452
Forage 335
Forge 9
Forgo 323
Forecast 296
Foremost 211
Foreshadow 295

Word Index

Foresight 354
Forestall 77
Formidable 445
Formulate 223
Fortuitous 406
Fossil 114
Foster 8
Fractious 91
Fracture 268
Fraternize 424
Friction 78
Frugal 433
Furnish 388
Futile 115

G

Garner 201, 322
Garrulous 436
Gauche 334
Gauge 106
Genial 406
Genuine 186
Geometric 116
Geothermal 311
Germinate 433
Glaze 283
Glean 155
Glee 436
Gnarl 283
Granary 212
Grandiose 199
Gratuitous 420
Greedy 320
Gregarious 394
Grimy 197
Grudge 145
Grueling 265

Gruesome 424
Grunt 280
Guileless 402
Gullible 394
Gush 306

H

Hallmark 374
Halt 225
Hamper 141, 419
Haphazard 420
Harbinger 424
Harbor 238
Harness 140
Hasty 424
Haughty 402
Haul 209
Hazard 202
Heal 174
Hedonist 416
Heed 437
Hefty 36
Hegemony 84
Heinous 394
Hence 348
Herald 292
Herbivore 102
Herbivorous 353
Hereditary 226
Heterogeneous 410
Hew 226
Hibernate 8
Hierarchical 152
Hieroglyphic 88
Hilarious 277
Hinder 50
Hinge 291

Word Index

Holistic 349
Homogeneous 73
Hone 198
Horrid 444
Hostile 85
Hover 229, 323
Hub 224
Hygiene 238
Hypnosis 199
Hypocrisy 407
Hypothesis 101

I

Identity 21
Idiosyncrasy 392
Ignite 12, 231
Illicit 243
Illiterate 21
Illuminate 182
Illusory 37
Illustrate 319
Immaculate 263
Immediate 170
Imminent 294
Immune 319
Impact 101, 209
Impartial 389
Impeccable 393
Impede 52, 298
Impel 198
Impend 224, 292
Impermanent 391
Impermeable 305
Impervious 104
Impetus 137
Impinge 171, 416
Implacable 37, 269

Implement 79
Implicit 241
Impose 78
Impoverish 308
Improvident 143
Imprudent 13
Impulsive 125
Inaccuracy 297
Inadequate 265
Inadvertent 444
Inalienable 390
Inanimate 390
Inarticulate 448
Inaugurate 240
Incarcerate 352
Incarnate 124
Incentive 310
Inception 189
Incipient 143
Incisive 420
Incite 26
Inclement 10
Incline 249
Inconceivable 187
Inconsequential 26
Inconsistent 297
Incontrovertible 26
Incorporate 167
Incorrigible 423
Incredible 36
Incredulous 231, 445
Increment 212
Incriminate 346
Incur 333
Indeterminate 423
Index 366
Indigenous 36, 226
Indignant 155
Indispensable 238
Indispose 339

Word Index

Induce 299
Indulge 22
Inert 139, 437
Inevitable 140, 309
Inexorable 158, 451
Inexplicable 92, 215
Infectious 60
Inference 113
Infest 129
Infiltrate 298
Infinitesimal 270
Inflate 296
Influential 297
Influx 184
Infrastructure 154
Infringe 269
Infuse 174
Ingest 61
Ingrate 299
Inhabit 31
Inhibit 102
Inhospitable 264
Inimical 90
Innate 381
Innovative 322
Inoculate 437
Inquiry 368
Inscribe 227
Inseminate 47
Insipid 430
Insolent 125
Instigate 347
Insufficient 251
Insulate 116
Insuperable 230
Insurmountable 229
Intact 187
Integral 102
Integrate 24
Intensify 335

Interact 237
Intercept 277
Interdisciplinary 352
Interfere 292
Intermediate 391
Intermittent 72, 306
Internecine 32
Intersperse 334
Intertwine 180, 334
Intervene 365
Intestine 239
Intimate 168, 228
Intimidate 49
Intricate 79, 285
Intrinsic 186
Introvert 382
Intuitive 173
Invariable 230
Inveigle 51
Inversion 363
Invigorate 195
Invoke 75
Irreparable 238, 363
Irrespective 216
Irrevocable 351
Irrigate 271
Irritate 352
Itinerant 212

J

Jaundiced 410
Jaunt 267
Jeer 406
Jeopardize 395
Jeopardy 45
Jubilant 403
Judicial 78

Word Index

Juvenile 143
Juxtapose 322

K

Kaleidoscope 168
Keen 156
Kinetic 403
Kinship 71
Kismet 402

L

Languid 395
Latent 267
Laudatory 433
Leeward 332
Legislative 378
Legitimacy 338
Lenient 362
Lessen 126
Lethal 139
Lethargic 403
Liability 417, 451
Liaison 118
Liberate 238
Lieu 240
Limb 159
Limber 437
Linger 31
Lithe 395
Longevity 410, 430
Lubricate 256
Lucrative 127
Lunacy 185
Lure 182

Lurid 424
Lurk 311
Lust 50

M

Magnificent 21
Magnify 112
Malady 105
Malediction 420
Malevolence 420
Malevolent 129
Malinger 431
Malleable 403
Malpractice 339
Manacle 252
Mandate 410
Manifest 263
Manifold 281
Manipulate 374
Mar 197
Marvel 38
Mature 159
Meager 407
Mechanism 379
Meddlesome 144
Mediate 72
Medicament 346
Mediocrity 433
Meek 155
Mellow 263
Menace 52
Mendacious 407
Mercurial 410, 433
Mesmerize 340
Meticulous 25, 157
Migrate 9
Milestone 160

Word Index

Milieu 310
Mimicry 280
Mingle 74
Misgiving 285
Mitigate 50, 353
Mock 294
Moderate 362
Modicum 417
Modify 127
Mollify 395, 421
Momentum 230
Monarchy 116
Monitor 292
Monopoly 76
Motif 166
Muffle 195
Multifarious 71
Multiplicity 281
Mundane 321
Municipal 66
Munificent 445
Murky 264
Mutate 294
Mutinous 184
Mutual 237
Myriad 34
Mythos 174

N

Nadir 223
Nascent 308
Nauseous 431
Nebulous 403
Nefarious 446
Negligible 420
Negotiate 87
Nettle 446

Neutralize 278
Niche 33, 282
Nihilism 318
Nimble 281
Nocturnal 395
Nomadic 115
Nonchalant 411
Nonplus 421
Norm 72
Nostalgia 171
Notify 417
Notwithstanding 360
Nourish 116
Nouveau 349
Novelty 210
Novice 159
Nuance 434
Nurture 417

O

Obese 407
Obligate 119
Oblige 196
Oblique 448
Oblivious 417
Obnoxious 404
Obscure 217
Obsessive 417
Obsolete 350
Obstacle 216
Obstinate 431
Obtain 45
Obtrusive 437
Obtuse 255
Occupy 213
Odor 131
Offshoot 153

Word Index

Offspring 49
Ominous 421
Onerous 203
Ongoing 332
Onset 366
Optical 253
Optimistic 339
Opulence 169
Opulent 396
Ordain 38
Ornament 283
Orthodox 446
Oscillate 141
Ossify 446
Ostentatious 19
Ostracism 333
Ostracize 411
Outbound 181
Outing 23
Outrageous 321
Outset 22
Outskirts 181
Overarch 379
Overcome 12
Overlap 227, 362
Oversee 227
Overthrow 90
Overwhelm 61

P

Pallid 451
Paradox 446
Parallel 362
Parameter 264
Paramount 65
Parch 254
Pariah 451

Parochial 73
Parody 105
Parsimonious 166
Partake 350
Pastoral 347, 391
Pathetic 228, 310
Patriarch 76
Patriotic 167
Patriotism 367
Patron 86
Patronage 87
Paucity 216
Pecuniary 350
Pedagogue 63
Peddle 446
Pending 297
Penetrate 48
Perceive 19, 158
Percolate 270
Perfunctory 24
Peripheral 152
Periphery 66
Perish 237
Perpetrate 351
Persecute 239, 318
Persistent 336, 374
Perspective 158
Persuade 201
Persuasive 350
Petrify 92
Petty 361
Phenomenon 292
Phonograph 195
Pictorial 366
Pigment 200
Pinnacle 368
Pioneer 199
Piquant 255
Pity 39
Pivot 141

Word Index

Placate 335
Placebo 335
Plague 47, 117, 285
Plateau 363
Pledge 92, 389
Plentitude 351
Plethora 210
Plunge 61
Polarize 449
Ponder 249
Pore 277
Portend 142, 418
Portray 199
Postpone 51
Postulate 100, 244
Potent 181
Potential 173
Pound 142
Pragmatic 160, 282
Pragmatism 438
Precede 295
Precedent 46
Precipitate 139
Precipitation 8
Precise 152
Precursor 293
Predecessor 183
Predetermine 297
Predicament 336
Predispose 285
Predisposed 78
Predisposition 351
Predominate 140, 225, 347
Preeminent 209
Prejudice 375
Preliminary 250
Premature 254
Premise 368
Preoccupied 85
Preponderance 265

Prerequisite 253
Prerogative 380
Prescribe 336
Presume 62, 244
Presumption 99
Prevail 21
Prevalent 140
Primary 216
Primogeniture 77
Primordial 72
Pristine 256
Probe 256
Proclaim 11
Proclamation 366
Procreate 46
Procure 281, 360
Prodigy 89
Prohibit 230
Profile 307
Profound 26
Proliferate 293
Prolong 237
Prominent 19, 253
Prompt 22
Prone 325
Propensity 351
Prophecy 209
Proponent 99, 379
Proprietor 185
Propulsion 231, 305
Prospect 311
Prosper 124
Protract 38
Provision 379
Provoke 293
Prowess 84
Proximity 252
Prudent 138
Pseudonym 199
Pugnacious 434

Word Index

Pulverize 392
Punctuality 361
Punitive 78
Purge 241
Pursue 86
Pursuit 33
Purview 366

Q

Quaint 184
Qualm 270
Quandary 225, 369
Quench 252
Querulous 405
Quintessence 172

R

Radical 312
Ramification 63
Rampant 242, 266
Rancorous 431
Rapid 34
Ratify 379, 407
Ravage 130
Raze 407
Realm 321
Rear 153
Rebut 105
Receding 268
Reciprocate 77
Reckon 12
Recur 351
Recurrent 254
Redundant 186

Refine 168
Reflective 309
Refrain 11
Regain 11
Regardless 158, 249
Regression 388
Regulate 59, 324
Reign 85
Reinforce 73, 333
Release 60
Reliable 181
Reliance 367
Relic 216
Reluctant 346
Remand 364
Reminiscence 404
Remnant 214
Remorse 243
Render 129
Renew 348
Renown 172
Renunciation 434
Repentance 278
Repercussion 239
Replace 145, 311
Replenish 59
Replicate 60
Reprehensible 438
Repudiate 396, 418
Reputation 86
Requisite 31
Rescind 154
Reshape 226
Residue 244
Resilient 284, 421
Respective 347, 363
Respiration 60, 324
Restitution 447
Restrict 38
Resurrect 282

Word Index

Retain 9
Retool 154
Retreat 8
Retribution 76
Retrogress 211
Retrospect 339
Revenue 85
Reverberate 152, 180
Reverence 174
Reverse 60, 212
Revitalize 223
Rigid 20
Ritual 325
Robust 241
Ruinous 102
Ruminant 393
Runoff 286
Rupture 89, 374
Ruthless 49

S

Sacred 127, 174
Sagacious 156
Salubrious 377
Saturate 139, 298
Savory 159
Scant 215
Scarce 74
Scarcity 65
Scatter 12, 117
Scheme 77
Scorch 377
Scrupulous 156
Scrutinize 195
Scrutiny 157
Secrete 278, 376
Secular 20, 88

Secularize 127
Sedentary 115
Seethe 11
Segment 282
Segregate 308
Seize 378
Sensuous 391
Sequence 113
Sequential 144
Serendipitous 318
Serenity 66
Sever 269
Severe 92
Shallow 375
Simulate 230
Simultaneous 308
Skeptic 203
Slipshod 393
Smother 187
Snap 376
Soar 229
Solace 447
Solemn 188
Solstice 266
Somber 284
Sophisticated 89
Sovereign 381
Span 130
Spate 253
Spawn 35
Specimen 105, 376
Spectacular 35, 180
Spectator 321
Speculative 111
Spew 100
Spiral 324
Splendid 188
Spontaneous 112
Spoof 38
Sporadic 283

Word Index

Spur 89
Spurious 438
Squander 47
Squirt 280
Stagger 158
Stagnate 32, 268
Staid 449
Stalk 253
Standstill 375
Staple 137, 210
Stark 23
Startle 244
Stationary 145, 298
Stave (off) 87
Sterile 291, 334
Stipend 91
Stoic 438
Stratify 78
Stride 375
Strip 322
Strive 291
Stun 51
Stupefy 198
Subdue 124
Submerge 375
Submit 90
Subordinate 117
Subsequent 63, 390
Subsidiary 76
Subsidize 240
Subsist 348
Subsistence 347
Substantial 98
Substitute 223
Subterranean 212, 293, 324
Subtle 249, 292
Successive 113
Succumb 281
Sufficient 89
Sully 439
Summit 126, 294
Superficial 125
Supernatural 77
Superstitious 166
Supervise 152, 338
Supplicate 52
Supposition 374
Suppress 10
Surge 210
Surplus 240
Surrealistic 319
Surrender 84
Surreptitious 408
Surrogate 447
Susceptible 266
Suspicion 367
Sustain 66, 306
Sustenance 34
Swath 116
Swell 124
Swift 201, 229
Symbiosis 237, 333
Symmetrical 362
Symmetry 323
Symptom 250
Synchronous 143
Synthetic 13

T

Tactics 338
Tandem 271
Tantalize 138
Taxing 266
Tedious 146
Tedium 438
Teem 185
Temerity 408

Word Index

Temper 278
Temperate 391
Tempestuous 117
Tempt 338
Tenable 73
Tenacious 396
Tendency 187
Tenet 172
Tentative 408
Tenuous 118
Tepid 404
Terminate 418
Terse 404
Testament 186
Therapeutic 421
Thereby 337
Threaten 285
Threshold 266
Thrive 7
Thrust 114
Thwart 363
Timorous 228, 411
Tinge 263
Tinker 183
Tirade 160
Toady 405
Toil 181
Toilsome 267
Tolerate 9
Topography 307
Torment 50
Torso 155
Tout 171
Trait 53
Tranquil 66
Tranquility 431
Transcend 349
Transform 64
Transgress 434
Transient 435

Transition 7
Translucent 200
Transmit 77
Transmute 447
Transparency 347
Transport 60
Traverse 141
Travesty 159
Tremendous 138
Tremor 296
Tribe 116
Tribute 126
Trickery 280
Trigger 351
Triumph 152
Trivial 349
Truncate 410
Tumultuous 367
Turbulence 308
Turmoil 127
Typify 313

U

Ubiquitous 104
Ultimate 378, 422
Unadulterated 116
Unanimous 117, 418
Unbiased 242
Unbridled 104
Undaunted 201, 377
Undercurrent 23
Undergo 338
Underlying 73
Undertake 142
Undoubtable 25
Unerring 264
Unify 36

Word Index

Unitary 157
Unkempt 404
Unleash 129
Unpalatable 396
Unparalleled 241
Unprecedented 365
Unravel 99
Unstinting 405
Untenable 435
Unwonted 144
Unyielding 439
Upheaval 118
Upswing 144
Urbanize 180
Urge 173
Usher 198, 348
Usurp 183
Utilitarian 431
Utilize 22

V

Vacate 418
Vacillate 211
Vague 142, 408
Vain 243
Validate 77
Valor 227
Vanish 99, 226
Vapid 195
Variation 293
Variegate 32
Vary 10, 131
Vast 227
Vehement 405
Velocity 270
Veneer 270
Vent 311

Ventilate 324
Verdant 439
Verify 99
Versatile 166
Vertebrate 47
Vertical 9
Vest 237
Vestige 269
Veto 381
Vex 39
Viable 14, 45
Vibrant 172
Vicarious 432
Vicious 138
Victim 376
Vigil 449
Vigilant 52
Vigorous 143
Vilify 445
Vindicate 435
Virtue 337
Virtuoso 435
Vital 59
Vitalize 418
Vivacious 396
Vivid 158
Void 293
Volatile 352
Voluble 144, 251
Voracious 36

W

Wan 397
Wane 252
Weaken 130
Weave 181
Weary 153

Word Index

Wherein 332
Whimsical 422
Wily 449
Winsome 452
Wither 129
Withhold 409
Withstand 11, 226
Worthwhile 142
Wrangle 105
Wrath 397
Wrest 129
Writ 422
Writhe 405

X

Xenophobia 422

Y

Z

Zealot 422
Zealous 397
Zenith 449
Zest 405

*The Most Effective Ways to Improve the Reading Score on the TOEFL iBT
(Korea Times, Education Column, 10/14/2013)*

William H. Shin

The reading section is the first section of the TOEFL iBT test. In this section, you must read three to five passages of approximately 700 words each and answer questions that test your comprehension after each passage. All the reading passages are about the same length, but the number of passages, questions, and amount of time for this section can vary. On any TOEFL iBT administration, you receive between three and five reading passages, and you have anywhere from 60 to 100 minutes to read the passages and answer the questions. Each passage can have 12 to 14 questions.

The time is divided as follows:

- 20 minutes for the first passage
- 40 minutes for the second and third passages
- 40 minutes for the fourth and fifth passages

General Reading Tactics and Strategies

1. Be prepared for your exam by knowing the organization of the section and the function of the various buttons on the screen. The time begins as soon as the Reading section begins, so you should not spend too much time reading the instructions that appear at the beginning of the section.

2. TOEFL reading passages are organized according to the basic outline for essays in English. Understanding this organization is essential to all four sections of the TOEFL iBT. The basic pattern for any passage is the paragraph, which is a group of sentences related to a common topic and/or purpose. Any reading passage or lecture has several paragraphs with brief breaks, or space, between one paragraph and the next, and each paragraph gives a part of the author's main idea. The entire passage can be broken into three main sections: the introduction, body, and conclusion.

3. Read actively. In other words, you must think while you read due to the level of description and explanation. The reading passages on the TOEFL iBT are dense, which means that they involve complex ideas. The concepts involve many aspects: multiple people, actions, states, and places. Reading actively is not skimming.

Many students skim the passage right away before they read the first question, but your first reading should be more thorough. Skimming is when you pass your eyes quickly over the words and you get a basic understanding of the topic but little understanding of the specifics of the passage. This is called getting the gist of a passage, but, in fact, it isn't enough for you to get the gist.

4. Inference is a vital skill for the Reading and Listening sections. To infer means to understand unstated or unwritten meaning based on certain details and logic. When you infer the idea, you understand it even though the writer (or speaker) didn't state it directly. Inference is related to implication; when a speaker or a writer implies an idea, he or she communicates the idea without mentioning it directly. A reader or listener then infers it based on some key detail and logic.

5. Pay attention to sequence, especially mixed sequence. In fact, the sequence, or order, of the ideas, events, steps, actions, or states in a passage is extremely important. A writer often, but not always, explains or describes the topic in chronological order. In other words, writer often starts at the beginning of an event or process and then moves to the end. The order of ideas in the passage matches their order in time. However, don't assume that events or steps take place in the same order that they are mentioned in the given passage.

6. Read the passage initially for comprehension, not note-taking. In other words, your aim should be to understand as much as possible about the passage from the first reading. Since your focus is on understanding the concepts and the connections among them, you shouldn't record very detailed notes.

It is not easy to reach an ideal score on the reading section of the TOEFL iBT. I am sure that the aforementioned tactics and strategies are extremely helpful for those who struggle to earn 22-25 on the Reading section.

The Most Effective Ways to Improve the Listening Score on the TOEFL iBT
(Korea Times, Education Column, 10/21/2013)

William H. Shin

The Listening section of the TOEFL iBT is the second part of the exam. This section includes both conversation and lectures: two or three conversations with five questions per conversation, and between four and six lectures with six questions per lecture. Depending on the number of passages, this section lasts 60 minutes or 90 minutes.

There are four things you need to do in order to perform well on the Listening section of the TOEFL iBT:

- Familiarize yourself with the question types

- Have the right skills to listen intelligently

- Take good notes

- Avoid incorrect answers

Listening Strategies and Tactics: Conversations and Lectures

1. Try to listen actively. You should think about what you are hearing. One of your major challenges as a TOEFL iBT student is that you must do many things while listening. You must recognize more than just names, places, and times. While you listen and take notes, you must also be able to anticipate, learn, connect ideas, organize, generalize, infer, assume, and conclude.

2. You must be able to anticipate key points based on the main idea. Anticipating means thinking about what might or will come next, and it is a part of active listening. In fact, anticipation will make listening much easier. Once you hear the main topic, you will certainly hear supporting ideas.

3. Try to infer meaning whenever possible. To infer means to understand unstated ideas, and inference is a part of active listening. You must be able to infer often

during the TOEFL iBT because meaning, organization, attitude, connections among ideas, and purpose are not always stated explicitly.

4. Do not waste time writing the exact words a speaker says. When you write notes, you must use your own words instead of copying the speaker exactly. If you understand an idea, you can record it in shorter or simpler words.

5. After you find a main idea, you can focus only on key supporting points, not minor ones. For instance, while listening to a history lecture about a famous battle, you must concentrate only on actors (attackers, defenders, civilians) and actions (attacking, defending, surrendering). A general marital status (single or married), on the other hand, probably doesn't have a major connection to the battle.

6. You must be prepared for the unique elements of spoken English. Although the speakers in the listening section use academic vocabulary and speak about academic topics, the lecturers and conversations in the TOEFL iBT have elements that are not found in academic writing. In other words, the speakers in the listening section do not sound like they are reading an essay. Instead, their speech is more natural and resembles everyday spoken English, which can include some or all of the following elements: interruptions, confusion and clarification, self-correction, and fragments.

7. You must avoid answer choices that repeat too many words exactly from the lecturer or conversation. Most of the listening sections are multiple-choice questions. The multiple-choice questions are followed by four possible answer choices, and you must choose one or more correct answers. Although some vocabulary such as names might be repeated, the correct answer usually paraphrases ideas from a conversation or lecture.

The Most Effective Ways to Improve the Speaking Score on the TOEFL iBT
(Korea Times, Education Column, 10/28/2013)

William H. Shin

The speaking section of the TOEFL iBT is the third section of the exam. It follows a mandatory ten-minute break after the Listening section, so you should be relaxed when you get to this portion.

There are six tasks in the Speaking section, and the entire section takes 20 minutes to complete.

First two tasks: Independent (which means that you speak about familiar topics without reading and listening to any passages beforehand)

Last four tasks: Integrated (which means that you must first read and/or listen to a passage, and then speak about what you have read and heard)

To perform well on the Speaking section of the TOEFL iBT, you must be able to generate ideas quickly, listen and read actively, record notes efficiently, speak clearly from fragmented notes, and accurately summarize passages in your own words. The following strategies review the necessary skills for each Speaking task on the exam. After reviewing each type, you can practice a question similar to the one you will get on the actual TOEFL iBT, and then read a sample response.

General Speaking Strategies: Independent and Integrated

1. You must be prepared to speak from notes, not a transcript. You won't have enough time on the actual exam to write out a transcript of your answer. Even for the independent tasks, you will only be able to record your ideas in note form. Also, the integrated tasks include some complex ideas that you must record or remember while you read and listen. Therefore, you must be able to speak clearly and directly with only notes as a guide.

2. You must organize your thoughts and speech as a paragraph, not a standard essay.

It means that your answers in the Speaking section are not spoken essays, but they must still be organized. Your answer must be relatively brief (45 seconds or one minute, maximum). You need to make your point quickly, so don't bother with an extended hook like those used in lectures and essays. Most importantly, there is no need, or time, for an introductory paragraph like the one in an essay or lecture.

3. You must use familiar vocabulary. It means that you use the vocabulary that you would normally use in a serious but friendly conversation about an academic topic. Although you may have to learn and use new vocabulary from a conversation or lecture, do not try to sound like a professor by thinking of long, unfamiliar words and sentences unnecessarily.

4. You must use short, simple sentences. Comfortable, natural speech in English doesn't sound like written English. Spoken English must still be grammatically correct, organized, and detailed. Yet native speakers use a more casual, relaxed style when speaking, even when they discuss academic topics. If you listen to them, most English speech is made up of sentences with one or two clauses.

5. You must vary your vocabulary and sentence structure. Speaking naturally does not mean speaking repetitively. Use different word forms when you discuss the same ideas or related ideas. It is not only more interesting but also demonstrates your vocabulary.

6. You must be able to use cohesive devices effectively. Cohesion means unity, and it refers to the number of connections among the ideas in a sentence and paragraph. There are many ways to add unity to your answer. Some of the most common cohesive devices are personal pronouns (he, she, they, etc.), demonstrative pronouns (that, this, etc.), adjectives (next, another, etc.), articles (a/an, the), synonyms, transitions (first, however, in fact, etc.), and using similar word forms (ex: inform, information, informative, etc.)

7. You must be able to use transitions appropriately. Throughout the speech, use transitions to indicate sequence (first, next, etc.), connection/similarity (moreover, furthermore, etc.), contrast (however, but, etc.), examples (for example, for instance, like, etc.), or explanation (therefore, because, due to, etc.). However, do not overuse them. Transitions can guide a listener when they are necessary, but they can waste time and confuse the listener if they are used excessively.

ARTICLES

The Most Effective Ways to Improve the Writing Score on the TOEFL iBT (Korea Times, Education Column, 11/04/2013)

William H. Shin

The writing section of the TOEFL iBT is the fourth and final section. There are two parts to this section. First, you will have an integrated task, in which you must read an academic passage, then listen to a related academic lecture, and finally write a summary of both. Second, you will have an independent persuasive essay similar to one you may have seen in the old computer-based TOEFL test.

Some of the strategies to be used here are similar to those used for the Speaking section, since the two Writing tasks resemble the second and fourth Speaking tasks. In fact, Writing tasks are longer than those in the Speaking section, which requires more planning and review.

General Writing Strategies: Independent and Integrated

- Organize your thoughts first because of the time limits. In order to write a complete essay spontaneously, you must be able to organize your ideas in your mind as you write.

- Do not spend two or three minutes on an outline before writing since you won't be marked on your outline. Decide quickly how you will organize your essay. Ask yourself, "What is the topic of each paragraph?" and "What detail will I discuss in each paragraph?" You can record these decisions in note form and use them as a guide while you write.

- You must use familiar and natural sentence structure. Like the spoken answers in the Speaking section, your written answers in the section should reflect your usual sentence structure. However, some students feel that they have to demonstrate complex grammatical structure in order to get higher marks. As a result, they try to write longer sentences with more dependent clauses than the sentences they would normally write. You may write awkward, confusing sentences, and you will almost certainly make more grammatical errors.

- You must be able to write as you speak but with better style and more care.

Generally, good writers write in the same voice, or style, in which they speak. This does not mean, however, that good writers use exactly the same words and structure in both writing and speaking. It just means that their writing doesn't differ radically from their speech. Most academic writing is more formal than speech, but the difference usually comes from the greater amount of time one has to choose words and edit written English as opposed to the shorter time one has when speaking.

- You must be able to vary your vocabulary and sentence structure. Like speakers, writers sometimes repeat the same word or sentence structure. This is natural because people develop habits over time, so they get used to expressing themselves in the same way. In fact, repetition may not be grammatically incorrect, but too much repetition is boring and suggests a limited knowledge of the language. Therefore, to get the highest mark possible, you should try to be versatile in your use of sentence structure and choice of work.

- You must edit your work. You must leave at least a few minutes to read over your writing at least once before you submit it. In fact, you need more than a minute. All writers, including professional writers, make mistakes, so don't expect or plan to write flawlessly. Many students make mistakes that they would normally not make simply because of the pressure and stress of the time limit. If you plan to review your work, and you know what kind of errors to look for, then you can improve your mark significantly.

www.ingramcontent.com/pod-product-compliance
Lightning Source LLC
Chambersburg PA
CBHW052006070526
44584CB00016B/1643